Ext JS in Action

Ext JS in Action

JESUS GARCIA

MANNING

Greenwich
(74° w. long.)

Manning Publications Co.
180 Broad St.
Suite 1323
Stamford, CT 06901

Development editor: Sebastian Stirling
Copyeditor: Linda Recktenwald
Proofreader: Katie Tennant
Typesetter: Dottie Marsico
Cover designer: Marija Tudor

ISBN 978-1-935182-11-5
Printed in the United States of America
1 2 3 4 5 6 7 8 9 10 – MAL – 15 14 13 12 11 10

brief contents

contents

vii

preface

It was early 2006, and I was spending many frustrating hours testing and learning many of the frameworks and libraries on the internet. Seemingly, out of nowhere, I stumbled upon an extension to YUI or YUI-ext, developed by an unknown at the time, Jack Slocum.

At last! An Ajax library that was easy to use and well-documented. All of this work was for a small web application that I was developing during a six-month contract. Keep in mind that Enterprise Web 2.0 apps were nonexistent, so I knew I was venturing into uncharted territory.

By late 2006, the project had come to a close, as did the contract, forcing me to reassess my career goals. I had a strong feeling that the Enterprise Rich Intranet Application was going to be very popular, so I decided to become as active as I could in the YUI-ext community, focusing my efforts on learning, implementing, and extending the framework. You could say that I became an evangelist of sorts.

Flash forward to the summer of 2008, when Michael Stephens at Manning Publications contacted me regarding the development of a book for their *In Action* series. Becoming an author of a book was something that I had never dreamed of.

Before the challenge of this book was presented to me, I had already spent countless hours on the Ext JS forums helping developers like you and me solve a myriad of problems. This was in addition to authoring articles published on various blogs, e-magazine articles, and online video tutorials, some of which are longer in duration than most shows on television! So, when Michael Stephens contacted me, I was immediately excited to explore this avenue of knowledge transfer.

After about a year and a half of work, I can reflect on the late nights and sacrificed weekends spent trying to figure out ways to explain complex concepts so that any developer could understand them. During that time, I did my best to interface with the MEAP (Manning Early Access Program) readers and Ext JS community, processing feedback to make this book what it is.

I hope this book is helpful to you. Please feel free to visit us at the Manning Author Online forum and provide your thoughts, comments, and suggestions.

About this book

Ext (pronounced *Eee-ecks-tee*) JS 3.0 is an extremely powerful cross-browser UI framework for building rich and robust applications, originally developed by Jack Slocum in 2006. Since then, Ext JS has endured explosive growth because it addresses the need for web developers to have a true UI framework, complete with a component and event model. That makes it still unique in the growing competitive space of Web 2.0 libraries.

Written by a member of the Ext JS community, this book walks you through the framework in great detail, from the perspective of a peer-to-peer conversation. It uses examples both small and large to demonstrate how to use Ext JS effectively. It also includes many custom illustrations to help accelerate learning of the material.

Ext JS is an extremely large framework and continues to grow with every release. Because of the size of the framework, this book focuses on the core concepts that all developers need to know to be effective when developing Ext JS apps. Such concepts include the Component lifecycle, each of the layouts, creating extensions and plug-ins, and so much more.

This book does not cover parts of the framework or modules such as state and cookie management, Direct, and Designer. Cookie and state management were passed up in favor of covering other key principle topics, such as developing applications. Ext Direct is a way to remotely call the client side from the server side and also allows for seamless communication between the client and server side, but isn't included because it requires specific knowledge of server-side languages and thus is too broad a concept for this publication. The Ext Designer application rapidly creates rich interfaces for Ext JS, but isn't covered because it wasn't available during the development of this book.

Who should read this book?

This book is designed for anyone who wants to learn Ext JS *and use it well*. Instead of just being a container for recipes, this book tries to give the reader a deep understanding of how Ext JS works from the inside out and how to apply it in their application development efforts. The examples are written so that novice and expert JavaScript developers alike find them useful.

Some skills are required to be able to understand the material in this book, however. You need to be fairly experienced with JavaScript, HTML, and CSS, though you needn't be an expert in these technologies. If you're charged with developing the server-side code, you should be up to speed on how to use your server-side language of choice to communicate from the web server to your database of choice.

Roadmap

This book is divided into five major parts, each progressively increasing in complexity.

Part 1, "Introduction to Ext JS," gets your feet wet and lays the foundation for the rest of the book. The goal of this part is to understand the core concepts of how to use the framework well, because they're essential for the comprehension of later parts of the book. By the end of this section, you'll know intricacies of the framework that you can carry well beyond this book.

Chapter 1 begins with a tour of the framework. In this tour, we take a brief look at some of the underlying machinery. This chapter concludes with a "Hello world" example.

Chapter 2 is meant to be more of an Ext JS boot camp, where essential topics, such as how to initialize Ext JS widgets properly, are covered. In this chapter, we also cover DOM manipulation and how to use the framework's template engines.

Chapter 3 closes part 1 by covering four key topics that drive the framework. These topics include event management, the Component model and lifecycle, and how Ext JS widgets manage other widgets, known as `Containers`.

In part 2, "Ext JS Components," we begin to exercise the various widgets in the framework that are not driven by a data model. We start off by exploring `TabPanels` and `Windows` and then show how to properly implement each of the layouts. This part closes with a comprehensive walk-through of the various form input fields.

Chapter 4 continues the momentum from chapter 3's concepts, exploring how `TabPanels`, `Windows`, and Ext JS `MessageBox` dialog boxes are used.

Chapter 5 springboards off the knowledge gained from chapter 4 and walks you through implementations of the various layout managers in the framework.

Chapter 6 is somewhat of a show-and-tell chapter, walking through each of the form input fields that the framework provides and explaining how to submit data via Ajax. In the end, it uses the layout concepts learned from chapter 5 to construct a complex multitab `FormPanel`.

In part 3, "Data-driven Components," you learn the intricacies of the data-driven widgets, such as the `GridPanel`, `EditorGridPanel`, `DataViews`, `Charts`, and `TreePanels`. The goal of this part is to get you familiar with these complex widgets and their underlying data model components.

Chapter 7 is a detailed analysis of the way data `Store` `GridPanels` function and explains how each of their supporting classes work together.

Chapter 8 teaches you how to use the `EditorGridPanel` widget and introduces key concepts for creating, updating, and deleting data.

Chapter 9 leverages what you know about the data `Store` to implement `DataViews` and `ListView` widgets. You also learn more about the `XTemplate` utility along the way.

Chapter 10 is all about `Charts`. You get an inside look at how to implement and customize them.

Chapter 11 walks you through implementing `TreePanels` and explains how the data for the `TreePanel` needs to be arranged.

Chapter 12 is all about `Toolbars`, `Menus`, and `Buttons`, and you'll learn how to create things such as custom `Menus` and `ButtonGroups`.

Part 4, "Advanced Ext," teaches you some of the more complex areas of the framework, such as drag and drop and how to create extensions and plug-ins. Drag and drop covers a lot of material, so it's divided into two chapters.

Chapter 13 is designed to ease you into the world of drag and drop, where you learn about the classes that make drag and drop possible with the framework. Here we implement basic drag and drop with DOM elements on the page.

Chapter 14 continues the momentum, focusing on drag and drop with the Ext JS `DataView`, `GridPanel`, and `TreePanel` widgets.

Chapter 15 explains how extensions and plug-ins work in the framework.

Part 5, "Building applications," focuses on piecing together what you've learned thus far and constructing a small web application. In this part, you'll learn essential concepts, such as how to organize your classes via namespaces and on your filesystem. You'll also learn how to create reusable components that are implemented in your application.

Chapter 16 teaches you application basics by walking you through the paces of understanding requirements and abstracting and creating the reusable components.

Chapter 17 ties together all of the reusable components that you created in chapter 16. Here you learn how to combine user interactions using events, providing full CRUD functionality for data `Records`.

Code conventions

The following typographical conventions are used throughout the book:

- `Courier` typeface is used in all code listings.
- `Courier` typeface is used within text for certain code words.
- *Italics* are used for emphasis and to introduce new terms.
- Code annotations are used in place of inline comments in the code. These highlight important concepts or areas of the code. Some annotations appear with numbered bullets like this ❶ that are referenced later in the text.

Code downloads

You can download the examples for chapters 1 through 15 of this book via http://extjsinaction.com/examples.zip and can view and exercise them online via http://examples.extjsinaction.com/. The source code downloads are also available from the publisher's website at www.manning.com/ExtJSinAction.

Author Online

The purchase of *Ext JS in Action* includes free access to a private forum run by Manning Publications where you can make comments about the book, ask technical questions, and receive help from the author and other users. You can access and subscribe to the forum at www.manning.com/ExtJSinAction. This page provides information on how to get on the forum once you're registered, what kind of help is available, and the rules of conduct in the forum.

Manning's commitment to our readers is to provide a venue where a meaningful dialogue among individual readers and between readers and the author can take place. It's not a commitment to any specific amount of participation on the part of the author, whose contribution to the book's forum remains voluntary (and unpaid). We suggest you try asking the author some challenging questions, lest his interest stray!

The Author Online forum and the archives of previous discussions will be accessible from the publisher's website as long as the book is in print. Finally, additions to the content will be added to the author's online blog for the book, located at http://extjsinaction.com.

About the title

By combining introductions, overviews, and how-to examples, the *In Action* books are designed to help learning and remembering. According to research in cognitive science, the things people remember are things they discover during self-motivated exploration.

Although no one at Manning is a cognitive scientist, we are convinced that for learning to become permanent, it must pass through stages of exploration, play, and, interestingly, retelling of what is being learned. People understand and remember new things, which is to say they master them, only after actively exploring them. Humans learn in action. An essential part of an *In Action* book is that it is example driven. It encourages the reader to try things out, to play with new code, and to explore new ideas.

There is another, more mundane reason for the title of this book: our readers are busy. They use books to do a job or solve a problem. They need books that allow them to jump in and jump out easily and learn just what they want, just when they want it. They need books that aid them in action. The books in this series are designed for such readers.

acknowledgments

This book is dedicated to my wife, Erika, and our two boys, Takeshi and Kenji. Because of you, I have the motivation to do what I do.

Erika, thank you for supporting me during the production of this book. Your dedication to taking care of our two very active boys and family matters allowed me to focus on this book. I am both grateful and lucky to have you in my life. I love you!

Takeshi and Kenji, thank you for always keeping me on my toes and for those five-minute slices of time. My hope is that this little accomplishment can serve as an inspiration to you someday to achieve what it is that you set your mind to.

Many thanks to Abe Elias, Aaron Conran, Tommy Maintz, and the rest of the Ext JS development team. Having the ability to interface directly with you and your team has allowed me to get the answers I needed to make some of this material possible.

This book exists because of the people at Manning. Sebastian Stirling, my development editor, spent many hours taking the seemingly mindless ramblings of this Ext JS developer and arranging them so they were understandable. Thank you, Sebastian, for helping to make this book what it is. Also, huge thanks to the production team, including Mary Piergies, Linda Recktenwald, Katie Tennant, and Dottie Marsico. My gratitude also goes out to Mitchell Simoens, a shining star in the Ext JS community, for technically reviewing the manuscript shortly before it went to press. Finally, to Michael Stephens and Marjan Bace: thank you very much for extending to me the opportunity of becoming a book author. This was a very personal experience for me, and I'm indebted to you for your support throughout this project.

Last, but not least, many thanks to all who contributed to the manuscript along the way. To Manning's Early Access readers and the Ext JS community for your support and unparalleled dedication to providing feedback: I cannot begin to express my gratitude for the time taken out of your busy lives to interact with me during the writing of this book. And many thanks to the following peer reviewers who read the manuscript at different stages of its development and provided invaluable insights: Robert Anderson, Robby O'Connor, Amos Bannister, Paul Holser, Anthony Topper, Orhan Alkan, Ric Peller, Dan McKinnon, Jeroen Benckhuijsen, Christopher Haupt, Patrick Dennis, Costantino Cerbo, Greg Vaughn, Nhoel Sangalang, Bernard Farrell, Chuck Hudson, George Jempty, and Rama Vavilala.

about the cover illustration

The figure on the cover of *Ext JS in Action* is captioned "Le voyageur," which means a traveling salesman. The illustration is taken from a 19th-century edition of Sylvain Maréchal's four-volume compendium of regional dress customs published in France. Each illustration is finely drawn and colored by hand. The rich variety of this collection reminds us vividly of how culturally apart the world's towns and regions were just 200 years ago. Isolated from each other, people spoke different dialects and languages. In the streets or in the countryside, it was easy to identify where they lived and what their trade or station in life was just by their dress.

Dress codes have changed since then and the diversity by region, so rich at the time, has faded away. It is now hard to tell apart the inhabitants of different continents, let alone different towns or regions. Perhaps we have traded cultural diversity for a more varied personal life—certainly for a more varied and fast-paced technological life.

At a time when it is hard to tell one computer book from another, Manning celebrates the inventiveness and initiative of the computer business with book covers based on the rich diversity of regional life of two centuries ago, brought back to life by illustrations from collections such as this one.

Part 1

Introduction to Ext JS

Welcome to *Ext JS in Action*, an in-depth guide into the world of Ext JS. In this book, in addition to learning how to get things done using the Ext JS Framework, you're going to learn how the different components and widgets that comprise the framework work and operate.

Chapters 1 through 3 are designed to give you the essential knowledge to understand many of the fundamental aspects of the framework. Your journey begins with chapter 1, where you'll learn the very basics of the framework. Chapter 2 is our "boot camp" chapter and is where you'll learn key items to bootstrap your applications properly. Chapter 3 covers some of the internal machinery of the framework, such as the Component and Container models.

After reading this part, you'll be ready to explore the many widgets that compose Ext JS.

A framework apart

This chapter covers

- A holistic view of Ext JS
- Learning about what's new in 3.0
- Downloading and unpacking the framework source code
- Exploring an Ajax-based "Hello world" example

Envision a scenario where you're tasked to develop an application with many of the typical UI (user interface) widgets such as menus, tabs, data grids, dynamic forms, and styled pop-up windows. You want something that allows you to programmatically control the position of widgets, which means it has to have layout controls. You also desire detailed and organized centralized documentation to ease your learning curve with the framework. Finally, this application needs to look mature and go into beta phase as quickly as possible, which means you don't have a lot of time to toy with HTML and CSS. Before entering the first line of code for the prototype, you need to decide on an approach for developing the frontend. What are your choices?

You do some recon on the common popular libraries on the market and quickly learn that all of them can manipulate the DOM, but only two of them have a mature UI library, YUI (Yahoo! User Interface) and Ext JS.

3

At first glance of YUI, you might think you need not look any further. You toy with the examples and notice that they look mature but are not exactly professional quality, which means you'll need to modify CSS. No way. Next, you look at the documentation at http://developer.yahoo.com/yui/docs. It's centralized and technically accurate, but it's far from user friendly. You look at all of the scrolling required to locate a method or class. Some classes are even cut off because the left navigation pane is too small. What about Ext JS? Surely it has to be better, right? What alternatives do we have?

In this chapter, we'll take a good look at Ext JS, and you'll learn about some of the widgets that compose the framework. After we finish the overview, you'll download Ext JS and take it for a test drive.

1.1   Looking at Ext JS

Having to develop an RIA with a set of rich UI controls, you turn to Ext JS and find that, out of the proverbial box, Ext JS provides a rich set of DOM utilities and widgets. Although you can get excited about what you see in the examples page, it's what is under the hood that's most exciting. Ext JS comes with a full suite of layout management tools to give you full control over organizing and manipulating the UI as requirements dictate. One layer down exists what's known as the Component model and Container model, each playing an important role in managing how the UIs are constructed.

> **Component and Container models**
>
> The Component and Container models play a key role in managing UIs with Ext JS and are part of the reason Ext JS stands out from the rest of the Ajax libraries and frameworks. The Component model dictates how UI widgets are instantiated, rendered, and destroyed in what's known as the component lifecycle. The Container model controls how widgets can manage (or *contain*) other child widgets. These are two key areas for understanding the framework, which is why we'll be spending a lot of time on these two topics in chapter 3.

Almost all UI widgets in the framework are highly customizable, affording you the option to enable and disable features, override functions, and use custom extensions and plug-ins. One example of a web application that takes full advantage of Ext JS is Conjoon. Figure 1.1 shows a screenshot of Conjoon in action.

Conjoon is an open source personal information manager and can be considered the epitome of web applications developed with Ext JS. It uses just about all of the framework's native UI widgets and demonstrates how well the framework can integrate with custom extensions such as `YouTubePlayer`, `LiveGrid`, and `ToastWindow`. You can get a copy of Conjoon by visiting http://conjoon.org.

You've learned how Ext JS can be used to create a full-page web application. But what if you have an application that's already in production? Next, you'll learn how Ext JS can be integrated into existing applications or websites.

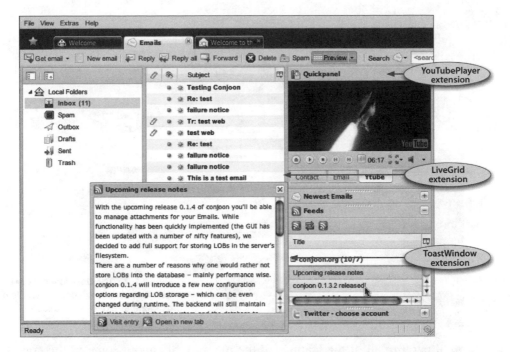

Figure 1.1 Conjoon is an open source personal information manager that's a great example of a web application that uses the framework to manage a UI that leverages 100 percent of the browser's viewport. You can download it at http://conjoon.org/.

1.1.1 Integration with existing sites

Any combination of widgets can be embedded inside an existing web page and or site with relative ease, giving your users the best of both worlds. An example of a public-facing site that contains Ext JS is the Dow Jones Indexes site, http://djindexes.com. Figure 1.2 shows Ext JS integrated with a page at djindexes.com.

This Dow Jones Indexes web page gives its visitors rich interactive views of data by utilizing a few of the Ext JS widgets such as the `TabPanel`, `GridPanel`, and `Window` (not shown). Its visitors can easily customize the view of the stocks by selecting a row in the main `GridPanel`, which invokes an Ajax request to the server, resulting in an updated graph below the grid. The non-Ext JS graph view can be modified as well by clicking one of the time period buttons below it.

You now know that Ext JS can be leveraged to build single-page applications or can be integrated into existing multipage applications. But we still haven't satisfied the requirement of API documentation. How does Ext JS solve this?

1.1.2 Rich API documentation

When opening the API documentation for the first time (figure 1.2), you get a sense of the polish that the framework has. Unlike competing frameworks, the Ext JS API Documentation leverages its own framework to present a clean and easy-to-use documentation tool that uses Ajax to provide the documentation.

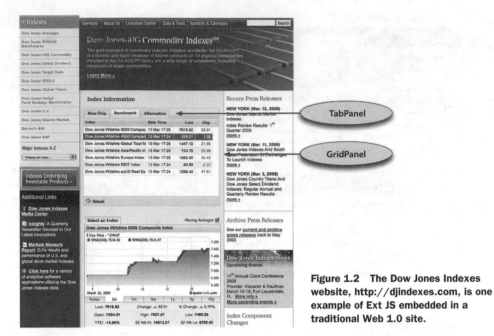

Figure 1.2   The Dow Jones Indexes website, http://djindexes.com, is one example of Ext JS embedded in a traditional Web 1.0 site.

We'll explore all of the features of the API and talk about some of the components used in this documentation tool. Figure 1.3 illustrates some of the components used in the Ext JS API Documentation application.

The API Documentation tool is chock-full of gooey GUI goodness and uses six of the most commonly used widgets, which include the Viewport, TreePanel, Toolbar with an embedded TextField and Toolbar Buttons, and TabPanel. I'm sure you're wondering what all of these are and what they do. Let's take a moment to discuss these widgets before we move on.

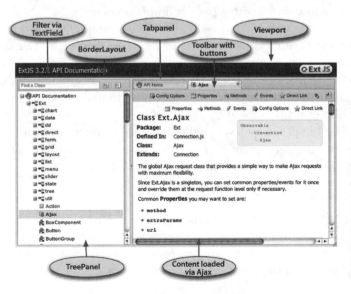

Figure 1.3   The Ext JS API Documentation contains a wealth of information and is a great resource for learning more about components and widgets. It contains most of what you need to know about the API, including constructor configuration options, methods, events, properties, component hierarchy, and more.

Looking from the outside in, the Viewport is a class that leverages all of the browser viewing space to provide an Ext JS–managed canvas for UI widgets. It's the foundation from which an entire Ext JS application is built upon. The BorderLayout layout manager is usually used, which divides the Viewport (or any container) into five regions. In this example three are used: North (top) for the page title, link, and Toolbar; West (left), which contains the TreePanel; and the Center (right) region, which contains the TabPanel to display documentation.

The Toolbar class provides a means to present commonly used UI components such as Buttons and Menus, but it can also contain, as in this case, any of the Ext.form.field subclasses. I like to think of the Toolbar as the common file-edit-view menus that you see in popular operating systems and desktop applications. The TreePanel widget displays hierarchical data visually in the form of a tree much like Windows Explorer displays your hard drive's folders. The TabPanel provides a means to have multiple documents or components on the canvas but allows only one to be active at a time.

Using the API is a cinch. To view a document, click the class node on the tree. This will invoke an Ajax request to fetch the documentation for the desired class. Each document for the classes is an HTML fragment (not a full HTML page). With the Text-Field in the Toolbar, you can easily filter out the class tree with a few strokes on the keyboard. If you're connected to the internet, you can search for API documentation in the API Home tab.

So the documentation is thorough. But what about rapid application development? Can Ext JS accelerate your development cycles?

1.1.3 Rapid development with prebuilt widgets

Ext JS can help you jump from conception to prototype because it offers many of the required UI elements already built and ready for integration. Having these UI widgets prebuilt, instead of having to engineer them, means that you save a lot of time. In many cases, the UI controls are highly customizable and can be modified to your application needs.

1.1.4 Works with Prototype, jQuery, and YUI, and inside AIR

Even though we discussed how Ext JS stands apart from other libraries such as YUI, it can easily be configured to leverage these frameworks as a base. This means if you're using these other libraries, you don't have to give them up to enjoy Ext JS UI goodness.

Although we won't cover development of Ext JS applications in Adobe AIR, it's worth noting that the framework has a complete set of utility classes to help with the integration of AIR. These utility classes include items like sound management, a video player panel, and access to the desktop clipboard. We won't go into AIR in this book, but we'll cover many of the important parts of the framework you'll need to know when developing with Ext JS in Adobe AIR.

NOTE   Because Adobe AIR is a development environment with features such as a sandbox, we won't be discussing how to develop applications with it. To learn more about Adobe AIR, visit http://www.adobe.com/devnet/air/.

Before we talk any more about Ext JS, we should set the playing field and discuss what types of skills are necessary to utilize the framework.

1.2   *What you need to know*

Although being an expert in web application development isn't required to develop with Ext JS, developers should have some core competencies before attempting to write code with the framework.

The first of these skills is a basic understanding of Hypertext Markup Language (HTML) and Cascading Style Sheets (CSS). It's important to have some experience with these technologies because Ext JS, like any other JavaScript UI library, uses HTML and CSS to build its UI controls and widgets. Although its widgets may look like and mimic typical modern operating system controls, it all boils down to HTML and CSS in the browser.

Because JavaScript is the glue that holds Ajax together, a solid foundation in JavaScript programming is suggested. Again, you need not be an expert, but you should have a good grasp of key concepts such as arrays, reference, and scope. It's a plus if you're familiar with object-oriented JavaScript fundamentals such as objects, classes, and prototypal inheritance. If you're new to JavaScript, you're in luck. JavaScript has existed since nearly the dawn of the internet. An excellent place to start is W3Schools.com, which offers a lot of free online tutorials and even has sandboxes for you to play with JavaScript online. You can visit them at http://w3schools.com/JS/.

If you're required to develop code for the server side, you're going to need a server-side solution for Ext JS to interact with as well as a way to store data. To persist data, you'll need to know how to interact with a database or filesystem with your server-side language of choice.

Naturally, the range of solutions available is quite large. For this book, we won't focus on a specific language. Instead, we'll use online resources at http://extjsinaction.com, where I've done the server-side work for you. This way, all you have to focus on is learning Ext JS.

We'll begin our exploration of Ext JS with a bird's-eye view of the framework, where you'll learn about the categories of functionality.

1.3   *A bird's-eye view of the framework*

The Ext JS framework not only provides UI widgets but also contains a host of other features. These fall into six major areas of purpose: Core, UI components, web remoting, data services, drag and drop, and general utilities. Figure 1.4 illustrates the six areas of purpose.

Knowing what the different areas of purpose are and what they do will give you an edge when developing applications, so we'll take a moment to discuss them.

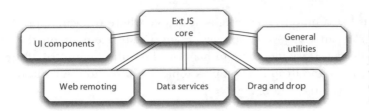

Figure 1.4 The six areas of purpose for Ext JS classes: Ext JS Core, UI components, web remoting, data services, drag and drop, and general utilities

CORE

The first feature set is the Ext JS Core, which comprises of many of the basic features such as Ajax communication, DOM manipulation, and event management. Everything else is dependent on the Core of the framework, but the Core isn't dependent on anything else.

> **Learn more about Ext Core**
>
> Ext Core is a library, which is a subset of the Ext JS base functionality and can be considered on par with jQuery, Prototype, and Scriptaculous. To learn more about Ext Core, visit http://extjs.com/products/core/.

UI COMPONENTS

The UI components contain all of the widgets that interface with the user.

WEB REMOTING

Web remoting is a means for JavaScript to (remotely) execute method calls that are defined and exposed on the server, which is commonly known as a Remote Procedure Call, or RPC. It's convenient for development environments where you'd like to expose your server-side methods to the client and not worry about all of the fuss of Ajax method management.

> **Learn more about Ext JS Direct**
>
> Because Direct is a server-side-focused product, we won't be covering it in this book. Ext JS has many online resources where you can learn about Direct, including examples for many of the popular server-side solutions. To learn more about Direct, visit http://extjs.com/products/direct/.

DATA SERVICES

The data services section takes care of all of your data needs, which include fetching, parsing, and loading information into stores. With the Ext JS data services classes, you can read Array, XML, and JSON (JavaScript Serialized Object Notation), which is a data format that's quickly becoming the standard for client-to-server communication. Stores typically feed UI components.

DRAG AND DROP

Drag and drop is like a mini framework inside Ext JS, where you can apply drag-and-drop capabilities to an Ext JS component or any HTML element on the page. It includes all of the necessary members to manage the entire gamut of all drag-and-drop operations. Drag and drop is a complex topic. We'll spend the entirety of chapters 13 and 14 on this subject alone.

UTILITIES

The utilities section comprises cool utility classes that help you perform some of your routine tasks easier. An example would be `Ext.util.Format`, which allows you to format or transform data easily. Another neat utility is the CSS singleton, which allows you to create, update, swap, and remove stylesheets as well as request the browser to update its rule cache.

Now that you have a general understanding of the framework's major areas of functionality, let's take some time to look at some of the more commonly used UI widgets that Ext JS has to offer.

1.3.1   *Containers and layouts at a glance*

Even though we'll cover these topics in detail in chapter 3, we should spend a little time here talking about containers and layouts. The terms *container* and *layout* are used extensively throughout this book, and I want to make sure you have at least a basic understanding of them before we continue. Afterwards, we'll begin our exploration of visual components of the UI library.

CONTAINERS

Containers are widgets that can manage one or more child items. A child item is generally any widget or component that's managed by a container or parent, thus the parent-child paradigm. You've already seen this in action in the API. The `TabPanel` is a container that manages one or more child items, which can be accessed via tabs. Please remember this term, because you'll be using it a lot when you start to learn more about how to use the UI portion of the framework.

LAYOUTS

Layouts are implemented by a container to visually organize the child items in the container's content body. Ext JS has 12 layouts from which to choose, which we'll go into in great detail in chapter 5 and shows the ins and outs of each layout. Now that you have a high level of understanding of containers and layouts, let's look at some containers in action.

In the figure 1.5, you see two subclasses of `Container`, `Panel` and `Window`, each engaged in parent-child relationships.

The `Panel` (left) and `Window` (right) in figure 1.5 each manage two child items. Child Panel 1 of each parent container *contains* HTML, whereas the children with the title Child Panel 2 manage one child panel each using the simple `ContainerLayout`, which is the base class for all other layouts. This parent-child relationship is the crux

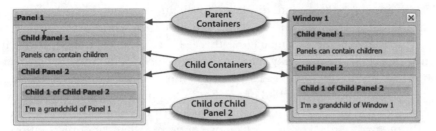

Figure 1.5 Here, you see two parent `Containers`, `Panel` (left) and `Window`
(right), managing child items, which include nested children.

of all of the UI management of Ext JS and will be reinforced and referenced repeat-
edly throughout this book.

You learned that `Containers` manage child items and use layouts to visually organize them. Now that you have these important concepts down, we'll move on to see
and discuss other `Containers` in action.

1.3.2 Other Containers in action

You saw `Panel` and `Window` being used when you learned about `Containers`. Figure 1.6
shows some other commonly used subclasses of `Container`.

In figure 1.6, you see the `FormPanel`, `TabPanel`, `FieldSet`, and `QuickTip` widgets.
The `FormPanel` works with the `BasicForm` class to wrap fields and other child items
with a `form` element.

Looking at this from a parent-child perspective, the `FormPanel` is being used to
manage three child items: two instances of `FieldSet` and one instance of `TabPanel`.

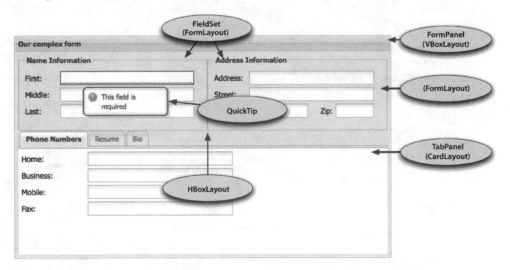

Figure 1.6 Commonly used subclasses of `Container`—`FormPanel`, `TabPanel`, `FieldSet`, and
`QuickTip`—and the layouts used to compose this UI `Panel`. We'll build this in chapter 6, where you
learn about forms.

FieldSets are generally used to display fields in a form much like a typical FieldSet tag does in HTML. These two FieldSets are managing child items, which are text fields. The TabPanel here is managing three direct children (tabs); in the first tab (Phone Numbers) it's managing many children, which are text fields. The QuickTip, which is used to display helpful text when the mouse is hovering over an element, is being displayed, but it isn't a child of any Ext JS component.

We'll spend some time building this complex UI in chapter 6, where you'll learn more about FormPanels. For now, let's move on to see what data presentation widgets the framework has to offer.

1.3.3 Grids, DataView, and ListView

You've already learned that the Data Services portion of the framework is responsible for the loading and parsing of data. The main consumers of the data that the data store manages are the GridPanel and the DataView and its subclass, the ListView. Figure 1.7 is a screenshot of the Ext JS GridPanel in action.

The GridPanel is a subclass of Panel and presents data in a table-like format, but its functionality extends far beyond that of a traditional table, offering sortable, resizable, and movable column headers and selection models such as RowSelectionModel and CellSelectionModel. You can customize its look and feel as you desire and couple it with a PagingToolbar to allow large datasets to be segmented and displayed in pages. It also has subclasses such as the EditorGridPanel, which allows you to create a grid where users can edit data on the grid itself, leveraging any of the Ext JS form data input widgets.

The grid is great for displaying data but is somewhat computationally expensive because of the many DOM elements that each row contains. To combat this, you can

ExtJS.com - Browse Forums		
Topic	Replies	Last Post ▾
[DONE]Ext.isSafari4 + related code savings Ext: Feature Requests Forum	16	Mar 24, 2009, 12:47 pm by mystix
adding a label after the combo box Ext: Help Forum	0	Mar 24, 2009, 12:47 pm by rjanos
extjs newbie stupid question Ext: Help Forum	0	Mar 24, 2009, 12:44 pm by SantaBarbarian
Masking a grid with a panel Ext: Help Forum	2	Mar 24, 2009, 12:44 pm by Deeeem
German umlauts UTF-8 problem Ext: Help Forum	14	Mar 24, 2009, 12:43 pm by makeflo
Ext JS Newbie Needs Help with Grids Ext: Help Forum	8	Mar 24, 2009, 12:26 pm by Bill@PAR
complex JSON problem Ext: Help Forum	3	Mar 24, 2009, 12:24 pm by Deeeem
Confusion using alignTo in a viewport based on Ext.example.msg (plz move->	5	Mar 24, 2009, 12:22 pm

Page 1 of 2067 ▶ ▶| ⟳ ☰ Show Preview   Displaying topics 1 - 25 of 51672

Figure 1.7   The GridPanel as seen in the Buffered Grid example in the Ext JS SDK

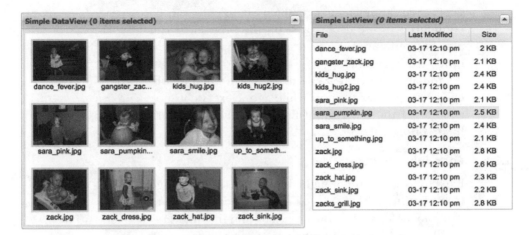

Figure 1.8   The `DataView` (left) and `ListView` (right) as shown in the Ext JS SDK examples

couple the `GridPanel` with a `PagingToolbar` or use one of the lighter-weight widgets to display data from a store, including the `DataView` and its subclass, the `ListView`, as shown in figure 1.8.

The `DataView` class consumes data from a store, paints it onscreen using a `Template`, and provides a simple selection model. An Ext JS `Template` is a DOM utility that allows you to create a *template*, with placeholders for data elements, which can be filled in by individual records in a store and stamped out on the DOM. In figure 1.8, the `DataView` (left) is displaying data from a store, which includes references to images. It uses a predefined template, which contains image tags, where the individual records are leveraged to fill in the location of the images. The `Template` then stamps out an image tag for each individual record, resulting in a nice collage of photos. The `DataView` can be used to display anything in a data store.

The `ListView`, as pictured in figure 1.8 (right), is displaying data from a store in a grid-like fashion but is a subclass of `DataView`. It's a great way to display data in a tabular format without the weight of the `GridPanel` if you're not looking to use some of the `GridPanel` features like sortable and resizable columns.

The `GridPanel` and `DataView` are essential tools for painting data onscreen, but they do have one major limitation. They can only show lists of records. They can't display hierarchical data. This is where the `TreePanel` fills the gap.

1.3.4 Make like a TreePanel and leaf

The `TreePanel` widget is an exception to the list of UI widgets that consume data, in that it doesn't consume data from a data store. Instead, it consumes hierarchical data via the usage of the `data.Tree` class. Figure 1.9 shows an example of an Ext JS `TreePanel` widget.

In figure 1.9, the `TreePanel` is being used to display the parent-child data inside the directory of an installation of the framework. The `TreePanel` can leverage a

TreeLoader to fetch data remotely via Ajax or can be configured to use data stored on the browser. It can also be configured to use drag and drop and has its own selection model.

You already saw TextFields in a form when we discussed containers a short while ago. Next, we'll look at some of the other input fields that the framework has to offer.

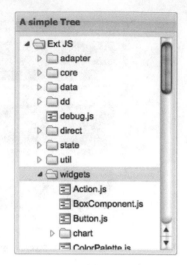

Figure 1.9   An Ext JS Tree, which is an example from the Ext JS SDK

1.3.5   *Form input fields*

Ext JS has a palette of eight input fields. They range from simple TextFields, as you've already seen, to complex fields such as the ComboBox and the HtmlEditor. Figure 1.10 is an illustration of some of the available Ext JS form field widgets that come out of the box.

As you can see in figure 1.10, some of the form input fields look like stylized versions of their native HTML counterparts. The similarities end here, however. With the Ext JS form fields, there's much more than meets the eye!

Each of the Ext JS fields (minus the HtmlEditor) includes a suite of utilities to perform actions like get and set values, mark the field as invalid, reset, and perform validations against the field. You can apply custom validation to the field via regex or custom validation methods, allowing you complete control over the data being

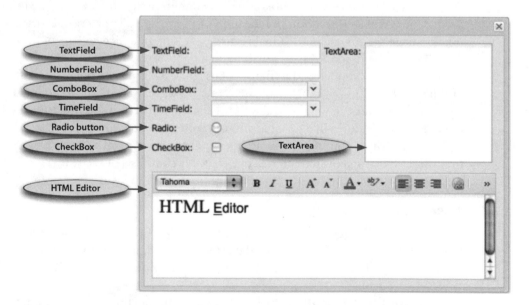

Figure 1.10   All of the out-of-the-box form elements displayed in an encapsulating Window

entered into the form. The fields can validate data as it's being entered, providing live feedback to the user.

TEXTFIELD AND TEXTAREA

The TextField and TextArea classes can be considered extensions of their generic HTML counterparts. NumberField, however, is a subclass of the TextField and is a convenience class, which utilizes regular expressions to ensure users can enter only numbers. With NumberField, you can configure decimal precision as well as specify the range of the value entered. The ComboBox and TimeField classes require a little extra time relative to the other fields, so we'll skip these two for now and jump back to them in a bit.

RADIO AND CHECKBOX

Like TextField, the Radio and Checkbox input fields are extensions of the plain old Radio and Checkbox but include all of the Ext JS Element management goodness and have convenience classes to assist with the creation of Checkbox and RadioGroups with automatic layout management. Figure 1.11 shows a small sample of how the Ext JS Checkbox and RadioGroup classes can be configured with complex layouts.

> **See all of the Radio and Checkbox examples**
>
> To see the entire set of examples, visit http://extjs.com/deploy/dev/examples/form/check-radio.html.

HTMLEDITOR

The HTML editor is WYSIWYG, like the TextArea on steroids. The HtmlEditor leverages existing browser HTML editing capabilities and can be considered somewhat of a black sheep when it comes to fields. Because of its inherent complexities (using IFrames and the like), it doesn't have a lot of the abilities like validation and can't be marked as invalid. There's much more to discuss about this field, which we're going to save for chapter 6. But for now, let's circle back to the ComboBox and its subclass, the TimeField.

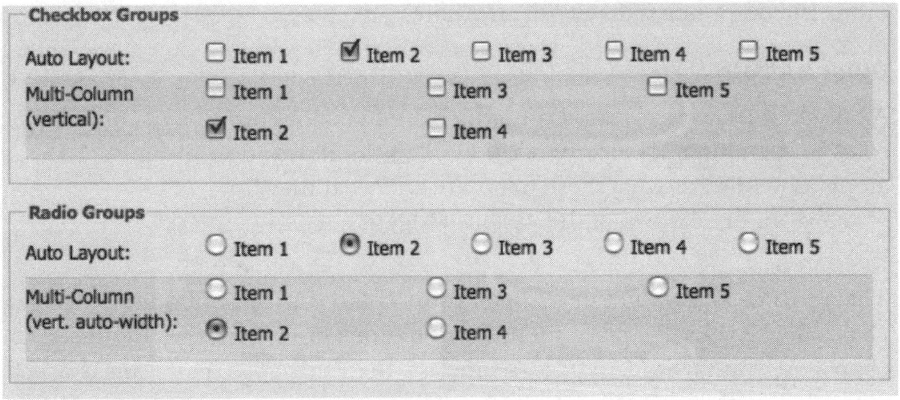

Figure 1.11 An example of the Checkbox and RadioGroup convenience classes in action with automatic layouts.

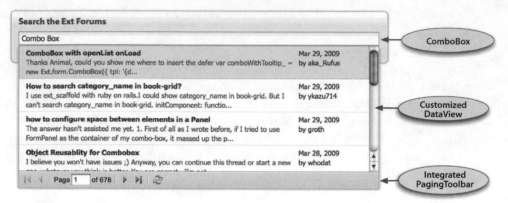

Figure 1.12   A custom `ComboBox`, which includes an integrated paging toolbar, as shown in the downloadable Ext JS examples

COMBOBOX AND TIMEFIELD

The `ComboBox` is easily the most complex and configurable form input field. It can mimic traditional option drop-down boxes or can be configured to use remote data-sets via the data store. It can be configured to autocomplete text, known as *type-ahead*, entered by the user and perform remote or local filtering of data. It can also be configured to use your own instance of an Ext JS `Template` to display a custom list in the drop-down area, known as the `ListBox`. Figure 1.12 is an example of a custom `Combo-Box` in action.

In figure 1.12, a custom combo box is being leveraged to search the Ext JS forums. The `ComboBox` here shows information like the post title, date, author, and a snippet of the post in the list box. Because some of the dataset ranges are so large, it's configured to use a paging toolbar, allowing users to page through the resulting data. Because the `ComboBox` is so configurable, we could also include image references to the resulting dataset, which can be applied to the resulting rendered data.

Here we are, on the last stop of our UI tour. Now we'll take a peek at some of the other UI components that work anywhere.

1.3.6   *Other widgets*

A bunch of UI controls stand out, which aren't major components but play supporting roles in a grander scheme of a UI. Look at the illustration in figure 1.13, and follow along as we discuss what these items are and what they do.

Here's a breakdown of the various widgets.

TOOLBAR

The `Toolbar` is a widget that allows you to place in it just about any widget that fits. Generally, developers place menus and buttons in it. When we discussed the custom `ComboBox`, you saw the `Toolbar`'s subclass, the `PagingToolbar`. `Panels` and just about any subclass thereof can use these toolbars on the top or bottom of their content body. The `Button` widget is a stylized version of the generic HTML button, which can include icons as well as text.

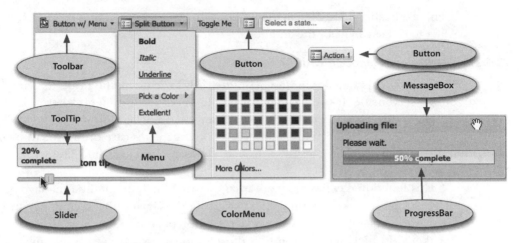

Figure 1.13 Miscellaneous UI widgets and controls

MENU

Menus can be displayed by clicking a button on the toolbar or shown on demand at any X and Y coordinates on screen. Although they typically contain menu items, such as the items shown and the color menu item, they can contain widgets such as ComboBoxes.

MESSAGEBOX

The MessageBox is a utility class, which allows you to easily provide feedback to the user without having to craft up an instance of Ext.Window. In this illustration, it's using an animated ProgressBar to display the status of an upload to the user.

SLIDER

The Slider is a widget that leverages drag and drop to allow users to change a value by repositioning the knob. Sliders can be styled with images and CSS to create your own custom look. The movement of the knob can be restricted so it moves only in increments. In this example, the slider has a ToolTip above the knob, displaying the value of the slider as the user moves it. In addition to the default horizontal orientation, Sliders can be configured as vertical.

You've learned how Ext JS can help you get the job done through a large palette of widgets. You've learned that you could elect to use Ext JS to build an application without touching an ounce of HTML or integrate it with existing sites. You also got a top-down view of the framework, which included a UI tour. All of the material discussed thus far existed for Ext JS 2.0. Let's take a moment to discuss what's new in Ext JS 3.0.

1.4 *New Ext JS 3.0 goodies*

Ext JS 2.0 introduced some radical changes, which made upgrading from 1.0 rather difficult. This was mainly because of the introduction to the more modern layout manager and a new, robust component hierarchy, which broke most of the user-developed Ext JS 1.x code. Thankfully, due to the great engineering of Ext JS 2.0, the migration from Ext JS 2.0 to 3.0 is much easier. Although the additions to Ext JS 3.0

aren't as drastic, there's excitement about this latest release, and it's certainly worthwhile to discuss some of the additions.

1.4.1 *Ext JS does remoting with Direct*

Web remoting is a means for JavaScript to easily execute method calls that are defined on the server side. It's convenient for development environments where you'd like to expose your server-side methods to the client and not have to worry about all of the muck with Ajax connection handling. `Ext.Direct` takes care of this for us by managing Ajax requests and acts as a bridge between the client-side JavaScript and any server-side language.

This functionality has great advantages, which include method management in a single location as well as unification of methods. Having this technology inside the framework will ensure consistency across the consumers, such as the data classes. Speaking of which, let's look at how the addition of `Ext.Direct` brings new classes to the data classes.

1.4.2 *Data class*

The `Ext.data` class is the nerve center for just about all data handling in the framework. The data classes manage every aspect of data management, including fetching, reading, and parsing data to create records, which are loaded into a store. With the addition of `Direct`, Ext JS has added additional convenience `Data` classes, `DirectProxy` and `DirectStore`, to facilitate ease of integration with your web remoting needs.

Now that we've reviewed some of the behind-the-scenes changes and additions to the framework, take a gander at some of the UI widgets that have been added.

1.4.3 *Meet the new layouts*

A total of six new layouts make their way into the Ext JS 3.0 framework, including `AutoLayout`, `MenuLayout`, `ToolbarLayout`, `BoxLayout`, `VBoxLayout`, and `HBoxLayout`. `MenuLayout` is an improvement on the way menu items were organized in the 2.0 version of the framework. Similarly, `ToolbarLayout` adds important features to the `Toolbar`, like overflow management, as illustrated in figure 1.14. Neither of these two layouts is designed to be implemented by their intended widgets, and neither is for end-developer use.

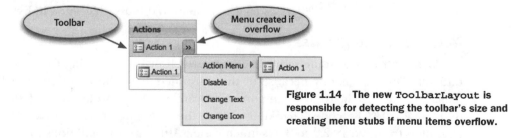

Figure 1.14 The new `ToolbarLayout` is responsible for detecting the toolbar's size and creating menu stubs if menu items overflow.

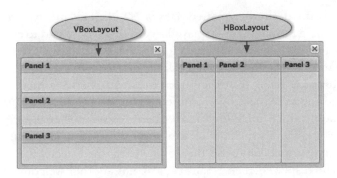

Figure 1.15 An example of the
VBox and HBox layouts in action

As shown in figure 1.14, ToolbarLayout will detect the overflow of toolbar items in a toolbar and will automatically create a menu that lists and contains the rest of the items. The changes to MenuLayout help support this effort.

The BoxLayout class is an abstract class that's meant to provide base functionality for the VBoxLayout and HBoxLayout classes and is not designed for end-developer use. The VBoxLayout and HBoxLayout are great additions to the list of end-developer-usable layouts. The HBoxLayout allows you to divide a container's content body into horizontal slices, whereas the VBoxLayout does the same except vertically, as illustrated in figure 1.15.

Many experienced Ext JS developers might think that the HBoxLayout looks like the ColumnLayout in practice. Although it does provide similar functionality, it extends way beyond the ColumnLayout's capabilities, where it will vertically and horizontally stretch children based on weights, which is known as flex. In contrast to the ColumnLayout, however, child items will never wrap around inside the Container's content body. These two layouts usher in a whole new era of layout capabilities within the framework.

In addition to the layout changes, the ColumnModel, a supporting class for the GridPanel, has undergone some fundamental changes. Let's look at some of these changes and see why they're going to help us in our development efforts.

1.4.4 *Grid ColumnModel enhancements*

The grid ColumnModel is a class that models how the columns are organized, sized, and displayed for the GridPanel widget. Prior to Ext JS 3.0, individual columns were generally configured as a list of configuration objects in an array, which is consumed by ColumnModel.

For each column in the ColumnModel, you could enhance or modify the way the data is displayed by creating a custom renderer, which is a method that's called for each data point for

Configuration objects

Many of the Ext JS constructors and some methods accept parameters listed in a configuration object. These configuration objects are nothing more than plain objects that contain a set of key-value pair parameters that will influence how a widget is rendered onscreen or how a method behaves.

that column and returns the desired formatted data or HTML. This means that if you wanted, let's say, a date to be formatted or displayed a certain way, you had to configure it, which many people found themselves doing a lot. In this release, the `ColumnModel` changed somewhat to make our jobs that much easier.

The individual `Column` has been abstracted from the `ColumnModel` and an entirely new class created called the `grid.Column`. From here, many convenience `Column` subclasses have been created, which include `NumberColumn`, `BooleanColumn`, `Template-Column`, and `DateColumn`, each of which allows you to display your data as you desire. To display formatted dates, you could use the `DateColumn` and specify a format in which the dates are to be displayed. The `TemplateColumn` is another welcome change because it allows you to leverage `XTemplates` and display them in a `GridPanel`, which are convenience methods to create and stamp out HTML fragments based on data. To use any of these `Column` subclasses, no custom renderers are required, though you can use them if you wish.

Many applications require data to be displayed in tabular format. Although the `GridPanel` is a great solution, it's computationally expensive for generic data displays that require little or no user interaction. This is where `ListView`, an extension of `DataView`, comes to the rescue.

1.4.5   ListView, like GridPanel on a diet

With this new addition to the framework, you can now display more data in a grid-like format without sacrificing performance. Figure 1.16 shows the `ListView` in action. Although it looks similar to the `GridPanel`, in order to achieve better performance, we sacrifice features such as drag-and-drop column reordering as well as keyboard navigation. This is mainly because the `ListView` doesn't have any of the elaborate, feature-rich supporting classes, such as the `ColumnModel` we discussed a moment ago.

Using `ListView` to display your data will ensure that you have faster response from DOM manipulation, but remember that it doesn't have all of the features of the `Grid-Panel`. Choosing which one to use will depend on your application requirements.

Simple ListView *(1 item selected)*		
File ▲	Last Modified	Size
dance_fever.jpg	03-17 12:10 pm	2 KB
gangster_zack.jpg	03-17 12:10 pm	2.1 KB
kids_hug.jpg	03-17 12:10 pm	2.4 KB
kids_hug2.jpg	03-17 12:10 pm	2.4 KB
sara_pink.jpg	03-17 12:10 pm	2.1 KB
sara_pumpkin.jpg	03-17 12:10 pm	2.5 KB
sara_smile.jpg	03-17 12:10 pm	2.4 KB
up_to_something.jpg	03-17 12:10 pm	2.1 KB
zack.jpg	03-17 12:10 pm	2.8 KB
zack_dress.jpg	03-17 12:10 pm	2.6 KB

Figure 1.16   The new `Ext.ListView` class, which is like a lightweight `DataGrid`

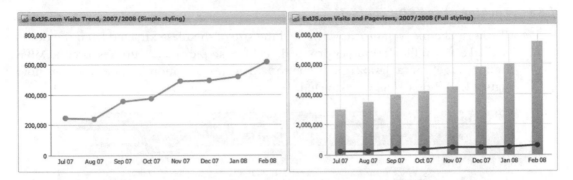

Figure 1.17 **These charts now bring rich graphical views of trend data to the framework. It's important to note that this new widget requires Flash.**

Ext JS has always been excellent at displaying textual data on screen, but it lacked a graphical means of data representation. Let's take a quick look at how this has changed with Ext JS 3.0.

1.4.6 Charts come to Ext JS

One thing that was missing in the 2.0 version of Ext JS was charts. Thankfully, the development team listened to the community and introduced them for version 3.0. These are a great addition, which adheres to the Ext JS layout models.

Use of these charts, however, requires Adobe Flash to be installed for the browser you're using, which you can download at http://get.adobe.com/flashplayer/. In addition to the `Line` and `Column` charts shown in figure 1.17, the framework has `Bar`, `Pie`, and `Cartesian` charts available for your data visualization needs.

You now have just about everything you need to lay down some code. Before you start on your path to becoming Ext JS Jedis, you must first download and set up the framework, and we'll have a discussion about development.

1.5 Downloading and configuring

Even though downloading Ext JS is a simple process, configuring a page to include Ext JS isn't as simple as referencing a single file in HTML. In addition to configuration, you'll learn about the folder hierarchy and what folders are and what they do.

The first thing you need to do is get the source code. Visit the following link: http://extjs.com/products/extjs/download.php.

The downloaded file will be the SDK in a zip file, which weighs in at over 6 MB in size. I'll explain why this file is so large in a bit. Now, extract the file in a place where you serve JavaScript. In order to leverage Ajax, you're going to need a web server. I typically use Apache configured locally on my computer, which is free and cross-platform, but IIS for Windows will do. Let's peek at what you just extracted.

1.5.1   *Looking at the SDK contents*

If you're like me, you probably checked the size of the files extracted from the down-loaded SDK zip file. If your jaw dropped, feel free to pick it back up. Yes, over 30 MB is rather large for a JavaScript framework. Pay no attention to the size for now; figure 1.18 shows what was extracted.

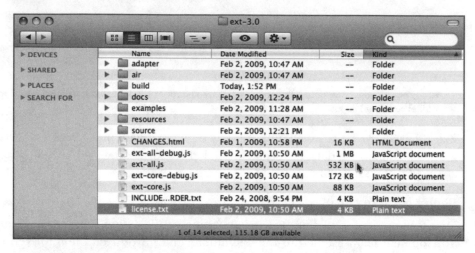

Figure 1.18   A view of the Ext JS SDK contents

Looking at the contents of the SDK, you see a lot of stuff. The reason there are so many folders and files is that the downloadable package contains a few copies of the entire code base and CSS. It's this way because you get the freedom to build or use Ext JS any way you see fit. Table 1.1 explains what each of the folders is and what it does.

Table 1.1   The contents of the Ext JS SDK

Folder	What it does
adapter	Contains the ext-base.js, which is the base Ext JS library, which is used for an all-Ext JS setup. It also contains necessary adapters and supported versions of Prototype, jQuery, or YUI libraries if you want to use any of those as a base.
air	Contains all of the required libraries to integrate Ext JS with Adobe AIR.
build	Has each of the files that compose the Ext JS framework with all of the unnecessary whitespace removed. It's a deflated version of the source directory.
docs	Holds the full API documentation.
examples	Holds all of the example source code, which is great source to learn by example (no pun intended).
resources	Contains all of the necessary images and CSS required to use the UI widgets. It contains all of the CSS files broken down by widget and an ext-all.css, which is a concatenation of all the framework's CSS.

Table 1.1   The contents of the Ext JS SDK *(continued)*

Folder	What it does
src	Holds the entire framework, including all of the comments.
ext-all.js	This is a minified version of the framework, which is intended for production applications.
ext-core.js	If you wanted to use the core library, which means none of the UI controls, you'd set up your page with ext-core.js.
*debug.js	Anything with *debug* in the name means that the comments are stripped to reduce file space, but the necessary indentation remains intact. When we develop, we're going to use ext-all-debug.js.

Although there are quite a few files and folders in the distribution, you need only a few of them to get the framework running in your browser. Now is a good time to talk about how to set up Ext JS for use.

1.5.2   Setting up Ext JS for the first time

In order to get Ext JS running in your browser, you need to include at least two required JavaScript files and at least one CSS file:

```
<link rel="stylesheet" type="text/css"
    href="extjs/resources/css/ext-all.css" />

<script type="text/javascript" src="extjs/adapter/ext/ext-base-debug.js">
</script>

<script type="text/javascript" src="extjs/ext-all-debug.js">
</script>
```

Here we're linking the three core files for an all-Ext JS configuration. The first thing we do is link to the ext-all.css file, which is all of the CSS for the framework in one file. Next, we include ext-base-debug.js, which is the underlying base of the framework. Last, we include ext-all-debug.js, which we'll use for development. When setting up your initial page, be sure to replace extjs in your path with wherever you plan to reference the framework on your development web server.

What if you want to use any of the other base frameworks? How do you include those?

1.5.3   Configuring Ext JS for use with others

In order for Ext JS to work with the previously mentioned frameworks, an *adapter* must be loaded after the external base framework. The adapter maps ext-base methods to the external library of choice, which is crucial. You can use the following patterns to use any of the other three base frameworks in addition to Ext JS:

First up, the Prototype library:

```
<link rel="stylesheet" type="text/css"
    href="extjs/resources/css/ext-all.css" />
```

```
<script type="text/javascript"
    src="extjs/adapter/prototype/prototype.js">
</script>

<script type="text/javascript"
    src="extjs/adapter/prototype/scriptaculous.js?load=effects.js">
</script>

<script type="text/javascript"
    src="extjs/adapter/prototype/ext-prototype-adapter-debug.js">
</script>

<script type="text/javascript"
    src="extjs/ext-all-debug.js"></script>
```

As you can see, this is like the generic Ext JS setup with two additional JS files. The Prototype and Scriptaculous libraries take the place of ext-base, and ext-prototype-adapter.js maps the external library methods to Ext. Note that we're still loading ext-all-debug.js. We'll continue to do so for the other two cases.

Next is jQuery:

```
<link rel="stylesheet" type="text/css"
    href="extjs/resources/css/ext-all.css" />

<script type="text/javascript"
    src="extjs/adapter/jQuery/jQuery.js">
</script>

<script type="text/javascript"
    src="extjs/adapter/jQuery/ext-jquery-adapter-debug.js">
</script>

<script type="text/javascript"
    src="extjs/ext-all-debug.js"></script>
```

Configuring jQuery is similar to the Prototype setup. The YUI configuration will be similar, the difference being that we're loading different base library and adapter files.

Lastly, YUI:

```
<link rel="stylesheet" type="text/css"
    href="extjs/resources/css/ext-all.css" />

<script type="text/javascript"
    src="extjs/adapter/yui/yui-utilities.js">
</script>

<script type="text/javascript"
    src="extjs/adapter/yui/ext-yui-adapter-debug.js">
</script>

<script type="text/javascript"
    src="extjs/ext-all-debug.js"></script>
```

And there you have it, the recipes for an Ext-all setup and the other three supported base JS libraries. Moving forward, we'll be using the Ext-all configuration, but you're free to use whichever base library you wish. Before we move on to coding, we need to talk about one final crucial step to setting up Ext, and that's configuring the reference for s.gif.

> **Place BLANK_IMAGE_URL configuration wisely**
>
> It's recommended that you set this parameter immediately after the inclusion of the Ext JS files or immediately before your application code is parsed. I'll show you an example of where to place it when we take Ext JS for a test drive.

1.5.4 Configuring BLANK_IMAGE_URL

The configuration of the Ext.BLANK_IMAGE_URL is one of those steps that developers often overlook and may lead to issues with the way the UI renders for your application. The BLANK_IMAGE_URL property specifies a location for the 1x1–pixel clear s.gif graphic (known as a spacer), which is an essential piece of the UI portion of the framework and is used to create items like icons. Out of the box, BLANK_IMAGE_URL points to http://extjs.com/s.gif. For most users, that's okay, but if you're in an area where extjs.com isn't accessible, this will become an issue. This also becomes a problem if you're using SSL, where s.gif is being requested via HTTP instead of HTTPS, which will invoke security warnings in browsers. In order to prevent these issues, set Ext.BLANK_IMAGE_URL to s.gif locally on your web server, like this:

```
Ext.BLANK_IMAGE_URL = 'extjs/resources/images/default/s.gif';
```

If you're like me, after all of this discussion, you're probably itching to start using Ext JS. So, what are you waiting for? Go ahead and dive in.

1.6 Take it for a test drive

For this exercise, you'll create an Ext JS Window, and you'll use Ajax to request an HTML file for presentation in the content body of the Window. You'll start by creating the main HTML file, from which you'll source all of your JavaScript files.

Listing 1.1 Creating our helloWorld.html

```
<link rel="stylesheet" type="text/css"
    href="/extjs/resources/css/ext-all.css" />          ❶ Include ext-all.css

<script type="text/javascript"
  src="/extjs/adapter/ext/ext-base-debug.js">            ❷ Load ext-base.js and
</script>                                                    ext-all-debug.js

<script type="text/javascript"
    src="/extjs/ext-all-debug.js"></script>              ❸ Configure Ext.
<script type="text/javascript">                              BLANK_IMAGE_URL
    Ext.BLANK_IMAGE_URL = '/extjs/resources/images/default/s.gif';
</script>

<script type="text/javascript" src='helloWorld.js'>     ❹ The soon-to-be-created
</script>                                                   helloWorld.js
```

Listing 1.1 includes the HTML markup for a typical Ext-only setup, which includes the concatenated CSS file, ext-all-css ❶ and the two required JavaScript files, ext-base.js and ext-all-debug.js ❷. Next, you create a JavaScript block ❸, where you set the ever-important Ext.BLANK_IMAGE_URL property. Last, you include our soon-to-be-created helloWorld.js file ❹.

If you haven't noticed it, we're using /extjs as the absolute path to our framework code. Be sure to change it if your path is different. Next, you create our helloWorld.js file, which will contain your main JavaScript code.

Listing 1.2   Creating helloWorld.js

```
function buildWindow() {
   var win =  new Ext.Window({            ❶ A new instance
       id        : 'myWindow',               of Ext.Window
       title     : 'My first Ext JS  Window',
       width     : 300,
       height    : 150,
       layout    : 'fit',                  ❷ An autoLoad
       autoLoad : {                          configuration object
          url     : 'sayHi.html',
          scripts : true
       }
   });                                    ❸ Calling upon our
   win.show();                              window to show()
}
                                          ❹ Passing buildWindow
Ext.onReady(buildWindow);                   to Ext.onReady
```

In listing 1.2, you create the function buildWindow, which will be passed to Ext.onReady for later execution. Inside this buildWindow, you create a new instance of Ext.Window and set up a reference to it called win ❶. You pass a single configuration object to Ext.Window, which has all of the properties required to configure the instance you're instantiating.

In the configuration object, you specify an id of 'myWindow', which will be used in the future to look up the window using the Ext.getCmp convenience method. You then specify a title for the window, which will appear as blue text on the topmost portion of the window, known as the title bar. Next, you specify the height and width of the window. You then go on to set the layout as 'fit', which ensures that whatever child item is managed by your window is stretched to the dimensions of its Content-Body. You then move on to specify an autoLoad configuration object ❷, which will instruct the window to automatically fetch an HTML fragment (specified via the url property) and execute a JavaScript if found (specified via scripts : true).

This ends the configuration object for your instance of Ext.Window. Next, you call on win.show ❸, which renders your window. This is where you find the conclusion of the buildWindow method. The last thing you do is call Ext.onReady ❹ and

HTML fragments

An HTML fragment is HTML that isn't enclosed by head and body tags and isn't considered a full page. Ext JS loads fragments because only one HEAD and BODY tag can exist in a page.

pass your method, `buildWindow`, as a reference. This ensures that `buildWindow` is
executed at the right time, which is when the
DOM is fully built and before any images are
fetched. Let's see how your window renders.
Go ahead and request helloWorld.html in
your browser. If you coded everything
properly, you'll see a window similar to the
one in figure 1.19, with a spinning icon next
to the "Loading…" text, known as a loading
indicator.

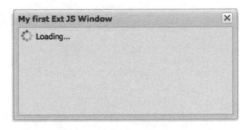

**Figure 1.19   Our first Ext JS window attempting
to load content via Ajax**

Why do you see this message? Because you haven't created sayHi.html, which you
referenced in the `url` property of the `autoLoad` configuration object. Essentially, you
instructed Ext JS to load something that wasn't on the web server. Next, you'll construct sayHi.html, where you'll create an HTML fragment, which will include some
JavaScript.

Listing 1.3   Creating sayHi.html

```
<div>Hello from the <b>world</b> of Ajax!</div>          ①  "Hello world" DIV tag

<script type='text/javascript'>
  function highlightWindow() {
    var win     = Ext.getCmp('myWindow');                    Highlight body
    var winBody = win.body;                              ②  of window
    winBody.highlight();
  }
                                                         ③  Delay execution
  highlightWindow.defer(1000);                              by one second
</script>
```

In listing 1.3, you create an HTML fragment file, sayHi.html. It contains a div ① from
which we have our "Hello world" message. After that, you have a `script` tag with some
JavaScript, which will get executed after this fragment is loaded by the browser. In our
code, we create a new function called `higlightWindow` ②, which will be executed
after a delay of one second. Inside that function, you perform a `highlight` effect on
the content body of the window. The execution of `highlightWindow` is delayed by one
second ③. Here's how this method works.

You start by creating a reference to the `Window` you created in our helloWorld.js file
by using a utility method called `Ext.getCmp`, which looks up an Ext JS component by
id. When you created your window, you assigned it an `id` of `'myWindow'`, which is what
you're passing to `Ext.getCmp`. This works because all components (widgets) are registered with the `ComponentMgr` upon instantiation. `Ext.getCmp` is a way to retrieve a reference by `id` from any context within your application.

After you get the reference of your `Window`, you create a reference, `winBody`, to its
content body via the `body` property. You then call its highlight method, which will

Figure 1.20   Our Ext JS `Window` **loading the our HTML fragment (left) and the highlight effect performed on the** `Window`**'s content body (right)**

perform the highlight (fade from yellow to white) operation on the element. This is where you conclude the `highlightWindow` method.

The last thing you do in this JavaScript block is call `highlightWindow.defer` and pass a value of `1000`, which defers the execution of `highlightWindow` by one thousand milliseconds (or one second).

If you've never heard of `defer` in the JavaScript language, that's because you're using an Ext-introduced method. Ext JS leverages JavaScript's extensibility to add convenience methods to important core language classes, such as `Array`, `Date`, `Function`, `Number`, and `String`. This means every instance of any of those classes has the new convenience methods. In this case, you're using `defer`, which is an extension of `Function`. If you're an old-timer, you're probably asking, "Why not use `setTimeout`?" The first reason is because of ease of use. Call `.defer` on any method and pass the length of time to defer its operation. That's it. Another reason to use it is because it allows us to control the scope from which the deferred method is being executed and pass custom parameters, which `setTimeout` lacks.

You then end your HTML fragment, which can now be fetched by your `Window`. Refresh helloWorld.html and you should see something like figure 1.20.

If you did everything correctly, your results should be exactly like those shown in figure 1.20, where the content body is being populated with the HTML fragment (left), and exactly one second later, the content body of the window highlights yellow (right). Pretty cool, huh? I suggest that you take some time to modify the example and use the API to do things like changing the color of the highlight effect. Here's a hint: Look under Ext JS > Fx for the list of effects and their parameters.

1.7   *Summary*

In this introduction to Ext JS, you learned how it can be used to build robust web applications or integrated into existing websites. You also learned how it measures up against other popular frameworks on the market and that it's the only UI-based framework to contain UI-centric support classes such as the `Component`, `Container`, and `Layout` models. Remember that Ext JS can ride on top of jQuery, Prototype, and YUI.

We explored many of the core UI widgets that the framework provides and showed that the number of prebuilt widgets helps rapid application development efforts. In doing that, we talked about some of the changes that Ext JS 3.0 has brought forth, such as Flash charts.

Last, we discussed where to download and how to set up the framework with each individual base framework. We created a "Hello world" example of how to use an Ext JS `Window` to retrieve an HTML fragment via Ajax with a few simple lines of JavaScript.

In the chapters to follow, we'll explore how Ext JS works from the inside out. This knowledge will empower you to make the best decisions when building well-constructed UIs and better enable you to leverage the framework effectively. This will be a fun journey.

Back to the basics

2

This chapter covers
- Learning how to bootstrap your JavaScript code properly
- Managing DOM elements with `Ext.Element`
- Loading HTML fragments via Ajax
- Exercising a simple highlight effect on an HTML element
- Implementing `Template`s and `XTemplate`s

When working on applications, I often think metaphorically, which helps me develop parallels for concepts in my mind. I like to think of the timing of an application's launch as similar to that of the space shuttle's launch, where timing can mean the difference between a successful launch and inevitable frustration. Knowing when to initialize your JavaScript is one of the most critical things when dealing with anything that manipulates the DOM. In this chapter you'll learn how to launch your JavaScript using Ext to ensure your application code initializes at the right time on each browser. We can then begin our discussion on using `Ext.Element` to manipulate the DOM.

As you know, DOM manipulation is one of the tasks that web developers are required to code for most of the time. Whether it's addition or removal of elements, I'm sure you've felt the pain of performing these tasks with the out-of-the-box JavaScript methods. After all, DHTML has been at the center of dynamic web pages for ages now.

We'll look at the heart of Ext, known as the `Ext.Element` class, which is a robust cross-browser DOM element-management suite. You'll learn to use `Ext.Element` to add and remove nodes from the DOM, and you'll see how it makes this task easier.

Once you're familiar with the `Ext.Element` class, you'll learn how to use templates to stamp out HTML fragments into the DOM. We'll also dive deep into the use of the `XTemplate`, which descends from `Template`, and you'll learn how to use it to easily loop through data and inject behavior-modification logic while you're at it. This is going to be a fun chapter. Before you can begin coding, however, you must learn the proper way of launching your code.

2.1 Starting off the right way

Since the early days, when most developers wanted to initialize their JavaScript, they typically would add an `onLoad` attribute to the `<body>` tag of the HTML page that's loading:

```
<body onLoad='initMyApp();'>
```

Although this method of invoking JavaScript works, it's not ideal for Ajax-enabled Web 2.0 sites or applications because the `onLoad` code is generally fired at different times for different browsers. For instance, some browsers fire this when the DOM is ready and all content has been loaded and rendered by the browser. For Web 2.0, this isn't a good thing, because the code generally wants to start managing and manipulating DOM elements when the DOM is ready but before any images are loaded. This is where you can achieve the right balance of timing and performance. I like to call this the "sweet spot" in the page-loading cycle.

Like many things in the world of browser development, each browser generally has its own way of knowing when its DOM nodes can be manipulated.

2.1.1 Fire only when ready!

There are native browser solutions for detecting that the DOM is ready, but they aren't implemented uniformly across each browser. For instance, Firefox and Opera fire the `DOMContentLoaded` event. Internet Explorer requires a script tag to be placed in the document with a `defer` attribute, which fires when its DOM is ready. WebKit fires no event but sets the `document.readyState` property to `complete`, so a loop must be executed to check for that property and fire off a custom event to tell your code that the DOM is ready. Boy, what a mess!

2.1.2 Let Ext JS pull the trigger

Luckily, you have `Ext.onReady`, which solves the timing issues and serves as the base from which to launch your application-specific code. Ext JS achieves cross-browser compatibility by detecting which browser the code is executing on and manages the detection of the DOM ready state, executing your code at just the right time.

`Ext.onReady` is a reference to `Ext.EventManager.onDocumentReady` and accepts three parameters: the method to invoke, the scope from which to call the method, and any options to pass to the method. The second parameter, scope, is used when you're calling an initialization method that requires execution within a specific scope.

> ### Getting a handle on scope
> The concept of scope is something that many JavaScript developers wrestle with early in their career. It's a concept that I think every JavaScript developer should master. A great resource to learn about scope can be found at http://www.digital-web.com/articles/scope_in_javascript/.d.

All of your Ext-based JavaScript code can be anywhere below (after) the inclusion of Ext JS script. This is important because JavaScript files are requested and loaded synchronously. Trying to call any Ext methods before Ext is defined in the namespace will cause an exception, and your code will fail to launch. Here's a simple example of using `Ext.onReady` to fire up an Ext `MessageBox` alert window:

```
Ext.onReady(function() {
    Ext.MessageBox.alert('Hello', 'The DOM is ready!');
});
```

In the preceding example, we pass what's known as an anonymous function to `Ext.onReady` as the only parameter, which will be executed when the DOM is ready to be manipulated. Our anonymous function contains a line of code to invoke an Ext `MessageBox`, as shown in figure 2.1.

An anonymous function is any function that has no variable reference to it or key reference in an object. `Ext.onReady` registers our anonymous function, which is to be executed when the internal `docReadyEvent` event is fired. In short, an event is like a message that something has occurred. A listener is a method that's registered to be executed, or called, when that event occurs, or fires.

Ext fires this `docReadyEvent` event when it finds *exactly* the right time (remember the sweet spot) in the page-loading cycle to execute our anonymous method and any other registered listeners. If the concept of events sounds a bit confusing, don't be alarmed. Event management is a complex topic, and we'll cover it later, in chapter 3.

I can't stress enough the importance of using `Ext.onReady`. All of our example code (and eventually your application code) *has to be launched* this way. Moving forward, if `Ext.onReady` isn't explicitly detailed in the examples, please assume that you must launch the code with it and wrap the example code in the following manner:

Figure 2.1   The result of our `Ext.onReady` call, an `Ext.MessageBox` window

```
Ext.onReady(function() {
    // ... Some code here ...
});
```

Now that you're comfortable with using `Ext.onReady` to launch your code, we should spend some time exploring the `Ext.Element` class, which is known as the heart of the framework. This is one of those essential topics that's used everywhere in the framework where DOM manipulation occurs.

2.2 The Ext.Element class

All JavaScript-based web applications revolve around a nucleus, which is the HTML `Element`. JavaScript's access to the DOM nodes gives us the power and flexibility to perform any action against the DOM we wish. These could include adding, deleting, styling, or changing the contents of any node in the document. The traditional method to reference a DOM node by ID is

```
var myDiv = document.getElementById('someDivId');
```

The `getElementById` method works well to allow you to perform some basic tasks such as changing the `innerHTML` or styling and assigning a CSS class. But what if you wanted to do more with the node, such as manage its events, apply a style on mouse click, or replace a single CSS class? You'd have to manage all of your own code and constantly update to make sure your code is fully cross-browser compatible. I honestly can't think of another thing that I wouldn't want to spend my time on than this. Thankfully, Ext takes care of this for you.

2.2.1 The heart of the framework

Let's turn to the `Ext.Element` class, which is known to many in the Ext JS community as the heart of Ext JS because it plays a role in every UI widget in the framework and can be generally accessed by the `getEl()` method or the `el` property.

The `Ext.Element` class is a full DOM element-management suite, which includes a treasure chest of utilities, enabling the framework to work its magic on the DOM and provide the robust UI that we've come to enjoy. This toolset and all of its power are available to us, the end developers.

Because of its design, its capabilities aren't relegated to simple management of DOM elements but rather to performing complex tasks such as managing dimensions, alignments, and coordinates with relative ease. You can also easily update an element via Ajax, manage child nodes, animate, enjoy full event management, and so much more.

2.2.2 Using Ext.Element for the first time

Using `Ext.Element` is easy and makes some of the hardest tasks simple. In order to exercise `Ext.Element`, you need to set up a base page. Set up a page where you include the Ext JavaScript and CSS, as we discussed in chapter 1. Next, include the following CSS and HTML:

```
<style type="text/css">
    .myDiv {
        border: 1px solid #AAAAAA;
```

```
        width: 200px;
        height: 35px;
        cursor: pointer;
        padding: 2px 2px 2px 2px;
        margin: 2px 2px 2px 2px;
    }
</style>

<div id='div1' class='myDiv'> </div>
```

What we're doing here is setting the stage for our examples by ensuring our target `div` tags have specific dimensions and a border so we can clearly see them on the page. We include one `div` with the `id` of `'div1'`, which we'll use as a target. If you set up your page correctly, the stylized `div` should be clearly visible, as shown in figure 2.2. This figure shows our generic HTML box, which we'll use to exercise the fundamental `Ext.Element` methods.

> **NOTE**   All of our `Ext.Element` example code will reference the base page we just set up. If you're interested in watching changes to the DOM occur live, I suggest using the multiline Firebug text editor inside of Firefox with these examples. If you're unfamiliar with Firebug, you can learn all about it via http://getfirebug.com/wiki/index.php/Main_Page. Conversely, you can place these examples inside generic script blocks. Just be sure to use `Ext.onReady()`.

According to the CSS, any `div` with the class `myDiv` is set to 35 pixels high and 200 pixels wide and looks a bit odd. Let's make that element perfectly square by setting the height to 200 pixels:

```
var myDiv1 = Ext.get('div1');
myDiv1.setHeight(200);
```

The execution of the previous two lines is pretty important. The first line uses `Ext.get`, which we pass the string `'div1'`, and returns an instance of `Ext.Element` referenced by the variable `myDiv1`. `Ext.get` uses `document.getElementById` and wraps it with the Ext element-management methods.

You leverage your newly referenced instance of `Ext.Element`, `myDiv1`, and call its `setHeight` method, passing it an integer value of 200, which grows the box to 200 pixels tall. Conversely, you could use its `setWidth` method to change the width of the element, but we'll skip that and jump to something more fun.

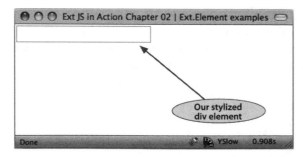

Figure 2.2   Our base page with our stylized `div` ready for some Ext Element action

"It now looks like a perfect square. Big deal!" you say. Well, let's change dimensions again; this time we'll use `setSize`. Let's make the `width` and `height` 350 pixels. We'll leverage the already created reference, `myDiv1`:

```
myDiv1.setSize(350, 350, {duration: 1, easing:'bounceOut'});
```

What happens when you execute this line of code? Does it animate and have a bouncing effect? That's better!

Essentially, the `setSize` method is the composite of `setHeight` and `setWidth`. For this method, you passed the target width and height and an object with two properties, `duration` and `easing`. A third property, if defined, will make `setSize` animate the size transition of the element. If you don't care for animation, omit the third argument, and the box will change size instantly, much like when you set the height.

Setting dimensions is a single facet of the many sides of element management with the `Element` class. Some of `Ext.Element`'s greatest power comes from its ease of use for full CRUD (create, read, update, and delete) of elements.

2.2.3 *Creating child nodes*

One of the great uses of JavaScript is the ability to manipulate the DOM, which includes the creation of DOM nodes. JavaScript provides many methods natively that give you this power. Ext JS conveniently wraps many of these methods with the `Ext.Element` class. Let's have some fun creating child nodes.

To create a child node, you use `Element`'s `createChild` method:

```
var myDiv1 = Ext.get('div1');
myDiv1.createChild('Child from a string');
```

This code adds a string node to the `innerHtml` of your target `div`. What if you wanted to create an element? Easy as pie:

```
myDiv1.createChild('<div>Element from a string</div>');
```

This usage of `createChild` will append a child `div` with the string `'Element from a string'` to the `innerHtml` of `div1`. I don't like to append children this way because I find the string representation of elements to be messy. Ext helps me with this problem by accepting a configuration object instead of a string:

```
myDiv1.createChild({
    tag  : 'div',
    html : 'Child from a config object'
});
```

Here, we're creating a child element by using a configuration object. We specify the `tag` property as `'div'` and the `html` as a string. This technically does the same thing as the prior `createChild` implementation but can be considered cleaner and self-documenting. What if you wanted to inject nested tags? With the configuration object approach, you can easily achieve this:

```
myDiv1.createChild({
    tag      : 'div',
    id       : 'nestedDiv',
```

```
    style     : 'border: 1px dashed; padding: 5px;',
    children : {
        tag   : 'div',
        html  : '...a nested div',
        style : 'color: #EE0000; border: 1px solid'
    }
});
```

In this code, you're creating one last child, which has an id, a bit of styling applied, and a child element, which is a div with some more styling. Figure 2.3 illustrates what the changes to the div look like.

In this illustration, you see all of the additions to myDiv1, including the live DOM view from Firebug, showing that you added a string node and three child divs, one of which has its own child div.

If you wanted to inject a child at the top of the list, you'd use the convenience method insertFirst, for instance:

```
myDiv1.insertFirst({
    tag  : 'div',
    html : 'Child inserted as node 0 of myDiv1'
});
```

Element.insertFirst will always insert a new element at position zero, even when no child elements exist in the DOM structure.

If you want to target the insertion of a child node at a specific index, the create-Child method can take care of that task. All you need to do is pass it the reference of where to inject the newly created node, for instance:

```
myDiv1.createChild({
    tag  : 'div',
    id   : 'removeMeLater',
    html : 'Child inserted as node 2 of myDiv1'
}, myDiv1.dom.childNodes[3]);
```

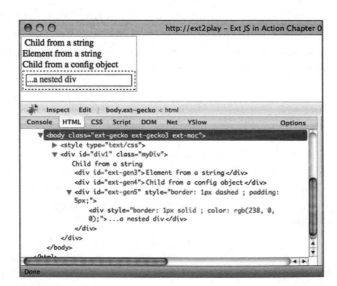

Figure 2.3   A composite of the element additions using `myDiv1.createChild()`

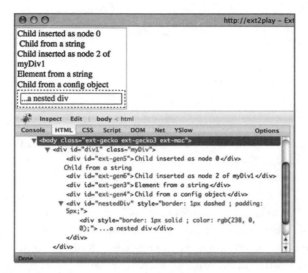

Figure 2.4   The results of our targeted DOM element insertions with `createChild()` using an index and `insertFirst()`

In this code, you're passing two arguments to `createChild`. The first is the configuration object representation of the newly created DOM element, and the second is the DOM reference of the target child node that `createChild` will use as the target to *inject* the newly created node. Please keep in mind the `id` that you set for this newly created item; you'll use this in a bit.

Notice that we're using `myDiv1.dom.childNodes`. `Ext.Element` gives you the opportunity to leverage all of the generic browser element-management goodness by means of the `dom` property.

> **NOTE** The `Element.dom` property is the same DOM object reference as returned by `document.getElementById()`.

Figure 2.4 shows what the inserted nodes look like in both the page view and the DOM hierarchy using the Firebug DOM inspection tool. As you can see in this figure, the node insertions functioned as we wanted them to. We used `insertFirst` to inject a new node at the top of the list and `createChild` to inject a node *above* child node 3. Remember to always count child nodes starting with the number 0 instead of 1.

Adding is something that we do often as web developers. After all, this is part of what DHTML is all about. But removing is equally important to know. Let's see how to remove some of the child elements using `Ext.Element`.

2.2.4   Removing child nodes

Removing nodes could be considered much easier than adding. All you need to do is locate the node with Ext and call its `remove` method. To exercise removal of child nodes, we're going to start with a clean and controlled slate. Create a new page with the following HTML:

```
<div id='div1' class="myDiv">
    <div id='child1'>Child 1</div>
    <div class='child2'>Child 2</div>
    <div class='child3'>Child 3</div>
    <div id='child4' class='sameClass'>
            <div id="nestedChild1" class='sameClass'>Nest Child 1</div>
    </div>
    <div>Child 5</div>
</div>
```

Examining this HTML, you find a parent div with the id of 'div1'. It has five direct descendants, the first of which has the id of 'child1'. The second and third children have no ids but have CSS classes of 'child2' and 'child3'. The fourth child element has an id of 'child4' and a CSS class of 'sameClass'. Likewise, it has a direct child with an id of "nestedChild1" and the same CSS class as its parent. The last child of div1 has no id or CSS class. The reason we have all this stuff going on is that we're going to start using CSS selectors as well as target directly the ids of the elements.

In the examples where we added child nodes, we always referenced the parent div (id='div1') by wrapping it in an Ext.Element class and leveraging its create methods. To remove a child node, the approach is different because we need to target specifically the node that's to be removed. Using the new DOM structure, we'll practice a few ways of doing this.

The first approach we'll examine is removing a child node for an already wrapped DOM element. We'll create an instance of Ext.Element wrapping div1 and then use it to find its first child node using a CSS selector:

```
var myDiv1 = Ext.get('div1');
var firstChild = myDiv1.down('div:first-child');
firstChild.remove();
```

In this example, we create a reference to div1 using Ext.get. We then create another reference, firstChild, to the first child using the Element.down method and pass a pseudo class selector, which causes Ext to query the DOM tree within the context of div1 for the first child, which is a div, and wrap it within an instance of Ext.Element.

The Element.down method queries the first-level DOM nodes for any given Ext.Element. It so happens that the element that's found is the one with the div id of 'child1'. We then call firstChild.remove, which removes that node from the DOM.

Here's how you could remove the last child from the list using selectors:

```
var myDiv1 = Ext.get('div1');
var lastChild = myDiv1.down('div:last-child');
lastChild.remove();
```

This example works similarly to the prior one. The biggest difference is that you use the selector 'div:last-child', which locates the last childNode for div1 and wraps it in an instance of Ext.Element. After that, you call lastChild.remove, and it's gone.

NOTE CSS selectors are a powerful way of querying the DOM for items. Ext JS supports the CSS3 selector specification. If you're new to CSS selectors, I highly advise visiting the following W3C page, which has a plethora of information on selectors: http://www.w3.org/TR/2005/WD-css3-selectors-20051215/#selectors.

What if you want to target an element by an `id`? You can use `Ext.get` to do your dirty work. This time, you'll create no reference and use *chaining* to take care of the job:

```
Ext.get('child4').remove();
```

Executing this code removes the child node with the `id` of `'child4'` and its child node. Always remember that removing a node with children will also remove its child nodes.

NOTE If you'd like to read more about chaining, Dustin Diaz, an industry-leading developer, has an excellent article on his site: http://www.dustindiaz.com/javascript-chaining/.

The last thing we'll look at is using `Ext.Element` to perform an Ajax request to load remote HTML fragments from the server and inject them into the DOM.

2.2.5 Using Ajax with Ext.Element

The `Ext.Element` class has the ability to perform an Ajax call to retrieve remote HTML fragments and inject those fragments into its `innerHTML`. To exercise this, you'll need to first write an HTML snippet to load:

```
<div>
    Hello there! This is an HTML fragment.
    <script type="text/javascript">
        Ext.getBody().highlight();
    </script>
</div>
```

In this HTML fragment, you have a simple `div` with an embedded `script` tag, which performs an `Ext.getBody` call and uses chaining to execute the results of that call to execute its `highlight` method. `Ext.getBody` is a convenience method to get a reference to the `document.body` wrapped by `Ext.Element`. Save this file as htmlFragment.html.

Next, you'll perform the load of this snippet:

```
Ext.getBody().load({
    url     : 'htmlFragment.html',
    scripts : true
});
```

In this snippet, you call the `load` method of the result of the `Ext.getBody` call and pass a configuration object specifying the `url` to fetch, which is the htmlFragment.html file, and set `scripts` to true. What happens when you execute this code? See figure 2.5.

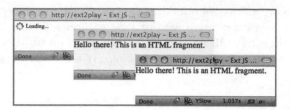

Figure 2.5   Loading an HTML fragment into the document body

When you execute this code snippet, you'll see that the document body performs an Ajax request to retrieve your htmlFragment.html file. While the file is being retrieved, it shows a loading indicator. Once the request is complete, the HTML fragment is injected into the DOM. You then see the entire body element highlighted in yellow, which is an indication that your JavaScript was executed. Now you see that using the Ext.Element.load utility method is a great convenience over having to manually code an Ext.Ajax.request call.

And there you have it. Adding and removing elements to and from the DOM is a cinch when using Ext.Element. Ext has another way to make adding elements even simpler, especially if you have repeatable DOM structures to be placed in the DOM. These are the Template and XTemplate utility classes.

2.3   Using Templates and XTemplates

The Ext.Template class is a powerful core utility that allows you to create an entire DOM hierarchy with slots that later can be filled in with data. Once you define a template, you can then use it to replicate one or more of the predefined DOM structures, with your data filling in the slots. Mastering templates will help you master UI widgets that use templates, such as the GridPanel, DataView, and ComboBox.

2.3.1   Exercising templates

You'll start out by creating an extremely simple template, and then you'll move on to create one that's much more complex:

```
var myTpl = new Ext.Template("<div>Hello {0}.</div>");

myTpl.append(document.body, ['Marjan']);
myTpl.append(document.body, ['Michael']);
myTpl.append(document.body, ['Sebastian']);
```

In this example, you create an instance of Ext.Template and pass it a string representation of a div with a slot, which is marked in curly braces, and store a reference in the variable myTpl. You then call myTpl.append and pass it a target element, document.body, and data to fill in the slots, which in this case happens to be a single element array that contains a first name.

You do this three consecutive times, which results in three divs being appended to the DOM, with each different first name filling in a slot. Figure 2.6 shows the result from our append calls.

As you can see, three `div`s were appended to the document body, each with a different name. The benefits of using templates should now be clear. You set the template once and apply it to the DOM with different values.

In the prior example, the slots were integers in curly braces, and you passed in single-item arrays. Templates can also map object key/values from plain objects. The following listing shows how to create a template that uses such syntax.

Listing 2.1   Creating a complex template

```
var myTpl = new Ext.Template(
    '<div style="background-color: {color}; margin: 10px;">',      ◁
        '<b> Name :</b> {name}<br />',                    Create complex
        '<b> Age :</b> {age}<br />',                      template ❶
        '<b> DOB :</b> {dob}<br />',
    '</div>'
);
                                     ❷ Compile template
myTpl.compile();    ◁                   for faster speed      ❸ Append template to
                                                                document body
myTpl.append(document.body,{                              ◁
    color : "#E9E9FF",
    name  : 'John Smith',
    age   : 20,
    dob   : '10/20/89'
});

myTpl.append(document.body,{
    color : "#FFE9E9",
    name  : 'Naomi White',
    age   : 25,
    dob   : '03/17/84'
});
```

When creating our complex `Template` ❶, the first thing you'll probably notice is that you pass in quite a few arguments. You do this because when creating a template, it's much easier to view the pseudo HTML in a tab-delimited format rather than a long string. The Ext developers were keen on this idea, so they programmed the `Template` constructor to read all of the *arguments* being passed, no matter how many.

In the `Template` pseudo HTML are slots for four data points. The first is `color`, which will be used to style the background of the element. The three other data points are `name`, `age`, and `dob`, which will be directly visible when the template is appended.

You then `compile` ❷ our template, which speeds up the `Template` by eliminating regular expression overhead. For these two operations you *technically* don't need to compile it because you wouldn't see the speed benefits, but for larger applications, where

Figure 2.6   Using our first template to append nodes to the DOM, shown in the exploded view in Firebug

many templates are stamped out, compiling has a clear benefit. To be safe, I always compile templates after instantiating them.

Last, you perform two `append` calls ❸, where you pass in the reference element and a data object. Instead of passing an array as you did when in your first exploration of templates, you pass in a data object, which has keys that match the template slots. Figure 2.7 shows the result of the complex template with a DOM view in Firebug.

By using the template, you were able to get two differently styled elements in the DOM without being displayed. What if you had an *array* of objects? For instance, what if an Ajax request

Figure 2.7   The result of our complex template with a DOM view in Firebug

returned an array of data objects, and you needed to apply a template for each data object? One approach could be looping through the array, which is easily done with a generic `for` loop or the more robust `Ext.each` utility method. I say nay to that approach. I'd use `XTemplate` instead, which makes the code much cleaner.

2.3.2   *Looping with XTemplates*

`XTemplate`s can *technically* be used for single data objects, but they can make life much easier when you have to deal with looping through arrayed data to stamp out HTML fragments onscreen. `XTemplate`s extends `Templates` and offers much more functionality. We'll start our exploration by creating an array of data objects and then create an `XTemplate`, which you'll use to stamp out HTML fragments, as in the following listing.

Listing 2.2   Using an `XTemplate` to loop through data

```
var tplData = [{
    color : "#FFE9E9",                      Data for
    name  : 'Naomi White',              ❶ XTemplate
    age   : 25,
    dob   : '03/17/84',
    cars  : ['Jetta', 'Camry', 'S2000']
},{
    color : "#E9E9FF",
    name : 'John Smith',
    age  : 20,
    dob  : '10/20/89',
    cars : ['Civic', 'Accord', 'Camry']
}];

                                            Instantiate new
                                        ❷ XTemplate
var myTpl = new Ext.XTemplate(
```

```
        '<tpl for=".">',
            '<div style="background-color: {color}; margin: 10px;">',
                '<b> Name :</b> {name}<br />',
                '<b> Age :</b> {age}<br />',
                '<b> DOB :</b> {dob}<br />',
            '</div>',
        '</tpl>'
);

myTpl.compile();

myTpl.append(document.body, tplData);
```

Append HTML fragments to DOM ❸

In listing 2.2 you first set up an array of data objects ❶, which are like the data objects you used in your last Template exploration, with the addition of a cars array, which you'll use in the next example.

Next, you instantiate an instance of XTemplate ❷, which looks much like the last Template configuration, except you encapsulate the div container with a custom tpl element with the attribute for, which contains the value ".". ❸ The tpl tag is like a logic or behavior *modifier* for the template and has two operators, for and if, which alter the way the XTemplate generates the HTML fragments. In this case, the value of "." instructs the

Figure 2.8 The result of using XTemplate with an exploded DOM view from Firebug

XTemplate to loop through the root of the array for which it's passed and construct the fragment based on the pseudo HTML encapsulated inside the tpl element. When you look at the rendered HTML, you'll see no tpl tags rendered to the DOM. The results of your efforts are identical to the Template example, as shown in figure 2.8.

Remember, the advantage of using XTemplates in this case is not having to write code to loop through the array of objects. You let the framework do the dirty work for you. The capabilities of XTemplates extend far beyond merely looping through arrays, which increase its usability exponentially.

2.3.3 *Advanced XTemplate usage*

You can configure XTemplates to loop through arrays within arrays and even have conditional logic. The example in the next listing will flex some XTemplate muscle and demonstrate many of these advanced concepts. Some of the syntax you're about to see will be foreign to you. Don't get discouraged. I'll explain every bit.

Listing 2.3 Advanced XTemplate usage

```
var myTpl = new Ext.XTemplate(
    '<tpl for=".">',
        '<div style="background-color: {color}; margin: 10px;">',
```

```
            '<b> Name :</b> {name}<br />',
            '<b> Age :</b> {age}<br />',
            '<b> DOB :</b> {dob}<br />',
            '<b> Cars : </b>',                    ❶ Loop through
            '<tpl for="cars">',                       cars data
                '{.}',                                            ❷ Display all
                '<tpl if="this.isCamry(values)">',                    data in array
                  '<b> (same car)</b>',                    Execute
                '</tpl>',                              ❸ this.isCamry method
                '{[ (xindex < xcount) ? ", " : "" ]}',
            '</tpl>',                                   Test for
            '<br />',                                 ❹ end of array
          '</div>',
        '</tpl>',                         ❺ Object containing
        {                                     one method
            isCamry : function(car) {
                return car === 'Camry';
            }
        }
    );

myTpl.compile();

myTpl.append(document.body, tplData);
```

This usage of XTemplate exercises quite a few advanced concepts, the first of which is looping within a loop ❶. Remember, the for attribute instructs the XTemplate to loop through a list of values. In this case, the for attribute has the value of 'cars', which differs from the value that's set for the first for attribute, ".". This instructs the XTemplate to loop this block of pseudo HTML for each individual car. Remember that cars is an array of strings.

Inside this loop is a string with "{.}" ❷, which instructs XTemplate to place the value of the array at the current index of the loop. In simple terms, the name of a car will be rendered at this position.

Next, you see a tpl behavior modifier with an if attribute ❸, which executes this.isCamry and passes values. The this.isCamry method is generated at the end of the XTemplate ❺. We'll speak more about this in a bit. The if attribute is more like an *if condition*, where the XTemplate will generate HTML fragments *if* the condition is met. In this case, this.isCamry must return true for the fragment that's encapsulated inside this tpl flag to be generated.

The values property is an internal reference of the values for the array you're looping through. Because you're looping through an array of strings, it references a single string, which is the name of a car.

In the next line, you're arbitrarily executing JavaScript code ❹. Anything encapsulated in curly braces and brackets ({[... JS code ...]}) will be interpreted as generic JavaScript; it has access to some local variables that are provided by XTemplate and can change with each iteration of the loop. In this case, you're checking to see if the current index (xindex) is less than the number of items in the array (xcount) and returning either a comma with a space or an empty string. Performing this test inline will ensure that commas are placed exactly between the names of cars.

The last item of interest is the object that contains your isCamry method ❺. Including an object (or reference to an object) with a set of members with the passing arguments to the XTemplate constructor will result in those members being applied directly to the instance of XTemplate itself. This is why you called this. isCamry directly in the if condition of one of the tpl behavior modifier pseudo elements. All of these member methods are called within the scope of the instance

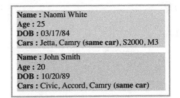

Figure 2.9   The results from the advanced XTemplate exercise

of the XTemplate for which they're being passed. This concept is extremely powerful but can be dangerous because you can override an existing XTemplate member, so please try to make your methods or properties unique. The isCamry method uses JavaScript shorthand to test whether the passed string, car, is equal to "Camry" and will return true if it is; otherwise, it will return false. Figure 2.9 shows the results of the advanced XTemplate exercise.

The results of the advanced XTemplate exercise show that all of our behavior injections worked as planned. All of the cars are listed, including proper comma placement. You can tell that our arbitrary JavaScript injection worked because the string "(same car)" is placed to the right of the Camry name.

As you can see, Templates and XTemplates have myriad benefits over generic DOM injections using Ext.Element to stamp out HTML fragments with data. I encourage you to look over the Template and XTemplate API pages for more details and examples of how to use these utilities. Your next exposure to Templates will be when you learn how to create a custom ComboBox.

2.4   Summary

In this chapter we discussed how JavaScript application logic was launched in the olden days with the onLoad handler of the <body> element. Remember that browsers typically have their own way of publishing when the DOM is ready for manipulation, which causes a code-management nightmare. In exercising Ext.onReady, you learned that it takes care of launching your application code at just the right time for each browser, so you can concentrate on the important stuff, application logic.

We then took an in-depth look the Ext.Element class, which wraps and provides end-to-end management for DOM nodes. We exercised a few of the management utilities for DOM nodes by adding and removing elements. All UI widgets use the Ext.Element, making it one of the most used components of the core framework. Each widget's element can be accessed via the (public) getEl method or the (private) el property, but only after it has been rendered.

Last, you learned about using the Template class to inject HTML fragments into the DOM. We also jumped into advanced techniques with XTemplates and showed how to embed behavioral modifying logic into the template definition itself, producing results depending on the data that provided.

Looking forward, we're going to focus on the UI side of the framework, where we'll jump right into the core concepts and models that drive the framework.

Events, Components, and Containers

This chapter covers

- Learning about software-driven events with `Observable`
- Getting to know the Component model and lifecycle
- Exploring the Ext JS Container model
- Managing parent-child relationship of widgets
- Implementing the Container model utility methods

I recall my early days with the Ext framework, when I started learning by toying with the examples and reading the API documentation. I spent many hours on some of the most important core UI concepts, such as adding user interaction, the reusability of widgets, and how one widget can contain or control another. For instance, how would I make the click of an anchor tag display an Ext `Window`? Sure, there's a generic JavaScript way of attaching an event handler, but I wanted to use Ext JS. Likewise, I needed to know how to get widgets to communicate with each other. For example, how would I reload a `GridPanel` when a row of another `GridPanel` is clicked? Also, how would I add and remove items dynamically from a `Panel`? Or how could I find a particular field within a form panel based on the type field?

This chapter is designed to cover these core concepts, which are essential to building rich and interactive user interfaces with the framework. Because we just covered Ext.Element in chapter 2, we'll leverage this information to set up native click handlers on DOM elements and learn how events flow in the DOM. We'll also touch on how widget events work from registration to firing the event.

We'll also explore the deep caverns of the fundamental UI building block, the Component class, and learn how it serves as the central model for all UI widgets by implementing a template for standard behaviors known as the Component lifecycle.

Last, we'll take some time discussing the Container class, where you'll get an in-depth understanding of how widgets can manage child items. You'll learn how to dynamically add and remove items to and from widgets like the Panel, which can be used as a building block for dynamically updating UIs.

3.1 Managing events with Observable

For me, one of the most fun tasks in developing web applications is coding to manage events. An event can be thought of as a signal that's sent by some source when something occurs that could require action. Understanding events is one of the key core concepts you must become familiar with, because this will aid you in developing user interfaces, which provide truly rich user interaction. For instance, what if you wanted to display a context menu on a GridPanel when a user right-clicks a row? You'd set up an event handler for the rowcontextmenu event, which will create and display the context menu.

Likewise, knowing how Ext Components communicate with each other via events is equally important. This section will give you the fundamental knowledge that you'll need.

3.1.1 Taking a step back

Although you may not have realized it, you use an event-driven operating system every day. All modern user interfaces are driven by events, which on a high level generally come from inputs such as a mouse or keyboard but can be synthesized by software. Events that are sent are dispatched, or fired. Methods that take actions on these events are listeners and are sometimes called handlers.

Like modern operating systems, the browser too has an event model, where it fires events because of user input. This powerful model allows us to leverage that input and perform complex tasks, such as refreshing a grid or applying a filter. Just about every interaction that's performed with the browser fires events that can be leveraged. These are known as DOM-based events.

3.1.2 DOM-based events

Recall that events can come from user input or be synthesized by software. We need to first explore DOM-based events, which are initiated by user input, before we can have fun with software-based events. A lot of old-school web developers attached listeners directly to HTML elements, such as the onclick attribute:

```
<div id="myDiv" onclick="alert(this.id + ' was clicked');">Click me</div>
```

This method of adding event handlers was standardized by Netscape many years ago and is considered to be ancient practice by most modern JavaScript developers. This is because it adds a dependency for embedded JavaScript in HTML and leads to a code-management nightmare in addition to memory leaks by some browsers. I suggest avoiding this method at all costs.

The way events are managed across browsers is added to our ever-growing list of cross-browser incompatibilities. Luckily for us, Ext JS takes care of that and presents a unified interface for us to leverage:

```
var el = Ext.get('myDiv');
el.on('click', doSomething);
```

Here, we use the utility method, `Ext.get`, which allows Ext to wrap its element management class, `Ext.Element`, around a referenced element, giving us the power to do pretty much anything we want with that element. Embedded with each instance of `Ext.Element` is the usage of the Ext event-management engine, `Ext.util.Observable`. It's important to remember that all event management with Ext stems from `Ext.util.Observable`, which serves as a base for all DOM elements and `Components` that need to manage events.

Next, we attach a listener by calling `el.on` and pass the native event to be handled and a method to perform an action on the event. Ext takes event listener registration a step further by allowing you to pass a reference to the `scope` from which the event handler is to be called and any parameters:

```
var el = Ext.get('myDiv');
el.on('click', doSomething, scopeRef, [opt1, opt2]);
```

It's important to note that the default `scope` is always the `object` from which the handler is being defined. If `scope` were not explicitly passed, the method `doSomething` would be called within the `scope` of the object `el`, which is an instantiation of `Ext.Element`.

Now that you've learned and exercised simple event handling on an `Element`, we'll take a quick glance at how events flow in the DOM.

3.1.3   *Event flow in the DOM*

In the early days of the internet, Netscape and Microsoft had two completely separate approaches with regard to event flow direction. In the Netscape model, events flowed downward from the document body to the source, which is known as *event capture*. The Microsoft model, known as *bubbling*, was exactly the inverse of capture, where the event is generated from the node from which the user action is performed and *bubbles up* to the `document` object, which performs a default action based on what type of node was clicked. Thankfully, the W3C model, shown in figure 3.1, combined these two models and is what we use now.

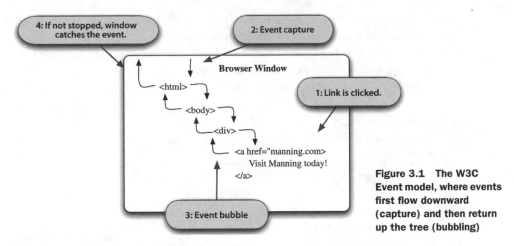

Figure 3.1 The W3C Event model, where events first flow downward (capture) and then return up the tree (bubbling)

As you can see, the user clicking the anchor tag generates a DOM-level click event. This causes the event-capture phase to occur, which cascades the event down the DOM tree, where it eventually lands at the target node, the anchor tag. If the event isn't stopped, it'll bubble back up to the browser window, where it'll cause the browser's location to change.

> **NOTE** If you're new to DOM events and want to learn more about the inner workings, Peter-Paul Koch has an excellent article on his site, in which he explains events in browsers in much greater detail than what is covered in this book. Here's the direct link: http://www.quirksmode.org/js/events_order.html.

Most of the time when you're developing event handlers for DOM events, you have to worry about bubbling. To demonstrate why this is important, we'll need to set up some HTML and attach event handlers to the node. We'll use the Firebug console to echo out messages. If you don't wish to use Firebug, the generic JavaScript `alert` box will work.

Suppose you have the following HTML, and you want to apply separate click listeners to both the `div` and the `anchor` tags:

```
<div id="myDiv">
    MyDiv Text
    <a href="#" id="myHref">
        My Href
    </a>
</div>
```

You'll register a click handler to the outermost element, `myDiv`, and use chaining so you don't have to set a static reference to the result of the `Ext.get` method call. You'll also pass an anonymous function as the second parameter instead of passing a reference to an existing function:

```
Ext.get('myDiv').on('click', function(eventObj, elRef) {
  console.log('myDiv click Handler, source elment ID: ' +  elRef.id);
});
```

After rendering the page, expand Firebug and click the anchor tag. You'll see a Firebug console message indicating that you clicked the myHref tag. Hold the phone—you only assigned a listener to the anchor's parent element, 'myDiv'. How could this be?

This is event bubbling in action. Remember that the click event generated from the anchor tag bubbled upward to the Container div, where you attached the click handler. That bubbled event triggered the event handler, causing its execution, thus the console message.

Next, attach a click handler to the anchor tag:

```
Ext.get('myHref').on('click', function(eventObj, elRef) {
    console.log('myHref click handler, source elment ID: ' + elRef.id);
});
```

Refresh your page and click the anchor again; you'll see two events fired, as shown in figure 3.2.

Having both event listeners fire could be troublesome and considered a waste of resources, especially if only one is needed. In order to stop this from happening, you need to stop the bubbling (propagation) of the click event in the anchor. Only then can you have separation from the anchor and the div element click event handlers.

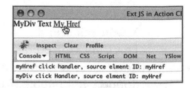

Figure 3.2 The results of our click event handlers in the Firebug console

3.1.4 *Burst the bubble*

To prevent both event handlers from triggering, you'll have to modify the anchor click event handler to include a stopEvent call on the instance of Ext.EventObject (eventObj) passed to the handler:

```
Ext.get('myHref').on('click', function(eventObj, elRef) {
    eventObj.stopEvent();
    console.log('myHref click handler, source elment ID: ' + elRef.id);
});
```

Refresh the page and click the anchor again. This time, you'll see only one Firebug console message per click, indicating that you've clicked the anchor tag. Likewise, clicking the div element will produce a message stating that you clicked the div.

The eventObj.stopEvent method call stops the event bubbling in its tracks. This is important to remember because there are other interactions for which you may want to cancel event propagation, such as contextmenu, where you'd want to show your own context menu instead of the browser's default menu.

We'll modify our example to listen to listen to the contextmenu event to perform this task:

```
Ext.get('myDiv').on('contextmenu', function(eventObj, elRef) {
    console.log('myDiv contextmenu Handler, source el ID: ' + elRef.id);
});

Ext.get('myHref').on('contextmenu', function(eventObj, elRef) {
```

```
    eventObj.stopEvent();
    console.log('myHref contextmenu Handler, source el ID: ' + elRef.id);

    if (!this.ctxMenu) {
        this.ctxMenu = new Ext.menu.Menu({
            items : [{
                text : "This is"
            },{
                text : "our custom"
            },{
                text : "context menu"
            }]
        });
    }
    this.ctxMenu.show(elRef);

});
```

In this example, we change the registered event from click to contextmenu for both the div and anchor elements. For the div event handler, we echo out a console message, providing an indication that the handler was triggered. For the anchor event handler, we stop the event propagation, log the event trigger in the Firebug console, create a new Ext menu, and display it below the anchor element.

If you right-click the div, you'll see the default browser context menu. But if you right-click the anchor (figure 3.3), you'll see your own custom menu because you halted the propagation of the contextmenu event, preventing it from bubbling back up to the browser.

As you can see, the registration of event handlers on DOM nodes is a simple task, but knowing whether you have to stop an event from bubbling up can be tricky. Certainly the contextmenu event is the only event that comes to mind that always needs to be stopped to prevent default browser behavior.

Next, we'll focus our attention on software-driven events, which is another key concept of the framework because inter-Component events are used extensively in the framework.

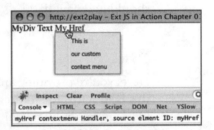

Figure 3.3 Displaying our custom context menu by means of a `contextmenu` event handler

3.1.5 *Software-driven events*

Almost every Ext widget or Component has custom events that it fires when it deems necessary. For instance, when a widget is finished rendering in the DOM, it fires a render event.

This is because just about everything extends Ext.util.Observable, which gives widgets the ability to exhibit similar behavior to complex UI environments such as your desktop UI. Events from widgets and Components can include DOM-based events that are bubbled up, such as click and keyup or Ext internal events such as beforerender and datachanged.

The API is a great place to read about events for a particular subclass of `Observable`. The last section of each API page is dedicated to public events from which other `Components` can register listeners and take action.

3.1.6   *Registration of events and event listeners*

Before an Ext-based event can be fired, it must be added to the list of events for that instance of `Observable`. This is typically done with the `addEvent` method, which stems from the `Observable` class. Let's instantiate a new instance of `Observable` and add a custom event:

```
var myObservable = new Ext.util.Observable();

myObservable.addEvents('sayHello');
myObservable.addEvents('sayGoodbye');
```

If you want to register more than one event, you can pass one event label per argument:

```
myObservable.addEvents('sayhello', 'saygoodbye');
```

Alternatively, you can pass in a configuration object that has a list of event labels and whether they should be enabled by default:

```
myObservable.addEvents({
  'sayHello'    : true,
  'sayGoodbye' : true
});
```

Now that you have your events registered, you need to register an event handler. This should look familiar:

```
myObservable.on('sayHello', function() {
    console.log('Hello stranger');
});
```

Here, you're providing an event handler for your custom event, `sayHello`. Notice that this is exactly how you registered events on the DOM. The handler will log a console message in Firebug as an indication that it was executed. Because you have your custom event defined and you have a listener registered, you need to fire the event so that you can watch the event handler get called:

```
myObservable.fireEvent('sayHello');
```

You can see in figure 3.4 that firing the event causes the handler to execute, resulting in a Firebug console message being displayed.

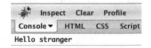

   Many events from the framework pass parameters when firing; among the parameters is a reference to the `Component` firing the event. Create an event handler for a custom `sayGoodbye` event so that it accepts two parameters, `firstName` and `lastName`:

Figure 3.4   A Firebug console message being displayed, indicating that the registered handler for the `sayHello` event was triggered

```
var sayGoodbyeFn = function(firstName, lastName) {
    console.log('Goodbye ' + firstName + ' ' + lastName + '!');
};
```

```
myObservable.on('sayGoodbye', sayGoodbyeFn);
```

Here, you define a method named sayGoodbyeFn, which accepts the two parameters. You then call myObservable.on, which is shorthand for myObservable.addListener, to register the event handler sayGoodbyeFn.

Next, fire the 'sayGoodbye' event and pass first and last names:

```
myObservable.fireEvent('sayGoodbye', 'John', 'Smith');
```

When calling fireEvent, the only required parameter is the first one, which is the event name. Parameters passed on thereafter are relayed to the event handler. The result of the 'sayGoodbye' event being fired with the firstName and lastName parameters passed should appear in your Firebug console, as shown in figure 3.5.

Figure 3.5   A Firebug console message displays as the result of the firing of the sayGoodbye event.

Remember that if you register an event handler without specifying scope, it will be called within the scope of the Component that's firing the event. As we continue our journey into the Ext JS world, we'll revisit events again because we'll use them to "wire" widgets together.

Just as the registration of event handlers is important to completing tasks, deregistration of event handlers is equally important to ensure proper cleanup when an event handler is no longer required. Fortunately, the method call to do so is extremely simple:

```
myObservable.removeListener('sayGoodbye', sayGoodbyeFn);
```

Here, we call myObservable.removeListener, passing in the event from which the listener is to be deregistered and the listener method to deregister. The shorthand for removeListener is un (opposite of on) and is commonly used in the framework and application code. The preceding code looks like this in shorthand:

```
myObservable.un('sayGoodbye', sayGoodbyeFn);
```

Managing events and event listeners is as straightforward as described. Using anonymous functions won't work with this approach because you have to specify which function you want to remove from the listener. Always remember to deregister event handlers when they're no longer needed. This will help reduce the memory footprint of your application and help ensure that no exceptions occur because of an event handler being triggered when it shouldn't be.

You're now familiar with registering events to DOM elements and have glanced at software-driven events; we can start to gravitate toward the UI portion of the framework. Before we dive into configuring and constructing widgets, we need to look at the Component model, which serves as the base model for all UI widgets. Having a solid grasp of how the Component model works in Ext JS 3.0 will allow you to better utilize the UI portion of framework, especially when managing child items of a Container.

3.2   *The Component model*

The Ext Component model is a centralized model that provides many of the essential Component-related tasks, which include a set of rules dictating how the Component instantiates, renders, and is destroyed, known as the Component lifecycle.

All UI widgets are subclasses of Ext.Component, which means that all of the widgets conform to the rules dictated by the model. Figure 3.6 partially depicts how many items subclass Component, directly or indirectly.

Knowing how each UI widget is going to behave introduces stability and predictability into the framework, which I enjoy. The Component model also supports direct instantiation of classes or deferred instantiation, known as XTypes. Knowing which to use when can enhance the responsiveness of your application.

3.2.1   *XTypes and Component Manager*

Ext 2.0 introduced a radical new concept known as an XType, which allows for lazy instantiation of Components, which can speed up complex user interfaces and can clean up our code quite a bit.

In short, an XType is nothing more than a plain JavaScript object, which generally contains an xtype property with a string value denoting which class the XType is for. Here's a quick example of an XType in action:

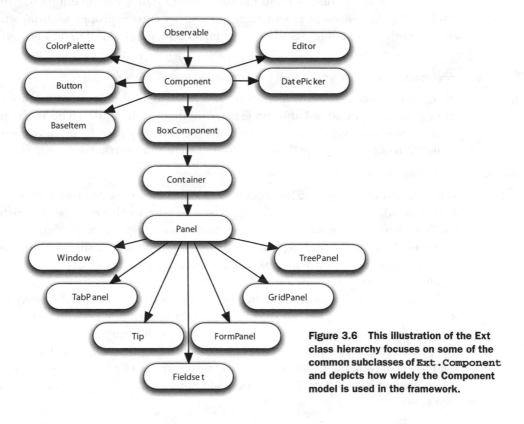

Figure 3.6   This illustration of the Ext class hierarchy focuses on some of the common subclasses of Ext.Component and depicts how widely the Component model is used in the framework.

```
var myPanel = {
    xtype    : 'panel',
    height   : 100,
    width    : 100,
    html     : 'Hello!'
};
```

In this configuration object, myPanel is an XType configuration object that would be used to configure an Ext.Panel widget. This works because just about every widget is registered to the Ext.ComponentMgr class with a unique string key and a reference to that class, which is then referred to as an XType. At the tail end of each Ext UI widget class, you'll find the registration of that widget in the Ext.ComponentMgr.

Registration of a Component is simple:

```
Ext.reg ('myCustomComponent', myApp.customClass);
```

The act of registering a Component to the ComponentMgr appends or replaces the new Component to the internal reference map of the ComponentMgr singleton. Once registration is complete, you can specify your custom Component as an XType:

```
new Ext.Panel({
    ...
    items : {
        xtype : 'myCustomComponent',
        ...
    }
});
```

When a visual Component, which can contain children, is initialized, it looks to see if it has this.items and will inspect this.items for XType configuration objects. If any are found, it will attempt to create an instance of that Component using Component-Mgr.create. If the xtype property isn't defined in the configuration object, the visual Component will use its defaultType property when calling ComponentMgr.create.

I realize that this may sound a tad confusing at first. I think you can better understand this concept if we demonstrate it. To do this, we'll create a window with an accordion layout that includes two children, one of which won't contain an xtype property. First, let's create our configuration objects for two of the children:

```
var panel1 = {
    xtype : 'panel',
    title : 'Plain Panel',
    html  : 'Panel with an xtype specified'
};

var panel2 = {
    title : 'Plain Panel 2',
    html  : 'Panel with <b>no</b> xtype specified'
};
```

Notice that panel1 has an explicit xtype value of 'panel', which in turn will be used to create an instance of Ext.Panel. Objects panel1 and panel2 are similar but have two distinct differences. Object panel1 has an xtype specified, whereas panel2 doesn't. Next, we'll create our window, which will use these xtypes:

```
new Ext.Window({
    width       : 200,
    height      : 150,
    title       : 'Accordion window',
    layout      : 'accordion',
    border      : false,
    layoutConfig : {
        animate : true
    },
    items : [
        panel1,
        panel2
    ]
}).show();
```

In our new instantiation of Ext.Window, we pass items, which are an array of references to the two configuration objects we created earlier. The rendered window should appear as illustrated in figure 3.7. Clicking a collapsed panel will expand and collapse any other expanded panels, and clicking an expanded panel will collapse it.

One of the lesser-known advantages of using XTypes is developing somewhat cleaner code. Because you can use plain object notation, you can specify all of your XType child items inline, resulting in cleaner and more streamlined code. Here is the previous example reformatted to include all of its children inline:

```
new Ext.Window({
    width        : 200,
    height       : 150,
    title        : 'Accordion window',
    layout       : 'accordion',
    border       : false,
    layoutConfig : {
        animate : true
    },
    items : [
        {
            xtype : 'panel',
            title : 'Plain Panel',
            html  : 'Panel with an xtype specified'
        },
        {
            title : 'Plain Panel 2',
            html  : 'Panel with <b>no</b> xtype specified'
        }
    ]
}).show();
```

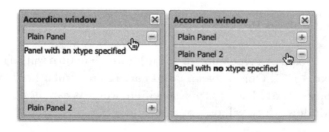

Figure 3.7   The results of our XType exercise: an Ext Window, which has two child panels derived from XType configuration objects

As you can see, we've included all of the child configuration items inline with the Window configuration object. The performance enhancements with using XTypes can't be seen with such a simple example. The biggest XType-based performance gains come in bigger applications, where there are a rather large number of Components to be instantiated.

Components also contain another performance-enhancing feature, lazy rendering. This means a Component is rendered only when necessary.

3.2.2 Component rendering

The Ext.Component class supports both direct and lazy (on-demand) render models. Direct rendering can happen when a subclass of Component is instantiated with either the renderTo or applyTo attribute, where renderTo points to a reference from which the Component renders itself and applyTo references an element that has HTML that's structured in such a way that allows the Component to create its own child elements based on the referenced HTML. You'd typically use these parameters when you wanted a Component to be rendered upon instantiation, for instance:

```
var myPanel = new Ext.Panel({
    renderTo : document.body,
    height   : 50,
    width    : 150,
    title    : 'Lazy rendered Panel',
    frame    : true
});
```

The result of this code would be the immediate render of the Ext.Panel, which sometimes is favorable and other times not. The times where it's not favorable can be when you want to *defer* rendering to another time in code execution or the Component is a child of another.

If you want to defer the rendering of the Component, omit the renderTo and applyTo attributes and call the Components render method when you (or your code) deem it necessary:

```
var myPanel = new Ext.Panel({
    height : 50,
    width  : 150,
    title  : 'Lazy rendered Panel',
    frame  : true
});

// ... some business logic...

myPanel.render(document.body);
```

In this example, you instantiate an instance of Ext.Panel and create a reference to it, myPanel. After some hypothetic application logic, you call myPanel.render and pass a reference to document.body, which renders the panel to the document body.

You could also pass an ID of an element to the render method:

```
myPanel.render('someDivId');
```

When passing an element ID to the render method, Component will use that ID with Ext.get to manage that element, which gets stored in its local el property. If this rings a bell, you may recall the conversation we had in the last chapter, when we were discussing Ext.Element, where you learned that you can access a widget's el property or use its *accessor* method, getEl, to get obtain the reference.

There's one major exception to this rule, however. You *never* specify applyTo or renderTo when the Component is a child of another. Components that *contain* other Components have a parent-child relationship, which is known as the Container model. If a Component is a child of another Component, it's specified in the items attribute of the configuration object, and its parent will manage the call to its render method when required. This is known as lazy or deferred rendering.

We'll investigate Containers later in this chapter, where you'll learn more about the parent-child relationship Components can have. But first, you need to understand the Component lifecycle, which details how Components are created, rendered, and eventually destroyed. Learning how each phase works will better prepare you for building robust and dynamic interfaces and can assist in troubleshooting issues.

3.3 *The Component lifecycle*

Ext Components, like everything in the real world, have a lifecycle where they're created, used, and destroyed. This lifecycle is broken up into three major phases: initialization, render, and destruction, as diagrammed in figure 3.8.

To better utilize the framework, you must understand in finer detail how the lifecycle works. This is especially important if you'll be building extensions, plug-ins, or composite Components. Quite a few steps take place at each phase of the lifecycle, which is controlled by the base class, Ext.Component.

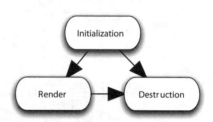

Figure 3.8 The Ext Component lifecycle always starts with initialization and always ends with destruction. The Component need not enter the render phase to be destroyed.

3.3.1 *Initialization*

The initialization phase is when a Component is born. All of the necessary configuration settings, event registration, and pre-render processes take place in this phase, as illustrated in figure 3.9.

Let's explore each step of the initialization phase:

1 *The configuration is applied*—When instantiating an instance of a Component, you pass a configuration object, which contains all of the necessary parameters and references to allow the Component to do what it's designed to do. This is done within the first few lines of the Ext.Component base class.

2 *Registration of the base Component events*—Per the Component model, each subclass of Ext.Component has, by default, a set of core events that are fired from the base class. These are fired before and after some behaviors occur: enable/

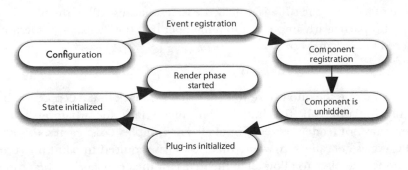

Figure 3.9 **The initialization phase of the `Component` lifecycle executes important steps such as event and `Component` registration as well as the calling the `initComponent` method. It's important to remember that a `Component` can be instantiated but may not be rendered.**

disable, show, hide, render, destroy, state restore, state save. The before events are fired and tested for a successful return of a registered event handler and will cancel the behavior before any real action has taken place. For instance, when `myPanel.show` is called, it fires the `beforeshow` event, which will execute any methods registered for that event. If the `beforeshow` event handler returns `false`, `myPanel` doesn't show.

3 *ComponentMgr registration*—Each `Component` that's instantiated is registered with the `ComponentMgr` class with a unique Ext-generated string ID. You can choose to override the Ext-generated ID by passing an `id` parameter in the configuration object passed to a constructor. The main caveat is that if a registration request occurs with a non-unique registration ID, the newest registration will override the previous one. Be careful to use unique IDs if you plan to use your own ID scheme.

4 *initComponent is executed*—The `initComponent` method is where a lot of work occurs for subclasses of `Component`, like registration of subclass-specific events, references to data stores, and creation of child `Components`. `initComponent` is used as a supplement to the constructor and is used as the main point to extending `Component` or any subclass thereof. We'll elaborate on extending with `initComponent` later on.

5 *Plug-ins are initialized*—If plug-ins are passed in the configuration object to the constructor, their `init` method is called, with the parent `Component` passed as a reference. It's important to remember that the plug-ins are called upon in the order in which they're referenced.

6 *State is initialized*—If the `Component` is state aware, it will register its state with the global `StateManager` class. Many Ext widgets are state aware.

7 *Component is rendered*—If the `renderTo` or `applyTo` parameter is passed into the constructor, the render phase begins at this time; otherwise, the `Component` then lies dormant, awaiting its `render` method to be called.

This phase of a `Component`'s life is usually the fastest because all of the work is done in JavaScript. It's particularly important to remember that the `Component` doesn't have to be rendered to be destroyed.

3.3.2   *Render*

The render phase is the one where you get visual feedback that a `Component` has been successfully initialized. If the initialization phase fails for whatever reason, the `Component` may not render correctly or at all. For complex `Components`, this is where a lot of CPU cycles get eaten up, where the browser is required to paint the screen and computations take place to allow all of the items for the `Component` to be properly laid out and sized. Figure 3.10 illustrates the steps of the render phase.

If `renderTo` or `applyTo` isn't specified, a call to the `render` method must be made, which triggers this phase. If the `Component` is not a child of another Ext `Component`, your code must call the `render` method, passing a reference of the DOM element:

```
someComponent.render('someDivId'');
```

If the `Component` is a child of another `Component`, its `render` method will be called by the parent `Component`. Let's explore the different steps of the render phase:

1   *beforerender is fired*—The `Component` fires the `beforerender` event and checks the return of any of the registered event handlers. If a registered event handler returns `false`, the `Component` halts the rendering behavior. Recall that step 2 of the initialization phase registers core events for subclasses of `Component` and that "before" events can halt execution behaviors.

2   *The `Container` is set*—A `Component` needs a place to live, and that place is known as its `Container`. If you specify a `renderTo` reference to an element, the `Component` adds a single child `div` element to the referenced element, known as its `Container`, and renders the `Component` inside that newly appended child. If an `applyTo` element is specified, the element referenced in the `applyTo`

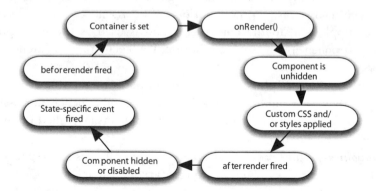

Figure 3.10   The render phase of the a `Component`'s life can utilize a lot of CPU because it requires elements to be added to the DOM and calculations to be performed to properly size and manage them.

parameter becomes the Component's Container, and the Component appends only those items to the referenced element that are required to render it. The DOM element referenced in applyTo will then be fully managed by the Component. You generally pass neither when the Component is a child of another Component, in which the container is the parent Component. It's important to note that you should pass only renderTo or applyTo, not both. We'll explore renderTo and applyTo later on, when you learn more about widgets.

3 *onRender is executed*—This is a crucial step for subclasses of Component, where all of the DOM elements are inserted to get the Component rendered and painted onscreen. Each subclass is expected to call its superclass.onRender first when extending Ext.Component or any subclass thereafter, which ensures that the Ext.Component base class can insert the core DOM elements needed to render a Component.

4 *The Component is unhidden*—Many Components are rendered hidden using the default Ext CSS class, like 'x-hidden'. If the autoShow property is set, any Ext CSS classes that are used for hiding Components are removed. It's important to note that this step doesn't fire the show event, so any listeners for that event won't be fired.

5 *Custom CSS classes or styles are applied*—Custom CSS classes and styles can be specified upon Component instantiation by means of the cls and style parameters. If these parameters are set, they're applied to the Container for the Component. It's suggested that you use cls instead of style, because CSS inheritance rules can be applied to the Component's children.

6 *The render event is fired*—At this point, all necessary elements have been injected into the DOM and styles applied. The render event is fired, triggering any registered event handlers for this event.

7 *afterRender is executed*—The afterRender event is a crucial post-render method that's automatically called by the render method within the Component base class and can be used to set sizes for the Container or perform any other post-render functions. All subclasses of Component are expected to call their superclass.afterRender method.

8 *The Component is hidden and/or disabled*—If either hidden or disabled is specified as true in the configuration object, the hide or disable method is called, which fires its respective before<action> event, which is cancelable. If both are true, and the before<action> registered event handlers don't return false, the Component is both hidden and disabled.

9 *State-specific events are fired*—If the Component is state aware, it will initialize its state-specific events with its Observable and register the this.saveEvent internal method as the handler for each of those state events.

10 Once the render phase is complete, unless the Component is disabled or hidden, it's ready for user interaction. It stays alive until its destroy method is called, in which it then starts its destruction phase.

The render phase is generally where a Component spends most of its life until it meets its demise with the destruction phase.

3.3.3   *Destruction*

As in real life, the death of a Component is a crucial phase in its life. Destruction of a Component performs critical tasks, such as removing itself and any children from the DOM tree, deregistration of the Component from ComponentMgr, and deregistration of event listeners, as depicted in figure 3.11.

The Component's destroy method could be called by a parent Container or by your code. Here are the steps in this final phase of a Component's life:

1   *beforedestroy is fired*—This, like many before<action> events, is a cancelable event, preventing the Component's destruction if its event handler returns false.

2   *beforeDestroy is called*—This method is first to be called within the Component's destroy method and is the perfect opportunity to remove any non-Component items, such as toolbars or buttons. Any subclass of Component is expected to call its superclass.beforeDestroy.

3   *Element and Element listeners are purged*—If a Component has been rendered, any handlers registered to its Element are removed and the Element is removed from the DOM.

4   *onDestroy is called*—Although the Component class itself doesn't perform any actions within the onDestroy method, subclasses are expected to use this to perform any post-destruction actions, such as removal of data stores. The Container class, which subclasses Component indirectly, manages the destruction of all registered children by the onDestroy method, alleviating the end developer of this task.

5   *Component is unregistered from ComponentMgr*—The reference for this Component in the ComponentMgr class is removed.

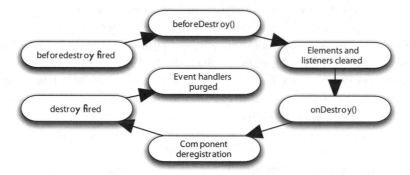

Figure 3.11   The destruction portion of a Component's life is equally as important as its initialization because event listeners and DOM elements must be deregistered and removed, reducing overall memory usage.

6 *The* destroy *event is fired*—Any registered event handlers are triggered by this event, which signals that the Component is no longer in the DOM.

7 *Component's event handlers are purged*—All event handlers are deregistered from the Component.

And there you have it, an in-depth look at the Component lifecycle, which is one of the features of the Ext framework that makes it so powerful and successful.

Be sure to not dismiss the destruction portion of a Component's lifecycle if you plan on developing your own custom Components. Many developers have gotten into trouble when they've ignored this crucial step and have code that has left artifacts such as data Stores that continuously poll web servers; or event listeners that are expecting an Element to be in the DOM were not cleaned properly and cause exceptions and the halt of execution of a crucial branch of logic.

Next, we'll look at the Container class, which is a subclass of Component and gives Components the ability to manage other Components in a parent-child relationship.

3.4 *Containers*

The Container model is a behind-the-curtains class that provides a foundation for Components to manage their child items, and is often overlooked by developers. This class provides a suite of utilities, which includes add, insert, and remove methods along with some child query, bubble, and cascade utility methods. These methods are used by most of the subclasses, including Panel, Viewport, and Window.

In order for you to learn how these tools work, we need to build a Container with some child items for us to use. The following listing is rather long and involved, but stay with me on this. The reward is just around the corner.

Listing 3.1 Building our first Container

```
var panel1 = {
    html   : 'I am Panel1',          ◁◺  First and second
    id     : 'panel1',               ❶  child panels
    frame  : true,
    height : 100
};

var panel2 = {
    html  : '<b>I am Panel2</b>',
    id    : 'panel2',
    frame : true
};

var myWin = new Ext.Window({
    id     : 'myWin',                ◁◺  Last child, a
    height : 400,                    ❷  form panel
    width  : 400,
    items  : [
        panel1,
        panel2
    ]
});

// myWin.show();
```

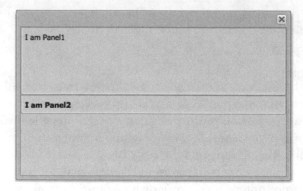

**Figure 3.12   The rendered
Container UI from listing 3.1**

Take a gander at listing 3.1. The first thing you do is create two vanilla panels ❶, and then you create myWin ❷, an instance of Ext.Window that *contains* the previously defined panels. The rendered UI should look like the one in figure 3.12.

We left some room at the bottom of myWin, which will come in handy when we add items. Each Container stores references to its children via an items property, which can be accessed via someContainer.items and is an instance of Ext.util.Mixed-Collection.

MixedCollection is a utility that allows the framework to store and index a mixed collection of data, which includes strings, arrays, and objects and provides a nice collection of handy utility methods. I like to think of it as the Array on steroids.

Now that we've rendered our Container, let's start to implement the addition of children to a container.

3.4.1   *Learning to tame children*

In the real world, learning to tame children can lead to frustration and many gray hairs, so we must learn to use the tools that are available to us. Mastering these utility methods will enable you to dynamically update your UI, which is in the spirit of Ajax web pages.

Adding Components is a simple task, in which we're provided two methods: add and insert. The add method only *appends* a child to the Container's hierarchy, whereas insert allows us to inject an item into the Container at a particular index.

Let's add to the Container that you created in listing 3.1. For this, we'll use our handy Firebug JavaScript console:

```
Ext.getCmp('myWin').add({
    title : 'Appended Panel',
    id    : 'addedPanel',
    html  : 'Hello there!'
});
```

Running the preceding code adds the item to the Container. Wait a cotton-picking second! Why didn't the new panel appear? Why does the Container still look like figure 3.1? It didn't show up because we didn't call the doLayout method for the Container. Let's see what happens when we call doLayout:

```
Ext.getCmp('myWin').doLayout();
```

Ah-ha! It showed up, but why? Well, the `doLayout` method forces the recalculation of the `Container` and its children and will render any unrendered children. The only reason you wouldn't need to call it is if the `Container` isn't rendered. We went down this path of pain so that you can learn the valuable lesson of calling `doLayout` when you add items to a `Container` at runtime.

Appending children is handy, but sometimes you need to be able to insert items at a specific index. Using the `insert` method and calling `doLayout` afterwards easily accomplishes this task:

```
Ext.getCmp('myWin').insert(1, {
    title : 'Inserted Panel',
    id    : 'insertedPanel',
    html  : 'It is cool here!'
});

Ext.getCmp('myWin').doLayout();
```

You insert a new `Panel` at index 1, which is right under `Panel1`. Because you call the `doLayout` method immediately after you do an insertion, you'll see the newly inserted panel in the `Window` instantaneously. The changes should look like figure 3.13.

As you can see, adding and inserting child `Components` is a cinch. Removing items is just as easy; it requires two arguments, the first of which is a reference to the `Component` or the `Component` ID from which you want the child to be removed. The second parameter, however, specifies whether or not the `destroy` method should be called for that `Component`, which gives you incredible flexibility, allowing you to move `Components` from one `Container` to another if you so desire. Here's how you'd remove one of the child panels that you recently added using your handy Firebug console:

```
var panel = Ext.getCmp('addedPanel');
Ext.getCmp('myWin').remove(panel);
```

After you execute this code, you'll notice that the panel immediately disappears. This is because you didn't specify the second parameter, which is by default `true`. You can override this default parameter by setting `autoDestroy` to `false` on a parent `Container`. Also, you don't need to call the parent's `doLayout` method, because the

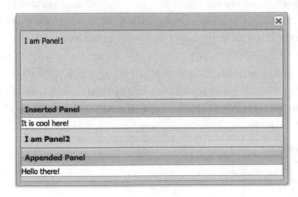

Figure 3.13 The rendered results of our dynamically added and inserted child panels

removed Component's destroy method is called, initiating its destruction phase and deleting its DOM element.

If you wanted to move a child to a different Container, you'd specify false as the remove's second parameter and then add or insert it into the parent, like this:

```
var panel = Ext.getCmp('insertedPanel');
Ext.getCmp('myWin').remove(panel, false);
Ext.getCmp('otherParent').add(panel);
Ext.getCmp('otherParent').doLayout();
```

The preceding code snippet assumes that you already have another parent Container instantiated with the ID of 'otherParent'. You create a reference to our previously inserted panel and perform a nondestructive removal from its parent. Next, you add it to its new parent and call its doLayout method to perform the DOM-level move operation of the child's element into the new parent's content body element.

The utilities offered by the Container class extend beyond the addition and removal of child items. They provide you the ability to descend deep into the Container's hierarchy to search for child Components, which becomes useful if you want to gather a list of child items of a specific type or that meet special criteria and perform an operation on them.

3.4.2 *Querying the Container hierarchy*

Of all of the query utility methods, the easiest is findByType, which is used to descend into the Container hierarchy to find items of a specific XType and return a list of items that it finds. For instance, here's how to find all of the text input fields for a given Container:

```
var fields = Ext.getCmp('myForm').findByType('field');
```

Executing the preceding code against a Container with the Component ID of 'myForm' will result in a list of all input fields at any level in its hierarchy. findByType leverages the Container's findBy method, which you can use as well. We're going to explore how findBy works. Please stay with me on this, because it may not make sense at first.

The findBy method accepts two parameters: a custom method that you use to test for your search criteria and the scope from which to call your custom method. For each of the custom Containers, your custom method gets called and is passed the reference of the child Component from which it's being called. If the custom search criteria are met, the custom method *needs to* return true, which instructs findBy to add that recently referenced Component to a list. Once all Components are exhausted, findBy returns the list, which contains any Components that met your criteria.

Okay, with that out of the way, let's explore this concept through code. For argument's sake, let's say you wanted to find all child items that are hidden. You could use findBy in the following way to do so:

```
var findHidden = function(comp) {
    if (! comp.isVisible()) {
        return true;
```

```
    }
}
var panels = Ext.getCmp('myContainer').findBy(findHidden);
```

In this rather simplistic findHidden query method, you're testing if the Component is *not* visible. If the Component's isVisible method returns anything but true, your findHidden method returns true. You then call findBy on the Container with the ID of 'myContainer' and pass it your custom findHidden method, with the results being stored in the panel's reference.

By now, you have the core knowledge necessary to manage child items. Let's shift focus to flexing some Ext-UI muscle by exploring some of the commonly used subclasses of Containers. You'll see how we can use Ext to create a UI using all of the browser's available viewing space.

3.4.3 *The Viewport Container*

The Viewport class is the foundation from which all web applications that depend solely on Ext are built by managing 100 percent of the browser's—you guessed it—viewport or display area. Weighing in at a tad over 20 lines, this class is extremely lightweight and efficient. Because it's a direct subclass of the Container class, all of the child management and layout usage is available to you. To leverage the viewport, you can use the following example code:

```
new Ext.Viewport({
    layout : 'border',
    items  : [
        {
            height : 75,
            region : 'north',
            title  : 'Does Santa live here?'
        },
        {
            width  : 150,
            region : 'west',
            title  : 'The west region rules'
        },
        {
            region : 'center',
            title  : 'No, this region rules!'
        }
    ]
});
```

The rendered Viewport from the code utilizes the entire browser's viewport and displays three panels organized by the border layout. If you resize the browser window, you'll notice that the center panel is resized automatically, which demonstrates how the Viewport listens and responds to the browser's window resize event (see figure 3.14).

The Viewport class provides the foundation for all Ext-based applications that leverage the framework as a complete web-based UI solution for their RIAs.

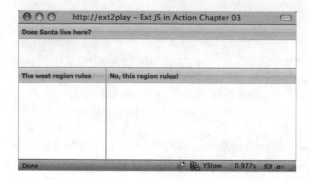

Figure 3.14 Our first `Viewport`, **which takes up 100 percent of the browser's available viewing space**

Many developers run into a brick wall when they attempt to create more than one `Viewport` in a fully managed Ext JS page to display more than one screen. To get around this, you can use the card layout with the viewport and flip through different application screens, which are resized to fit the viewport. We'll dive into layouts in chapter 5, where you'll get to understand key terms like *fit* and *flip* in the context of layouts.

We've covered quite a few important core topics, which help you manage child items in a `Container`. You also learned how to use the `Viewport` to help manage all of the browser's viewing space to lay out Ext UI widgets.

3.5   *Summary*

In this chapter we took a deep look at three fundamental areas of Ext JS. In doing so, you learned about managing the DOM level, where you exercised the registration of event listeners for DOM elements and learned how to stop them from bubbling up the DOM hierarchy. We also glanced at `Component`-level events and showed how to register an event and fire that event.

We took a real in-depth look at the Component model, which gives the Ext framework a unified method of managing instances of `Components`. The `Component` lifecycle is one of the most important concepts for the UI portion of the framework, which is why we covered it before we went too deep into learning about the many widgets.

Last, we explored the world of `Containers` and showed how they're used to manage child `Components`. In doing so, you also learned about the `Viewport` class and how it's the foundation for web applications that are based entirely on Ext JS.

You now have the foundation that will help propel you forward as you start to exercise the framework's UI machinery. Next, we'll explore the `Panel`, which is the most commonly used UI widget to display content.

Part 2

Ext JS Components

At this point, you've gained core knowledge that's vital to leveraging the framework properly. In this part, you'll begin the exploration of the Ext JS Components that are not driven by data models and take an in-depth walk through the various layout managers.

We kick off this part with chapter 4, where you learn about Containers, leveraging what you learned from chapter 3. Chapter 5 is all about Layouts and how to use them effectively. We close out this part with a walk through the FormPanel and various input items in chapter 6.

By the end of this part, you'll have a solid understanding of many of the widgets and layout managers that Ext JS has to offer.

A place for Components

This chapter covers

- Exploring the `Panel`
- Implementing the many `Panel` content areas
- Displaying an `Ext.Window`
- Using `Ext.MessageBox`
- Learning about and creating `TabPanels`

When developers start to experiment or build applications with Ext, they often start by copying examples from the downloadable SDK. Although this approach is good for learning how a particular layout was accomplished, it falls short in explaining how the stuff works, which leads to those throbbing forehead arteries. In this chapter, I'll explain some of the core topics, which are some of the building blocks to developing a successful UI deployment.

Here we'll cover `Containers`, which provide the management of child items and are one of the most important concepts in the Ext framework. We'll also dive into how the `Panel` works and explore the areas where it can display content and UI widgets. We'll then explore `Windows` and the `MessageBox`, which float above all other content on the page. Toward the end, we'll dive into using `TabPanels` and explore some of the usability issues that may occur when working with this widget.

Upon completion of this chapter, you'll have the ability to manage the full CRUD (create, read, update, and delete) lifecycle for Containers and their child items, which you'll depend on as you develop your applications.

4.1   The Panel

The Panel, a direct descendant of Container, is considered another workhorse of the framework because it's what many developers use to present UI widgets. A fully loaded panel is divided into six areas for content, as shown in figure 4.1. Recall that Panel is also a descendant of Component, which means that it follows the Component lifecycle. Moving forward, I'll use the term *Container* to describe any descendent of Container. This is because I want to reinforce the notion that the UI widget in context is a descendant of Container.

The Panel's title bar is a busy place that offers both visual and interactive content for the end user. As in Microsoft Windows, you can place an icon at the top left of the Panel, offering your users a visual queue as to what type of Panel they're seeing. In addition to the icon, you can display a title on the Panel.

On the right-most area of the title bar is a section for tools, which is where miniature icons can be displayed that will invoke a handler when clicked. Ext provides many icons for tools, which include many common user-related functions like help, print, and save. To view all of the available tools, visit the Panel API.

Of the six content areas, the Panel body is arguably the most important, which is where the main content or child items are housed. As dictated by the Container class, a layout must be specified upon instantiation. If a layout isn't specified, the Container-Layout is used by default. One important attribute about layouts is that they can't be swapped for another layout dynamically.

Let's build a complex panel with top and bottom Toolbars, with two Buttons each.

4.1.1   Building a complex Panel

Because the Toolbar will have Buttons, you need a method to be called when they're clicked:

```
var myBtnHandler = function(btn) {
  Ext.MessageBox.alert('You Clicked', btn.text);
}
```

Figure 4.1   An example of a fully loaded Panel, which has a title bar with an icon and tools, top and bottom Toolbars, and a button bar on the bottom

This method will be called when a Button on any Toolbar is clicked. The Toolbar Buttons will call handlers, passing themselves as a reference, called btn. Next, let's define your toolbars; see the following listing.

Listing 4.1 Building Toolbars for use in a Panel

```
var myBtnHandler = function(btn) {                          Button click
    Ext.MessageBox.alert('You Clicked', btn.text);      1   handler method
}
var fileBtn =  new Ext.Button({            2   File Button
    text    : 'File',
    handler : myBtnHandler
});
var editBtn = new Ext.Button({             3   Edit Button
    text    : 'Edit',
    handler : myBtnHandler
});                                            "Greedy"
var tbFill = new Ext.Toolbar.Fill();       4   Toolbar fill
var myTopToolbar = new Ext.Toolbar({           Top Toolbar
    items : [                               5   instantiation
        fileBtn,
        tbFill,
        editBtn
    ]
});                                            Bottom Toolbar
var myBottomToolbar = [                     6   array configuration
    {
        text    : 'Save',
        handler : myBtnHandler
    },
    '-',
    {
        text    : 'Cancel',
        handler : myBtnHandler
    },
    '->',
    '<b>Items open: 1</b>',
];
```

In the preceding code example, you do quite a lot and display two different ways of defining a Toolbar and its child Components. First, you define myBtnHandler ❶. By default, each Button's handler is called with two arguments, the Button itself and the browser event wrapped in an Ext.Event object. You use the passed Button reference (btn) and pass that text to Ext.MessageBox.alert to provide the visual confirmation that a Button was clicked.

Next, you instantiate the File ❷ and Edit ❸ Buttons and the "greedy" toolbar spacer ❹, which will push all toolbar items after it to the right. You assign myTopToolbar to a new instance of Ext.Toolbar ❺, referencing the previously created Buttons and spacer as elements in the new toolbar's items array.

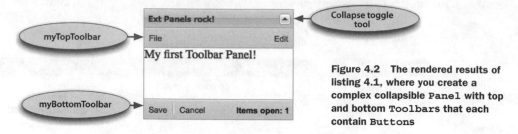

Figure 4.2 The rendered results of listing 4.1, where you create a complex collapsible `Panel` with top and bottom `Toolbars` that each contain `Buttons`

That was a lot of work for a relatively simple `Toolbar`. I had you do it this way to "feel the pain" of doing things the old way and to better appreciate how much time (and end developer code) the Ext shortcuts and XTypes save. The `myBottomToolbar` ❻ reference is a simple array of objects and strings, which Ext translates into the appropriate objects when its parent container deems it necessary to do so. To get references to the top `Toolbar`, you can use `myPanel.getTopToolbar()` and, inversely, to get a reference to the bottom, `myPanel.getBottomToolbar()`. You'd use these two methods to add or remove items dynamically to or from either `Toolbar`. We'll cover `Toolbars` in much greater detail later. Next, you'll create your `Panel` body:

```
var myPanel = new Ext.Panel({
    width        : 200,
    height       : 150,
    title        : 'Ext Panels rock!',
    collapsible  : true,
    renderTo     : Ext.getBody(),
    tbar         : myTopToolbar,
    bbar         : myBottomToolbar,
    html         : 'My first Toolbar Panel!'
});
```

You've created `Panels` before, so just about everything here should look familiar except for the `tbar` and `bbar` properties, which reference the newly created `Toolbars`. Also, there's a `collapsible` attribute; when `collapsible` is set to `true`, the `Panel` creates a toggle `Button` on the top right of the title bar. Rendered, the `Panel` should look like the one in figure 4.2. Remember, clicking any of the `Toolbar` `Buttons` will result in an `Ext.MessageBox` displaying the `Button`'s text, giving you visual confirmation that the click handler was called.

`Toolbars` are great places to put content, `Buttons`, or `Menus` that are outside the `Panel` body. There are two areas you still need to explore, `Buttons` and `tools`. To do this, you'll add to the `myPanel` example in the next listing, but you'll do it using the Ext shortcuts with XTypes inline with all of the other configuration options.

Listing 4.2 Adding `Buttons` and `tools` to your existing `Panel`

```
var myPanel = new Ext.Panel({        ❶  Properties from
    ...                                  previous example
    buttons      : [                              ❷  buttons
        {                                            array begins
```

```
        text    : 'Press me!',              ◁—❸ 'Press me!' button
        handler : myBtnHandler
    }
],                              ❹  tools array begins
tools     : [                      ◁
    {                                    ❺ 'gear' tool and
        id      : 'gear',              ◁┘  inline click handler
        handler : function(evt, toolEl, panel) {
            var toolClassNames = toolEl.dom.className.split(' ');
            var toolClass      = toolClassNames[1];
            var toolId         = toolClass.split('-')[2];

            Ext.MessageBox.alert('You Clicked', 'Tool ' + toolId);
        }
    },
    {                                  ❻ 'help' tool and
        id      : 'help',           ◁┘  inline click handler
        handler : function() {
            Ext.MessageBox.alert('You Clicked', 'The help tool');
        }
    }
    ]
});
```

In listing 4.2, you added to the previous set of config options ❶ and included two shortcut arrays, one for buttons and the other for tools. Because you specified a buttons array ❷, when the Panel renders, it will create a footer div, a new instance of Ext.Toolbar with a special CSS class x-panel-fbar, and render it to the newly created footer div. The 'Press me!' Button ❸ will be rendered in the newly created footer Toolbar, and when clicked it will invoke your previously defined myBtnHandler method.

If you look at the myBottomToolbar shortcut array in listing 4.1 and the buttons shortcut array in listing 4.2, you'll see some similarities. This is because all of the Panel Toolbars (tbar, bbar, and buttons) can be defined using the same shortcut syntax because they will all get translated into instances of Ext.Toolbar and rendered to their appropriate position in the Panel.

You also specified a tools array ❹ configuration object, which is somewhat different than the way you define the Toolbars. Here, to set the icon for the tool, you must specify the id of the tool, such as 'gear' ❺ or 'help' ❻. For every tool that's specified in the array, an icon will be created in the tools. Panel will assign a click event handler to each tool, which will invoke the handler specified in that tool's configuration object. The rendered version of the newly modified myPanel should look like the one in figure 4.3.

The preceding example is meant to display all of the items that can be utilized on a Panel, but it isn't the best example of elegant and efficient user interface design. Although it may be tempting to load up your Panels with Buttons and Toolbars, you must be careful not to overload a Panel with too much onscreen gadgetry, which could overwhelm your user and take up valuable screen real estate.

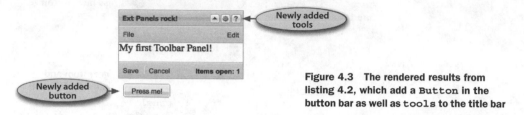

Figure 4.3   The rendered results from listing 4.2, which add a `Button` in the button bar as well as `tools` to the title bar

Now that you have some experience with the `Panel` class, let's look at one of its close descendants, the `Window`, which you can use to float content above everything else on the screen and to replace the traditionally lame browser-based pop-up.

4.2   *Popping up Windows*

The `Window` UI widget builds upon the `Panel`, providing you the ability to float UI `Components` above all of the other content on the page. With `Windows`, you can provide a modal dialog box, which masks the entire page, forcing the user to focus on the dialog box, and prevents any mouse-based interaction with anything else on the page. Figure 4.4 is a perfect example of how you can leverage this class to focus the user's attention and request input.

Working with the `Window` class is a lot like working with the `Panel` class, except you have to consider issues like whether you want to disable resizing or want the `Window` to be constrained within the boundaries of the browser's viewport. Let's look into how you can build a window. For this, you'll need a vanilla Ext `Page` with no widgets loaded, as shown in the following listing.

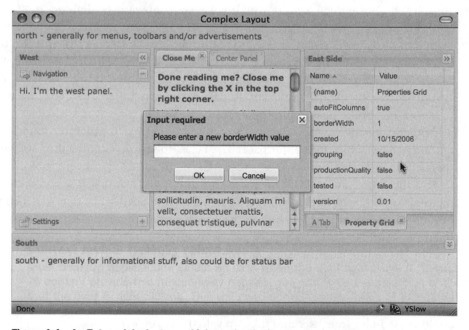

Figure 4.4   An Ext modal `Window`, which masks the browser's viewport

---

Listing 4.3 Building an animated `Window`

```
var win;
var newWindow = function(btn) {                    ❶ Handler creates
    if (!win) {                                        new Window
        win = new Ext.Window({                     ❷ Instantiate
            animateTarget : btn.el,                    new Window
            html          : 'My first vanilla Window',
            closeAction   : 'hide',                ❸ Prevent destruction
            id            : 'myWin',                   on close
            height        : 200,
            width         : 300,                   ❹ Constrain Window to
            constrain     : true                       browser's viewport
        });
    }
    win.show();

}                                                  ❺ Create Button that
new Ext.Button({                                       launches Window
    renderTo : Ext.getBody(),
    text     : 'Open my Window',
    style    : 'margin: 100px',
    handler  : newWindow
});
```

In listing 4.3, you do things a little differently in order to see the animation for your
Window's close and hide method calls. The first thing you do is create a global variable, win, for which you'll reference the soon-to-be-created Window. You create a
method, newWindow, ❶ that will be the handler for your future Button and is responsible for creating the new Window ❷.

Let's take a moment to examine some of the configuration options for your
Window. One of the ways you can instruct the Window to animate upon show and hide
method calls is to specify an animateEl property, which is a reference to some element in the DOM or the element ID. If you don't specify the element in the configuration options, you can specify it when you call the show or hide methods, which take
the exact same arguments. In this case, you're launching the Button's element.
Another important configuration option is closeAction ❸, which defaults to close
and destroys the Window when the close tool is clicked. You don't want that in this
instance, so you set it to hide, which instructs the close tool to call the hide method
instead of close. You also set the constrain ❹ parameter to true, which instructs the
Window's drag-and-drop handlers to prevent the Window from being moved from outside the browser's viewport.

Last, you create a Button ❺ that, when clicked, will call your newWindow method,
resulting in the window animating from the Button's element. Clicking the (x) close
tool will result in the window hiding. The rendered results will look like figure 4.5.

Because you don't destroy the Window when the close tool is clicked, you can show
and hide the Window as many times as you wish, which is ideal for Windows that you
plan to reuse. Whenever you deem that it's necessary to destroy the Window, you can
call its destroy or close method. Now that you have experience in creating a reusable

Figure 4.5   The rendered results from listing 4.3, where you create a `Window` that animates from the `Button`'s element when clicked

`Window`, you can begin exploring other configuration options to further alter the behavior of the `Window`.

4.2.1   *Further Window configuration exploration*

There are times when you need to make a `Window` behave to meet requirements of your application. In this section, you'll learn about some of the commonly used configuration options.

Sometimes you need to produce a `Window` that's modal and rigid. To do this, you need to set a few configuration options, as shown in the next listing.

Listing 4.4   Creating a rigid modal `Window`

```
var win = new Ext.Window({
    height      : 75,
    width       : 200,
    modal       : true,              ❶ Ensure page
    title       : 'This is one rigid window',   is masked
    html        : 'Try to move or resize me. I dare you.',
    plain       : true,
    border      : false,             ❷ Prevent
    resizable   : false,                resizing      ❸ Disable Window
    draggable   : false,                              movement
    closable    : false,             ❹ Prevent Window
    buttonAlign : 'center',             closure
    buttons     : [
        {
            text    : 'I give up!',
            handler : function() {
                win.close();
            }
        }
    ]
})
win.show();
```

In listing 4.4, you create an extremely strict modal `Window`. To do this, you have to set quite a few options. The first of these, `modal` ❶, instructs the `Window` to mask the rest of the page with a semitransparent `div`. Next, you set `resizable` ❷ to `false`, which

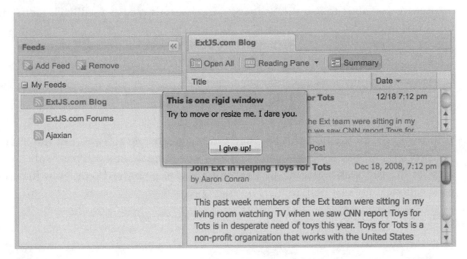

Figure 4.6   Our first strict modal `Window` rendered in the Ext SDK feed viewer example

prevents the `Window` from being resized via mouse actions. To prevent the `Window` from being moved around the page, you set `draggable` ❸ to `false`. You want only a single center `Button` to close the `Window`, so `closable` ❹ is set to `false`, which hides the close tool. Last, you set some cosmetic parameters, `plain`, `border`, and `button-Align`. Setting `plain` to `true` will make the content body background transparent. When coupled with setting the `border` to `false`, the `Window` appears to be one unified cell. Because you want to have the single `Button` centered, you specify the `button-Align` property as such. The rendered example should look like figure 4.6.

Other times you want to relax the restrictions on the `Window`. For instance, there are situations where you need a `Window` to be `resizable`, but not less than specific dimensions. For this, you allow resize (`resizable`) and specify `minWidth` and `min-Height` parameters. Unfortunately, there's no easy way to set boundaries as to how large a `Window` can grow.

Although there are many reasons for creating your own `Windows`, there are times when you need something quick and dirty, for instance, to display a message or prompt for user data. The `Window` class has a stepchild known as the `MessageBox` to fill this need.

4.2.2   *Replacing alert and prompt with MessageBox*

The `MessageBox` class is a reusable, yet versatile, singleton class that gives you the ability to replace some of the common browser-based message boxes such as alert and prompt with a simple method call. The most important thing to know about the `MessageBox` class is that it *does not* stop JavaScript execution like traditional alerts or prompts do, which I consider an advantage. While the user is digesting or entering information, your code can perform Ajax queries or even manipulate the UI. If specified, the `MessageBox` will execute a callback method when the `Window` is dismissed.

Before you start to use the `MessageBox` class, let's create a callback method. You'll need this later on.

```
var myCallback = function(btn, text) {
    console.info('You pressed '  + btn);
    if (text) {
        console.info('You entered : ' + text)
    }
}
```

Your `myCallback` method will leverage Firebug's console to echo out the `Button` that was pressed and the text you entered, if any. The `MessageBox` will pass only two parameters to the callback method: the `Button` ID and any entered text. Now that you have your callback, let's launch an alert message box:

```
var msg   = 'Your document was saved successfully';
var title = 'Save status:'
Ext.MessageBox.alert(title, msg);
```

Here, you call the `MessageBox.alert` method, which will generate a `Window`, which will look like figure 4.7 (left) and will dismiss when OK is clicked. If you want `myCallback` to get executed upon dismissal, add it as the third parameter. Now that we've looked at alerts, let's see how you can request user input with the `MessageBox.prompt` method:

```
var msg   = 'Please enter your email address.';
var title = 'Input Required'
Ext.MessageBox.prompt(title, msg, myCallback);
```

You call the `MessageBox.prompt` method, which you pass the reference of your callback method; it will look like figure 4.7 (right). Enter some text and click Cancel. In the Firebug console, you'll see the `Button` ID pressed and the text entered.

And there you have it, `MessageBox` alert and prompt at a glance. I find these handy, because I don't have to create my own singleton to provide these UI widgets. Remember them when you're looking to implement a `Window` class to meet a requirement.

I have to confess a little secret. The alert and prompt methods are actually shortcut methods for the much larger and highly configurable `MessageBox.show` method. Next up is an example of how you can use the `show` method to display an icon with a multiline `TextArea` input box.

Figure 4.7   The `MessageBox`'s alert (left) and prompt (right) modal dialog `Windows`

4.2.3 *Advanced MessageBox techniques*

The MessageBox.show method provides an interface to display the MessageBox using any combination of the 24 available options. Unlike the previously explored shortcut methods, show accepts the typical configuration object as a parameter. Let's display a multiline TextArea input box along with an icon:

```
Ext.Msg.show({
    title      : 'Input required:',
    msg        : 'Please tell us a little about yourself',
    width      : 300,
    buttons    : Ext.MessageBox.OKCANCEL,
    multiline  : true,
    fn         : myCallback,
    icon       : Ext.MessageBox.INFO
});
```

When the preceding example is rendered, it will display a modal dialog box like the one in figure 4.8 (left). Next, let's see how to create an alert box that contains an icon and three Buttons.

```
Ext.Msg.show({
    title      : 'Hold on there cowboy!',
    msg        : 'Are you sure you want to reboot the internet?',
    width      : 300,
    buttons    : Ext.MessageBox.YESNOCANCEL,
    fn         : myCallback,
    icon       : Ext.MessageBox.ERROR
})
```

The preceding code example will display your tri-button modal alert dialog Window, like the one in figure 4.8 (right).

Although everything in our two custom MessageBox examples should be self-explanatory, I think it's important to highlight two of the configuration options, which pass references to MessageBox public properties.

The buttons parameter is used as a guide for the singleton to know which Buttons to display. Although you pass a reference to an existing property, Ext.Message-Box.OKCANCEL, you can display no Buttons by setting buttons to an empty object, such as {}. Otherwise, you can customize which Buttons you want to display. To display Yes and Cancel Buttons, pass { yes : true, cancel : true} and so on. The singleton

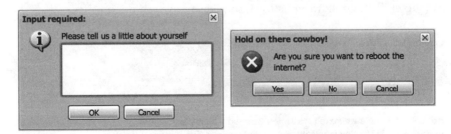

Figure 4.8   A multiline input box with an icon (left) and a tri-button icon alert box (right)

already has a set of predefined popular combinations, which are CANCEL, OK, OKCANCEL, YESNO, and YESNOCANCEL.

The icon parameter works in the same way as the button parameter, except it's a reference to a string. The MessageBox class has three predefined values: INFO, QUESTION, and WARNING. These are references to strings that are CSS classes. If you wish to display your own icon, create your own CSS class and pass the name of your custom CSS class as the icon property. Here's an example of a custom CSS class:

```
.icon-add {
    background-image: url(/path/to/add.png) !important;
}
```

Now that you have your feet wet with some advanced MessageBox techniques, we can explore how to leverage the MessageBox to display an animated dialog box, which you can use to offer the user live and updated information regarding a particular process.

4.2.4   *Showing an animated wait MessageBox*

When you need to stop a particular workflow, you must display some sort of modal message box, which can be as simple and *boring* as a modal dialog box with a "Please wait" message. I prefer to introduce some spice into the application and provide an animated "wait" dialog box. With the MessageBox class, you can create a seemingly effortless and infinitely looping progress bar:

```
Ext.MessageBox.wait("We're doing something...", 'Hold on...');
```

This will produce a wait box like the one shown in figure 4.9. If the syntax seems a little strange, it's because the first parameter is the message body text, with the second parameter being the title. It's exactly opposite of the alert or prompt calls. Let's say you want to display text in the body of the animating progress bar itself. You could pass a third parameter with a single text property, such as {text: 'loading your items'}. Figure 4.9 (right) also shows what it would be like if you added progress bar text to your dummy wait dialog box.

Although this may seem cool at first, it's not interactive because the text is static and you're not controlling the progress bar status. You can customize the wait dialog box by using the handy show method and passing in some parameters. Using this method, you now have the leeway to update the progress bar's advancement as you see fit. In order to create an auto-updating wait box, you need to create a rather involved loop (shown in the following listing), so please stay with me on this.

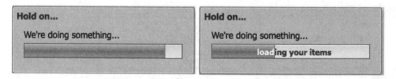

Figure 4.9   A simple animated MessageBox wait dialog where the ProgressBar is looping infinitely at a predetermined fixed interval (left) and a similar message box with text in the progress bar (right)

Listing 4.5 Building a dynamically updating `ProgressBar`

```
Ext.MessageBox.show({
    title        : 'Hold on there cowboy!',
    msg          : "We're doing something...",
    progressText : 'Initializing...',
    width        : 300,
    progress     : true,
    closable     : false
});

var updateFn = function(num){
    return function(){
        if(num == 6){
            Ext.MessageBox.updateProgress(100,
                'All Items saved!');
            Ext.MessageBox.hide.defer(1500,
                Ext.MessageBox);
        }
        else{
            var i = num/6;
            var pct = Math.round(100 * i);
            Ext.MessageBox.updateProgress(i,
                pct + '% completed');
        }
    };
};
for (var i = 1; i < 7; i++){
    setTimeout(updateFn(i), i * 500);
}
```

① Show ProgressBar

② Update progress text

③ Update percentage and text

④ Defer MessageBox dismissal

⑤ Update progress if limit not met

⑥ Looping .5 second timeout

In listing 4.5, you show a `MessageBox`, with the `progress` option **①** set to `true`, which will show your progress bar. Next, you define a rather involved updater function, aptly named `updateFn` **②**, which is called at a predefined interval. In that function, if the number passed equals your limit of 6, you update the progress bar to 100 percent wide and show the completion text **③**. You also defer the dismissal of the message box by one and a half seconds **④**. Otherwise, you'll calculate a percentage completed and update the progress bar width and text accordingly **⑤**. Last, you create a loop that calls `setTimeout` **⑥** six consecutive times, which delays your calls of `updateFn` by the iteration times one-half second. The results of this rather lengthy example will look like figure 4.10.

Figure 4.10 Your automatically updating wait `MessageBox` (left) with the final update (right) before automatic dismissal

With some effort you can dynamically update your users with a status of operations that are taking place before they can move further.

In this section, you learned how to create both flexible and extremely rigid Windows to get the user's attention. We also explored a few different ways of using one of Ext's super singletons, the Ext MessageBox class. Let's now shift focus to the TabPanel class, which provides a means to allow a UI to contain many screens but display them only one at a time.

4.3   Components can live in tab panels too

The Ext.TabPanel class builds on Panel to create a robust tabbed interface, which gives the user the ability to select any screen or UI control associated with a particular tab. Tabs within the TabPanel can be unclosable, closable, disabled, and even hidden, as illustrated in figure 4.11.

Unlike other tab interfaces, the Ext TabPanel supports only a top or bottom tab strip configuration. This is mainly because most modern browsers don't support CSS version 4.0, where vertical text is possible. Although configuring a TabPanel may seem straightforward by looking at the API, there are two options that if not understood could cause bleeping to occur in the office.

4.3.1   Remember these two options

It's amazing that just two of these options could cause developers pain and fill up the office expletive jars, providing free lunch or coffee for fellow team members. Exploring these may help keep those jars empty and your wallets fuller. Before you build your TabPanel, I think it's important to lay these out first, so you can get on to the fun!

One of the reasons that the CardLayout is so darn fast is because it makes use of a common technique called lazy or deferred rendering for its child Components. This is controlled by the deferredRender parameter, which is set to true by default. *Deferred render* means that only cards that get activated are rendered. It's fairly common for TabPanels to have multiple children that have complex UI controls, such as the one in figure 4.12, which can require a significant amount of CPU time to render. Deferring

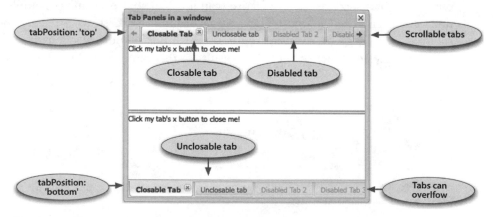

Figure 4.11   Exploring top- and bottom-positioned tabs

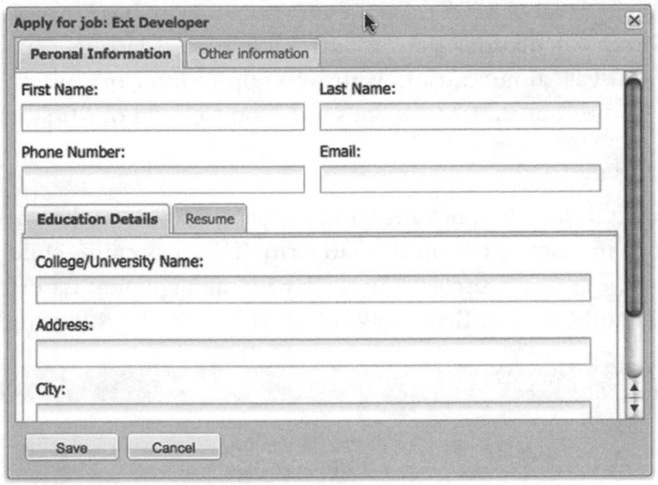

Figure 4.12 A `TabPanel` with children that have complex layouts

the render of each child until it's activated accelerates the `TabPanel`'s initial rendering and gives the user a better-responding widget.

There's one major disadvantage to allowing `deferredRender` to be `true`, and it has to do with the way form panels work. The form's `setValues` method doesn't apply values across any of the unrendered member fields, which means that if you plan on populating forms with tabs, be sure to set `deferredRender` to `false`; otherwise you might be adding to the jar!

Another configuration option that fellow developers often overlook is `layoutOnTabChange`, which forces a `doLayout` method call on child items when that tab is activated. This is important because in deeply nested layouts, sometimes the parent's resize event may not cascade down properly, forcing a recalculation on child items that are supposed to conform to the parent's content body. If your UI starts to look funky, like the one in figure 4.13, I suggest setting this configuration option to `true`, and the issue will be solved.

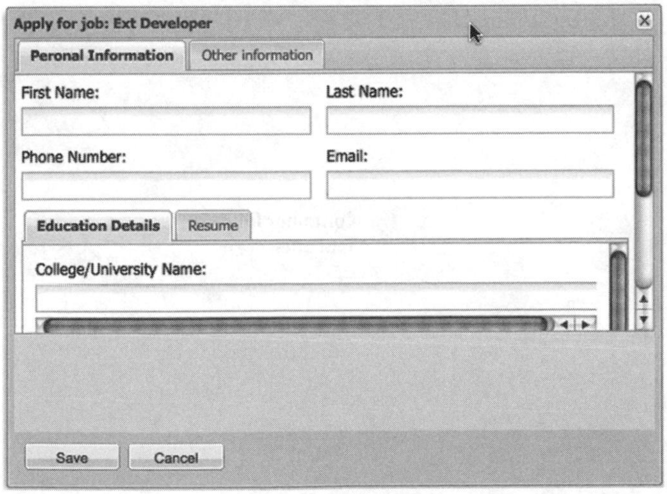

Figure 4.13 A child `Panel` whose layout has not been properly recalculated after a parent's resize

I suggest setting `layoutOnTabChange` to `true` only when you have problems. The `doLayout` method forces calculations that in extremely nested layouts can require a considerable amount of CPU time, causing your web app to jitter or stutter. Now that we've covered some of the `TabPanel` basics, let's move on to build our first `TabPanel`.

4.3.2   *Building our first TabPanel*

The `TabPanel` is a direct descendant of `Panel` and makes clever use of the `CardLayout`. `TabPanel`'s main job is managing tabs in the tab strip. This is because child management is performed by the `Container` class and the layout management is performed by the `CardLayout`. Let's build out our first `TabPanel`, as shown in the following listing.

Listing 4.6   Exploring a `TabPanel`

```
var disabledTab = {                          ➊ A simple,
    title    : 'Disabled tab',                 static tab
    id       : 'disabledTab',
    html     : 'Peekaboo!',
    disabled : true,
    closable : true
}
                                             ➋ A simple,
var closableTab = {                            closable tab
    title    : 'I am closable',
    html     : 'Please close when done reading.',
    closable : true
}
                                             ➌ A closable yet
var disabledTab = {                            disabled tab
    title    : 'Disabled tab',
    id       : 'disabledTab',
    html     : 'Peekaboo!',
    disabled : true,
    closable : true
}

var tabPanel = new Ext.TabPanel({           ➍ Our TabPanel
    activeTab       : 0,
    id              : 'myTPanel',
    enableTabScroll : true,
    items           : [
        simpleTab,
        closableTab,
        disabledTab,
    ]
});
                                             ➎ Container for our
new Ext.Window({                               TabPanel
    height : 300,
    width  : 400,
    layout : 'fit',
    items  : tabPanel
}).show();
```

Although you could have defined all of the items in this code in a single large object, I thought it would be best to break it up so things are readily apparent. The first three variables define your TabPanel's children in generic object form, with the assumption that the defaultType (XType) for the TabPanel class is Panel. The first child is a simple and nonclosable tab ❶. One thing to note here is that all tabs are nonclosable by default. This is why your second tab ❷ has closable set to true. Next, you have a closable *and* disabled tab.

You then go on to instantiate your TabPanel ❸. You set the activeTab parameter to 0. You do this because you want the first tab to be activated after the TabPanel ❹ is rendered. You can specify any index number in the TabPanel's item's mixed collection. Because the mixed collection is an array, the first item always starts with 0. You also set enableTabScroll to true, which instructs the TabPanel class to scroll your tab strip *if* the sum of the tab widths exceeds that of the viewable tab strip. Last, your Tab-Panel's items array has your three tabs specified.

Next, you create a Container for your TabPanel, an instance of Ext.Window ❺. You specify a Fit layout for the Window and set the tabPanel reference as its single item. The rendered code should look should look like the TabPanel shown in figure 4.14.

Now that you have your first Tab-Panel rendered, you can start to have fun with it. You've probably closed the "I am closable" tab, which is okay. If you haven't done so, feel free to explore the rendered UI control and close out the only closable tab when you're comfortable doing so, which will leave only two tabs available, "My first tab" and "Disabled tab."

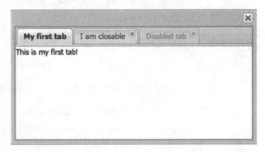

Figure 4.14 Your first TabPanel rendered inside a Window

4.3.3 Tab management methods you should know

Because the TabPanel class is a descendant of Container, all of the common child-management methods are available to utilize. These include add, remove, and insert. There are a few other methods, however, that you'll need to know in order to take full advantage of the TabPanel.

The first of these is setActiveTab, which activates a tab, as if the user had selected the item on the tab strip, and accepts either the index of the tab or the Component ID:

```
var tPanel = Ext.getCmp('myTPanel');

tPanel.add({
    title : 'New tab',
    id    : 'myNewTab'
});

tPanel.setActiveTab('myNewTab');
```

Executing the prior code will result in a new tab with the title of "New closable tab," which gets activated automatically. Calling `setActiveTab` after an add operation is akin to calling `doLayout` on a generic container. You also have the capability to enable and disable tabs at runtime, but this requires a different approach than simply calling a method on the `TabPanel`.

The `TabPanel` doesn't have enable or disable methods, so in order to enable or disable a child, you need to call those methods of the child items themselves. You can leverage listing 4.6 to enable our disabled tab.

```
Ext.getCmp('disabledTab').enable();
```

Yes, that's all there is to it. The tab strip item (tab UI control) now reflects that the item is no longer disabled. This happens because the `TabPanel` subscribes to the child item's—you guessed it—`enable` and `disable` events to manage the associated tab strip items.

In addition to enabling and disabling tabs, you can also hide them. To hide a tab, however, the `TabPanel` does have a utility method, `hideTabStripItem`. This method accepts a single parameter but three possible data values: the tab index number, the tab `Component` ID, or a reference to the `Component` instance itself. In your case, you'll use the ID because that's a known:

```
Ext.getCmp('myTPanel').hideTabStripItem('disabledTab');
```

The inverse of this is `unhideTabStripItem`:

```
Ext.getCmp('myTPanel').unhideTabStripItem('disabledTab');
```

There you have it, managing tab items. Although there are many advantages to using the `TabPanel` in your web application, we should explore some of the usability problems that you may encounter. After all, you need to keep that swear jar as empty as possible.

4.3.4   *Caveats and drawbacks*

Although the `TabPanel` opened new doors for UI control, it does have some limitations that we should explore. Two of these are related to the size of the tabs and the width of the bounding area for which the `TabPanel` is being displayed. If the sum of the widths of the tabs is greater than the viewport, the tabs can be pushed offscreen. This can happen because the tab widths are too large or the total number of tabs exceeds the allowable viewing space. When this issue occurs, the usability of the `TabPanel` is somewhat reduced.

To offer some relief of these shortcomings, the `TabPanel` can be configured to resize tabs automatically or even scroll them if they go beyond the viewport. Although these features help ease the problem, they don't solve them.

In order for you to fully understand these issues, we should explore them further. Let's start out with a `TabPanel` inside a `Viewport`, shown in the following listing.

Listing 4.7   Exploring scrollable tabs

```
Ext.QuickTips.init();

new Ext.Viewport({
    layout : 'fit',
    title  : 'Exercising scrollable tabs',
    items  : {
        xtype            : 'tabpanel',
        activeTab        : 0,
        id               : 'myTPanel',
        enableTabScroll  : true,
        items            : [
            {
                title : 'our first tab'
            }
        ]
    }
});

(function (num) {
    for (var i = 1; i <= 30; i++) {
        var title = 'Long Title Tab # ' + i;
        Ext.getCmp('myTPanel').add({
            title    : title,
            html     : 'Hi, i am tab ' + i,
            tabTip   : title,
            closable : true
        });
    }
}).defer(500);
```

❶ Ext Viewport with embedded TabPanel

❷ Deferred anonymous function execution

In listing 4.7, you create a viewport with your TabPanel ❶, which contains a single child. Next, you create an anonymous function ❷ and defer its execution by half a second. You specify 30 as the number of dynamic tabs to create dynamically in the for loop. For each new tab that you create, you include the tab number in the tab title, html, and tabTip. The rendered code should look like the tab panel in figure 4.15.

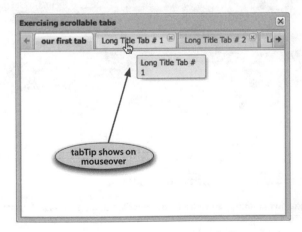

Figure 4.15   A TabPanel with a scrolling tab strip, which includes mouseover tooltips for the dynamic tabs

Now that you have your `TabPanel` rendered, scroll over to find "Long Title Tab # 14." Took a while, huh? Even with an extra-wide display, the tabs will still scroll. One way to remedy this situation is to set a minimum tab width. Let's modify our example by adding the following configuration parameters to the `TabPanel` XType configuration:

```
resizeTabs  : true,
minTabWidth : 75,
```

Refreshing the newly modified `TabPanel` in figure 4.16 (bottom) results in tabs that are either unusable or hard to use. Specifying `resizeTabs` as `true` instructs the `Tab-Panel` to reduce the width of a tab as much as it needs to in order to display the tabs without scrolling. Autosizing a tab works if the tab title doesn't get truncated or hidden. This is where the diminishing usability of `TabPanels` becomes apparent. If the tab title isn't completely visible, the user must activate each tab in order to find the correct one. Otherwise, if the tab tooltips are enabled, the user must mouseover each tab in order to locate the one they wish to activate. As you can see in figure 4.16, the tooltips can enhance the speed of the tab search but don't remedy the issue completely.

No matter which route you choose for implementing the `TabPanel`, always keep in mind that too many tabs could lead to trouble by reducing usability or even reducing performance of the web application.

In exploring the `TabPanel`, you learned how to create tabs that could be static, controlled, disabled, or even hidden and to programmatically control them. You also learned of two of the configuration options, `deferredRender` and `layoutOnTab-Change`, that could cause some of your hair to fall out. We exercised some of the common tab-management methods and discussed some of the caveats for using this UI control.

There you have it. You have now seen how easy it is to create a scrolling `TabPanel`. Always remember to enabling scrolling when the number of tabs can increase beyond the width of the `TabPanel`.

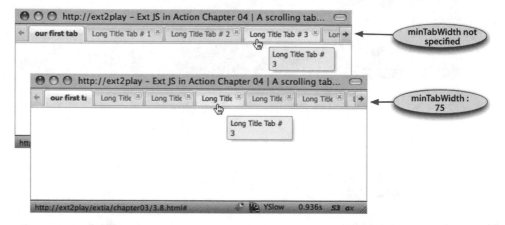

Figure 4.16   A `TabPanel` that has no minimum tab width (top) specified and a `TabPanel` (bottom) that has a minimum tab width of 75 specified

4.4 *Summary*

We covered a lot of material about the Swiss army knife of UI display widgets, the `Panel`, which is enough to make just about any developer's head spin. In exploring the `Panel` class, you saw how it provides a plethora of options to display user interactive content, including `Toolbars`, `Buttons`, title bar icons, and miniature `tools`.

You used the `Window` class as a general container and mastered the art of adding and removing children dynamically, providing you the ability to dynamically and drastically change an entire UI or a single widget or control.

In exercising the `Window` class and its cousin, the `MessageBox`, you learned how you could replace the generic alert and prompt dialog boxes to get the user's attention to display or request user input. You also had some fun fooling with the animated wait `MessageBox`.

Finally, we examined the `TabPanels`, showing how to dynamically manage tab items, as well as a few of the usability pitfalls that the UI control brings.

In the next chapter, we'll explore the many Ext `Layout` schemes, where you'll learn the common uses and pitfalls of these controls.

Organizing Components

This chapter covers
- Learning the various layout systems
- Exploring the `Layout` class inheritance model
- Exercising programmatic management of the `CardLayout`

When building an application, many developers struggle with how to organize their UI and which tools to use to get the job done. In this chapter, you'll gain the necessary experience to be able to make these decisions in a more educated manner. We'll explore all of the numerous layout models and identify some of the best practices and common issues that you'll encounter.

The layout management schemes are responsible for the visual organization of widgets onscreen. They include simple layout schemes such as Fit, where a single child item of a `Container` will be sized to fit the `Container`'s body, or complex layouts such as a `BorderLayout`, which splits a `Container`'s content body into five manageable slices, or regions.

When exploring some of the layouts, we'll hit upon examples that are verbose, and thus lengthy, and can serve as a great springboard or starting point for your layout endeavors. We'll start our journey with taking a look at the `ContainerLayout`, which is the nucleus of the entire layout hierarchy.

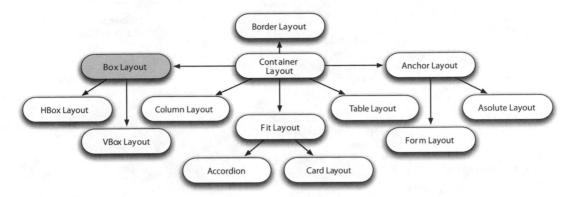

Figure 5.1   The layout class hierarchy, where layouts are subclasses of the `ContainerLayout`

5.1   *The simple ContainerLayout*

As you may recall, the `ContainerLayout` is the *default* layout for any instance of `Container` and places items on the screen, one on top of another. I like to think of it as the Lincoln Logs of the Ext layouts.

Though the `ContainerLayout` doesn't explicitly resize child items, a child's width may conform to the `Container`'s content body if it isn't constrained. It also serves as the base class for all other layouts, providing much of the base functionality for the subclass layouts. Figure 5.1 illustrates the `Ext.layout` class hierarchy.

A `ContainerLayout` is the easiest to implement, requiring only that you add and remove child items. In order to see this, you need to set up a dynamic example, using quite a few components, as shown in the following listing.

Listing 5.1   Implementing the `ContainerLayout`

```
var childPnl1 = {                              First child item,
    frame  : true,                          ❶ a Panel
    height : 50,
    html   : 'My First Child Panel',
    title  : 'First children are fun'
};                                             ❷ Third child item,
                                                 another Panel
var childPnl2 = {
    width  : 150,
    html   : 'Second child',
    title  : 'Second children have all the fun!'
};
                                               ❸ Window with
var myWin = new Ext.Window({                      two child items
    height    : 300,
    width     : 300,
    title     : 'A window with a container layout',   ❹ Allow content
    autoScroll : true,                                  body to scroll
    items     : [
        childPnl1,                             Child items are
        childPnl2                           ❺ referenced
    ],
```

```
        tbar : [
           {
              text    : 'Add child',
              handler : function() {
                 var numItems = myWin.items.getCount() + 1;
                 myWin.add({
                    title       : 'Child number ' + numItems,
                    height      : 60,
                    frame       : true,
                    collapsible : true,
                    collapsed   : true,
                    html        : 'Yay, another child!'
                 });
                 myWin.doLayout();
              }
           }
        ]
    });
```

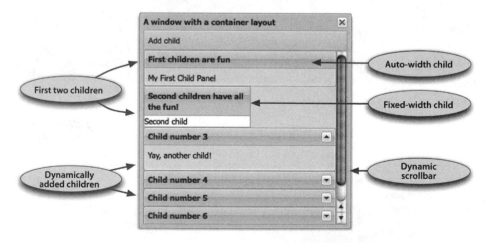

Toolbar with
6 add child Button

In listing 5.1, you do quite a lot to exercise the `ContainerLayout` because I want you to be able to see how the items stack and don't resize.

The first thing you do is instantiate object references using `XTypes` for the two child items that will be managed by a `Window`: `childPnl1` **1** and `childPnl2` **2**. These two child items are static.

Next, you begin your `myWin` **3** reference, which is an instance of `Ext.Window`. You also set the `autoScroll` property **4** to `true`. This tells the `Container` to add the CSS attributes `overflow-x` and `overflow-y` to `auto`, which instructs the browser to show the scroll bars only when it needs to.

Notice that you set the child `items` **5** property to an array. The `items` property for any container can be an instance of an array used to list multiple children *or* an object reference for a single child. The `Window` contains a toolbar **6** that has a single `Button` that, when clicked, adds a dynamic item to the `Window`. The rendered `Window` should look like the one in figure 5.2.

Figure 5.2   The results of our first implementation of the `ContainerLayout`

Although the ContainerLayout provides little to manage the size of child items, it's not completely useless. It's lightweight relative to its subclasses, which makes it ideal if you want to display child items that have fixed dimensions. There are times, however, when you'll want to have the child items dynamically resize to fit the container's content body. This is where the AnchorLayout can be useful.

5.2 The AnchorLayout

The AnchorLayout is similar to the ContainerLayout, in that it stacks child items one on top of another, except it adds dynamic sizing into the mix using an anchor parameter specified on each child. This anchor parameter is used to calculate the size of the child item relative to the parent's content body size and is specified as a percentage, an offset, which is an integer. The anchor parameter is a string, using the following format:

```
anchor : "width, height" // or "width height"
```

In the following listing you take your first stab at implementing an anchor layout using percentages.

Listing 5.2 The AnchorLayout using percentages

```
var myWin = new Ext.Window({
    height      : 300,
    width       : 300,
    layout      : 'anchor',
    border      : false,
    anchorSize  : '400',
    items       : [
        {
            title  : 'Panel1',
            anchor : '100%, 25%',
            frame  : true
        },
        {
            title  : 'Panel2',
            anchor : '0, 50%',
            frame  : true
        },
        {
            title  : 'Panel3',
            anchor : '50%, 25%',
            frame  : true
        }
    ]
});
myWin.show();
```

❶ The parent container, myWin

❷ layout set to 'anchor'

❸ 100% width, 25% of parent's height

❹ 100% width, 50% of parent's height

❺ 50% width, 25% of parent's height

In listing 5.2, you instantiate a myWin ❶, an instance of Ext.Window, specifying the layout as 'anchor' ❷. The first of the child items, Panel1, has its anchor parameters ❸ specified as 100 percent of the parent's width and 25 percent of the parent's height. Panel2 has its anchor parameters ❹ specified a little differently, where the width

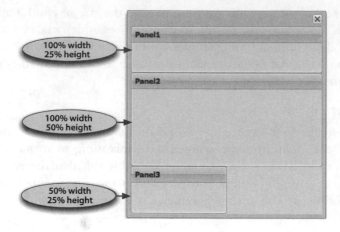

Figure 5.3   The rendered results of our first implementation of the AnchorLayout

parameter is 0, which is shorthand for 100 percent. You set `Panel2`'s `height` to 50 percent. `Panel3`'s anchor parameters **5** are set to 50 percent relative `width` and 25 percent relative `height`. The rendered item should look like figure 5.3.

Relative sizing with percentages is great, but you also have the option to specify an offset, which allows greater flexibility with the Anchor layout.

Offsets are calculated as the content body dimension plus the offset. In general, offsets are specified as negative numbers to keep the child item in view. Let's put on our algebra hats on for a second and remember that adding a negative integer is exactly the same as subtracting an absolute integer. Specifying a positive offset would make the child's dimensions greater than the content body's, requiring a scroll bar.

We'll explore offsets by using the previous example, modifying only the child item `XTypes` from listing 5.2:

```
items : [
  {
    title    : 'Panel1',
    anchor   : '-50, -150',
    frame    : true
  },
  {
    title    : 'Panel2',
    anchor   : '-10, -150',
    frame    : true
  }
]
```

The rendered `Panel` from the preceding layout modification should look like figure 5.4. We reduced the number of child items to two to more easily explain how offsets work and how they can cause you a lot of trouble.

It's important to dissect what's going on, which will require us to do a little math. Through inspecting the DOM with Firebug, I learned that the `Window`'s content body is 285 pixels high and 288 pixels wide. Using simple math, we can determine what the dimensions of `Panel1` and `Panel2` should be:

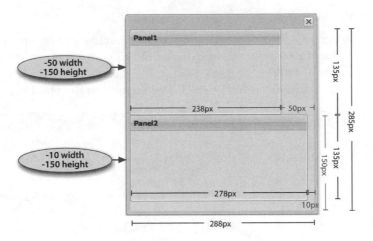

Figure 5.4 Using offsets
with an **AnchorLayout**
with sizing calculations

```
Panel1 Width  = 288px - 50px  = 238px
Panel1 Height = 285px - 150px = 135px

Panel2 Width  = 288px - 10px  = 278px
Panel2 Height = 285px - 150px = 135px
```

You can easily see that both child Panels fit perfectly within the Window. If you add the height of both Panels, you see that they fit, with a total of only 270 px. But what happens if you resize the Window vertically? Notice anything strange? Increasing the Window's height by any more than 15 pixels results in Panel2 being pushed offscreen and scroll bars appearing in the windowBody.

Recall that with this layout, the child dimensions are relative to the parent's content body minus a *constant*, which is the offset. To combat this problem, you can mix anchor offsets with fixed dimensions. To explore this concept, you'll only need to modify Panel2's anchor parameters and add a fixed height:

```
{
    title     : 'Panel2',
    height    : '150',
    anchor    : '-10',
    frame     : true
}
```

This modification makes Panel2's height a fixed 150 pixels. The newly rendered Window can now be resized to virtually any size, and Panel1 will grow to Window content body minus 150 pixels, which leaves just enough vertical room for Panel2 to stay onscreen. One neat thing about this is that Panel2 still has the relative width.

Anchors are used for a multitude of layout tasks. A sibling of the AnchorLayout, the FormLayout, is leveraged by the Ext.form.FormPanel class by default, but it can be used by any Container or subclass that can contain other child items, such as Panel or Window.

5.3 *The FormLayout*

The FormLayout, shown in listing 5.3, is just like the AnchorLayout, except it wraps each child element in a div with the class x-form-item, which makes each item stack vertically like an outline. It adds a label element in front of each of the child items, using the element's for attribute, which when clicked focuses on the child item.

Listing 5.3   The FormLayout

```
var myWin = new Ext.Window({
    height       : 240,
    width        : 200,
    bodyStyle    : 'padding: 5px',
    layout       : 'form',                    ❶ Use the
    labelWidth   : 50,                           FormLayout   ❷ Set field label
    defaultType  : 'textfield',                               widths to 50 px
    items        : [                          ❸ Set default XType
        {                                        to 'field'
            fieldLabel : 'Name',
            width      : 110                  ❹ First child Item
        },                                       with static width
        {
            fieldLabel : 'Age',
            width      : 25
        },                                    ❺ Third child, a
        {                                        ComboBox
            xtype      : 'combo',
            fieldLabel : 'Location',
            width      : 120,
            store      : [ 'Here', 'There', 'Anywhere' ]
        },                                    ❻ Fourth child,
        {                                        a TextArea
            xtype      : 'textarea',
            fieldLabel : 'Bio'
        },                                    ❼ A Panel with
        {                                        instructions
            xtype         : 'panel',
            fieldLabel    : '',
            labelSeparator : '',
            frame         : true,
            title         : 'Instructions',
            html          : 'Please fill in the form',
            height        : 55
        }
    ]
});

myWin.show();
```

There is a heck of a lot that you're doing here to achieve a fairly complex form layout. Like all of the other layouts, you set the Window's layout ❶ to 'form'. You set a layout-specific attribute, labelWidth ❷, to 50 pixels. Remember the label element we discussed earlier? This attribute sets the width of that element. Next, you specify the default XType by setting the 'defaultType' ❸ attribute to 'field', which is used for the first ❹ and second child items and which automatically creates an instance of Ext.form.Field. The third child item ❺ is an xtype definition of a static combination autocomplete and drop-down box, known as a combo box or Ext.form.ComboBox. The fourth child item ❻ is a simple xtype for a text area, whereas the last child item ❼ is a fairly complex xtype object, specifying a Panel.

In order to keep the field label element but show no text, you must set the fieldLabel's property to a string, containing a single space character. You also must remove the label separator character, which is a colon (:) by default, by setting it as an empty string. The rendered code should look like figure 5.5.

Figure 5.5
Using the FormLayout

Remember that it's an ancestor to the AnchorLayout, which makes it powerful for dynamically resizing child items. Although the layout in figure 5.5 works, it's static and could be improved. What if you wanted the Name, Location, and Bio fields to dynamically size with their parent? Remember those anchor parameters? Let's use offsets to improve our use of the FormLayout, as shown in the following listing.

Listing 5.4   Using offsets with the FormLayout

```
{
    fieldLabel : 'Name',
    anchor     : '-4'
},
{
    fieldLabel : 'Age',
    width      : 25
},
{
    xtype      : 'combo',
    fieldLabel : 'Location',
    anchor     : '-4',
    store      : [ 'Here', 'There', 'Anywhere' ]
},
{
    xtype      : 'textarea',
    fieldLabel : 'Bio',
    anchor     : '-4, -134'
},
{
    xtype          : 'panel',
    fieldLabel     : ' ',
    labelSeparator : '',
    frame          : true,
    title          : 'Instructions',
    html           : 'Please fill in the form',
    anchor         : '-4'
}
```

In the preceding code, you add `anchor` parameters to the child items originally defined in listing 5.3. The rendered changes should look like figure 5.6. When you resize the example `Window`, you'll see how well the child items resize and conform to their parent container.

Always try to remember that the `FormLayout` is a direct subclass of the `AnchorLayout`. This way you won't forget to set proper `anchor` parameters for dynamically resizable forms.

There are times when you need complete control over the positioning of the widget layout. The `Absolute-Layout` is perfect for this requirement.

Figure 5.6 Using offsets to create a much fuller form

5.4   *The AbsoluteLayout*

Next to the `ContainerLayout`, the `AbsoluteLayout` is by far one of the simplest to use. It fixes the position of a child by setting the CSS "position" attribute of the child's element to `'absolute'` and sets the `top` and `left` attributes to the x and y parameters that you set on the child items. Many designers place HTML elements as a `position: absolute` with CSS, but Ext leverages JavaScript's DOM-manipulation mechanisms to set attributes to the elements themselves, without having to muck with CSS.

In the following listing you'll create a `Window` with an `AbsoluteLayout`.

Listing 5.5   An `AbsoluteLayout` in action

```
var myWin = new Ext.Window({
    height     : 300,
    width      : 300,
    layout     : 'absolute',          ❶ Use the
    autoScroll : true,                  AbsoluteLayout
    border     : false,
    items      : [
        {
            title : 'Panel1',         ❷ Panel one's x and
            x     : 50,                 y coordinates
            y     : 50,
            height : 100,
            width  : 100,
            html   : 'x: 50, y:50',
            frame  : true
        },
        {
            title  : 'Panel2',        ❸ Panel2's x and y
            x      : 90,                coordinates
            y      : 120,
            height : 75,
            width  : 77,
            html   : 'x: 90, y: 120',
            frame  : true
        }
```

```
    ]
});

myWin.show();
```

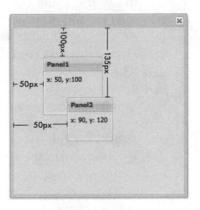

By now, most of this code should look familiar to you, except for a few new parameters. The first noticeable change should be the Window's layout ❶ being set to 'absolute'. You attach two children to this Window. Because you're using the AbsoluteLay-out, you need to specify the x and y coordinates.

The first child, Panel1, has its x ❷ (CSS left attribute) coordinate set to 50 pixels and y (CSS top attribute) coordinate set to 50. The second child, Panel2, has its x ❸ and y coordinates set to 90 pixels and 120 pixels. The rendered code should look like figure 5.7.

Figure 5.7 The results of our AnchorLayout implementation

One of the apparent attributes about this example is that Panel2 overlaps Panel1. Panel2 is on top because of its placement in the DOM tree. Panel2's element is below Panel1's element, and because Panel2's CSS position attribute is set to 'absolute' as well, it's going to show above Panel1. Always keep the risk of overlapping in mind when you implement this layout. Also, because the positions of the child items are fixed, the AbsoluteLayout isn't an ideal solution for parents that resize.

If you have one child item and want it to resize with its parent, the FitLayout is the best solution.

5.5 Making components fit

The FitLayout, shown in the following listing, forces a Container's single child to "fit" to its body element and is, by far, the simplest of the layouts to use.

Listing 5.6 The FitLayout

```
var myWin = new Ext.Window({
    height    : 200,
    width     : 200,
    layout    : 'fit',              ❶ The Window's
    border    : false,                 layout set to 'fit'
    items     : [
        {
            title : 'Panel1',       ❷ The single
            html  : 'I fit in my parent!',   child widget
            frame : true
        }
    ]
});

myWin.show();
```

In the preceding example, you set the Window's layout to 'fit' ❶ and instantiate a single child, an instance of Ext.Panel ❷. The child's XType is assumed by the Window's defaultType attribute, which is automatically set to 'panel' by the Window's prototype. The rendered Panels should look like figure 5.8.

The FitLayout is a great solution for a seamless look when a Container has one child. Often, however, multiple widgets are housed in a container. All other layout-management schemes are generally used to manage multiple children. One of the best-looking layouts is the AccordionLayout, which allows you to vertically stack items, which can be collapsed, showing the user one item at a time.

**Figure 5.8
Using the FitLayout for the
first time**

5.6   *The AccordionLayout*

The AccordionLayout, shown in the next listing, a direct subclass of the FitLayout, is useful when you want to display multiple Panels vertically stacked, where only a single item can be expanded or contracted.

Listing 5.7   The AccordionLayout

```
var myWin = new Ext.Window({
    height       : 200,
    width        : 300,
    border       : false,
    title        : 'A Window with an accordion layout',
    layout       : 'accordion',
    layoutConfig : {
        animate : true
    },
    items        : [
        {
            xtype        : 'form',
            title        : 'General info',
            bodyStyle    : 'padding: 5px',
            defaultType  : 'field',
            labelWidth   : 50,
            items        : [
                {
                    fieldLabel : 'Name',
                    anchor     : '-10'
                },
                {
                    xtype      : 'numberfield',
                    fieldLabel : 'Age',
                    width      : 30
                },
                {
                    xtype      : 'combo',
                    fieldLabel : 'Location',
```

❶ Creates delegate instSpecify an AccordionLayoutance

❷ Layout configuration options

❸ First child item, a FormPanel

```
            anchor    : '-10',
            store     : [ 'Here', 'There', 'Anywhere' ]
        }
    ]
},
{
    xtype  : 'panel',
    title  : 'Bio',
    layout : 'fit',
    items  : {
        xtype : 'textarea',
        value : 'Tell us about yourself'
    }
},
{
    title : 'Instructions',
    html  : 'Please enter information.',
    tools : [
        {id : 'gear'}, {id:'help'}
    ]
}
    ]
});
```

A Panel,
containing a
④ TextArea

An empty
Panel with
⑤ tools

`myWin.show();`

Listing 5.7 is quite large to demonstrate the usefulness of the AccordionLayout. The first thing you do is instantiate a Window, myWin, which has its layout set to 'accordion' ❶. A configuration option you haven't seen thus far is layoutConfig ❷. Some layout schemes have specific configuration options, which you can define as configuration options for a Component's constructor.

These layoutConfig parameters can change the way a layout behaves or functions. In this case, you set the layoutConfig for the AccordionLayout, specifying animate: true, which instructs the AccordionLayout to animate the collapse and expansion of a child item. Another behavior-changing configuration option is activeOnTop, which if set to true will move the active item to the top of the stack. When working with a layout for the first time, I suggest consulting the API for all the options available to you.

Next, you start to define child items, which leverage some of the knowledge you've gained thus far. The first child is a FormPanel ❸, which uses the anchor parameters you learned about earlier in this chapter. Next, you specify a Panel ❹ that has its layout set to 'fit' and *contains* a child TextArea. You then define the last child item ❺ as a vanilla Panel with some tools. The rendered code should look like figure 5.9.

Another way to configure layouts

Instead of using both the layout (String) as well as the layout-Config (Object) configurations, you can set the layout configuration to an Object that contains both the layout type and any options for that layout. For example:

```
layout : {
    type    : 'accordion',
    animate : true
}
```

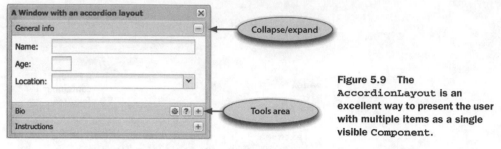

Figure 5.9 The `AccordionLayout` is an excellent way to present the user with multiple items as a single visible `Component`.

It's important to note that the `AccordionLayout` can function well only with a `Panel` and two of its subclasses, `GridPanel` and `TreePanel`. This is because the `Panel` (and the two specified subclasses) has what's required for the `AccordionLayout` to function properly. If you desire anything else inside an `AccordionLayout` such as a `TabPanel`, wrap a `Panel` around it and add that `Panel` as a child of the `Container` that has the `AccordionLayout`.

Although the `AccordionLayout` is a good solution for having more than one `Panel` onscreen, it has limitations. For instance, what if you needed to have 10 `Components` in a particular `Container`? The sum of the heights of the title bars for each item would take up a lot of valuable screen space. The `CardLayout` is perfect for this requirement, because it allows you to show and hide child `Components` or flip through them.

5.7   *The CardLayout*

A direct subclass of the `FitLayout`, the `CardLayout` ensures that its children conform to the size of the `Container`. Unlike the `FitLayout`, however, the `CardLayout` can have multiple children under its control. This tool gives you the flexibility to create `Components` that mimic wizard interfaces.

Except for the initial active item, the `CardLayout` leaves all of the flipping to the end developer with its publicly exposed `setActiveItem` method. In order to create a wizard-like interface, you need to create a method to control the card flipping:

```
var handleNav = function(btn) {
    var activeItem    = myWin.layout.activeItem;
    var index         = myWin.items.indexOf(activeItem);
    var numItems      = myWin.items.getCount() - 1;
    var indicatorEl   = Ext.getCmp('indicator').el;

    if (btn.text == 'Forward' && index < numItems - 1) {
        index++;
        myWin.layout.setActiveItem(index);
        index++;
        indicatorEl.update(index + ' of ' + numItems);
    }
    else if (btn.text == 'Back' && index > 0) {
        myWin.layout.setActiveItem(index - 1);
        indicatorEl.update(index + ' of ' + numItems);
    }
}
```

In the preceding code, you control the card flipping by determining the active item's index and setting the active item based on whether the Forward or Back Button is pressed. You then update the indicator text on the bottom toolbar. Next, let's implement your CardLayout. The code example in the following listing is rather long and involved, so please stick with me.

Listing 5.8 The `CardLayout` in action

```
var myWin = new Ext.Window({
    height      : 200,
    width       : 300,
    border      : false,
    title       : 'A Window with a Card layout',      ❶ Set layout
    layout      : 'card',                                  to 'card'
    activeItem  : 0,                                   ❷ Set Container's
    defaults    : { border : false },                      active item to 0
    items       : [
        {
            xtype       : 'form',
            title       : 'General info',
            bodyStyle   : 'padding: 5px',
            defaultType : 'field',
            labelWidth  : 50,
            items       : [
                {
                    fieldLabel : 'Name',
                    anchor     : '-10',
                },
                {
                    xtype      : 'numberfield',
                    fieldLabel : 'Age',
                    width      : 30
                },
                {
                    xtype      : 'combo',
                    fieldLabel : 'Location',
                    anchor     : '-10',
                    store      : [ 'Here', 'There', 'Anywhere' ]
                }
            ]
        },
        {
            xtype : 'panel',
            autoEl : {},
            title : 'Bio',
            layout : 'fit',
            items : {
                xtype : 'textarea',
                value : 'Tell us about yourself'
            }
        },
        {
            title : 'Congratulations',
```

```
        html  : 'Thank you for filling out our form!'
      }
    ],
    bbar : [
      {
        text     : 'Back',
        handler : handleNav
      },'-',
      {
        text     : 'Forward',
        handler : handleNav
      },'->',
      {
        xtype  : 'box',
        id     : 'indicator',
        style  : 'margin-right: 5px',
        autoEl :  {
           tag  : 'div',
           html : '1 of 3'
        }
      }
    ]
});

myWin.show();
```

❸ **Back and Forward Buttons**

❹ **BoxComponent with id of 'indicator'**

Listing 5.8 details the creation of a `Window`, which leverages the `CardLayout`. Although most of this should be familiar to you, I should point out a few things. The first obvious item is the `layout` ❶ property, which is set to `'card'`. Next is the `activeItem` property ❷, which the `Container` passes to the layout at render time. You set this to `0` (zero), which tells the layout to call the child `Component`'s `render` method when the `Container` renders.

Next, you define the bottom toolbar, which contains the Forward and Back ❸ Buttons, which call your previously defined `handleNav` method and the `BoxComponent` ❹ that you use to display the `index` of the current active item. The rendered `Container` should look like the one in figure 5.10.

Clicking Forward or Back will invoke the `handleNav` method, which will take care of the card flipping and update the indicator `BoxComponent`. Remember that with the `CardLayout`, the logic of the active item switching is completely up to the end developer to create and manage.

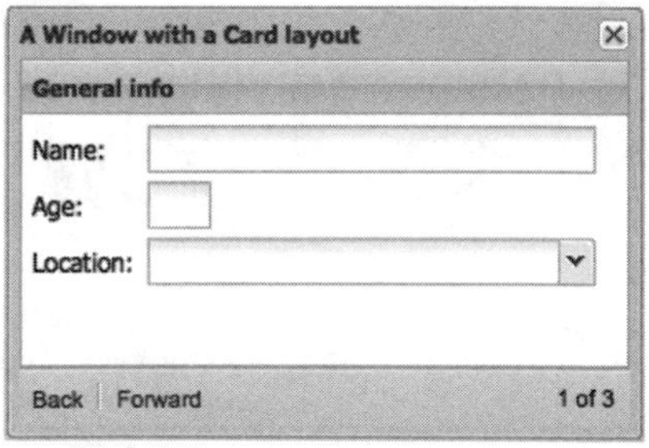

In addition to the previously discussed layouts, Ext offers a few more schemes. The `ColumnLayout` is one of the favorite schemes among UI developers for organizing UI columns that can span the entire width of the parent `Container`.

Figure 5.10   Our first `CardLayout` implementation with a fully interactive navigation `Toolbar`

5.8   *The ColumnLayout*

Organizing components into columns allows you to display multiple Components in a Container side by side. Like the AnchorLayout, the ColumnLayout allows you to set the absolute or relative width of the child Components. There are some things to look out for when using this layout. I'll highlight these in a bit, but first let's construct a ColumnLayout Window in the next listing.

Listing 5.9   Exploring the ColumnLayout

```
var myWin = new Ext.Window({
    height      : 200,
    width       : 400,
    autoScroll  : true,                                 ❶ Automatically
    id          : 'myWin',                                 scroll Container
    title       : 'A Window with a Card layout',
    layout      : 'column',                             ❷ Set layout
    defaults    : {                                        to 'column'
        frame : true
    },
    items       : [
        {
            title       : 'Col 1',
            id          : 'col1',                       ❸ Set relative column
            columnWidth : .3                               width of 30%
        },
        {
            title       : 'Col 2',
            html        : "20% relative width",
            columnWidth : .2
        },
        {
            title : 'Col 3',
            html  : "100px fixed width",                ❹ Set fixed width
            width : 100                                    of 100 pixels
        },
        {
            title       : 'Col 4',
            frame       : true,
            html        : "50% relative width",         ❺ Another
            columnWidth : .5                               relative width
        }
    ]
});

myWin.show();
```

In a nutshell, the ColumnLayout is easy to use. Declare child items, and specify relative or absolute widths or a combination of both, as you do here. In listing 5.9, you set the autoScroll ❶ property of the Container to true, which ensures that scroll bars will appear if the composite of the child Component dimensions grows beyond those of the Container. Next, you set the layout property to 'column' ❷. You then declare four child Components, the first of which has its relative width set to 30 percent via the

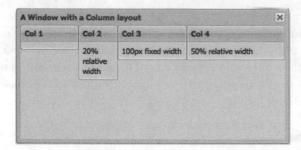

Figure 5.11 Our first `ColumnLayout`, which uses relative column widths with a fixed width entity

columnWidth ❸ attribute. Set the second child's relative width to 20 percent. You mix things up a bit by setting an absolute width for the third child, 100 pixels ❹. Last, you set a relative width ❺ for the last child, 50 percent. The rendered example should look like figure 5.11.

If you tally up the relative widths, you'll see that they total up to 100 percent. How can that be? Three Components, taking 100 percent width, *and* a fixed-width Component? To understand how this is possible, you need to dissect how the ColumnLayout sets the sizes of all of the child Components. Put your math cap back on for a moment.

The meat of the ColumnLayout is its onLayout method, which calculates the dimensions of the Container's body, which in this case is 388 pixels. It then goes through all of its direct children to determine the amount of available space to give to any of the children with relative widths.

To do this, it first subtracts the width of each of the absolute-width child Components from the known width of the Container's body. In our example, we have one child with an absolute width of 100 pixels. The ColumnLayout calculates the difference between 388 and 100, which equals 288 (pixels).

Now that the ColumnLayout knows exactly how much horizontal space it has left, it can set the size of each of the child Components based on the percentage. It goes through each of the children and sizes each based on the known available horizontal width of the Container's body. It does this by multiplying the percentage (decimal) by the available width. Once complete, the sum of the widths of relatively sized Components turns out to be about 288 pixels.

Now that you understand the width calculations for this layout, let's change our focus to the height of the child items. Notice how the height of the child Components doesn't equal the height of the Container body? This is because the ColumnLayout doesn't manage the height of the child Components. This causes an issue with child items that may grow beyond the height of its Container's body. This is precisely why you set autoScroll to true for the Window. You can exercise this theory by adding an extra-large child to the 'Col 1' Component by entering the following code inside Firebug's JavaScript input console. Make sure you have a virgin copy of listing 5.9 running in your browser.

```
Ext.getCmp('col1').add({
  height : 250,
```

```
    title  : 'New Panel',
    frame  : true
  });
Ext.getCmp('col1').doLayout();
```

You should now see a `Panel` embedded into the 'Col 1' panel with its height exceeding that of the `Window`'s body. Notice how scroll bars appear in the `Window`. If you didn't set `autoScroll` to `true`, your UI would look cut off and might have its usability reduced or halted. You can scroll vertically and horizontally. The reason you can scroll vertically is that `Col1`'s overall height is greater than that of the `Window`'s body. That's acceptable. The horizontal scrolling is the problem in this case. Recall that the `ColumnLayout` calculated only 288 pixels to properly size the three columns with relative widths. Because the vertical scroll bar is now visible, the physical amount of space from which the columns can be displayed is reduced by the width of the vertical scroll bar. To fix this issue, you must call `doLayout` on the parent `Container`, `Ext.getCmp('myWin').doLayout()`, which will force a recalculation of the available horizontal space and resize the relatively sized columns so the `Container`'s body need not scroll horizontally. Remembering to call the parent's `doLayout` method when adding a `Component` to any of the direct children will help keep your UIs looking great.

As you can see, the `ColumnLayout` is great for organizing your child `Components` in columns. With this layout, however, there are two limitations. All child items are always left justified, and their heights are unmanaged by the parent `Container`. Ext provides us with the `HBoxLayout` that overcomes the limitations of the `ColumnLayout` and extends far beyond its capabilities.

5.9 The HBox and VBox layouts

New to version 3.0 are the HBox and VBox layouts. The `HBoxLayout`'s behavior is similar to the `ColumnLayout`, where it displays items in columns but allows for much greater flexibility. For instance, you can change the alignment of the child items both vertically and horizontally. Another great feature of this layout scheme is the ability to allow the columns or rows to stretch to their parent's dimensions if required. Let's dive into the `HBoxLayout`, shown in the following listing, where you'll create a `Container` with three child `Panels` to manipulate.

Listing 5.10   HBoxLayout, exploring the packing configuration

```
new Ext.Window({                              ❶ Set layout
    layout       : 'hbox',                       to 'hbox'
    height       : 300,
    width        : 300,
    title        : 'A Container with an HBox layout',
    layoutConfig : {                          ❷ Specify layout
       pack : 'start'                           configuration
    },
    defaults : {
       frame : true,
    },
```

```
    items : [
        {
            title  : 'Panel 1',
            height : 100
        },
        {
            title  : 'Panel 2',
            height : 75,
            width  : 100
        },
        {
            title  : 'Panel 3',
            height : 200
        }
    ]
}).show();
```

In listing 5.10, you set the layout to 'hbox' ❶ and specify the layoutConfig ❷ configuration object. You create the three child Panels with irregular shapes, allowing you to properly exercise the different layout configuration parameters for which you can specify two, pack and align, where pack means "vertical alignment" and align means "horizontal alignment." Being able to understand the meanings for these two parameters is important because they're flipped for the HBoxLayout's cousin, the VBoxLayout. The pack parameter accepts three possible values: start, center, and end. In this context, I like to think of them as left, center, and right. Modifying that parameter in listing 5.10 will result in one of the rendered Windows in figure 5.12. The default value for the pack attribute is 'start'.

The align parameter accepts four possible values: 'top', 'middle', 'stretch', and 'stretchmax'. Remember that with the HBoxLayout, the align property specifies vertical alignment.

The default parameter for align is 'top'. In order to change how the child panels are vertically aligned, you need to override the default, by specifying it in the layoutConfig object for the Container. Figure 5.13 illustrates how you can change the way the children are sized and arranged based on a few different combinations.

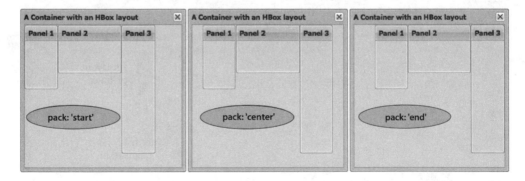

Figure 5.12   Different results with the three pack options

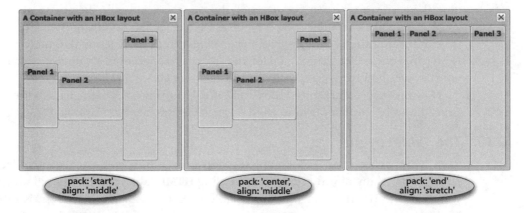

Figure 5.13 The 'stretch' alignment will always override any height values specified by the child items.

Specifying a value of 'stretch' for the align attribute instructs the HBoxLayout to resize the child items to the height of the Container's body, which overcomes one limitation of the ColumnLayout.

The last configuration parameter that we must explore is flex, which is similar to the columnWidth parameter for the columnLayout and gets specified on the child items. Unlike the columnWidth parameter, the flex parameter is interpreted as a weight or a priority instead of a percentage of the columns. Let's say, for instance, you'd like each of the columns to have equal widths. Set each column's flex to the same value, and they'll all have equal widths. If you wanted to have two of the columns expand to a total of one half of the width of the parent's Container and the third to expand to the other half, make sure that the flex value for each of the first two columns is exactly half that of the third column. For instance:

```
items : [
   {
      title   : 'Panel 1',
      flex    : 1
   },
   {
      title   : 'Panel 2',
      flex    : 1
   },
   {
      title   : 'Panel 3',
      flex    : 2
   }
]
```

Stacking items vertically is also possible with the VBoxLayout, which follows exactly the same syntax as the HBoxLayout. To use the VBoxLayout, modify listing 5.10, change the layout to 'vbox', and refresh the page. Next, you can apply the flex parameters described previously to make each of the Panels relative in height to the parent Container. I like to think of VBoxLayout as the ContainerLayout on steroids.

Contrasting the VBoxLayout with the HBoxLayout, there's one parameter change. Recall that the align parameter for the HBoxLayout accepts a value of top. For the VBoxLayout, however, you specify left instead of top.

Now that you've mastered HBox and VBox layouts, we'll switch gears to the Table-Layout, where you can position child Components, such as a traditional HTML table.

5.10 *The TableLayout*

The TableLayout gives you complete control over how you visually organize your Components. Many of you are used to building HTML tables the traditional way, where you write the HTML code. Building a table of Ext Components, however, is different because you specify the content of the table cells in a single-dimension array, which can get a little confusing. I'm sure that once you've finished these exercises, you'll be an expert in this layout. In the following listing you'll create a basic 3 x 3 TableLayout.

Listing 5.11 A vanilla TableLayout

```
var myWin = new Ext.Window({
    height       : 300,
    width        : 300,
    border       : false,
    autoScroll   : true,
    title        : 'A Window with a Table layout',      ❶ Specify layout
    layout       : 'table',                                 as 'table'
    layoutConfig : {                                    ❷ Three columns
        columns : 3                                        for the table
    },                                              ❸ Default size for
    defaults     : {                                    box is 50 x 50
        height : 50,
        width  : 50
    },
    items        : [
        {
            html : '1'
        },
        {
            html : '2'
        },
        {
            html : '3'
        },
        {
            html : '4'
        },
        {
            html : '5'
        },
        {
            html : '6'
```

```
      },
      {
        html : '7'
      },
      {
        html : '8'
      },
      {
        html : '9'
      }
    ]
});

myWin.show();
```

The code in listing 5.11 creates a `Window Container` that has nine boxes stacked in a 3 x 3 formation like in figure 5.14. By now, most of this should seem familiar to you, but I want to highlight a few items. The most obvious of these should be the `layout` parameter ❶ being set to 'table'. Next, you set a `layoutConfig` ❷ object, which sets the number of columns. Always remember to set this property when using this layout. Last, you set the defaults ❸ for all of the child items to 50 pixels wide by 50 pixels high.

Often you need sections of the table to span multiple rows or multiple columns. To accomplish this, you must specify either the `rowspan` or `colspan` parameter explicitly on the child items. Let's modify your table so the child items can span multiple rows or columns, as shown in the following listing.

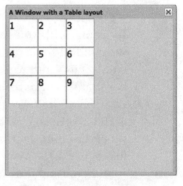

Figure 5.14 The results of our first simple `TableLayout`

```
items : [
    {
      html    : '1',
      colspan : 3,
      width   : 150
    },
    {
      html    : '2',
      rowspan : 2,
      height  : 100
    },
    {
      html : '3'
    },
    {
      html    : '4',
      rowspan : 2,
      height  : 100
```

❶ Set colspan to 3, width to 150 px

❷ Set rowspan to 2, height to 100 px

❸ Set rowspan to 2, height to 100 px

```
      },
      {
        html : '5'
      },
      {
        html : '6'
      },
      {
        html : '7'
      },
      {
        html : '8'
      },
      {
        html    : '9',
        colspan : 3,
        width   : 150
      }
  ]
```

④ **Set colspan to 3,
width to 150 px**

In listing 5.12, you reuse the existing Container code from listing 5.11 and replace the child items array. You set the colspan attribute for the first panel ❶ to 3 and manually set its width to fit the total known width of the table, which is 150 pixels. Remember that you have three columns of default 50 x 50 child containers. Next, you set the rowspan of the second child ❷ item to 2 and its height to the total of two rows, which is 100 pixels. You do the same thing for panel 4 ❸. The last change involves panel 9, which has the exact same attributes as panel 1 ❹. The rendered change should look like figure 5.15.

When using the TableLayout, you should remember a few things. First is to determine the total number of columns that will be used and specify it in the layoutConfig parameter. Also, if you're going to have Components span rows and/or columns, be sure to set their dimensions accordingly; otherwise the Components laid out in the table won't seem to be aligned correctly.

The TableLayout is extremely versatile and can be used to create any type of box-based layout that your imagination conjures up, with the main limitation being that there's no parent-child size management.

Moving to our last stop on the Ext layout journey, we reach the ever-so-popular BorderLayout, where you can divide any container into five collapsible regions that manage their children's size.

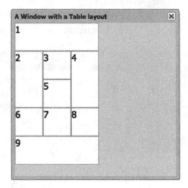

Figure 5.15 When using the TableLayout, you could specify rowspan and colspan for a particular Component, which will make it occupy more than one cell in the table.

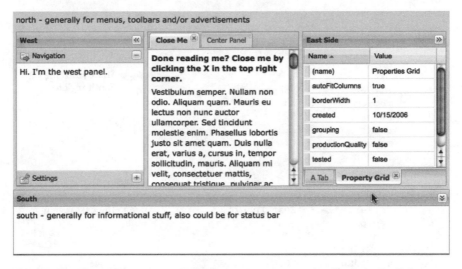

Figure 5.16 The `BorderLayout` is what attracts many new developers to the Ext Framework and is widely used in many applications to divide the screen into task-specific functional areas.

5.11 *The BorderLayout*

The `BorderLayout` made its début in 2006, back when Ext was more than a mere extension to the YUI Library and had matured into an extremely flexible and easy-to-use layout that provides full control over its subparts, or regions. These regions are aptly named by polar coordinates: North, South, East, West, and Center. Figure 5.16 illustrates a `BorderLayout` implementation from the Ext SDK.

Each region of a `BorderLayout` is managed by the `BorderLayout.Region` class, which is what provides all of the UI and programmatic controls to that specific division of the layout scheme. Depending on the configuration options provided, the region can be resized or collapsed by the user. There are also options to limit the resize of the region or prevent it from being resized altogether.

To explore the `BorderLayout` and the `Region` class, we'll use the `Viewport` class because it will make it easier for us to see the final result of our exercise.

Listing 5.13 Flexing the `BorderLayout`

```
new Ext.Viewport({
    layout   : 'border',
    defaults : {
        frame : true,
        split : true
    },
    items : [
        {
            title       : 'North Panel',
            region      : 'north',
```

❶ Split regions, allowing for resize

❷ Static North region

```
        height      : 100,
        minHeight   : 100,
        maxHeight   : 150,
        collapsible : true
    },
    {
        title       : 'South Panel',
        region      : 'south',
        height      : 75,
        split       : false,
        margins     : {
            top : 5
        }
    },
    {
        title       : 'East Panel',
        region      : 'east',
        width       : 100,
        minWidth    : 75,
        maxWidth    : 150,
        collapsible : true
    },
    {
        title        : 'West Panel',
        region       : 'west',
        collapsible  : true,
        collapseMode : 'mini'
    },
    {
        title  : 'Center Panel',
        region : 'center'
    }
  ]
});
```

❸ Static resizable South region

❹ The East region

❺ Mini-collapse West region

In listing 5.13, you accomplish quite a lot using the Viewport a bit in a few lines of code. You set layout to 'border' ❶ and set split to true in the default configuration object. There's a lot going on here at once, so feel free to reference figure 5.17, which depicts what the rendered code will look like.

Although all regions are technically divided, the split parameter instructs the BorderLayout to render a 5-pixel high (or wide) divider between the center and the regions. This divider is used as the resize handles for the regions. In order to work this magic, the BorderLayout employs the BorderLayout.SplitRegion class, which creates an absolute-position invisible div that intercepts the click-and-drag action of the user. When the drag action occurs, a proxy div appears, which is a direct sibling of the split bar handle div, allowing users to preview exactly how wide or high they're about to resize a region.

Next, you begin to instantiate child items, which have BorderLayout.Region-specific parameters. In order to review many of them, you'll make each region's behavior different from the other.

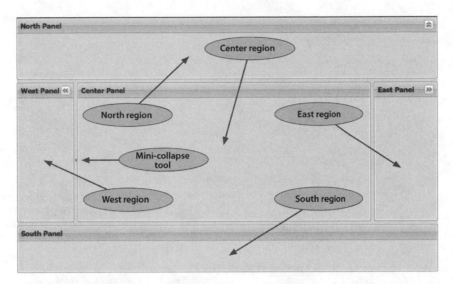

Figure 5.17 The BorderLayout's versatility and ease of use make it one of the most widely used in Ext-based RIAs.

For the first child ❷, you set the region property to 'north' to ensure that it's at the top of the BorderLayout. You play a little game with the BoxComponent-specific parameter, height, and the region-specific parameters, minHeight and maxHeight. By specifying a height of 100, you're instructing the region to render the Panel with an initial height of 100 pixels. The minHeight instructs the region to not allow the split bar to be dragged beyond the coordinates that would make the northern region the minimal height of 100. The same is true for the maxHeight parameter, except it applies to expanding the region's height. You also specify the Panel-specific parameter of collapsible as true, which instructs the region to allow it to be collapsed to a mere 30 pixels high.

Defining the South region, the viewport's second child ❸, you play some games to prevent it from being resized but work to keep the layout's 5-pixel split between the regions. Setting the split parameter to false, you instruct the region to not allow it to be resized. Doing so also instructs the region to omit the 5-pixel split bar, which would make the layout somewhat visually incomplete. In order to achieve a façade-split bar, you specify a region-specific margins parameter, which specifies that you want the South region to have a 5-pixel buffer between itself and anything above it. One word of caution about this, however: although the layout now looks complete, end users may try to resize it, possibly causing frustration on their end.

The third child ❹ is defined as the East region. This region is similarly configured to the north panel except it has sizing constraints that are a bit more flexible. Where the northern region starts its life out at its minimum size, the eastern region starts its life between its minWidth and maxWidth. Specifying size parameters like these allows the UI to present a region in a default or suggested size but allows the Panel to be resized beyond its original dimensions.

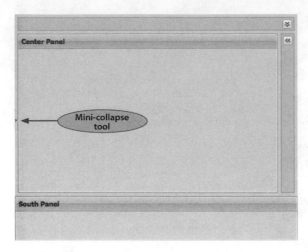

Figure 5.18   Our `BorderLayout` **where two of the regions, North and East, are collapsed in regular mode and the West panel is collapsed in miniature mode**

The West region ❺ has a special region-specific parameter, `collapseMode`, set to the string `'mini'`. Setting this parameter that way instructs Ext to collapse a `Panel` to a mere 5 pixels, providing more visual space for the Center region. Figure 5.18 illustrates how small. By allowing the `split` parameter to stay as `true` (remember our `defaults` object) and not specifying minimum or maximum size parameters, the western region can be resized as far as the browser will physically allow, as shown in figure 5.18.

The last region is the Center region, which is the only *required* region for the `BorderLayout`. Although the Center region seems a bit bare, it's special indeed. The Center region is generally the canvas in which developers place the bulk of their RIA UI components, and its size is dependent on its sibling regions' dimensions.

For all of its strengths, the `BorderLayout` has one huge disadvantage, which is that once a child in a region is defined/created, it can't be changed. Because the `Border-Layout.Region` is a base class and doesn't extend `Container`, it doesn't have the power to replace a child once it's instantiated. The fix for this is extremely simple. For each region where you wish to replace `Components`, specify a `Container` as a region. Let's exercise this by replacing the Center region section for listing 5.13:

```
{
    xtype  : 'container',
    region : 'center',
    layout : 'fit',
    id     : 'centerRegion',
    autoEl : {},
    items  : {
        title : 'Center Region',
        id    : 'centerPanel',
        html  : 'I am disposable',
        frame : true
    }
}
```

Remember that the Viewport can be created only once, so a refresh of the page where the example code lies is required. The refreshed Viewport should look nearly identical to figure 5.18, except the Center region now has HTML showing that it's disposable. In the previous example, you define the Container XType with the layout of fit and an id that you can leverage with Firebug's JavaScript console.

Recalling our prior discussion and exercises over adding and removing child Components to and from a Container, can you remember how to get a reference to a Component via its id and remove a child? If you can, excellent work! If you can't, I've already worked it out for you. But be sure to review the prior sections because they're extremely important to managing the Ext UI. Take a swipe at replacing the Center region's child Component; see the following listing.

Listing 5.14 Replacing a Component in the Center region

```
var centerPanel  = Ext.getCmp('centerPanel');
var centerRegion = Ext.getCmp('centerRegion');

centerRegion.remove(centerPanel, true);
centerRegion.add({
    xtype        : 'form',
    frame        : true,
    bodyStyle    : 'padding: 5px',
    defaultType  : 'field',
    title        : 'Please enter some information',
    defaults     : {
        anchor : '-10'
    },
    items        : [
        {
            fieldLabel : 'First Name'
        },
        {
            fieldLabel : 'Last Name'
        },
        {
            xtype      : 'textarea',
            fieldLabel : 'Bio'
        }
    ]
});
centerRegion.doLayout();
```

Listing 5.14 leverages everything you've learned thus far regarding Components, Containers, and Layouts, providing you with the flexibility to replace the Center region's child, a Panel with a FormPanel, with relative ease. You can use this pattern in any of the regions to replace items at will.

5.12 Summary

We took a lot of time to explore the many and versatile Ext layout schemes. In doing so, you learned some of the strengths, weaknesses, and pitfalls. Remember that although many layouts can do similar things, each has its place in a UI. Finding the correct layout to display Components may not be immediately apparent and will take some practice if you're new to UI design altogether.

If you aren't 100 percent comfortable with the material as you exit this chapter, I suggest moving forward and returning to it after some time has passed and the material has had some time to sink in.

Now that you have many of the core topics behind you, put your seatbelt on because you're going to be in for a wild ride, where you learn more about and use Ext's UI widgets, starting off with form Panels.

Ext JS takes form

This chapter covers

- Getting to know the basics of `FormPanel` input fields
- Creating custom `ComboBox` templates
- Creating a complex layout `FormPanel`

We just finished exploring how to organize UI widgets with the various layout managers in the Ext framework. From here, we'll spring into learning how to instantiate and manage Ext JS form elements. After all, what's any application without user input?

It should be no surprise to hear that developing and designing forms is a common task for web developers. Managing form validation is what JavaScript was mainly used for just a few years ago. Ext JS goes beyond typical form validation, building on the basic HTML input fields to both add features for the developer and enhance the user experience. For instance, let's say a user is required to enter HTML into a form. Using an out-of-the-box `TextArea` input field, the user would have to write the HTML content by hand. This isn't required with the Ext JS `HtmlEditor`, where you get a full WYSIWYG input field, allowing the user to input and manipulate richly formatted HTML easily.

121

In this chapter, we'll look into the FormPanel, and you'll learn about many of the Ext JS form input classes. You'll also see how to leverage what you know about layouts and the Container model to build a complex form and use that implementation to submit and load the data via Ajax.

Because there are so many things to cover with input fields, this chapter will follow more of a cookbook style, where I walk you through the various input fields and discuss how to implement them. Once you get a solid grasp on the various input fields, we'll tie things together by implementing and discussing the FormPanel class.

6.1   *The TextField*

The Ext TextField adds features to the existing HTML input field such as basic validations, a custom validation method, automatic resizing, and keyboard filtering. To utilize some of the more powerful features such as keyboard filters (masks) and automatic character stripping, you'll need to know a little about regular expressions.

> ### Learn more about regex with JavaScript
> If you're new to regular expressions, there's a plethora of information on the internet. One of my favorite sites to learn about this topic is http://www.regular-expressions.info/javascript.html.

We're going to explore quite a few features of the TextField at once. Please stay with me, because some of example code can be lengthy.

Because the TextField class is a subclass of Component, you could renderTo or applyTo an element on the page. Instead, you'll build them as children of a Form-Panel, which will provide a better presentation. To start, you'll create the items array, which will contain the XType definitions of the different TextFields, as shown in the following listing.

Listing 6.1   Our text fields

```
Ext.QuickTips.init();

var fpItems =[
    {
        fieldLabel : 'Alpha only',        ◄─❶ The fieldLabel      ❷ Enable basic
        allowBlank : false,                                          blank validation
        emptyText  : 'This field is empty!',
        maskRe     : /[a-z]/i                                     ❸ Empty field
    },                                          Alpha-only
    {                                        ❹ characters
        fieldLabel : 'Simple 3 to 7 Chars',
        allowBlank : false,
        minLength  : 3,
        maxLength  : 7          ◄   Allow min/max
    },                            ❺ number of characters
    {
```

```
        fieldLabel   : 'Special Chars Only',
        stripCharsRe : /[a-zA-Z0-9]/ig
    },
    {
        fieldLabel : 'Web Only with VType',
        vtype      : 'urlOnly'
    }
];
```

⬅ ⑥ **Allow only special characters**

⬅ **Use our** ⑦ **custom VType**

In listing 6.1 you must work a lot of angles to demonstrate the capabilities of the simple `TextField`. You create four text fields in the `fpItems` array. One of the redundant attributes that each child has is `fieldLabel` ❶, which describes to the `FormLayout` (remember that the `FormPanel` uses the `FormLayout` by default) what text to place in the `label` element for the `field` element.

For the first child, you ensure that the field can't be blank by specifying `allowBlank` ❷ as `false`, which ensures that you use one of Ext's basic field validations. You also set a string value for `emptyText` ❸, which displays helper text and can be used as a default value. One important thing to be aware of is that it gets sent as the field's value during its form submission. Next, you set `maskRe` ❹, a regular expression mask, to filter keystrokes that resolve to anything other than alpha characters. The second text field is built so it can't be left blank and must contain from three to seven characters to be valid. You do this by setting the `minLength` ❺ and `maxLength` parameters. The third text field can be blank, but it has automatic alphanumeric character stripping. You enable automatic stripping by specifying a valid regular expression for the `stripCharsRe` ❻ property. For the last child ❼ item, we're going to veer off course for a bit to explore `VTypes`.

The last child item is a plain-text field that makes use of a custom `VType` ❼, which we'll build out shortly. A `VType` is a custom validation method that's called automatically by the form field by a field losing focus or sometime after the field is modified. To create your own `VType`, you can use a regular expression *or* a custom function. The anatomy of a `VType` is simple and can contain up to three ingredients. The validation method is the only required item; the input mask regular expression and invalid text string are optional. The name of the `VType` is the validation method, whereas the mask and text properties are a concatenation of the name with "Mask" or "Text." Let's create our custom `VType`:

```
var myValidFn = function(v) {
    var myRegex = /https?:\/\/([-\w\.]+)+(:\d+)?(\/([\w/_\.]*(\?\S+)?)?)?/;
    return myRegex.test(v);
};

Ext.apply(Ext.form.VTypes, {
    urlOnly     : myValidFn,
    urlOnlyText : 'Must be a valid web URL'
});
```

Don't run away! The regular expression is scary, I know. It does serve a purpose, though, and you'll see what I mean in a bit. Our validation method, `myValidFn`, contains our monster regular expression and returns the result of using its test method, where we pass v, which is the value of the TextField at the time the VType's validation method is called. Next, we apply an object to the Ext.form.VTypes single-ton, which contains urlOnly—the reference to our validation method. Our VType is now known to Ext.form.VTypes as urlOnly and is why we set the vtype property as such on the last TextField. We also set the urlOnlyText property for the vtype as a string with our custom error message. Okay, now that we've explored VTypes, let's build the form in which our TextFields will live, as shown in the following listing.

Listing 6.2   Building the FormPanel for our TextFields

```
var fp = new Ext.form.FormPanel({
    renderTo     : Ext.getBody(),
    width        : 400,
    height       : 160,
    title        : 'Exercising textfields',
    frame        : true,
    bodyStyle    : 'padding: 6px',
    labelWidth   : 126,                    ❶ Set default XType
    defaultType  : 'textfield',               to textfield
    defaults     : {
        msgTarget : 'side',                ❷ Set validation
        anchor    : '-20'                     message target
    },
    items        : fpItems
});
```

Because we've already gone over the FormLayout, most of the code construct in listing 6.2 should be familiar to you. But let's review a few key items relating to the FormLayout and Component model. You override the default Component XType by set-ting the defaultType ❶ property to 'textfield', which, if you recall, will ensure your objects are resolved into text fields. You also set up some defaults ❷, which ensure your error message target is to the right side of the field and your anchor prop-erty is set. Last, you reference the FormPanel's items to the fpItems variable that you created earlier, which contains the four TextFields. The rendered FormPanel should look like figure 6.1.

Notice in figure 6.1 that there's a little extra space to the right of the TextFields. This is because we wanted to ensure that validation error messages are displayed to the right of the fields. This is why we set msgTarget to 'side' for our default object in our FormPanel definition. You can invoke validation one of two ways: focus and blur

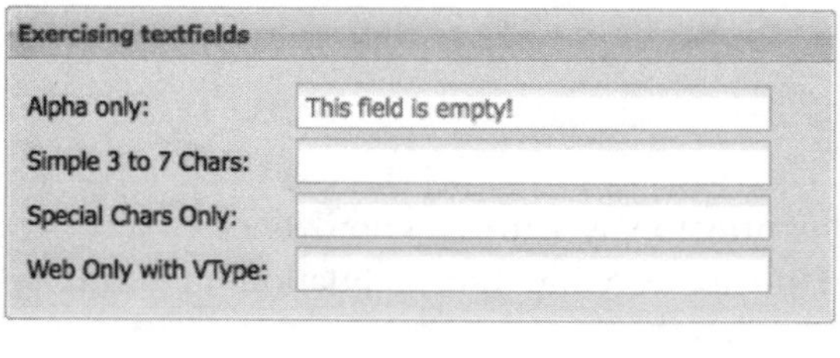

Figure 6.1   The rendered results of our FormPanel, which contains four TextFields

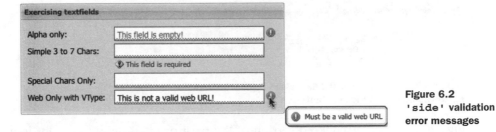

Figure 6.2
'side' validation
error messages

(lose focus) of a field or invoke a form-wide isValid method call, fp.getForm().
isValid(). Figure 6.2 shows what the fields look like after validation has occurred.

Each field can have its own msgTarget property, which can be any of five possible
attributes:

- qtip—Displays an Ext quicktip on mouseover
- title—Shows the error in the default browser title area
- under—Positions the error message below the field
- side—Renders an exclamation icon to the right side of the field
- [element id]—Adds the text of the error message as the innerHTML of the target element

It's important to note that the msgTarget property affects only how the error message
is displayed when the field is inside a FormLayout. If the TextField is rendered to
some arbitrary element somewhere on the page (that is, using renderTo or applyTo),
the msgTarget will be set only to title. I encourage you to spend some time experi-
menting with the different msgTarget values; that way, when it comes down to building your first real-world form, you'll have a good understanding of the way they work.
Let's see how to create password and file upload fields using the TextField.

6.1.1 *Password and file select fields*

To create a password field in HTML, you set its type attribute to 'password'. Likewise, for a file input field, you set type to 'file'. In Ext, to generate these, enter the
following:

```
var fpItems =[
    {
        fieldLabel : 'Password',
        allowBlank : false,
        inputType  : 'password'
    },
    {
        fieldLabel : 'File',
        allowBlank : false,
        inputType  : 'file'
    }
];
```

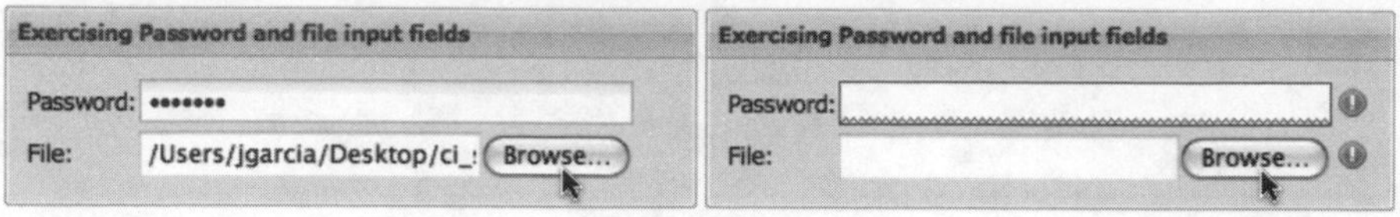

Figure 6.3 Our password and file upload fields with data filled in (left) and an example of the side validation error icons (right)

Figure 6.3 shows a rendered version of the password and file input fields in a Form-Panel.

When using file upload fields, remember to configure the underlying form element with fileUpload : true; otherwise, your files will never get submitted. Also, in case you haven't noticed it, the file upload field in figure 6.3 (right) doesn't have a red bounding box around it. This is because of the browser's security model preventing styling of the upload field.

We've covered a lot about the generic TextField, field validations, and the password and file upload fields. We'll now move on to looking at other input fields.

6.1.2 Building a TextArea

The TextArea extends TextField and is a multiline input field. Constructing a Text-Area is like constructing a TextField, except you have to take the Component's height into consideration. Here's an example TextArea with a fixed height but a relative width:

```
{
    xtype       : 'textarea',
    fieldLabel  : 'My TextArea',
    name        : 'myTextArea',
    anchor      : '100%',
    height      : 100
}
```

It's as easy as that. Let's take a quick look at how you can leverage the NumberField, which is another subclass of TextField.

6.1.3 The convenient NumberField

Sometimes requirements dictate that you place an input field that allows only numbers to be entered. You could do this with the TextField and apply your own validation, but why reinvent the wheel? The NumberField does pretty much all of the validation for you for integers and floating numbers. Let's create a NumberField that accepts floating-point numbers with the precision to thousandths and allows only specific values:

```
{
    xtype           : 'numberfield',
    fieldLabel      : 'Numbers only',
    allowBlank      : false,
```

```
        emptyText          : 'This field is empty!',
        decimalPrecision : 3,
        minValue           : 0.001,
        maxValue           : 2
}
```

In this example, you create your `NumberField` configuration object. In order to apply your requirements, you specify the `decimalPrecision`, `minValue`, and `maxValue` properties. This ensures that any floating number written with greater precision than 3 is rounded up. Likewise, the `minValue` and `maxValue` properties are applied to ensure that valid range is 0.001 to 2. Any number outside of this range is considered invalid and Ext will mark the field as such. The `NumberField` looks exactly like the `TextField` when rendered. There are a few more properties that can assist with the configuration of the `NumberField`. Please see the API documentation at http:// extjs.com/docs/?class=Ext.form.NumberField for further details.

Now that we've looked at the `TextField` and two of its subclasses, the `TextArea` and `NumberField`, let's look at its distant cousin, the `ComboBox`.

6.2   TypeAhead with the ComboBox

The cleverly named `ComboBox` input field is like a Swiss army knife of all text input fields. It's a *combination* of a general text input field and a general drop-down box to give you a flexible and highly configurable combination input field. The `ComboBox` has the ability for automatic text completion (known as *type-ahead*) in the text input area, and coupled with a *remote* data `Store`, it can work with the server side to filter results. If the combo box is performing a remote request against a large dataset, you can enable result paging by setting the `pageSize` property. Figure 6.4 illustrates the anatomy of a remote loading and paging `ComboBox`.

Before we look at how the `ComboBox` works, we should explore how to construct one. Because you're familiar with how to lay out child items, I think this is an excellent opportunity to leverage your new newly gained experience. So moving forward, when we discuss items that don't contain children, such as fields, I'll leave it up to you to build a `Container`. Hint: You can use the `FormPanel` from listing 6.2.

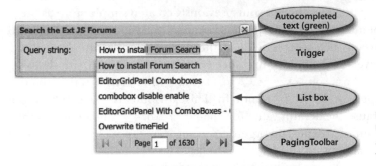

Figure 6.4   An example UI of a remote loading and paging `ComboBox` with type-ahead

6.2.1 *Building a local ComboBox*

Creating a TextField is simple compared to building a ComboBox. This is because the ComboBox has a direct dependency on a class called the data Store, which is the main tool to manage data in the framework. We'll just scratch the surface of this supporting class here and will go much further into detail in chapter 7. In the following listing you'll build your first ComboBox using an XType configuration object.

Listing 6.3   Building your first ComboBox

```
var mySimpleStore = new Ext.data.ArrayStore({      ←──❶ Build your first ArrayStore
    data    : [
        ['Jack Slocum'], ['Abe Elias'], ['Aaron Conran'], ['Evan Trimboli']
    ],
    fields : ['name']
});

var combo = {
    xtype        : 'combo',
    fieldLabel   : 'Select a name',        ❷ Specify store in
    store        : mySimpleStore,      ◁──┘  the ComboBox
    displayField : 'name',                 ←──❸ Set display field
    typeAhead    : true,
    mode         : 'local'        ◁──┐ Set ComboBox
};                                 ❹ to local mode
```

In listing 6.3, you construct a simple Store that reads array data, known as an Array-Store ❶ (a preconfigured extension of the Ext.data.Store class, which makes it easy for you to create a store that digests array data. You populate the consumable array data and set it as the data property for the configuration object. Next, you specify the fields property as an array of data points from which the data Store will read and organize records. Because you have only one data point per array in your array, you specify only a single point and give it a name of 'name'. Again, we'll go into much greater detail on the data Store later on, where you'll learn the entire gamut from records to connection proxies.

You specify your combo as a simple POJSO (Plain Old JavaScript Object), setting the xtype property as 'combo' to ensure that its parent Container calls the correct class. You specify the reference of your previously created simple store as the store ❷ property. Remember the fields property you set for the store? Well, the display-Field ❸ is directly tied to the fields of the data Store that the ComboBox is using. Because you have a single field, you'll specify your displayField with that single field, which is 'name'. Last, you set mode ❹ to 'local', which ensures that the data Store doesn't attempt to fetch data remotely. This attribute is extremely important to remember because the default value for mode is 'remote', which ensures that all data is fetched via remote requests. Forgetting to set it to 'local' will cause some problems. Figure 6.5 show what the ComboBox looks like rendered.

To exercise the filtering and type-ahead features, you can immediately start to type inside the text input field. Now your record set contains only four records, but you can begin to see how this works. Entering a simple a into the text field will filter the

list and display only two names in the list box. At
the same time, the ComboBox will type-ahead the
rest of the first match, which will show up as 'be
Elias'. Likewise, entering aa will result in the
store filtering out all but a single record, and the
type-ahead will fill in the rest of the text, 'ron
Conran'. There you have it, a nice recipe for a local
ComboBox.

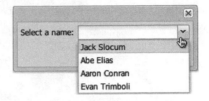

**Figure 6.5 An example rendering of
our ComboBox from listing 6.3 inside
a Window**

Using a local ComboBox is great if you have a
minimal amount of static data. It does have its advantages and disadvantages, however.
Its main advantage is that the data doesn't have to be fetched remotely. This, however,
ends up being a major disadvantage when there's an extreme amount of data to parse
through, which would make the UI slow down, sputter, or even grind to a halt, showing that dreaded "This script is taking too long" error box. This is where the remote
loading ComboBox can be called into service.

6.2.2 Implementing a remote ComboBox

Using a remote ComboBox is somewhat more complicated than a static implementation. This is because you have server-side code to manage, which will include some
type of server-side store like a database. To keep your focus on the ComboBox, you'll
use the preconstructed PHP code at http://extjsinaction.com/dataQuery.php on my
site, which contains randomly generated names and addresses. Let's get on to implementing our remote ComboBox, as shown in the next listing.

Listing 6.4 Implementing a remote loading ComboBox

```
var remoteJsonStore = new Ext.data.JsonStore({
    root          : 'records',          ◁┓ Specify root
    baseParams    : {                   ① property
      column : 'fullName'
    },
    fields        : [
      {
          name    : 'name',
          mapping : 'fullName'
      },
      {
          name    : 'id',
          mapping : 'id'
      }
    ],
    proxy : new Ext.data.ScriptTagProxy({
      url : 'http://extjsinaction.com/dataQuery.php'
    })
});

var combo = {
    xtype         : 'combo',
    fieldLabel    : 'Search by name',
```

```
    forceSelection : true,
    displayField   : 'name',
    valueField     : 'id',
    hiddenName     : 'customerId',
    loadingText    : 'Querying....',         ❷  Number of characters
    minChars       : 1,                          for autocomplete
    triggerAction  : 'name',
    store          : remoteJsonStore
};
```

In listing 6.4, you change the data `Store` type to a `JsonStore` ❶, a preconfigured extension of the `Ext.data.Store` class, to allow you to easily create a store that can consume JSON data. For the store, you specify a `baseParams` property, which ensures that base parameters are sent out with each request. For this instance, you have only one parameter, `column`, which is set to `'fullName'` and specifies which column in the database the PHP code is to query from. You then specify `fields`, which is now an array containing a single object, and you translate the inbound `'fullName'` property to `'name'` with the `name` and `mapping` attributes. You also create a mapping for the ID for each record, which you'll use for submission. You could have set fields to an array of strings, as you did in your local `ArrayStore`, but that makes the mapping order dependant. If you specify name and mapping, the order of the properties in each record won't matter, which I prefer. Finally, for the store, you specify a `proxy` property where you create a new instance of `ScriptTagProxy`, a tool that's used to request data from across domains. You instruct the `ScriptTagProxy` to load data from a specific URL via the `url` property.

In creating your `ComboBox`, you specify `forceSelection` to `true`, which is useful for remote filtering (and `typeAhead`, for that matter), but it keeps users from entering arbitrary data. Next, you set the `displayField` to `'name'`, which shows the name data point in the `TextField`, and you specify the `valueField` as `'id'`, which ensures that the ID is used to send data when the combo's data is being requested for submission. The `hiddenName` property is greatly overlooked but important. Because you're displaying the name of the person but submitting the ID, you need an element in the DOM to store that value. Because you specified `valueField` previously, a hidden input field is being created to store the field data for the record that's being selected. To have control over that name, you specify `hiddenName` as `'customerId'`.

You also customize the list box's loading text by specifying a `loadingText` string. The `minChars` ❷ property defines the minimum number of characters that need to be entered into the text field before the combo executes a data `Store` load and you override the default value of 4. Last, you specify `triggerAction` as `'all'`, which instructs the combo to perform a data `Store` load querying for all of the data. An example of our newly constructed combo can be seen in figure 6.6.

Exercise the rendered results, and you'll see how remote filtering can be a joy for a user to work with. Let's look at how the data coming back from the server is formatted, as shown in figure 6.7.

In examining a snippet of the resulting JSON in figure 6.7, you can see the root that we specified in our remote combo's JSON store and the `fullName` field we mapped to. The root contains an array of objects, which the data `Store` will translate and pluck out any of the properties we map as `"fields"`. Notice how the `id` is the first property in the record and `fullName` is the second. Because we used `name` and `mapping` in our store's `fields` array, our store will ignore `id` and all other properties in the records.

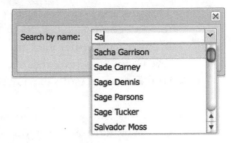

Figure 6.6 An example rendition of our remote loading `ComboBox` from listing 6.4

Following the format in figure 6.6 when implementing your server-side code will help ensure that your JSON is properly formatted. If you're unsure, you can use a free online tool at `http://jsonlint.com`, where you can paste in your JSON and have it parsed and verified.

When exercising the example code in listing 6.4, you might notice that when you click the trigger, the UI's spinner stops for a brief moment. This is because all of the 2,000 records in the database are being sent to the browser and parsed, and DOM manipulation is taking place to clear the list box and create a node. The transfer and parsing of the data are relatively quick for this large dataset. DOM manipulation, however, is one of the main reasons for JavaScript slowing down and is why you'd see the spinner animation stop. The amount of resources required to inject the 2000 DOM elements is intense enough for the browser to halt all animation and focus its attention on the task at hand, not to mention that bombarding the user with that many records may present a usability issue. To mitigate these issues, you should enable paging.

To do this, your server-side code needs to be aware of these changes, which is the hardest part of this conversion. Luckily, the PHP code that you're using already has the code in place necessary to adapt to the changes you're going to make. The first change is adding the following property to your JSON store:

```
totalProperty : 'totalCount'
```

Next, you need to enable paging in your combo box. This can be done by adding a `pageSize` property to your combo box:

```
pageSize : 20
```

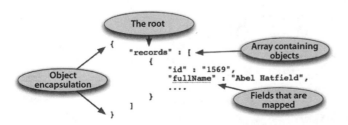

Figure 6.7 An exploded view of a slice of the served-up JSON

That's it! Ext is now ready to enable pagination to your combo box. Refresh the code in your browser, and either click the trigger or enter a few characters into the text input field, and you'll see the results of your changes, as shown in figure 6.8.

Thus far, we've explored the UI of the `ComboBox` and implemented both local and remote versions of using both the `Array` and JSON stores. Although we've covered many aspects of the `ComboBox`, we've just been using it as an enhanced version of a drop-down box and have not discussed how to customize the result-

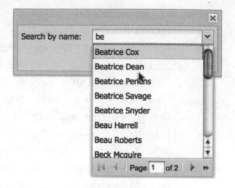

Figure 6.8 Adding pagination to our remote `ComboBox`

ing data's appearance. In order to show why we'll be changing some things, such as the template and `itemSelector`, we need take a quick glance at the innards of the combo.

6.2.3 *The ComboBox deconstructed*

At the nucleus of the `ComboBox` lie two helper classes. We've touched on the data `Store`, which provides the data fetching and loading, but we haven't discussed the `DataView`, which is the component responsible for displaying the result data in the list box as well as providing the events necessary to allow users to select the data. `Data-Views` work by binding to data `Stores` by subscribing to events such as `'beforeload'`, `'datachanged'`, and `'clear'`. They leverage the `XTemplate`, which provides the DOM manipulation to stamp out the HTML based on the HTML template you provide. Now that we've taken a quick look at the `Components` of a `ComboBox`, let's move forward in creating our custom `ComboBox`.

6.2.4 *Customizing our ComboBox*

When we enabled pagination in our `ComboBox`, we saw only names. But what if we wanted to see the full address along with the names that we're searching? Our data store needs to know of the fields. In modifying listing 6.4, you'll need to add the mappings for address, city, state, and ZIP. I'll wait here while you finish doing that.

Ready? Okay, before you can create a `Template`, you must create some CSS that you'll need:

```
.combo-result-item {
    padding:  2px;
    border:   1px solid #FFFFFF;
}

.combo-name {
    font-weight:      bold;
    font-size:        11px;
    background-color: #FFFF99;
}
.combo-full-address {
```

```
    font-size:   11px;
    color:       #666666;
}
```

In the preceding CSS, you create a class for each of the `divs` in our `Template`. Now you now need to create a new `Template` so your list box can display the data that you want. Enter the following code before you create your combo:

```
var tpl = new Ext.XTemplate(
  '<tpl for="."><div class="combo-result-item">',
    '<div class="combo-name">{name}</div>',
    '<div class="combo-full-address">{address}</div>',
    '<div class="combo-full-address">{city} {state} {zip}</div>',
  '</div></tpl>'
);
```

We won't go too in depth into the `XTemplate` because it deserves its own section. It's important to note that any string encapsulated in curly braces (`{}`) is directly mapped to the record. Notice how we have all of our data points except for `'id'`, which we don't need to show and are just using for submission. The last change you need to make is to the combo itself. You need to reference the newly created template and specify an `itemSelector`:

```
tpl           : tpl,
itemSelector  : 'div.combo-result-item'
```

It's worth noting that the string for the `itemSelector` property is part of a pseudo sub-language called Selectors, which are patterns for which a query against the DOM can match. In this case, the `Ext.DomQuery` class is being used to select the `div` with the class `'combo-result-item'` when any of its children are clicked. Your changes are now ready to be tested. If you did things correctly, your results should look similar to figure 6.9.

What we did to customize our `ComboBox` is the tip of the iceberg! Because you have complete control of the way the list box is being rendered, you can even include images or `QuickTips` in the list box.

In this section, you learned how to create a local and a remote `ComboBox`. You also learned about the `ArrayStore` and `Json-Store` data `Store` classes. You had some fun adding pagination to your remote implementation, dissected the `ComboBox`, and customized the list box. The `ComboBox` has a subclass, the `TimeField`, which assists with creating a `ComboBox` to select times from specific ranges. Let's see how to create a `TimeField`.

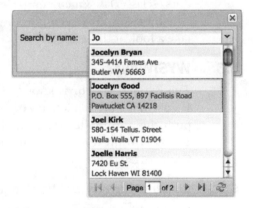

Figure 6.9 An example rendition of our customized `ComboBox`

6.2.5   *Finding the time*

`TimeField` is another convenience class that allows you to easily add a time selection field to a form. To build a generic `TimeField`, you can create a configuration object with the `xtype` set to `'timefield'`, and you'll get a `ComboBox` that has selectable items from 12:00 A.M. to 11:45 P.M. Here's an example of how to do that:

```
{
    xtype      : 'timefield',
    fieldLabel : 'Please select time',
    anchor     : '100%'
}
```

Figure 6.10 shows an example of how this field would render.

The `TimeField` is configurable, however, and you can set the range of time, increments, and even the format. Let's modify our `TimeField` by adding the following properties, which will allow us to use military time, set an increment of 30 minutes, and allow only from 9:00 A.M. to 6:00 P.M.:

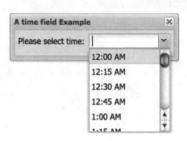

Figure 6.10   Our rendered generic `TimeField`

```
...
    minValue  : '09:00',
    maxValue  : '18:00',
    increment : 30,
    format    : 'H:i'
```

In this property list, we set the `minValue` and `maxValue` properties, which set the range of time that we want our `TimeField` to have. We also set the increment property to 30 and format to `'H:i'`, or 24 hours and two-digit minutes. The `format` property must be valid per the `Date.parseDate` method. You should consult the full API documentation if you intend to use a custom format. Here's the direct API link: http://extjs.com / docs/?class=Date&member=parseDate.

Now that you've seen how the `ComboBox` and its subclass, the `TimeField`, work, let's take a look at the `HtmlEditor`.

6.3   *WYSIWhat?*

The Ext `HtmlEditor` is known as a WYSIWYG, or *What You See Is What You Get*, editor. It's a great way to allow users to enter rich HTML-formatted text without having to push them to master HTML and CSS. It allows you to configure the `Buttons` on the `Toolbar` to prevent certain interactions by the user. Let's move on to building our first `HtmlEditor`.

6.3.1   *Constructing our first HtmlEditor*

Just like building the `TextField`, constructing a generic HTML editor is simple:

```
var htmlEditor = {
    xtype      : 'htmleditor',
    fieldLabel : 'Enter in any text',
```

```
    anchor    : '100% 100%'
}
```

Our `HtmlEditor` rendered to a form will look like figure 6.11.

We discussed how the `HtmlEditor`'s `Toolbar` could be configured to prevent some items from being displayed. This is easily done by setting the `enable<someTool>` properties to `false`. For instance, if you wanted to disable the font size and selection menu items, you'd set the following properties as `false`:

```
enableFontSize : false,
enableFont     : false
```

And that's all there is to it. After making the changes, refresh your page. You'll no longer see the text drop-down menu and the icons to change font sizes. To see a full list of the available options, be sure to visit the API. The `HtmlEditor` is a great tool, but it, like many things, has some limitations.

6.3.2 Dealing with lack of validation

The single biggest limitation to the `HtmlEditor` is that it has no basic validation and no way to mark the field as invalid. When developing a form using the field, you'll have to create your own custom validation methods. A simple `validateValue` method could be created as such:

```
var htmlEditor = {
    xtype         : 'htmleditor',
    fieldLabel    : 'Enter in any text',
    anchor        : '100% 100%',
    allowBlank    : false,
    validateValue : function() {
        var val = this.getRawValue();
        return (this.allowBlank ||
            (val.length > 0 && val != '<br>')) ? true : false;
    }
}
```

Although this `validateValue` method will return `false` if the message box is empty or contains a simple line-break element, it won't mark the field as such. We'll talk about how to test the form for validity before form submissions a little later in this chapter. For now, we'll switch gears and look at the date field.

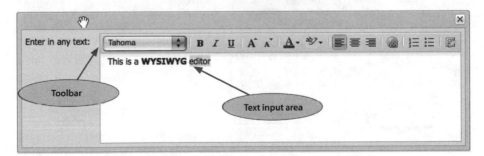

Figure 6.11 Our first `HtmlEditor` in an `Ext` `Window`

6.4 *Selecting a date*

The `DateField` is a fun little form widget that's chock full of UI goodness that allows a user to either enter a date via an input field or select one via the leveraged `DatePicker` widget. Let's build out a `DateField`:

```
var dateField = {
    xtype      : 'datefield',
    fieldLabel : 'Please select a date',
    anchor     : '100%'
}
```

Yes, it's that easy. Figure 6.12 shows how the `DateField` renders.

This widget can be configured to prevent days from being selected by setting a date property, which is an array of strings that match the *format* property. The format property defaults to m/d/Y, or 01/01/2001. Here are some recipes for disabling dates using the default format:

```
["01/16/2000", "01/31/2009"] disables these two exact dates
["01/16"] disables this date every year
["01/../2009"] disables every day in January for 2009
["^01"] disables every month of January
```

Now that you're comfortable with the `DateField` and the rest of the `TextField` subclasses, let's move on to explore the `Checkbox` and `Radio` fields and learn how you can use the `CheckboxGroup` and `RadioGroup` classes to create clusters of fields.

6.5 *Checkboxes and Radios*

In this section, we're not only going to focus on instantiating `Checkboxes` and `Radios`, but we'll also show how to stack them side by side and on top of one another. This will aid you in developing forms that allow for complex data selection.

The Ext `Checkbox` field wraps Ext element management around the original HTML `Checkbox` field, which includes layout controls as well. Like with the HTML `Checkbox`,

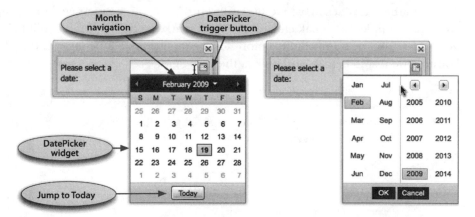

Figure 6.12 The `DateField` the `DatePicker` exposed (left) and the `DatePicker`'s month and year selection tool (right)

you can specify the value for the Checkbox, overriding the default Boolean value. Let's create some Checkboxes, where we use custom values, as shown in the following listing.

Listing 6.5 Building `Checkbox`es

```
var checkboxes = [
    {
        xtype        : 'checkbox',
        fieldLabel   : 'Which do you own',
        boxLabel     : 'Cat',
        inputValue   : 'cat'
    },
    {
        xtype         : 'checkbox',
        fieldLabel    : '',
        labelSeparator : ' ',
        boxLabel      : 'Dog',
        inputValue    : 'dog'
    },
    {
        xtype         : 'checkbox',
        fieldLabel    : '',
        labelSeparator : ' ',
        boxLabel      : 'Fish',
        inputValue    : 'fish'
    },
    {
        xtype         : 'checkbox',
        fieldLabel    : '',
        labelSeparator : ' ',
        boxLabel      : 'Bird',
        inputValue    : 'bird'
    }
];
```

❶ Set the box label text

❷ The default input value

The code in listing 6.5 builds out four Checkboxes, where you override the default `inputValue` for each node. The `boxLabel` ❶ property creates a field label to the right of the input field, and the `inputValue` ❷ overrides the default Boolean value. An example rendering of this code is shown in figure 6.13.

Although this will work for many forms, for some large forms it's a waste of screen space. In the following listing you'll use the CheckboxGroup to automatically lay out your Checkboxes.

Figure 6.13 Our first four `Checkbox`es

Listing 6.6 Using a `CheckboxGroup`

```
var checkboxes = {
    xtype      : 'checkboxgroup',
    fieldLabel : 'Which do you own',
    anchor     : '100%',
```

```
items        : [
    {
        boxLabel    : 'Cat',
        inputValue : 'cat'
    },
    {
        boxLabel    : 'Dog',
        inputValue : 'dog'
    },
    {
        boxLabel    : 'Fish',
        inputValue : 'fish'
    },
    {
        boxLabel    : 'Bird',
        inputValue : 'bird'
    }
  ]
};
```

Using the `CheckboxGroup` in this way will lay out your check boxes in a single horizontal line, as shown in figure 6.14. Specifying the number of columns is as simple as setting the `columns` attribute to the number of desired columns.

Figure 6.14   Two implementations of the `CheckboxGroup`: single horizontal line (left) and a two-column layout (right)

Your implementation of the `CheckboxGroup` will depend on your requirements. Implementing the `Radio` and `RadioGroup` classes is nearly identical to using the `Checkbox` and `CheckboxGroup` classes. The biggest difference is that you can *group* radios by giving them the same name, which allows only one item to be selected at a time. Let's build a group of `Radios`, as shown in figure 6.15.

Because the `RadioGroup` class extends the `CheckboxGroup` class, the implementation is identical, so I'll save you from going over the same material. Now that we've explored the `Checkbox` and `Radio` classes and their respective `Group` classes, we'll begin to tie these together by taking a more indepth look at the `FormPanel`, where you'll learn to perform form-wide checks and complex form layouts.

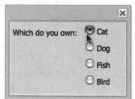

Figure 6.15   A single column of `Radios`

6.6   *The FormPanel*

With the Ext `FormPanel` you can submit and load data using Ajax and provide live feedback to users if a field is deemed invalid. Because the `FormPanel` is a descendant

> ### File uploads aren't really Ajax
> The XMLHttpRequest object in most browsers can't submit file data. To give the appearance of an Ajax-like submission, Ext JS uses an IFRAME to submit forms that contain file input elements.

of the Container class, you can easily add and remove input fields to create a truly dynamic form.

An added benefit is the FormPanel's ability to leverage other layouts or Components, such as the TabPanel with the CardLayout, to create robust forms that take considerably less screen space than traditionally laid-out single-page forms. Because the FormPanel is a subclass of Panel, you get all of Panel's features, which include top and bottom Toolbars and the button footer bar (fbar).

Like the other Container subclasses, the FormPanel class can leverage any layout that's available from the framework to create exquisitely laid-out forms. To assist with the grouping fields, the FormPanel has a cousin called the Fieldset. Before we build our Components, take a sneak peak of what we're going to achieve (figure 6.16).

To construct your complex form, you'll have to construct two FieldSets: one for the name information and another for the address information. In addition to the FieldSets, you'll set up a TabPanel that has a place for some TextFields and two HtmlEditors. In this task, you'll leverage all of what you've learned thus far, which means we'll go over quite a bit of code.

Now that you know what you'll be constructing, let's start by building out the FieldSet that will contain the TextFields for the name information.

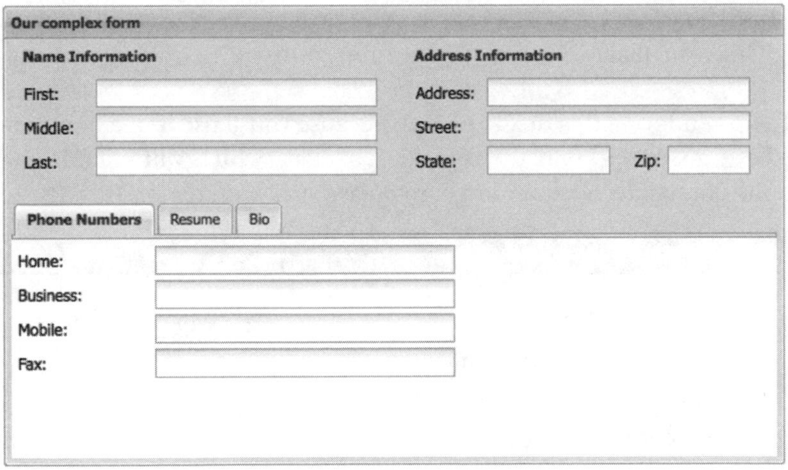

Figure 6.16 A sneak peek of the complex FormPanel we're going to build

Listing 6.7   Constructing our first `FieldSet`

```
var fieldset1 = {
    xtype       : 'fieldset',                    ◁┐  Set xtype
    title       : 'Name',                        ❶  to 'fieldset'
    flex        : 1,
    border      : false,
    labelWidth  : 60,
    defaultType : 'field',
    defaults    : {
        anchor    : '-10',
        allowBlank : false
    },
    items : [
        {
            fieldLabel : 'First',
            name       : 'firstName'
        },
        {
            fieldLabel : 'Middle',
            name       : 'middle'
        },
        {
            fieldLabel : 'Last',
            name       : 'firstName'
        }
    ]
};
```

In constructing your first `fieldset` ❶ xtype, the parameters may look like those of a `Panel` or `Container`. This is because the `FieldSet` class extends `Panel` and adds some functionality for the collapse methods to allow you to include fields in a form or not, which we don't exercise here. The reason you're using the `FieldSet` in this instance is that it's giving you that neat little title up top and you're getting exposure to this `Component`.

You'll skip rendering this first `FieldSet` because you'll use it in a `FormPanel` a little later on. Let's go on to build the second `FieldSet`, which will contain the address information. This listing is rather large, so please stick with me on this.

Listing 6.8   Building our second `FieldSet`

```
var fieldset2 = Ext.apply({}, {                  ◁┐  Copy properties
    flex        : 1,                             ❶  from first FieldSet
    title       : 'Address Information',
    items       : [
        {
            fieldLabel : 'Address',
            name       : 'address'
        },
        {
            fieldLabel : 'Street',
            name       : 'street'
        },
```

```
{
    xtype       : 'container',          ❷ ColumnLayout
    border      : false,                    containers
    layout      : 'column',
    anchor      : '100%',
    items       : [
        {
            xtype  : 'container',       ❸ FormLayout
            layout : 'form',                container
            width  : 200,
            items  : [
                {
                    xtype     : 'textfield',    ◀——❹ State TextField
                    fieldLabel : 'State',
                    name       : 'state',
                    anchor     : '-20'
                }
            ]
        },
        {
            xtype       : 'container',          ❺ Another FormLayout
            layout      : 'form',                  container
            columnWidth : 1,
            labelWidth  : 30,
            items       : [
                {                               ❻ ZIP code
                    xtype     : 'textfield',        TextField
                    fieldLabel : 'Zip',
                    anchor     : '-10',
                    name       : 'Zip'
                }
            ]
        }
    ]
}
}, fieldset1);
```

In listing 6.8, you leverage Ext.apply ❶ to copy many of the properties from fieldset1 and apply them to fieldset2. This utility method is commonly used to copy or override properties from one object or another. We'll talk more about this method when we look into Ext's utility toolbelt. To accomplish the desired layout of having the State and ZIP code fields side by side, you must create quite a bit of nesting. The child ❷ of your second FieldSet is a Container, which has its layout set to column. The first child of that Container is a FormLayout Container ❸, which contains the State TextField ❹. The second child ❺ of your ColumnLayout Container is another FormLayout Container, which contains the ZIP code TextField ❻.

You might be wondering why there are so many nested containers and perhaps why the code to get this done is so darn long. The Container nesting is required to use different layouts within other layouts. This might not make sense to you immediately. I think the picture will be clearer to you when you render the form. For now, let's move on to building a place for these two FieldSets to live.

In order to achieve the side-by-side look of the form, you'll need to create a container for it that's set up to leverage the HBoxLayout. In order to have equal widths in the HBoxLayout, you must set both of your FieldSets' stretch properties to 1. Let's build a home for the two FieldSets:

```
var fieldsetContainer = {
   xtype        : 'container',
   layout       : 'hbox',
   height       : 120,
   layoutConfig : {
      align : 'stretch'
   },
   items   : [
      fieldset1,
      fieldset2
   ]
};
```

In the preceding code block, you create a Container that has a fixed height but has no width set. This is because this Container's width will be automatically set via the VBox layout, which your future FormPanel will use.

Now that you've done that, you'll build a TabPanel with three tabs, one for the phone number form elements and the other two for HtmlEditors. This will use the bottom half of the FormPanels' available height. You'll configure all of the tabs in one shot, so the following listing is pretty lengthy. Please bear with me on this one also.

Listing 6.9   Building a TabPanel with form items

```
var tabs = [
   {
      xtype      : 'container',                    ❶ Container with
      title      : 'Phone Numbers',        ◁┘      four TextFields
      layout     : 'form',
      bodyStyle  : 'padding:6px 6px 0',
      defaults   : {
         xtype : 'textfield',
         width : 230
      },
      items: [
         {
            fieldLabel : 'Home',
            name       : 'home'
         },
         {
            fieldLabel : 'Business',
            name       : 'business'
         },
         {
            fieldLabel : 'Mobile',
            name       : 'mobile'
         },
         {
            fieldLabel : 'Fax',
```

```
                name        : 'fax'
            }
        ]
    },
    {
        title : 'Resume',
        xtype : 'htmleditor',
        name  : 'resume'
    },
    {
        title : 'Bio',
        xtype : 'htmleditor',
        name  : 'bio'
    }
];
```

❷ Two HtmlEditors
   as tabs

Listing 6.9 contains a lot of code to construct an array that comprises three tabs that will serve as children to your future TabPanel. The first tab ❶ is a Container that leverages the FormLayout and has four TextFields. The second ❷ and third tabs are HtmlEditors that will be used to enter a resume and a short biography. Let's move on to building our TabPanel:

```
var tabPanel = {
    xtype             : 'tabpanel',
    activeTab         : 0,
    deferredRender    : false,
    layoutOnTabChange : true,
    border            : false,
    flex              : 1,
    plain             : true,
    items             : tabs
}
```

In the preceding code block, you configure a TabPanel object that contains your tabs. You set deferredRender to false because you want to ensure that the tabs are built and in the DOM when you get around to loading your data. You also set layoutOnTab-Change to true to ensure that the doLayout method for the tab you're activating is called, which ensures that the tab is properly sized.

Your task in the next listing will be to construct the FormPanel itself, which is relatively trivial compared to all of its child items.

Listing 6.10   Piecing it all together

```
var myFormPanel  = new Ext.form.FormPanel({
    renderTo     : Ext.getBody(),
    width        : 700,
    title        : 'Our complex form',
    height       : 360,
    frame        : true,
    id           : 'myFormPanel',
    layout       : 'vbox',
    layoutConfig : {
        align : 'stretch'
```

```
    },
    items          : [
        fieldsetContainer,
        tabPanel
    ]
});
```

Here, you're finally getting to create your `FormPanel`. You set `renderTo` to ensure that the `FormPanel` is automatically rendered. In order to have the `fieldsetContainer` and the `TabPanel` properly sized, you use the `VBoxLayout` with `layoutConfig`'s `align` property set to `'stretch'`. You specify only a height for the `fieldsetContainer`. You do this because other than the height of the `fieldsetContainer` you let the `VBox-Layout` do its job in managing the size of the child items of the `FormPanel`. Take a look at figure 6.17 to see what this beast of a form renders to.

In the preceding figure, I highlighted the different `Containers` that compose the first half of the form, which include our `fieldsetContainer`, two `FieldSets`, and their child `Components`. In using this many `Containers`, you're ensuring complete control over how the UI is laid. It's common practice to have these long code batches to create a UI with this type of complexity. In exercising our newly built `FormPanel`, you can flip through the three tabs and reveal the `HtmlEditors` underneath.

By now you've seen how combining multiple `Components` and layouts can result in something that's both usable and space saving. You now must focus your attention on learning to use forms for data submission and loading; otherwise, your forms will be useless.

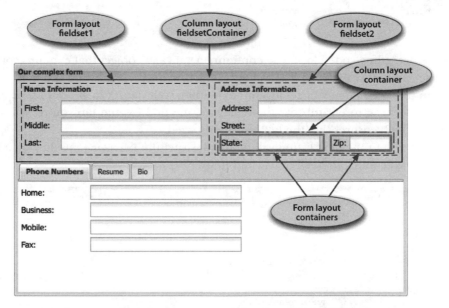

Figure 6.17   The results of our first complex layout form with the different `Containers` used to compose the complex layouts

6.7 *Data submission and loading*

Submitting data via the basic form-submit method is one of the areas new developers most commonly get tripped up on. This is because for so many years we were used to submitting a form and expecting a page refresh. With Ext, the form submission requires a bit of know-how. Likewise, loading a form with data can be a little confusing for some, so we'll explore the few ways you can do that as well.

6.7.1 *Submitting the good old way*

As I said before, submitting your form the good old way is extremely simple, but you need to configure the FormPanel's underlying form element with the standardSubmit property set to true. To perform the submission you call

```
Ext.getCmp('myFormPanel').getForm().submit();
```

This will call the generic DOM form submit method, which will submit the form the old-fashioned way. If you're going to use the FormPanel in this way, I'd still suggest that you review submitting via Ajax, which will point out some of the features that you can't use when using the older form-submission technique.

6.7.2 *Submitting via Ajax*

To submit a form, you must access the FormPanel's BasicForm component. To do this, you use the accessor method getForm or FormPanel.getForm(). From there, you have access to the BasicForm's submit method, which you'll use to send data via Ajax. The code is shown in the following listing.

Listing 6.11 Submitting our form

```
var onSuccessOrFail = function(form, action) {
    var formPanel = Ext.getCmp('myFormPanel');
    formPanel.el.unmask();

    var result = action.result;                             ① Display message
    if (result.success) {                                      driven by JSON
       Ext.MessageBox.alert('Success',action.result.msg);
    }
    else {
       Ext.MessageBox.alert('Failure',action.result.msg);
    }
}

var submitHandler = function() {
    var formPanel = Ext.getCmp('myFormPanel');
    formPanel.el.mask('Please wait', 'x-mask-loading');

    formPanel.getForm().submit({                            Perform form
       url      : 'success.true.txt',                    ② submission
       success : onSuccessOrFail,
       failure : onSuccessOrFail
    });
}
```

In listing 6.11, you create a success and failure handler called `onSuccessOrFail`, which will be called if the form-submission attempt succeeds or fails. It will display an alert `MessageBox` ❶ depending on the status of the returning JSON from the web server. You then create the submission handler method, `submitHandler`, which performs the form submission ❷ Although you specify the URL on the submit call, you could have specified it at the `BasicForm` or `FormPanel` level, but you specify it here because I wanted to point out that the target URL could be changed at runtime. Also, if you're providing any type of wait message, as you do here, you should have success and failure handlers.

At minimum, the returning JSON should contain a `'success'` Boolean with the value of `true`. Your success handler is expecting a `msg` property as well, which should contain a string with a message to return to the user:

```
{success: true, msg : 'Thank you for your submission.'}
```

Likewise, if your server-side code deems that the submission was unsuccessful for any reason, the server should return a JSON object with the `success` property set to `false`. If you want to perform server-side validation, which can return errors, your return JSON could include an `errors` object as well. Here's an example of a failure message with attached errors:

```
{
   success : false,
   msg      : 'This is an example error message',
   errors   : {
      firstName : 'Cannot contain "!" characters.',
      lastName  : 'Must not be blank.'
   }
}
```

If the returning JSON contains an `errors` object, the fields that are identified by that name will be marked invalid. Figure 6.18 shows the form with the JSON code served to it.

In this section, you learned how to submit your form using the standard submit methods as well as the Ajax way. You also saw how to leverage the `errors` object to provide server-side validation with UI-level error notification. Next, we'll look at loading data into the form using the `load` and `setValues` methods.

6.7.3 *Loading data into our form*

The use cycle of just about every form includes saving and loading data. With Ext, we have a few ways to load data, but we must have data to load, so we'll dive right into creating some data to load. Let's create some mock data and save it in a file called data.txt.

```
var x = {
   success : true,
   data     : {
       firstName : 'Jack',
       lastName  : 'Slocum',
```

```
        middle      : '',
        address     : '1 Ext JS Corporate Way',
        city        : 'Orlando',
        state       : 'Florida',
        zip         : '32801',
        home        : '123 346 8832',
        business    : '832 932 3828',
        mobile      : '',
        fax         : '',
        resume      : 'Skills:<br><ul><li>Java Developer</li>' +
                      '<li>Ext JS Senior Core developer</li></ul>',
        bio         : 'Jack is a stand-up kind of guy.<br>'
    }
}
```

Just like with form submission, the root JSON object must contain a `success` property with the value of `true`, which will trigger the `setValues` call. Also, the values for the form need to be in an object, whose reference property is `data`. Likewise, it's great practice to keep your form element names inline with the data properties to load. This will ensure that the right fields get filled in with the correct data. For the form to load the data via Ajax, you can call the `BasicForm`'s `load` method, whose syntax is just like `submit`:

```
var formPanel = Ext.getCmp('myFormPanel');

formPanel.el.mask('Please wait', 'x-mask-loading');
formPanel.getForm().load({
    url     : 'data.txt',
    success : function() {
        formPanel.el.unmask();
    }
});
```

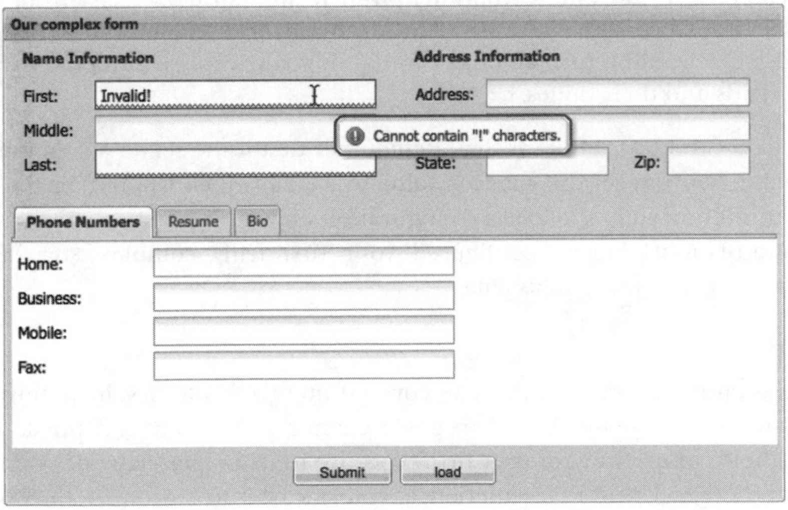

Figure 6.18 The results from our server-side errors object using the standard QuickTip error msg

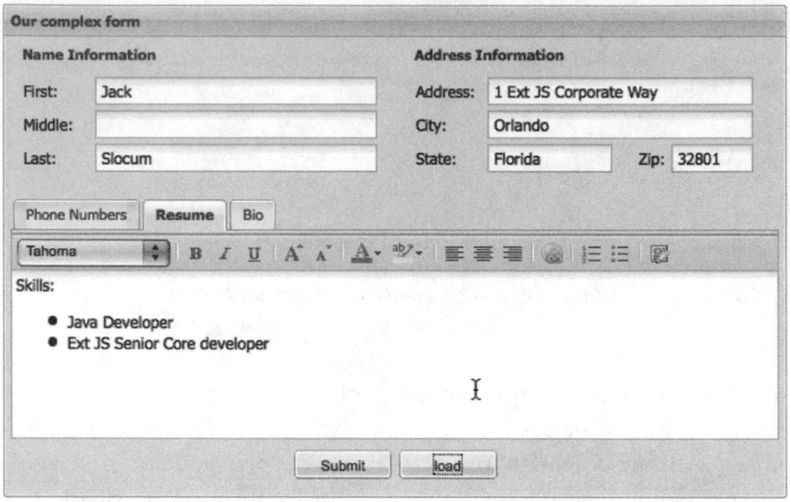

Figure 6.19   The results of loading our data via XHR

Executing this code will result in your form panel performing an XHR (XMLHttp-Request) and ultimately the form being filled in with the values, as illustrated in figure 6.19.

If you have the data on hand, let's say from another component such as a DataGrid, you can set the values via myFormPanel.getForm().setValues(dataObj). Using this, dataObj would contain only the proper mapping to element names. Likewise, if you have an instance of Ext.data.Record, you could use the form's loadRecord method to set the form's values.

> **TIP**   To retrieve the values from any given form, call getValues from the FormPanel's BasicForm instance. For example, myFormPanel.getForm().getValues() would return an object containing keys representing the names of the fields and their values.

Loading data can be as simple as that. Remember that if the server side wants to deny data loading, you can set the success value to false, which will trigger the failure method as referenced in the load's configuration object.

Congratulations! You've configured your first truly complex FormPanel and learned how to load and save its data.

6.8   *Summary*

In focusing on the FormPanel class, we covered quite a few topics, including many of the commonly used fields. You even got a chance to take an in-depth look at the ComboBox field, where you got your first exposure to its helper classes, the data Store and the DataView. Using that experience, you saw how to customize the ComboBox's resulting list box. We also took some time to build a relatively complex layout form and used our new tool to submit and load data.

Moving forward, we're going to take an in-depth look at the data `GridPanel`, where you'll learn about its inner `Components` and see how to customize the look and feel of a grid. You'll also see how to leverage the `EditorGridPanel` class to edit data inline. Along the way, you'll learn more about the data `Store`. Be sure to get some candy; this is going to be a fun ride!

Part 3

Data-driven Components

In this part, we'll look at the widgets in the framework that consume data, including the GridPanel, DataView, Charts, and TreePanel. Here you'll learn about the intricacies of the supporting classes, such as the data Store.

Chapter 7 is where we take a detailed look at how the GridPanel works and discuss its supporting classes. This chapter includes an in-depth discussion of the data Store class and how it leverages several supporting classes to control data flow within the framework.

In chapter 8 you'll add to your newly found knowledge of GridPanels and data Stores and learn to implement the EditorGridPanel. Here you'll learn how to use the data Writer class, allowing you to create a UI that allows full CRUD capabilities for your users.

Chapter 9 is dedicated to exploring the DataView and its subclass the List-View. In addition to learning about these widgets, you'll learn how to bind them together with a FormPanel to create a screen with a workflow that can be implemented in any application.

You'll learn how to visualize data by using the framework's various charting widgets in chapter 10.

In chapter 11, you'll learn about displaying hierarchical data with the TreePanel widget. You'll also learn how to use the TreeEditor class to enable full CRUD against data nodes.

We'll close this section out by taking a deep look at Buttons, Menus, and Tool-bars in chapter 12.

While completing this section, you'll learn about and experience almost all of the framework's widgets.

The venerable GridPanel 7

This chapter covers

- Learning about the GridPanel Component
- Becoming an expert at Ext JS data Stores
- Setting up custom column renderers
- Configuring GridPanel mouse interaction event handlers
- Enabling GridPanel pagination with the PagingToolbar
- Implementing a custom context menu on the GridPanel

Since the early days of Ext JS, the GridPanel has been the centerpiece of the Ext Framework. It can display data like a table, but is much more robust. In many respects, I believe this holds true today, and the GridPanel is arguably one of its more complicated widgets, because directly depends on five directly supporting classes.

In this chapter, you'll learn a lot about the GridPanel and the class that feeds it data, the data Store. We'll start by constructing GridPanel that feeds from a Store that reads local in-memory array data. At each step of the process, you'll learn more about both the data Store and the GridPanel and their supporting classes.

Once you become more familiar with the data Store and GridPanel, we'll move on to building a remote-loading data Store that can parse JSON that will feed a paging toolbar.

7.1   Introducing GridPanel

At a first glance, the `GridPanel` may look like a glorified HTML table, which has been used for ages to display data. If you take a moment to look at one of the Ext JS grid examples, you'll come to the realization that this is no ordinary HTML table. You can see one example implementation of the `GridPanel` that uses an array store at http://extjs.com/deploy/dev/examples/grid/array-grid.html. If you're not online, that's all right. I've included a snapshot of it in figure 7.1.

In the array grid example, you can see that the features provided by this widget extend beyond those of a typical HTML table. These include column-management features such as sorting, resizing, reordering, showing, and hiding. Mouse events are also tracked, out of the box, to allow you to highlight a row by hovering over it and even select it by clicking it.

The example also demonstrates how the `GridPanel`'s view (known as the `GridView`) can be customized with what are known as custom renderers, which are applied to the Change and % Change columns. These custom renderers color the text based on negative and positive values.

This example merely skims the surface when it comes to how the `GridPanel` can be configured or extended. In order to fully understand the `GridPanel` and why it's so extensible, you need to know more about its supporting classes.

7.1.1   Looking under the hood

The key supporting classes that drive the `GridPanel` are the `ColumnModel`, `GridView`, `SelectionModel`, and data `Store`. Let's take a quick glance at an implementation of a grid panel and see how each class plays a role in making the `GridPanel` work (figure 7.2).

In figure 7.2, you see a `GridPanel` and its five supporting classes highlighted. Starting from the beginning, the data source, you see the data `Store` class. Data `Stores` work by leveraging a reader, which is used to "map" data points from a data source

Array Grid				
Company	Price	Change	% Change	Last Updated
3m Co	$71.72	0.02	0.03%	09/01/2009
Alcoa Inc	$29.01	0.42	1.47%	09/01/2009
Altria Group Inc	$83.81	0.28	0.34%	09/01/2009
American Express Company	$52.55	0.01	0.02%	09/01/2009
American International Group, Inc.	$64.13	0.31	0.49%	09/01/2009
AT&T Inc.	$31.61	-0.48	-1.54%	09/01/2009
Boeing Co.	$75.43	0.53	0.71%	09/01/2009
General Electric Company	$34.14	-0.08	-0.23%	09/01/2009
General Motors Corporation	$30.27	1.09	3.74%	09/01/2009
Hewlett-Packard Co.	$36.53	-0.03	-0.08%	09/01/2009

Figure 7.1   The array grid example, found in the examples folder of the downloadable SDK

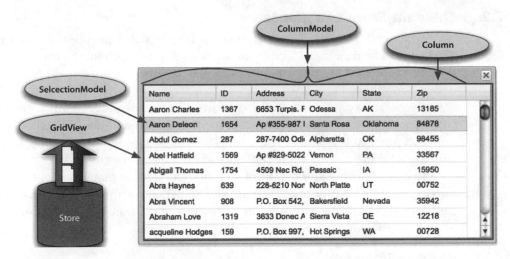

Figure 7.2 The `GridPanel`'s five supporting classes: data `Store`, `GridView`, `ColumnModel`, `Column`, and `SelectionModel`

and populate the data store. They can be used to read array, XML, or JSON data via the array, XML, and JSON readers. When the reader parses data, it's organized into records, which are organized and stored inside the data `Store`.

This should be somewhat familiar to you, because you leveraged it when creating `ComboBoxes`. As you learned earlier, data `Stores` can get their data from either local or remote sources. Like the `ComboBox`, the data `Store` feeds a view. In this case, it's the `GridView`.

The `GridView` class is the UI component of the `GridView`. It's responsible for reading the data and controlling the painting of data onscreen. It leverages the `Column-Model` to control the way the data is presented onscreen.

The `ColumnModel` is the UI controller for each individual column. It's what provides the functions for `columns`, such as resize, sort, and so on. In order to do its job, it has to leverage one or more instances of `Column`.

`Columns` are classes that map the data `fields` from each individual record for placement on screen. They do this by means of a `dataIndex` property, which is set for each column and is responsible for displaying the data it obtains from the field it's mapped to.

Finally, the `SelectionModel` is a supporting class that works with a view to allow users to select one or more items onscreen. Out of the box, Ext supports `Row`, `Cell`, and `Checkbox` `SelectionModels`.

You have a nice head start on `GridPanels` and their supporting classes. Before you construct your first grid, you should learn more about the data `Store` class, which many widgets in the framework depend on for data.

7.2   *The data Store at a glance*

As you learned a bit ago, the data `Store` is the class that provides the data for the `GridPanel`. The data `Store` feeds quite a few widgets throughout the framework wherever data is needed. To put this into plain view, figure 7.3 enumerates the classes that depend on the data `Store`.

As you can see, the data `Store` supports quite a few widgets, which include the `DataView`, `ListView`, `ComboBox`, `Charts`, the `GridPanel`, and all of its subclasses. The only exception to this pattern is the `TreePanel`. The reason for this is the data `Store` contains a list of records, whereas `TreePanel`s require hierarchical data.

As a quick warning, this may be one of those "dry" areas that you might not think is important—but hold on one second. Remember all of those classes that the data `Store` feeds data to? Being proficient in this area of the framework better enables you to easily use any of those consumer widgets.

7.2.1   *How data Stores work*

When you got your first real exposure to the data `Store`, you learned how to use subclasses of the data `Store`, `ArrayStore`, and `JsonStore`, to read array and JSON data. These subclasses are convenience classes, or preconfigured versions of the actual data `Store`, which take care of things for us like attaching the correct reader for data consumption. We used these convenience methods in the earlier chapters because they make life easier for us, but there's a lot going on under the hood that's not immediately exposed and is important to know as well. We'll start by looking at exactly how the data flows from a data source to the store. We'll begin with a simple flow illustration, shown in figure 7.4.

As you can see, the data always starts from a `DataProxy`. The `DataProxy` classes facilitate the retrieval of unformatted data objects from a multitude of sources and contain their own event model for communication for subscribed classes such as the `DataReader`. In the framework, there's an abstract class aptly called `DataProxy`, which serves as a base class for the subclasses, which are responsible for retrieving data from specific sources, as shown in figure 7.5.

The most commonly used proxy is the `HttpProxy`, which leverages the browser's XHR object to perform generic AJAX requests. The `HttpProxy` is limited, however, to

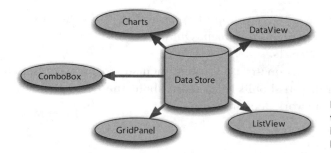

Figure 7.3   The data `Store` and the classes it feeds data to. This illustration doesn't depict class hierarchy.

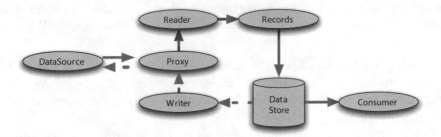

Figure 7.4   The data flow from a data source to a data `Store` consumer

the same domain because of what is known as the "same-origin policy." This policy dictates that XHR requests via XHR can't be performed outside of the domain from which a specific page is being loaded. This policy was meant to tighten security with XHRs but has been construed as more of an annoyance than a security measure. The Ext developers were quick to come up with a workaround for this "feature," which is where the `ScriptTagProxy` (`STP`) comes into the picture.

The `STP` cleverly leverages the script tag to retrieve data from another domain and works well, but it requires that the requesting domain return JavaScript instead of generic data snippets. This is important to know because you can't just use the `STP` against any third-party website to retrieve data. The `STP` requires the return data to be wrapped in a global method call, passing the data in as the only parameter. You'll learn more about the `STP` in a bit because we'll be using it to leverage extjsinaction.com to retrieve data from our examples.

The `MemoryProxy` class offers Ext the ability to load data from a memory object. Although you can load data directly to an instance of data `Store` via its `loadData` method, use of the `MemoryProxy` can be helpful in certain situations. One example is the task of reloading the data `Store`. If you use data `Store.loadData`, you need to pass in the reference to the data, which is to be parsed by the reader and loaded into the store. Using the `MemoryProxy` makes things simple, because you only need to call the data `Store.reload` method and let Ext take care of the dirty work.

The `DirectProxy` is new to Ext JS 3.0 and allows the data `Store` to interact with the `Ext.direct` remoting providers, allowing for data retrievals via remote procedure calls (RPCs). We won't be covering usage of `Direct` because there's a direct dependency on server-side language to provide the `remoting` methods.

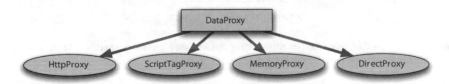

Figure 7.5   The `DataProxy` and its four subclasses. Each is responsible for retrieving data from a specific data source.

NOTE   If you're interested in learning more about Ext.direct, I suggest visiting http://extjs.com/products/extjs/direct.php for details on specific server-side implementations.

After a proxy fetches the raw data, a Reader then reads or parses it. A Reader is a class that takes the raw, unformatted data objects and abstracts the data points, known as dataIndexes, and arranges them into name data pairs, or generic objects. Figure 7.6 illustrates how this mapping works.

As you can see, the raw and unformatted data is organized and fed into Records that the Reader then creates. These Records are then spooled into the data Store and are now ready to be consumed by a widget.

Ext provides readers for the three common data types: array, XML, and JSON. As the reader chews on Records, it creates a Record for each row of data, which is to be inserted into the data Store.

A Record is a fully Ext-managed JavaScript object. Much like Ext manages Element, the Record has getter and setter methods and a full event model for which the data Store is bound. This management of data adds usability and some cool automation to the framework.

For example, changing a value of a Record in a store that's bound to a consumer, like the GridPanel, will result in the UI being updated when the Record is committed. You'll learn much more about management of Records in the next chapter, when we discuss editable grids. After the Records are loaded into the data Store, the bound consumer refreshes its view and the load cycle completes.

Now that you have some fundamental knowledge of the data Store and its supporting classes, we can begin to build our first GridPanel.

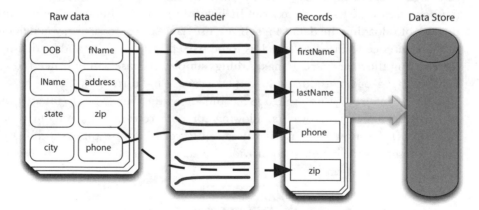

Figure 7.6   A Reader maps raw or unformatted data so that it can be inserted into Records, which then get spooled into a data Store.

7.3 Building a simple GridPanel

When implementing GridPanels, I typically start by configuring the data Store. The reason for this is that the configuration of the ColumnModel is directly related to the configuration of the data Store. This is where you'll start too.

7.3.1 Setting up an ArrayStore

In the example shown in listing 7.1, we'll create a complete end-to-end data Store that reads data already present in memory. This means that we're going to instantiate instances of all of the supporting classes from the Proxy to the Store. This exercise will help you see the working parts being configured and instantiated. Afterwards, you'll learn how to use some of the preconfigured Data Store convenience classes to make constructing certain types of stores easier with much less code.

Listing 7.1 Creating a data Store that loads local array data

```
var arrayData = [                            Create local
    ['Jay Garcia',     'MD'],             ❶ array data
    ['Aaron Baker',    'VA'],
    ['Susan Smith',    'DC'],
    ['Mary Stein',     'DE'],
    ['Bryan Shanley',  'NJ'],
    ['Nyri Selgado',   'CA']
];
                                          ❷ Create Ext.data.Record
var nameRecord = Ext.data.Record.create([    constructor
    { name : 'name',  mapping : 1  },
    { name : 'state', mapping : 2  }
]);
                                             ❸ Instantiate an
var arrayReader = new Ext.data.ArrayReader({}, nameRecord);    ArrayReader

var memoryProxy  = new Ext.data.MemoryProxy(arrayData);     Construct new
                                                          ❹ MemoryProxy
var store = new Ext.data.Store({    ❺ Build our Store
    reader : arrayReader,
    proxy  : memoryProxy
});
```

In listing 7.1, you implement the full gamut of data Store configuration. You start by creating an array of arrays, which is referenced by the variable arrayData ❶. Please pay close attention to the format the array data is in, because this is the expected format for the ArrayReader class. The reason the data is an array of arrays is that each child array contained within the parent array is treated as a singular Record.

Next, you create an instance of data.MemoryProxy, which is what will load your unformatted data from memory and is referenced by the variable memoryProxy ❷. You pass in the reference arrayData as the only argument.

You create an instance of data.Record ❸ and reference it in the variable name-Record, which will be used as the template to map your array data points to create records. You pass an array of object literals, which are known as fields ❹, to the Record.create method, and detail each field name and its mapping. Each of these object literals is a configuration object for the `Ext.data.Field` class, which is the smallest unit of managed data within a `Record`. In this case, you map the field `personName` to the first data point in each array record and the `state` field to the second data point.

> **NOTE** Notice that we're not calling new `Ext.data.Record()`. This is because `data.Record` is a special class that's able to create constructors by using its `create` method, which returns a new record *constructor*. Understanding how `data.Record.create` works is essential to performing additions to a data `Store`.

You then create an instance of `ArrayReader` **5**, which is what's responsible for sorting out the data retrieved by the proxy and creating new instances of the record constructor you just created. The `ArrayReader` reads each `Record` and creates a new instance of `nameRecord, passing the parsed data to it,` which is then loaded into the store.

Last, you create your data `Store`, for which you pass the reader and proxy you created, which completes the creation of your `ArrayStore`. This completes our end-to-end example of how to create a store that reads array data. With this pattern, you can change the type of data the store is able to load. To do this, you swap out the `Array-Reader` with either a `JsonReader` or an `XmlReader`. Likewise, if you wanted to change the data source, you could swap out the `MemoryProxy` for another such as the `Http-Proxy`, `ScriptTagProxy`, or `DirectProxy`.

Recall that I mentioned something a bit earlier about convenience classes to make our lives a little easier. If you were to re-create the `Store` using the `ArrayStore` convenience class, this is what your code would look like using the previous `arrayData`:

```
var store = new Ext.data.ArrayStore({
   data   : arrayData,
   fields : ['personName', 'state']
});
```

As you can see in this example, you use shortcut notation for the fields to create an instance of `Ext.data.ArrayStore`. You achieve this by passing a reference of the data, which is your `arrayData` and a list of fields, which provide the `mapping`. Notice how the `fields` property is a simple list of strings? This is a completely valid configuration of field mappings because Ext is smart enough to create the name and index mapping based on the string values passed in this manner. You could have a mixture of objects and strings in a `fields` configuration array. For instance, the following configuration is completely valid:

```
fields : [ 'fullName', { name : 'state', mapping : 2} ]
```

Having this flexibility is something that can be really cool to leverage. Just know that having a mixture of field configurations like this can make the code a bit hard to read.

Using this convenience class saved you from having to create a proxy, record template, and reader to configure the store. Use of the `JsonStore` and `XmlStore` is equally as simple, which you'll learn more about later. Moving forward, we'll be using the convenience classes to save us time.

For now, we'll move on to creating the ColumnModel, which defines the vertical slices of data that our GridPanel will display along with our GridView component.

7.3.2 Completing our first GridPanel

As we discussed before, the ColumnModel has a direct dependency on the data Store's configuration. This dependency has to do with a direct relationship between the data field records and the column. Just as the data fields map to a specific data point in the raw inbound data, columns map to the record field *names*.

To finish your GridPanel construction, you need to create a ColumnModel, Grid-View, and SelectionModel, and then you can configure the GridPanel itself, as shown in the following listing.

Listing 7.2 Creating an ArrayStore and binding it to a GridPanel

```
var colModel = new Ext.grid.ColumnModel([          ←  ❶ Create
    {                                                     ColumnModel
        header     : 'Full Name',
        sortable   : true,
        dataIndex  : 'fullName'
    },                                             ←  ❷ Map dataIndexes
    {                                                   to columns
        header     : 'State',
        dataIndex  : 'state'
    }
]);

var gridView = new Ext.grid.GridView();            ←  ❸ Instantiate
                                                        new GridView

var selModel = new Ext.grid.RowSelectionModel({    ←  ❹ Create single-selection
    singleSelect : true                                 RowSelectionModel
});

var grid = new Ext.grid.GridPanel({                ←  ❺ Instantiate
    title      : 'Our first grid',                      our Grid
    renderTo   : Ext.getBody(),
    autoHeight : true,
    width      : 250,
    store      : store,                            ←  ❻ Reference
    view       : gridView,                              supporting
    colModel   : colModel,                              classes
    selModel   : selModel
});
```

In listing 7.2, you configure all of the supporting classes before constructing the Grid-Panel itself. The first thing you do is create a reference for a newly instantiated instance of a ColumnModel ❶, for which you pass in an array of configuration objects. Each of these configuration objects is used to instantiate instances of Ext.grid.Column (or any subclasses thereof), which is the smallest managed unit of the ColumnModel. These configuration objects ❷ detail the text that's to be populated in the column *header* and which Record field the column maps to, which is specified by the dataIndex property. This is where you see the direct dependency on the configuration of the

Store's fields and the ColumnModel's columns. Also, notice that you set sortable to true for the Full Name column and not the State column. This will enable sorting on that one column.

You then create an instance of Ext.grid.GridView ❸, which is responsible for managing each individual row for the grid. It binds key event listeners to the data Store, which it requires to do its job. For instance, when the data Store performs a load, it fires the datachanged event. The GridView listens for that event and will perform a full refresh. Likewise, when a record is updated, the data Store fires an update event, for which the GridView will only update a single row. You'll see the update event in action in the next chapter, when you learn how to leverage the EditableGrid.

Next, you create an instance of Ext.grid.RowSelectionModel ❹ and pass a configuration object that instructs the selection model to allow only single selection of rows to occur. There are two things to know in this step. The first is that by default the GridPanel always instantiates an instance of RowSelectionModel and uses it as the default selection model if you don't specify one. But you did create one because by default the RowSelectionModel allows for multiple selections. You can elect to use the CellSelectionModel in place of the RowSelectionModel. The CellSelectionModel doesn't allow for multiple selections of items, however.

After you instantiate your selection model, you move on to configure your Grid-Panel ❺. GridPanel extends Panel, so all of the Panel-specific configuration items apply. The only difference is you *never* pass a layout to the GridPanel because it will get ignored. After you set the Panel-specific properties, you set your GridPanel-specific properties. This includes configuring the references for the data Store, ColumnModel, GridView, and Selection Model ❻. Loading the page will generate a grid panel that looks like the one in figure 7.7.

You can see that the data isn't in the order specified. This is because before I took the snapshot, I clicked the Full Name column, which invoked the click handler for that column. The click handler checks to see if this column is sortable (which it is) and invokes a data Store sort method call, passing in the data field (dataIndex), which is fullName. The sort method call then sorts all of the records in the store based on the field that was just passed. It first sorts in ascending order, then toggles to descending. A click on the State column would result in no sorting because we didn't specify sort : true as we did for the Full Name column.

Figure 7.7 **Our first grid rendered onscreen demonstrating the single-select configured RowSelectionModel and the sortable Full Name Column**

The `ColumnModel` has other features that you can use. You can drag and drop the columns to reorder them, resize them by dragging the resize handle, or click the column menu icon, which appears whenever the mouse hovers over a particular column.

To use the `SelectionModel`, select a row by clicking it. Once you've done that, you can use the keyboard to navigate rows by pressing the up- and down-arrow keys. To exercise the multiselect `RowSelectionModel`, you can modify the `SelectionModel` by removing the `singleSelect: true` property, which defaults to `false`. Reloading the page will allow you to select many items by using typical operating system multiselect gestures such as Shift-click or Ctrl-click.

Creating our first grid was a cinch, wasn't it? Obviously, there's much more to `GridPanel`s than displaying data and sorting it. Features like pagination and setting up event handlers for gestures like right mouse clicks are used frequently. These advanced usages are exactly where we're heading next.

7.4 Advanced GridPanel construction

In the previous section, we built a `GridPanel` that used static in-memory data. We instantiated every instance of the supporting classes, which helped us get some exposure to them. Like many of the `Components` in the framework, the `GridPanel` and its supporting classes have alternate configuration patterns. In building our advanced `GridPanel`, we'll explore some of these alternate patterns in a couple of the supporting classes.

7.4.1 What we're building

The `GridPanel` we'll construct will leverage some advanced concepts, the first of which is using a remote data `Store` to query against a large data set of randomly generated data, giving us the opportunity to use a `PagingToolbar`. You'll learn how to construct custom renders for two of these columns. One of these will apply color to the ID column, and the other will be more advanced, concatenating the address data into one column. After we build this `GridPanel`, we're going to circle around and set up a `rowdblclick` handler. You'll be introduced to context menus as you learn to use the `GridPanel`'s `rowcontextmenu` event. Put on your propeller hat if you have one; we'll be spending the rest of this chapter on this task and will be covering a lot of material.

7.4.2 Creating the store using shortcuts

When creating your store in listing 7.3, you'll learn some of the common shortcuts, which will save you time. If you need to customize the configuration beyond what's covered here, you can mix and match shortcuts with longhand versions of the configuration.

Listing 7.3   Creating an `ArrayStore`

```
var recordFields = [
    { name : 'id',        mapping : 'id'        },
    { name : 'firstname', mapping : 'firstname' },
    { name : 'lastname',  mapping : 'lastname'  },
    { name : 'street',    mapping : 'street'    },
    { name : 'city',      mapping : 'city'      },
    { name : 'state',     mapping : 'state'     },
    { name : 'zip',       mapping : 'zip'       },
    { name : 'country',   mapping : 'country'   }
];

var remoteJsonStore = new Ext.data.JsonStore({
    fields        : recordFields,
    url           : 'http://extjsinaction.com/dataQuery.php',
    totalProperty : 'totalCount',
    root          : 'records',
    id            : 'ourRemoteStore',
    autoLoad      : false,
    remoteSort    : true
});
```

❶ Fields mapped to raw data points

❷ Shortcut config of remote JsonStore

In this code, you're configuring a remote `JsonStore` using some shortcuts. The first thing you do is create a reference, `recordFields` ❶, which is an array of field configuration objects. In this array, you're mapping a lot of data fields, some of which you'll specify in the column model.

If the field labels map the data point labels, and you want to further simplify the mappings, you could specify an array of string values:

```
var recordFields = [
    'id','firstname','lastname','street','city','state','zip','country'
];
```

You could also specify a mixture of objects and strings for the list of fields. When I build applications, I always configure objects instead of strings because I like to think of the code as self-documenting. Also, if the data point on the backend needs to change, all you need to modify is the mapping attribute compared to having to modify the mapping *and* column model if you were to use just strings.

You then move on to configure your `JsonStore` ❷, which will fetch data remotely. When configuring this `Store`, you set the `fields` property to the reference of the `recordFields` array you just created. Ext uses this `fields` configuration array to automatically create the `data.Record` that it will use to fill the store.

Next you pass a `url` property, which is one of the shortcuts we're using. Because you pass this property, the `Store` class will use it to instantiate a `Proxy` to fetch data. Also, because this is a remote URL, an instance of `ScriptTagProxy` will be used. Remember that the `ScriptTagProxy` requires that the data get passed as the first parameter to the callback method that it automatically produces. Figure 7.8 illustrates the format in which the server must respond.

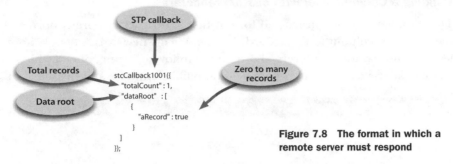

Figure 7.8 The format in which a remote server must respond

In this figure, you see that the server returns a method call to `stcCallback1001`. The callback method name the server responds with is passed to the server in the request via a `callback` property during each request. The number will increment for each STP request.

The `totalCount` property is an optional value, which specifies how many records are available for viewing. In configuring your remote `JsonStore`, you specified the `totalProperty` configuration property as `totalCount`. This property will be leveraged by the `PagingToolbar` to calculate how many pages of data are available.

The most important property is the data `root`, which is the property that contains our array of data. You specified the `root` configuration property as `records` in the remote `JsonStore` configuration.

You then instruct the store not to automatically fetch the data from the data source. You'll need to specially craft the first request so you don't fetch all of the records in the database for the query that you're performing.

You also set a static `id`, `ourRemoteStore`, for the `Store`, which you'll use later to get a reference of the `Store` from the `Ext.StoreMgr`, which is to data `Stores` what the `ComponentMgr` is to `Components`. Each instance of `Data Store` can have a unique ID assigned to it or will assign one to itself and is registered to the `StoreMgr` singleton upon instantiation. Likewise, deregistration of the store occurs when a store is destroyed.

> **NOTE** We could configure the `JsonStore` using the `XType` `jsonstore`, but because we're binding it to the `GridPanel` *and* the `PagingToolbar`, we must use an instance of `Ext.data.Store`.

Last, you enable remote sorting by specifying `remoteSort` as the Boolean value of `true`. Because you're paging, sorting locally would cause your UI to behave abnormally because the data sorting and page count would mismatch.

Now that we have that out of the way, we can move on to configure our advanced `ColumnModel`.

7.4.3　Building a ColumnModel with custom renderers

The ColumnModel we constructed for our first GridPanel was pretty boring. All it did was map the column to the record data field. This new ColumnModel, however, will leverage two custom renderers, shown in the following listing, one of which will allow us to make use of the Address data fields to build composite and stylized cells.

Listing 7.4　Creating two custom renderers

```
var colorTextBlue = function(id) {
    return '<span style="color: #0000FF;">' + id + '</span>';
};

var stylizeAddress = function(street, column, record) {
    var city  = record.get('city');
    var state = record.get('state');
    var zip   = record.get('zip');

    return String.format('{0}<br>{1} {2}, {3}', street, city, state, zip );
};
```

In listing 7.4, you construct two custom renderers (methods) that will be used by two different columns. The first method, colorTextBlue, returns a concatenated string that consists of a span tag that wraps the id argument being passed to it. The span tag has a CSS-style property that will result in blue text.

The second custom renderer, stylizeAddress, is a much more complex method that will create a composite view of all of the address data available to us minus the country. All custom renderers are called with six arguments. You're using the first and third in this case. The first is the field value that the column is bound to. The second is the column metadata, which you're not using. The third is a reference to the actual data Record, which you'll use heavily.

In this method, you create references to the city and state values of the record by using its get method, passing in the field for which you want to retrieve data. This gives you all the references you need to construct your composite data value.

The last thing you do in this method is return the result of the String.format method call, which is one of the lesser-known power tools that Ext offers. The first argument is a string that contains integers wrapped in curly braces, which get filled in by the subsequent values passed to the method. Using this method is a nice alternative to the string concatenation you performed previously.

Excellent. Your custom renderers are set and you can now proceed to construct your column configuration. This next listing is rather long because you're configuring five columns, which requires quite a few configuration parameters. Please stick with me on this. Once you start to see the pattern, reading through this will be rather easy.

Listing 7.5　Configuring our advanced ColumnModel

```
var columnModel = [
    {
        header    : 'ID',
```

```
           dataIndex : 'id',
           sortable  : true,
           width     : 50,
           resizable : false,
           hidden    : true,                    ❶ Hide
           renderer  : colorTextBlue              ID column
   },
   {                                            ❷ Bind colorTextBlue
                                                  to ID column
           header    : 'Last Name',
           dataIndex : 'lastname',
           sortable  : true,
           hideable  : false,
           width     : 75
   },
   {
           header    : 'First Name',
           dataIndex : 'firstname',
           sortable  : true,
           hideable  : false,
           width     : 75
   },
   {
           header    : 'Address',
           dataIndex : 'street',
           sortable  : false,
           id        : 'addressCol',            ❸ Bind stylizeAddress
           renderer  : stylizeAddress             to Address column
   },
   {
           header    : 'Country',
           dataIndex : 'country',
           sortable  : true,
           width     : 150
   }
];
```

Configuring this `ColumnModel` is much like configuring the `ColumnModel` for our previous grid. The biggest difference is that instead of instantiating an instance of `Ext.grid.ColumnModel`, you're using the shortcut method by creating an array of objects, which will be translated to a list of `Ext.grid.Columns`. But you do some things differently. For instance, the ID column is hidden ❶ and bound to the `colorText-Blue` ❷ custom renderer.

You also set both the `hideable` property for the Last Name and First Name columns to `false`, which will prevent them from being hidden via the `Columns` menu. You'll get a chance to see this in action after you render the `GridPanel`.

The Address column is a bit special because you disable sorting. This is because you're binding the column to the street field but are using the `stylizeAddress` custom renderer ❸ to provide cells based on a composite of other fields in the record, such as `city`, `state`, and `zip`. You do, however, enable sorting on each individual column. This column also has an `id` property set to `addressCol` and no `width` property. It's configured this way because you're going to configure the `GridPanel` to automatically expand this column so that it takes all of the available width after all of the statically sized columns are rendered.

Now that you've constructed the array of Column configuration objects, we can move on to piece together our paging GridPanel.

7.4.4 *Configuring our advanced GridPanel*

You now have just about all of the pieces required to configure our paging GridPanel. In order to do this, however, you'll need to first configure the paging toolbar, which will be used as the bottom toolbar, or bbar, in the GridPanel, as shown in the following listing.

Listing 7.6   Configuring our advanced `GridPanel`

```
var pagingToolbar = {
    xtype       : 'paging',                          PagingToolbar
    store       : remoteJsonStore,              ❶   using XType
    pageSize    : 50,
    displayInfo : true
};
                                                ❷   Shorthand GridPanel
var grid = {                                        configuration object
    xtype            : 'grid',
    columns          : columnModel,
    store            : remoteJsonStore,
    loadMask         : true,
    bbar             : pagingToolbar,
    autoExpandColumn : 'addressCol'
};
```

In listing 7.6, you use the XType as a shortcut to configure both the PagingToolbar and the GridPanel.

For the PagingToolbar configuration ❶, you bind the remote JsonStore you configured earlier and set the pageSize property to 50. This will enable the PagingToolbar to bind to the data Store, allowing it to control requests. The pageSize property will be sent to the remote server as the limit property and will ensure that the data Store receives bundles of 50 (or fewer) records per request. The PagingToolbar will leverage this limit property along with the server's returning totalCount property to calculate how many "pages" there are for the dataset. The last configuration property, displayInfo, instructs the PagingToolbar to display a small block of text, which displays the current page position and how many records (remember totalCount) are available to be flipped through. I'll point this out when we render the GridPanel.

You then configure a GridPanel XType configuration object ❷. In this configuration, you bind the earlier created configuration variables columnModel, remoteJsonStore, and pagingToolbar. Because you set the columns property, Ext will automatically generate an instance of Ext.grid.ColumnModel based on the array of configuration objects in the columnModel variable.

You set the loadMask property to true, which will instruct the GridPanel to create an instance of Ext.LoadMask and bind it to the bwrap (body wrap) element, which is the tag that ultimately wraps or contains all of the elements below the `titlebar` of a `Panel`. These elements include the top toolbar, content body, bottom toolbar, and `fbar`, which is the bottom button footer bar. The `LoadMask` class binds to various events that the `Store` publishes to show and hide itself based on the situation the `Store` is in. For instance, when the `Store` initiates a request, it will mask the `bwrap` element, and when the request completes, it will unmask that element.

You then set the `bbar` property to our `pagingToolbar` XType configuration object, which will render an instance of the `PagingToolbar` widget with that configuration data as the bottom toolbar in the `GridPanel`.

Last, you set the `autoExpandColumn` property to the string of `'addressCol'`, which is the ID of your Address column, ensuring that this column will be dynamically resized based on all of the available viewport width minus the other fixed-width columns.

Our `GridPanel` is now configured and ready to be placed in a `Container` and rendered. We could render this `GridPanel` to the document body element, but I'd like to place it as a child of an instance of `Ext.Window`; this way we can easily resize the `GridPanel` and see how features like the automatic sizing of the Address column work.

7.4.5 Configuring a Container for our GridPanel

We'll now move on to create the `Container` for our advanced `GridPanel`, as shown in the following listing. Once we render the `Container`, we'll initiate the first query for the remote data `Store` we created just a while ago.

Listing 7.7   Placing our `GridPanel` inside a `Window`

```
new Ext.Window({                          ◁⌐  Render GridPanel
    height : 350,                          ❶  in a Window
    width  : 550,
    border : false,
    layout : 'fit',
    items  : grid
}).show();

Ext.StoreMgr.get('ourRemoteStore').load({    ◁⌐  Perform initial
    params : {                               ❷  load request
        start : 0,
        limit : 50
    }
});
```

In listing 7.7, you perform two tasks. The first is the creation of `Ext.Window` ❶, which uses the `FitLayout` and has our `GridPanel` as its only item. Instead of creating a reference to the instance of `Ext.Window` and then calling the `reference.show` method, you use chaining to call the `show` method directly from the result of the constructor call.

Then you use the `Ext.StoreMgr.get` method ❷, passing it our remote `Store` ID string, and again use chaining to call the result's `load` method. You pass an object, which contains a `params` property, which itself is an object specifying `start` and `limit` properties.

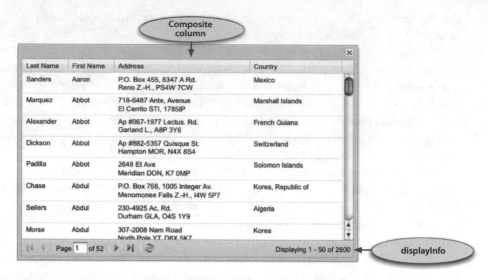

Figure 7.9 The results of our advanced paging `GridPanel` implementation.

The `start` property is instructed by the server as to which `Record` or row number to begin the query. It will then read the start plus the limit to return a "page" of data. You have to call this `load` method because the `PagingToolbar` doesn't initiate the first `Store` load request on its own. You have to nudge it a little to get it started.

Your rendered `GridPanel` should look like the one in figure 7.9. As you can see from the fruits of our labor, our `GridPanel`'s Address column displays a composite of the address fields in one neat column that's dynamically sized and can't be sorted, whereas all of the other columns start life with a fixed size and can be sorted.

A quick look at the communication from the first request via Firebug will show us the parameters sent to the server. Figure 7.10 illustrates those parameters. We covered the `callback`, `limit`, and `start` parameters a short while ago when we discussed the paging toolbar. What you see new here are the `_dc` and `xaction` parameters.

The `_dc` parameter is what's known as a *cache buster* parameter that's unique for every request and contains the timestamp for which the request was made in the UNIX epoch format, which is the number of seconds since the beginning of computer time, or 12 A.M. on January 1, 1970. Because the value for each request is unique, the

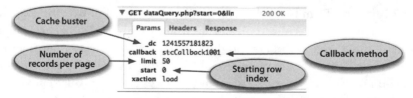

Figure 7.10 A list of parameters sent to the remote server to request paged data

Figure 7.11 Enabling the ID column via the Columns menu

request bypasses proxies and prevents them from intercepting the request and return-ing cached data.

The xaction parameter is used by Ext.direct to instruct the controller as to which action to execute, which in this case happens to be the load action. The xaction parameter is sent with every request generated by stores and can safely be ignored if needed.

I'm not sure if you've detected this already, but we haven't seen our ID column in action. This is because we configured it as a hidden column. In order to enable it, we can leverage the Columns menu and check the ID column, as shown in figure 7.11.

After checking the ID column in the Columns menu, you'll see it appear in the GridView. In this menu, you can also specify the direction in which a column is to be sorted. One thing you may notice right away by looking at the Columns menu is that the menu options for the First Name and Last Name columns are missing. This is because we set the hideable flag to false, which prevents their respective menu options from being rendered. The Columns menu is also a great way to sort a column directly by the order that you desire.

Cool; we have our GridPanel constructed. We can now configure some event han-dlers for the GridPanel that will allow us to interact more with it.

7.4.6 *Applying event handlers for interaction*

In order to create row-based user interaction, you need to bind event handlers to events that are published by the GridPanel. Here, you'll learn how to leverage the rowdblclick event to pop up a dialog box when a double-click is detected on a row. Likewise, you'll listen for a contextmenu (right-click) event to create and show a sin-gle-item context menu using the mouse coordinates.

You'll begin by creating a method to format a message for the Ext alert message box and then move on to create the specific event handlers, as shown in the following listing. You can insert this code anywhere *before* your GridPanel configuration.

Listing 7.8   Creating event handlers for our data grid

```
var doMsgBoxAlert = function(record) {                          Show Ext alert
    var record    = thisGrid.selModel.getSelected();        ❶  message box
    var firstName = record.get('firstname');
    var lastName  = record.get('lastname');

    var msg = String.format('The record you chose:<br /> {0}, {1}',
            lastName , firstName);

    Ext.MessageBox.alert('', msg);
};                                                      ❷  rowdbleclick
var doRowDblClick = function(thisGrid)  {                   event handler
    doMsgBoxAlert(thisGrid);
};                                                    rowcontextmenu  ❸
                                                       event handler
var doRowCtxMenu = function(thisGrid, rowIndex, evtObj) {
    evtObj.stopEvent();                                     Hide browser's
                                                        ❹  context menu
    thisGrid.getSelectionModel().selectRow(rowIndex);

    if (! thisGrid.rowCtxMenu) {                            Create static
        thisGrid.rowCtxMenu = new Ext.menu.Menu({           instance of
            items : {                                   ❺  Ext menu
                text    : 'View Record',
                handler : function() {
                    doMsgBoxAlert(thisGrid);
                }
            }
        });
    }

    thisGrid.rowCtxMenu.showAt(evtObj.getXY());
};
```

In listing 7.8, you create three methods. The first of these, doMsgBoxAlert ❶, is a utility method that accepts thisGrid as its only argument, which is a pointer to the Grid-Panel generating the event. It leverages the RowSelectionModel getSelected method to obtain a reference to the selected record and record.get method to extract the first and last name fields and uses them to display an Ext alert message box that contains a message with those two properties.

Next, you create the first handler, doRowDblClick ❷, which is configured to accept two of the parameters that the event publishes, the reference to the GridPanel firing the event. All this method does is execute the doMsgBoxAlert method that we discussed previously.

Context menus typically select items

Most desktop applications select an item when the user right-clicks it. Because Ext JS doesn't provide this functionality natively, you can force the selection of the item that the user is right-clicking. This will give your application more of a desktop feel.

The last method, doRowCtxMenu ❸, is much more complicated and accepts three parameters. The first is the reference to the grid, thisGrid, and the second is the index of the row, rowIndex, for which the event occurred. The third parameter is an instance of Ext.EventObject. Knowing this is important because on some browsers such as Firefox for OS X you need to prevent the browser's own context menu from displaying. This is why it calls evtObj.stopEvent ❹ as the first task. Calling stopEvent stops the native browser context menu from showing.

Next, this handler uses the rowIndex parameter to force the selection of the row for which the event was generated by calling the RowSelectionModel's selectRow method, passing in the rowIndex parameter.

You then select the record based on the rowIndex argument. Doing so will provide the necessary feedback to the user. You then test to see whether thisGrid has a rowCtxMenu property, which on the first execution of this method will be true and the interpreter will dive into this branch of code. You do this because you want to create the menu once if it doesn't exist. Without this fork in the logic, you'd be creating menus every time the context menu is called, which would be wasteful.

You then assign the rowCtxMenu property ❺ to thisGrid as the result of a new instance of Ext.menu.Menu, which has one item, written in typical XType shorthand. The first property of the menu item is the text that will be displayed when the menu item is shown. The other is a handler method that's defined inline and causes doMsgBoxAlert to be called with the referenced record.

The last bit of code calls upon the newly created rowCtxMenu's showAt method, which requires the X and Y coordinates to display the menu. You do this by directly passing the results of the evtObj.getXY() to the showAt method. The EventObject.getXY will return the exact coordinates where the event was generated.

Your event handlers are now armed and ready to be called upon. Before you can use them in the grid, you need to configure them as listeners, as shown in the following listing.

Listing 7.9 Attaching your event handlers to your grid

```
var grid = {
    xtype            : 'grid',
    columns          : columnModel,
    store            : remoteJsonStore,
    loadMask         : true,
    bbar             : pagingToolbar,
    autoExpandColumn : 'addressCol',
    selModel         : new Ext.grid.RowSelectionModel({
        singleSelect : true
    }),
    stripeRows       : true,                          ❶ Attach event
    listeners        : {                                handlers to grid
        rowdblclick    : doRowDblClick,
        rowcontextmenu : doRowCtxMenu
    }
};
```

To configure the event handlers to the grid, you add a `listeners` ❶ configuration object, with the event to handle mapping. Because your event handlers can handle only one selected record, you have to enforce single selection. To do this, you add a `RowSelectionModel` with the `singleSelect` option set to `true`.

Refresh the page and generate some double-click and right-click gestures on the grid. What happens? See figure 7.12.

Now double-clicking any record will cause the Ext alert message box to appear. Likewise, right-clicking a row will cause your custom context menu to appear. If you click the View Record menu item, the Ext alert box will then appear.

Adding user interaction to a grid can be as simple as that. One key to effective development of UI interactions is not to instantiate and render widgets only once and when needed, as you did with the context menu. Although this technique works to prevent duplicate items, it falls short of cleanup. Remember the destruction portion of the `Component` lifecycle? You can attach a quick method to destroy the context menu when the grid panel is destroyed by adding a `destroy` handler method to the list of listeners:

```
listeners         : {
    rowdblclick       : doRowDblClick,
    rowcontextmenu : doRowCtxMenu,
    destroy           : function(thisGrid) {
        if (thisGrid.rowCtxMenu) {
            thisGrid.rowCtxMenu.destroy();
        }
    }
}
```

In this code snippet, you add the `destroy` event handler inline instead of creating a separate referenced method for it. The `destroy` event always passes the `Component` that's publishing the event, which is labeled `thisGrid`. In that method, you test for the existence of the `rowCtxMenu` variable. If this item exists, you call its `destroy` method.

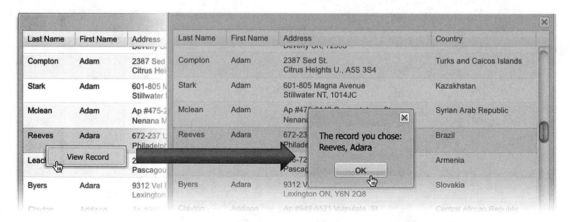

Figure 7.12   The results of adding the context menu handler to our advanced grid

Context menu cleanup is one of those topics that developers often miss and can lead to lots of leftover DOM node garbage, which chews up memory and can contribute to application performance degradation over time. If you're attaching context menus to any Component, always be sure to register a destroy event handler for that Component that destroys any existing context menus.

7.5 Summary

In this chapter, you learned quite a bit about the GridPanel and the data Store classes. You started by constructing a local data-feeding GridPanel and learned about the supporting classes for both the data Store and GridPanel.

While building your first GridPanel, you got to see how the data Store uses proxies to read data, uses a reader to parse it, and spools up Records, which are Ext-managed data objects. You also learned how the GridView knows when to render data from the Store by listening to events.

When you constructed your remote-loading GridPanel, you learned about some of the shortcuts that can be used to configure the GridPanel and many of its supporting classes. You learned more about the ColumnModel and how it can have hidden columns or columns that can't be hidden. While doing this, you configured the JSON-reading data Store that allows for remote sorting as well.

Last, you added grid interactions to the GridPanel, where mouse double-click and right-click gestures were captured and the UI responded. In doing this, you got a quick glance at menus and learned the importance of cleaning up menu items after their parent Component is destroyed.

Many of the concepts that you learned in this chapter will carry forward when you learn how to use the EditorGridPanel and its subclass, the PropertyGrid.

The *EditorGridPanel*

8

This chapter covers

- Implementing an `EditorGridPanel`
- Learning to exercise full data CRUD cycles
- Deploying the `DataWriter`

In the last chapter, you learned about the `GridPanel` and how it can be used to display data. We integrated a `PagingToolbar` into our complex `GridPanel` to allow us to flip through large amounts of paginated data.

In this chapter, we'll build on our previous work to construct a working `Editor-GridPanel`, which will allow you to modify data inline much like you can in popular desktop spreadsheet applications like Microsoft Excel. You'll also learn how to integrate context menus and toolbar buttons with Ajax requests for CRUD operations.

You'll start out by creating your first `EditorGridPanel`, where you'll get an introduction to what an `EditorGridPanel` is and how edits are possible. We'll discuss the ins and outs of setting up UI widgets for interaction to support insert and delete CRUD operations as well as how to get modified `Record`s from the store or even reject changes. Building up an `EditorGridPanel` without saving the data is useless, so we'll take advantage of this opportunity to show how to code for CRUD operations.

Afterward, we'll integrate `Ext.data.DataWriter` and show how it can save you time by doing a lot of the heavy lifting and reducing the amount of code that you need to write.

This is going to be one of the most intense chapters yet.

8.1 A close look at the EditorGridPanel

The `EditorGridPanel` class builds on the `GridPanel` class, which works with the `ColumnModel`, to allow the use of Ext form fields to edit data on the fly without the use of a separate `FormPanel`. It uses the `CellSelectionModel` by default and has an internal event model to detect user input, such as clicks and keyboard keystrokes, to trigger the cell selection and even the rendering or repositioning of the editor fields. It can leverage the `Ext.data.DataWriter` class to automatically save data after it's been edited, which we'll explore later in this chapter.

Excited yet? Before we break ground, we should discuss what you're going to be constructing.

We'll expand on the complex `GridPanel` you constructed in the last chapter, but with some changes to allow you to edit data. The first obvious change is the use of the `EditorGridPanel` instead of the `GridPanel` widget.

Another change you'll make is to split up the composite Address column into separate columns for each `dataIndex`, which will allow you to easily edit the separate address information instead of having to craft a complex editor. Figure 8.1 illustrates what your `EditorGridPanel` panel will look like.

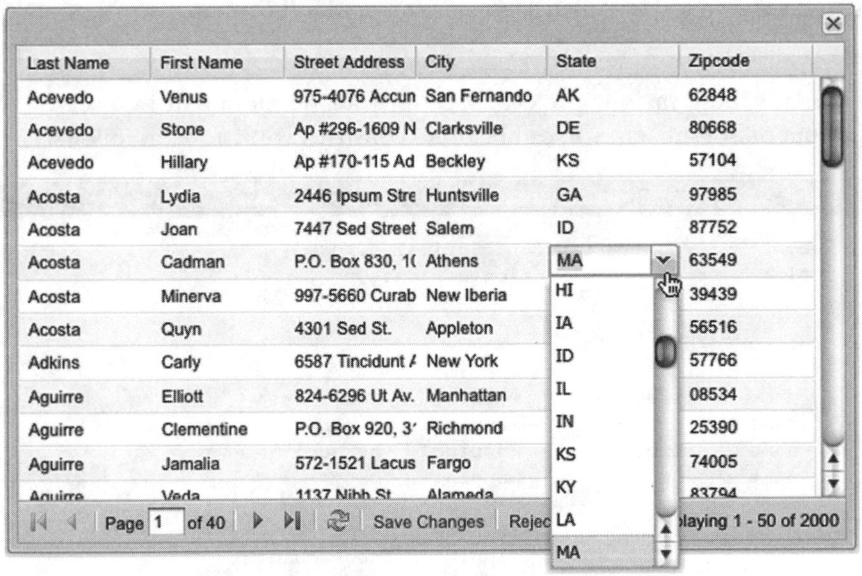

Figure 8.1 A quick peek at what you'll be constructing

In building this `EditorGridPanel`, you'll leverage the necessary UI components to construct something that could be considered a mini-application, because it will have simulated CRUD (create, read, update, and delete) capabilities for `Records`. The reason it's simulated is that you can't make Ajax requests to a different domain, and in order to keep server-side code out of the picture, you need to create some static responses.

To enable CRUD, you'll add two `Buttons` to the `PagingToolbar` that will allow you to save or reject changes. Likewise, you'll create a usable context menu to add or delete rows based on which cell is right-clicked. This will be the most complex code thus far, and you'll perform this in phases.

The first phase is getting the `EditorGridPanel` functioning. You'll then circle back and add slices of each CRUD action, one slice at a time.

8.2   *Building your first EditorGridPanel*

Because you're expanding on the complex `GridPanel` you built in the last chapter, you'll see some of the exact same code and patterns. We're doing it this way so the flow of the code is as smooth as possible. In most cases, there'll be changes, so please take the time to read through every bit. I'll point out all of the pertinent modifications.

Before you begin, you need to create two files that contain some JSON that will enable the simulation of server-side responses to calls you're going to make for the CRUD actions. The first of these will be called successTrue.js and will contain

```
{success : true}
```

The second one will be called successFalse.js and will contain

```
{success: false}
```

Please save these in your project space on your development web server. Once you have that out of the way, you can begin to construct your store, as follows.

Listing 8.1   Creating our remote store

```
var remoteProxy = new Ext.data.ScriptTagProxy({
    url : 'http://extjsinaction.com/dataQuery.php'
});

var recordFields = [
    { name : 'id',          mapping : 'id'          },
    { name : 'firstname',   mapping : 'firstname'   },
    { name : 'lastname',    mapping : 'lastname'    },
    { name : 'street',      mapping : 'street'      },
    { name : 'city',        mapping : 'city'        },
    { name : 'state',       mapping : 'state'       },
    { name : 'zipcode',     mapping : 'zip'         },
    { name : 'newRecordId', mapping : 'newRecordId' }
];

var remoteJsonStore = new Ext.data.JsonStore({
    proxy           : remoteProxy,
    storeId         : 'ourRemoteStore',
```

```
    root            : 'records',
    autoLoad        : false,
    totalProperty   : 'totalCount',
    remoteSort      : true,
    fields          : recordFields,
    idProperty      : 'id'
});
```

You begin by creating your `ScriptTagProxy`, which will allow you to fetch data from a remote domain. You then move on to create a list of fields, which map to the data points in the raw data. Remember, these are used to create instances of `Ext.data.field`, which are the smallest parts of an `Ext.data.Record`. Notice that the last field is added to the list. Our fictitious server-side controller will use this `'new-RecordId'` for insert operations. We'll discuss this further later on when we talk about saving inserted records and see why only new records will have this property.

Last, you create your `remoteJsonStore`, which uses your `remoteProxy` and `record-Fields`. You could have set `remoteJsonStore` as an XType configuration object, but you'll need that reference later on when you create some of the handlers for your CRUD actions. This will keep things simple for you down the road, I promise. For the `JsonStore`, you also set the `idProperty` to `'id'`, which will ensure that the data `Store` tracks IDs, allowing you to monitor insert operations down the road.

Your next step is to create the field editors that will be used for the `ColumnModel` later on, shown in the following listing.

Listing 8.2 Creating `ComboBox` and `NumberField` editors

```
var textFieldEditor = new Ext.form.TextField();          ◁─┐ Create
                                                             │ TextField
var comboEditor = {                    ◁─┐ XType configuration ❶ editor
    xtype           : 'combo',            ❷ for ComboBox
    triggerAction : 'all',
    displayField  : 'state',
    valueField    : 'state',
    store           : {
        xtype   : 'jsonstore',
        root    : 'records',
        fields  : ['state'],
        proxy   :   new Ext.data.ScriptTagProxy({
            url :   'http://extjsinaction.com/getStates.php'
        })
    }
};
                                    ❸ NumberField
var numberFieldEditor = {        ◁─┐  configuration object
    xtype       : 'numberfield',
    minLength : 5,
    maxLength : 5
};
```

When creating your editors, you use two techniques: direct and lazy instantiation. You directly instantiate an instance of `Ext.form.TextField` ❶ because you're going to be using it multiple times, and it would be wasteful to use an XType configuration.

Conversely, the `comboEditor` ❷ and `numberFieldEditor` ❸ use XType configurations because they'll be used for only a single column. The `comboEditor` is an XType configuration for the `Ext.Form.ComboBox` and has a nested XType configuration for an `Ext.data.JsonStore`, which uses a `ScriptTagProxy` so you can get a list of states from the remote database. Likewise, the `numberFieldEditor` is an XType configuration for the `Ext.form.NumberField` class. You're using this in the ZIP Code column, so you set two basic validation rules that dictate the minimum and maximum character lengths for the field. Because the editor is a `NumberField`, no alpha characters can be entered, and only values with five integers will be accepted.

You can now begin creating the `ColumnModel`, where you'll use the editors you just configured. As was the case for our complex `GridPanel`, this listing is relatively lengthy. The patterns should be obvious, however.

Listing 8.3   Creating `ColumnModel`

```
var columnModel = [
    {
        header    : 'Last Name',
        dataIndex : 'lastname',
        sortable  : true,                    ❶ Use
        editor    : textFieldEditor            TextField editor
    },
    {
        header    : 'First Name',
        dataIndex : 'firstname',
        sortable  : true,
        editor    : textFieldEditor
    },
    {
        header    : 'Street Address',
        dataIndex : 'street',
        sortable  : true,
        editor    : textFieldEditor
    },
    {
        header    : 'City',
        dataIndex : 'city',
        sortable  : true,
        editor    : textFieldEditor
    },
    {
        header    : 'State',
        dataIndex : 'state',
        sortable  : true,                    ❷ Specify ComboBox
        editor    : comboEditor                configuration object
    },
    {
        header    : 'Zip Code',
        dataIndex : 'zipcode',
        sortable  : true,                    ❸ Set numberFieldEditor
        editor    : numberFieldEditor          to column
    }
];
```

As we review the `ColumnModel` configuration array, you'll see familiar properties such as `header`, `dataIndex`, and `sortable`. You'll also see a new kid on the block, `editor`, which allows you to specify an editor for each of the `Columns`.

Notice that the `textFieldEditor` ❶ is used in four of the of the six `Column` configuration objects. The main reason for this is performance. Instead of using an XType configuration object and having one instance of `Ext.form.TextField` instantiated for each column, the single `TextField` class is merely rendered and positioned where it's needed, which saves memory and reduces DOM bloat. Consider this a performance-saving technique. You'll see this in action when we get around to rendering our `EditorGridPanel`.

Last, you have the `comboEditor` ❷ used for the State column and the `numberFieldEditor` ❸ used for the ZIP Code column. Remember that because these are used only once, using an XType configuration object is okay.

You now have your `Store`, editors, and `ColumnModel` configured. You can now move on to creating your `PagingToolbar` and `EditorGridPanel`, as in the following listing.

Listing 8.4 Creating the `PagingToolbar` and `EditorGridPanel`

```
var pagingToolbar = {
    xtype       : 'paging',
    store       : remoteJsonStore,
    pageSize    : 50,
    displayInfo : true
};

var grid = {
    xtype       : 'editorgrid',          ❶ Specify 'editorgrid'
    columns     : columnModel,              xtype property
    id          : 'myEditorGrid',
    store       : remoteJsonStore,
    loadMask    : true,
    bbar        : pagingToolbar,
    stripeRows  : true,
    viewConfig : {
        forceFit : true
    }
};

new Ext.Window({
    height  : 350,
    width   : 550,
    border  : false,
    layout  : 'fit',
    items   : grid
}).show();

remoteJsonStore.load({              ❷ Load the Store
    params : {
        start : 0,
        limit : 50
    }
});
```

In this code, you create the rest of your `EditorGridPanel`, starting with the `Paging-Toolbar`, which uses your `remoteJsonStore` and has the `pageSize` set to 50 records. Next, you create your `EditorGridPanel` ❶, which has its `xtype` property set to `'editorgrid'` and uses your `columnModel`, `remoteJsonStore`, and `pagingToolbar`.

You then move on to create the container for your `EditorGridPanel`, which is an instance of `Ext.Window`, and has its `layout` set to `'fit'`. You use chaining to show the `Window` immediately after it's instantiated.

Last, you call `remoteJsonStore.load` ❷ and pass a configuration object that specifies the parameters to send to the server. This ensures you start at record 0 and limits the number of returning records to 50.

All of the pieces of the puzzle are in place for this phase. You can now render your `EditorGridPanel` and begin to edit data. Figure 8.2 shows the `EditorGridPanel` in action.

You can see that our `EditorGridPanel` and `PagingToolbar` have rendered with data just waiting to be modified. Initially this seems like a normal `GridPanel`. But under the covers lies a whole new level of functionality just waiting to be unleashed. We'll take a moment to discuss exactly how you can use it.

8.3 *Navigating our EditorGridPanel*

You can use mouse or keyboard gestures to navigate through the cells and enter or leave editing mode.

To initiate editing mode via the mouse, double-click a cell and the editor will appear, as in figure 8.2. You can then modify the data and click or double-click another cell or anywhere else on the page to cause the blur of the editor to occur. Repeat this process to update as many cells as you wish.

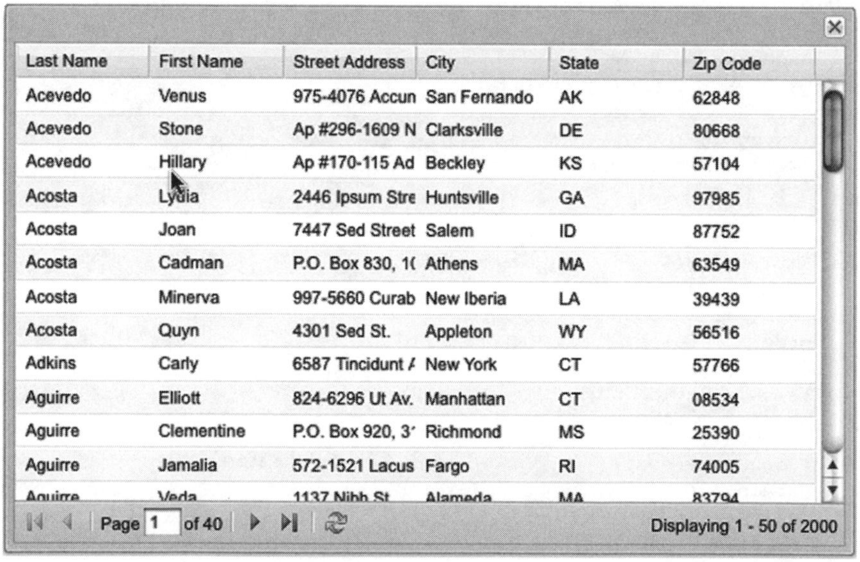

Figure 8.2 Our first `EditorGridPanel`

You can modify how many clicks it takes to edit a cell by adding a `clicksToEdit` property to the `EditorGridPanel` configuration object and specifying an integer value. Some applications allow editing via a single click of a cell; if so, so you'd set `clicksToEdit` to 1 and be done.

Being a command line junkie, I feel that keyboard navigation offers you much more power than the mouse. If you're a power user of Excel or a similar spreadsheet application, you know what I'm talking about. To initiate keyboard navigation, I like to use the mouse to focus on the first cell I want to edit. This immediately places focus exactly where I need it. I can use the Tab key or Shift-Tab key combination to move left or right. I can also use the arrow keys to focus on any cell at will.

To enter edit mode using the keyboard, press Enter, which displays the editor for that cell. While in edit mode, you can modify adjacent cells by pressing Tab to move one cell to the right or Shift-Tab to move one cell to the left.

To exit edit mode, you can press Enter again or press Esc. If the data you entered or modified validates properly, the record will be modified and the field will be marked as dirty. You can see quite a few fields being modified in figure 8.3.

When exiting an editor, depending whether the field has a `validator` and the results of the validation, the data will be discarded. To test this, edit a ZIP Code cell and enter more or fewer than five integers. Then exit edit mode by pressing Enter or Esc.

You can now edit data, but the edits are useless unless you save your changes. This is where you enter the next building phase, adding the CRUD layers.

8.4 Getting the CRUD in

With `EditorGridPanel`, CRUD server requests can be fired either automatically or manually. Automatic requests take place whenever a `Record` is modified or when modifications occur and a preset timer expires in the client-side logic, firing off a request

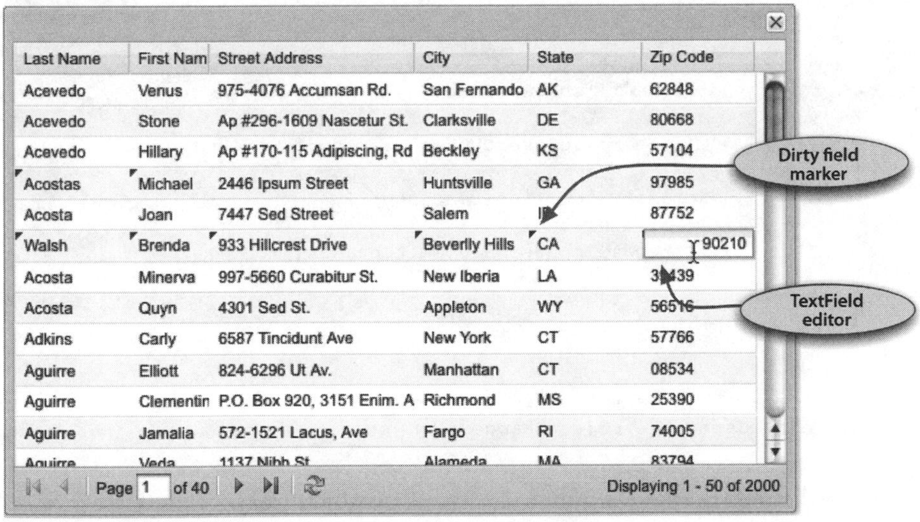

Figure 8.3 Our first `EditorGridPanel` with an editor and dirty field markers

to the server. To set up automatic CRUD, you can create your own logic to send the requests, or you can do things the easy way and use the `Ext.data.DataWriter` class, which is exactly what you'll do later in this chapter.

For now, we'll focus on manual CRUD, which is when the user invokes an action via UI, such as clicking a menu `Item` or a `Button` somewhere. The reason we're focusing on manual CRUD is that even though `Ext.data.DataWriter` is helpful, it won't satisfy everyone's needs, and going through this exercise will give you valuable exposure to what's going on with the `Store` and `Records` when data is modified. Also, because `Create` and `Delete` are CRUD actions, you'll explore how to insert and delete `Records` from the `Store`.

8.4.1   *Adding save and reject logic*

You'll begin by creating the save and change rejection methods, which you'll tie into `Buttons` that will live in your `PagingToolbar`. The following code is quite complicated, so please bear with me. We'll have an in-depth discussion about it, in which I'll walk you through just about every bit.

Listing 8.5   Setting up your save and change rejection handlers

```
var onSave = function() {                                           ❶ Get list of
    var modified = remoteJsonStore.getModifiedRecords();              modified Records
    if (modified.length > 0) {
        var recordsToSend = [];                                     ❷ Gather Record data
        Ext.each(modified, function(record) {                         into list to send
            recordsToSend.push(record.data);
        });

        var grid = Ext.getCmp('myEditorGrid');                      ❸ Manually mask
        grid.el.mask('Updating', 'x-mask-loading');                   grid's element
        grid.stopEditing();

        recordsToSend = Ext.encode(recordsToSend);                  ❹ Encode JSON to
                                                                      be sent over wire
        Ext.Ajax.request({
            url     : 'successTrue.js',                             ❺ Send
            params  : {                                               Ajax.request
                recordsToInsertUpdate : recordsToSend
            },
            success : function(response) {
                grid.el.unmask();
                remoteJsonStore.commitChanges();
            }
        });
    }
};

var onRejectChanges = function() {
    remoteJsonStore.rejectChanges();
};
```

In this listing you have two methods: `onSave`, which will be called when Save Changes is clicked, and `onRejectChanges`, which will be called when Reject Changes is clicked.

onSave contains quite a few lines to achieve your goal of data updates by means of Ajax requests. It begins with retrieving a list of modified Records by calling the remoteJsonStore's getModifiedRecords ❶ method, which returns a list of Record instances. In essence, whenever a Record Field is modified, it's marked as *dirty* and placed into the Store's modified list, which getModifiedRecords returns. You test to see if the length of the returned array is greater than zero, which indicates that you have data to save. You then create an empty array, recordsToSend, which you populate by looping through the modified records using Ext.each ❷. When calling Ext.each, you pass two parameters, the modified records list and an anonymous method, which Ext.each will call for each item in the modified list. The anonymous method takes a single parameter, record, which changes with each item in the modified list. Inside the anonymous method, you push the record.data reference, which is an object that contains every data point in the record.

You then mask the EditorGridPanel's element via the mask method ❸. You pass two properties to the mask method; the first is a message to display while the mask is visible, and the second is a CSS class that Ext JS uses to show a spinner loading graphic.

The recordsToSend reference is then overwritten with the result of the Ext.encode method call ❹, for which you pass the original recordsToSend list. This "stringifies" your list of JSON objects so you can send it over the wire.

Next, you perform your Ajax.request ❺, which is where the fun begins. You pass Ext.Ajax.request a configuration object that has three properties to get the job done.

The first is the url for which you have your successTrue.js dummy response file. Naturally, there would be some business logic here on the server side to insert or update Records. This dummy file assumes the role of a central controller for all of your CRUD operations.

The second property, params, is an object that contains the recordsToInsert-Update property with its value set to the stringified JSON, recordsToSend. Setting the params object ensures that the XHR being lobbed over at the server has a parameter or parameters sent to it, which in this case will be one parameter. The last property of the Ajax.request single parameter is success, which is a method to be called if the server returns successful status codes, such as 200 and so on.

Because this is a simulation, you don't check the response from the request. In here, you'd generally have some type of business logic to do something based on the results returned. For now, you unmask the grid's element and call the remoteJson-Store's commitChanges method.

Know the JSON tools

Ext.encode is a shortcut for Ext.util.JSON.encode. Its counterpart is Ext.decode or Ext.util.JSON.decode. The Ext.util.JSON class is a modified version of Douglas Crockford's JSON parser but doesn't modify the Object prototype. Please see http://www.json.org/js.html for more details on Douglas Crockford's JSON parser.

This is an important step because it clears the dirty flag from the Records and Fields that were modified, which clears the dirty flag on the modified cells within the EditorGridPanel. Failing to do this after a successful submission will result in Fields not being cleared in the UI and the modified Records not being purged from the Store's internal modified list.

The last method, onRejectChanges, calls the remoteJsonStore's rejectChanges method, which reverts the data to the original values in the Fields and clears the dirty flag from the UI.

The supporting methods for save and rejection are all set up. You can move on to modifying our PagingToolbar to include the two Buttons that will call these methods, as shown in the following listing.

> **Listing 8.6   Reconfiguring the PagingToolbar to include save and reject Buttons**

```
var pagingToolbar = {
    xtype       : 'paging',
    store       : remoteJsonStore,
    pageSize    : 50,
    displayInfo : true,
    items       : [                         ❶ Vertical line spacer
        '-',                                    for a cleaner UI
        {
            text    : 'Save Changes',
            handler : onSave
        },
        '-',
        {
            text    : 'Reject Changes',
            handler : onRejectChanges
        },
        '-'
    ]
};
```

In this listing you reconfigure the PagingToolbar XType configuration object to include items ❶, which consists of five entities. The string entities that you see with the hyphens ('-') are shorthand for the Ext.Toolbar.Separator, which will place a tiny vertical bar between toolbar child items. You're doing this because you want to show some separation between the Buttons and the generic PagingToolbar navigational items.

Also in the list are generic objects, which are translated to instances of Ext. Toolbar.Button. Figure 8.4 shows the Save Changes and Reject Changes Buttons, which have their respective handlers set. As you can see in the figure, the save and reject Buttons are placed neatly inside the PagingToolbar's center, which normally is empty space, and the Buttons are separated by neat Button separators. You can now begin to edit data and exercise your newly modified PagingToolbar functionality and newly created CRUD methods.

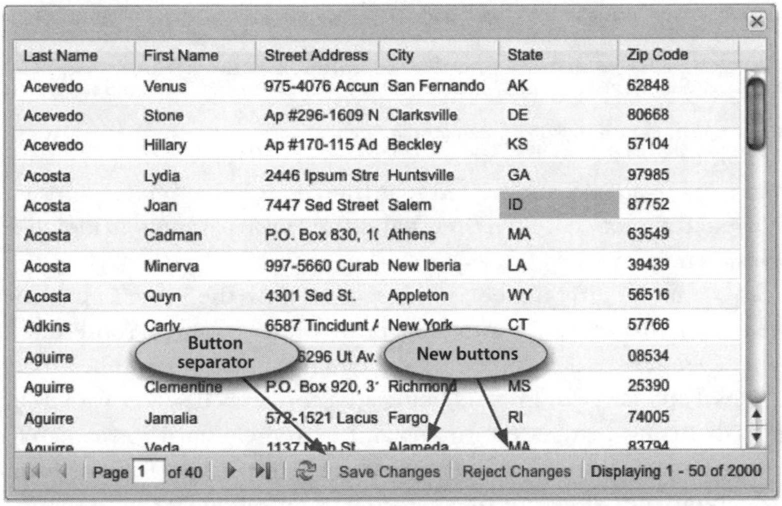

Figure 8.4 Our `EditorGridPanel` with Save Changes and Reject Changes buttons added

8.4.2 *Saving or rejecting your changes*

To use your save and reject buttons, you first need to modify data. Leveraging what you know about using the `EditorGridPanel`, change some data and click Save Changes. You should see the `EditorGridPanel`'s element mask appear briefly and then disappear once the save completes and the cells that are marked as dirty are marked clean or committed. Figure 8.5 shows the masking in action.

Remember that your `onSave` method retrieved a list of modified records and used the `Ext.encode` method to convert the raw list of JavaScript objects to stringified

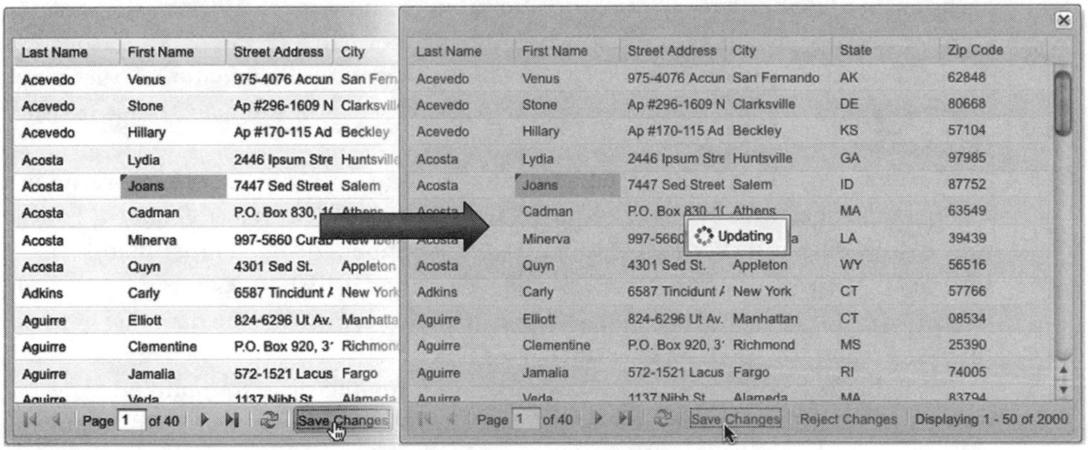

Figure 8.5 The load mask shows when save requests are being sent to the server.

Figure 8.6   Inspecting our `Ajax.request` POST parameter in Firebug

JSON. It then used that JSON and posted it as the `records` parameter sent by the Ajax request. Figure 8.6 shows what the request and the POST parameters look like in Firebug's XHR inspection view.

As you can see in the Firebug request inspection view, the `records` parameter is an array of items. In this case, it's two JavaScript objects, which represent the data records. Whenever you're developing or debugging, always remember that you can inspect the POST and GET parameters being sent to the web server via Firebug. Also, sometimes JSON BLOBs can get enormous and extremely hard to read. What I typically do is copy the JSON from Firebug and paste it in the web form at http://JSON-Lint.com, which tab indents and formats the data so it's readable.

If you were to have actual code on the server side to handle this update request, you'd read the `records` parameter, `decode` the JSON, and test to see if it's an instance of an array. If so, you'd loop through each object inside that array and search the database for the ID that's presented in the object instance. If the ID is in the database, you'd code the proper SQL `update`. Once the updates occur, you return a JSON object with `{success:true}` and an optional `msg` or `errors` property, which could contain a message from the server or a list of IDs for which the records could not be updated due to some business rules. You could then use the `success` or `failure` callback handlers, which you send to the `Ajax.request` method, to inspect what's sent back from the server and perform commits or post error messages accordingly.

The last bit we need to discuss regarding saving modifications has to do with sorting and pagination. Remember that changing data in a sorted column throws off the sorting completely. What I typically do after a successful change in a sorted column is call the `Store`'s `reload` method, which requests a new copy of the data set from the server and fixes sorting in the UI. Remember that you're simulating a successful server-side save, which is why you don't reload the `Store` in the `Ajax.request`'s success handler.

You've saved your data and seen what it looks like going over the wire. You have yet to reject changes though. Let's see what happens when you reject changes. To test this, modify data and click Reject Changes. What happened? Remember that the handler called the remote `Store`'s `rejectChanges` method, which looks at each `Record` in its `modified` list and calls its `reject` method. This, in turn, clears the dirty flag both on the `Record` and the UI. That's it—no magic.

Now that you've seen what it takes to perform remote saves to modified `Records`, you'll add create and delete functionality to your `EditableGrid`, which will complete your CRUD actions.

8.4.3 *Adding create and delete*

When configuring the UI for your save and reject functionality, you added `Buttons` to the `PagingToolbar`. Although you could add the create and delete functionality the same way, it's best to use a context menu because it's much smoother to delete and add from a context menu. Think about it for a second. If you've ever used a spreadsheet application, you know that right-clicking a cell brings up a context menu that, among other things, has insert and delete menu items. We're going to introduce the same paradigm here.

As you did with the previously added functionality, you'll develop the supporting methods in the following listing before you construct and configure the UI components. We're going to ratchet up the complexity.

Listing 8.7   Constructing your delete and new `Record` methods

```
var doDelete = function(rowToDelete) {                          ❶ Method for
    var grid  = Ext.getCmp('myEditorGrid');                        delete operations
    var recordToDelete = grid.store.getAt(rowToDelete);

    if (recordToDelete.phantom) {                               ❷ Delete
        grid.store.remove(recordToDelete);                         phantom Records
        return;
    }

    grid.el.mask('Updating', 'x-mask-loading');

    Ext.Ajax.request({                                          ❸ Request to
        url          : 'successTrue.js',                           delete Records
        parameters : {
            rowToDelete   : recordToDelete.id
        },
        success : function() {
            grid.el.unmask();
            grid.store.remove(recordToDelete);
        }
    });
};
                                                                ❹ Delete menu
var onDelete = function() {                                        item handler
    var grid      = Ext.getCmp('myEditorGrid');
    var selected = grid.getSelectionModel().getSelectedCell();

    Ext.MessageBox.confirm(                                     ❺ Get confirmation
        'Confirm delete',                                          from user
        'Are you sure?',
        function(btn) {
            if (btn == 'yes') {
                doDelete(selected[0]);
            }
        }
    );

};
```

I hope you haven't run away, but chances are that if you're reading this right now, you're still with me. Awesome. Some of this will look familiar to you from the save feature you added to your EditorGridPanel panel earlier.

The first method in the listing, doDelete ❶, will be called by the delete menu item handler that you create just after it. Its only argument is rowToDelete, which is an integer indicating the index of the record that you're to delete. This method is responsible for removing Records from the Store. Here's how it works.

This method first gets a reference to the EditorGridPanel panel via the ComponentMgr's get method. It immediately gets the Record that the Store is to remove using the Store's getAt method and passes the rowToDelete argument. Then it checks to see if the Record is a phantom (new Record) or not.

If it is, the Record is immediately removed ❷ from the Store, and this method is aborted with a return call. When the Record is removed from the Store, the Grid-View immediately shows the change by removing the Record's row in the DOM.

If the Record isn't a phantom, the grid's element is masked, preventing any further user interaction, and provides feedback that something is taking place. Ajax.request ❸ is then called to your server-side simulation file, successTrue.js, with the single parameter rowToDelete, which is the ID of the Record in the database. The success handler of this Ajax.request will unmask the element and remove the Record from the Store.

The onDelete handler ❹ method will query the selected cell from the selection model and request a confirmation from the user. If the user clicks the Yes button, it will call the doDelete method. Here's how it works.

When onDelete is first called, it gets a reference to your EditorGridPanel via the Ext.getCmp method. It then gets the selected cell via calling the EditorGridPanel's SelectionModel.getSelectCell method. What getSelectedCell returns is an array with two values, which are the coordinates of the cell: the row and column number.

A call to Ext.MessageBox.confirm ❺ is made, passing in three arguments: title, message body, and button handler, which is an anonymous method. The button handler determines whether the button pressed was 'yes' and calls your doDelete method, passing the first value of the cell coordinates, which is the row of the selected cell.

Before you move on to deploy delete, you should add the insert handler. This one is relatively small:

```
var onInsertRecord = function() {
    var newRecord        = new remoteJsonStore.recordType({
        newRecordId : Ext.id()
    });
    var grid             = Ext.getCmp('myEditorGrid');
    var selectedCell     = grid.getSelectionModel().getSelectedCell();
    var selectedRowIndex = selectedCell[0];

    remoteJsonStore.insert(selectedRowIndex, newRecord);
    grid.startEditing(selectedRowIndex,0);
}
```

The purpose of this method is to locate the row index that was right-clicked and insert a phantom Record at the index. Here's how it works.

First it creates a new record via a call to new remoteJsonStore.recordType. It does this by passing an object with a single property, newRecordId, which is a unique value by virtue of the Ext.id utility method call. Having this unique newRecordId will aid the server side in inserting new records and returning a mapping for the client to register real ids for each of the new Records. We'll discuss this more a little later, when we explore what the server side could be doing with the data we're submitting.

All data Stores have the default Record template accessible via the recordType property. Remember that to instantiate a new instance of a Record, you must use the new keyword.

Next, you create a reference, rowInsertIndex, to the row of the newly selected cell. You do this because it ends up in easier-to-read code when you use it in the following two statements.

A call is then made to the remoteJsonStore's insert method, which requires two parameters. The first is the index for which you wish to insert the Record, and the second is a reference to an actual Record. This effectively inserts a Record above the row that's right-clicked, emulating one of the spreadsheet features we discussed earlier.

Last, you want to initiate editing of that Record immediately. You accomplish this by a call to the EditorGridPanel's startEditing method, passing it the row for which you inserted the new Record and 0, which means the first column.

This concludes the supporting methods for the create and delete functions. You can now move on to create the context menu handler and reconfigure the grid to listen to the cellcontextmenu event, as shown in the following listing.

Listing 8.8   Setting up your context menu handler for the EditorGridPanel

```
var doCellCtxMenu = function(editorGrid,
    rowIndex, cellIndex, evtObj) {                    ◁┐  Cell context menu
    evtObj.stopEvent();                               ❶  listener method

    if (!editorGrid.rowCtxMenu) {                              ◁┐  Create context
        editorGrid.rowCtxMenu = new Ext.menu.Menu({            ❷  menu object
            items : [
                {
                    text    : 'Insert Record',
                    handler : onInsertRecord
                },
                {
                    text    : 'Delete Record',
                    handler : onDelete
                }
            ]                                                    Select  ❸
        });                                               right-clicked
    }                                                             cell
    editorGrid.getSelectionModel().select(rowIndex,cellIndex);  ◁┘
    editorGrid.rowCtxMenu.showAt(evtObj.getXY());
};
```

Listing 8.8 contains doCellCtxMenu ❶, a method to handle the cellcontextmenu event from the EditorGridPanel, which is responsible for creating and showing the context menu for the insert and delete operations. Here's how it works.

doCellCtxMenu accepts four arguments, which are passed by the cellcontextmenu handler. They are editorGrid, a reference to the EditorGridPanel that fired the event, rowIndex and cellIndex, which are the coordinates of the cell that was right-clicked, and evtObj, an instance of Ext.EventObject.

The first function that this method performs is preventing the right-click event from bubbling upward by calling the evtObj.stopEvent, preventing the browser from displaying its own context menu. If you didn't prevent the event from bubbling, you'd see the browser context menu on top of yours, which would be silly and unusable.

doCellCtxMenu then tests ❷ to see if the EditorGridPanel has a rowCtxMenu property and creates an instance of Ext.menu.Menu and stores the reference as the rowCtxMenu property on the EditorGridPanel. This effectively allows for the creation of a single Menu, which is more efficient than creating a new instance of Ext.menu.Menu every time the event is fired and will last until the EditorGridPanel is destroyed, as you'll see later.

You pass a configuration object to the Ext.menu.Menu constructor, which has a single property, items, that's an array of configuration objects that get translated to an instance of Ext.menu.MenuItem. The MenuItem configuration objects both reference the respective handlers to match the Item text.

The last two functions that this method performs are selecting the cell that was right-clicked and showing the context menu at the correct X and Y coordinates onscreen. It does this by calling the select ❸ method of the EditorGridPanel's CellSelectionModel and passing it the rowIndex and cellIndex coordinates. Last, you display the context menu using the coordinates where the right-click event occurred.

Before you execute your code, you'll have to reconfigure the grid to register the context menu handler. Please add the following to your grid configuration object:

```
listeners : {
    cellcontextmenu : doCellCtxMenu
}
```

You now have everything you need to start using our new UI features. I want to see this thing in action.

8.4.4   *Using create and delete*

At this point, you have your insert and delete handlers developed and ready to be used. You just finished creating the context menu handler and reconfigured your grid to call it when the cellcontextmenu event is fired.

You'll start your exploration by creating and inserting a new Record, as shown in figure 8.7.

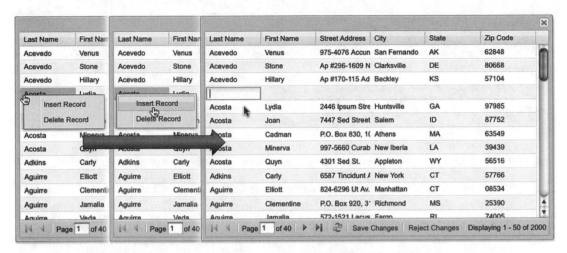

Figure 8.7   Adding a new `Record` with our newly configured Insert Record menu item

As illustrated in figure 8.7, you can display the context menu by right-clicking any cell, which calls the `doCellCtxMenu` handler. This causes the selection to occur and displays the custom Ext menu at the mouse's coordinates. Clicking the Insert Record menu `Item` forces the call to the registered handler, `onInsertRecord`, which inserts a new `Record` at the index of the selected cell and begins editing on the first column. Cool!

Now, in order to save changes, you need to modify the newly inserted `Record` and then click the Save Changes `Button` that you created earlier. Figure 8.8 shows this screen.

Clicking Save Changes invokes the `onSave` handler, which performs the `Ajax.request` to our mock server handler, the successTrue.js file. Figure 8.9 shows what the JSON looks like being submitted in Firebug's XHR inspection tool.

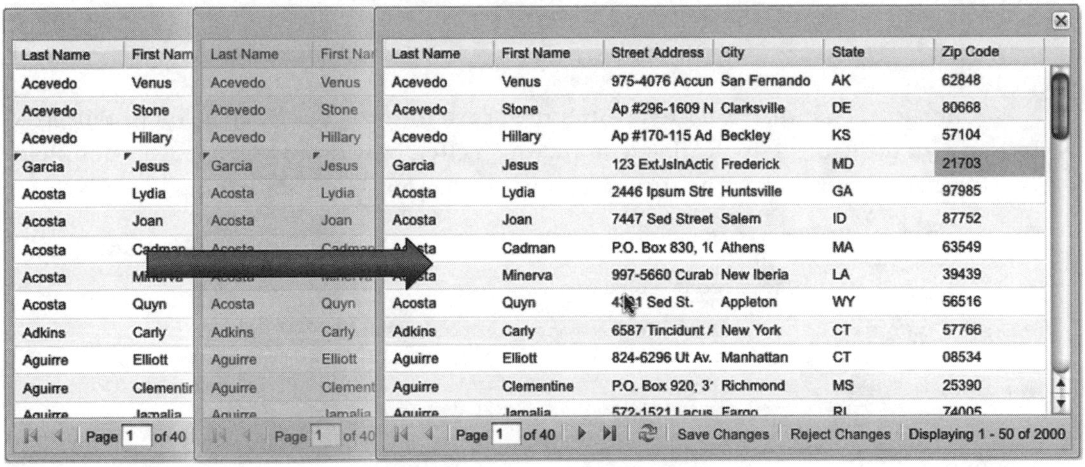

Figure 8.8   The UI transitions when saving our newly inserted `Record`

Figure 8.9   Using Firebug to inspect the JSON being submitted for our newly inserted `Record`

As you can see, there's no `id` associated with this `Record`, but there is a `newRecordId` property, which is a telltale sign that it's a new `Record`. This property is important because the controller code on the server could use this to know that this is a new record to be inserted versus an update operation. Remember that our `onSave` handler is set up to handle both inserts and update operations; thus, the theoretical controller needs to be able to handle both situations. Here's a quick overview of how things might work if you have server code to submit to.

The server would receive the `records` parameter and decode the JSON. It would then loop through the array and perform inserts on any of the records that have this `newRecordIdProperty` and return a list of database `ids` for the records that you've newly inserted. Instead of a generic return of `{ success : true }`, it could return something much more intelligent, like a list of objects that map the `newRecordId` to the `Record`'s database `id`, which would look something like this:

```
{
    success : true,
    records : [
        {
            newRecordId : 'ext-gen85',
            id          : 2213
        }
    ]
}
```

Your success handler can then search the `Store` for the `Records` that you just inserted and set the `Records` to the database `id`, which effectively makes the `Record` a nonphantom, or a real `record`. The success handler code would look something like this:

```
success : function(response) {
    grid.el.unmask();
    remoteJsonStore.commitChanges();

    var result = Ext.decode(response.responseText);
    Ext.each(result.records, function(o) {
        var rIndex = remoteJsonStore.find('newRecordId', o.newRecordId);
        var record = remoteJsonStore.getAt(rIndex);

        record.set('id', o.id);
        delete record.data.newRecordId;
    });
}
```

In this snippet, you use `Ext.decode` to decode the returning JSON, which is the `response.responseText` property. You then use `Ext.each` to loop through the resulting array of objects. For each object in the list, you get the `Record index` by using the `remoteJsonStore`'s `find` method and pass two properties. The first is the field you're searching for, which is `newRecordId`, and the other is the returned object's `new-RecordId`. You get the reference of the `Record` by calling the `remoteJsonStore`'s `getAt` method and pass the `Record index` that you just obtained. You use the `Record`'s `set` method to set the database `id` you just got back from the server and then move on to delete the `Record`'s `newRecordId` property. This ensures that any further modifications to that `Record` will only result in an update because it will pass its database `id` to the controller. Figure 8.10 shows what an update to the recently inserted record looks like in Firebug.

In this figure, you can see that the `newRecordId` is being sent to the server for insertion. The server then returns the database `id` as 9999, and our newly modified success handler sets the `Record`'s database `id` and removes the `newRecordId`. Whoa, that's a lot of material just for the creation of `Records`. What about delete? Surely that's simpler, right?

Absolutely! Before we discuss the process of deleting records, we'll examine how the UI works.

When you right-click a `Record`, an `Ext.MessageBox` displays to confirm the delete operation, as shown in figure 8.11. You click Yes, and an `Ajax.request` is made to the controller to delete the records.

Figure 8.12 shows what the delete request looks like in Firebug's XHR inspection tool.

This works because our `onDelete` handler called `MessageBox.confirm` and will call our `doDelete` method, which checks to see if this is a new `Record` or not. Because you happened to request a deletion of a nonphantom `Record`, an `Ajax.request` was made to the central controller with one parameter, `rowToDelete`, which is the database `id` of the `Record`. If the record had been a phantom, the request would have never been made and the `Record` would have been immediately moved from the `Store`.

You did a lot of work to get manual CRUD operations set up for your first `Editor-GridPanel`. In doing so, you learned more about `Stores` and `Records` and how to

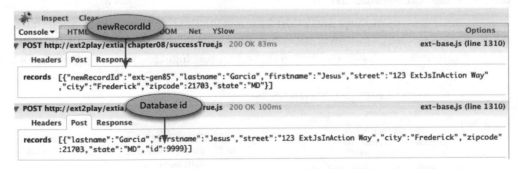

Figure 8.10   A Firebug view of a newly inserted `Record` followed by a subsequent update

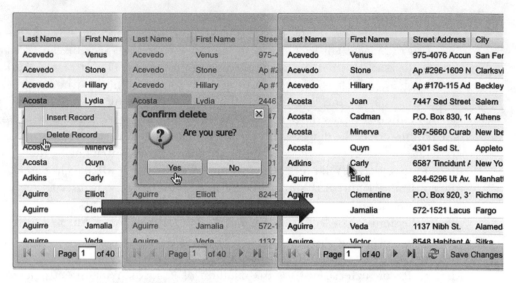

Figure 8.11 **The UI workflow for deleting a** `Record`

detect changes and save them using `Ajax.requests`. Along the way you got a chance to see a real-life case of an Ext confirmation `MessageBox` in action. Cool!

Now that you've learned the nuts and bolts of manual CRUD, you can switch tracks to learn how you can leverage `Ext.data.DataWriter` to manage CRUD operations easily and even automatically.

8.5 Using Ext.data.DataWriter

In our last example you learned how to code manual CRUD actions, which meant you had to code your own `Ajax.requests`. But what if you wanted the `EditorGridPanel` to automatically save when you're editing? In order to do this without a `Writer`, you'd have to write an entire event model that fired off requests when a CRUD UI action took place. This would have to take into account exception handling, which means you'd have to code for the rollback changes. I can personally tell you that it's a lot of work. Luckily, you don't have to do all of this for easy and automated CRUD.

8.5.1 Enter Ext.data.DataWriter

`Writer` saves you time and effort by removing the requirement for you to have to code `Ajax.requests` and exception handling, giving you more time to do more of the important stuff, like building out the business logic for your application. Before you

Figure 8.12 **The controller request to delete a** `Record` **as viewed in Firebug's XHR inspection tool**

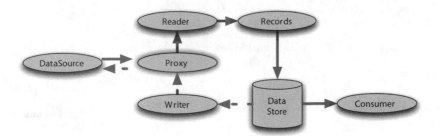

Figure 8.13   A depiction of the flow for data reads and writes when a data `Store` is used

start coding your `Writer` implementation, you should have a quick review of how `Writer` fits into the picture.

Please recall our discussion about the operation of data `Store`s from the last chapter, where you learned about the flow of data from the source to the consumer. Remember that `Proxy` is the intermediary connection class for reads as well as writes. If this still seems a little fuzzy, figure 8.13 should help clear things up.

In order to user `Writer`, you'll need to reconfigure your data `Store` and the supporting `Proxy`. Instead of configuring a `url` property for the `Proxy`, you'll create a configuration object known as the `api`. The proxy `api` is a new concept for you, and we'll discuss it more in detail in a bit, when we review the example code.

You'll then need to create an instance of `Writer` and plug it into your data `Store` as well as add some new configuration properties to the `Store`'s configuration object itself, thus completing the reconfiguration of the `Store`.

To reconfigure the `EditorGridPanel` and the CRUD actions, you'll keep all of the UI changes but remove the supporting code for the `Ajax.requests`. Because you're familiar with most of this code, we'll be moving at a faster pace, but we'll slow down for the new material.

8.5.2   Adding DataWriter to our JsonStore

Now that you have an understanding of what you'll be doing, you can get out your shovels and start digging. As before, you'll begin by reconfiguring your `Store`, as shown in the following listing.

Listing 8.9   Reconfiguring data `Store` to use `Writer`

```
var remoteProxy = new Ext.data.ScriptTagProxy({                      Configuring
    api : {                                                          ScriptTagProxy api
        read    : 'http://extjsinaction.com/dataQuery.php',
        create  : 'http://extjsinaction.com/dataCreate.php',
        update  : 'http://extjsinaction.com/dataUpdate.php',
        destroy : 'http://extjsinaction.com/dataDelete.php'
    }
});

var recordFields = [
    { name : 'id',          mapping : 'id'          },
```

```
    { name : 'firstname',    mapping : 'firstname'  },
    { name : 'lastname',     mapping : 'lastname'   },
    { name : 'street',       mapping : 'street'     },
    { name : 'city',         mapping : 'city'       },
    { name : 'state',        mapping : 'state'      },
    { name : 'zipcode',      mapping : 'zip'        }
];

var writer = new Ext.data.JsonWriter({         ◁┐  New instance of
    writeAllFields : true                        ❷ JsonWriter
});

var remoteJsonStore = new Ext.data.JsonStore({
    proxy            : remoteProxy,
    storeId          : 'ourRemoteStore',
    root             : 'records',
    autoLoad         : false,
    totalProperty    : 'totalCount',
    remoteSort       : true,
    fields           : recordFields,
    idProperty       : 'id',
    autoSave         : false,
    successProperty  : 'success',               ◁┐  New options for
    writer           : writer,                    ❸ JsonStore
    listeners        : {
        exception : function () {
            console.info(arguments);
        }
    }
});
```

In listing 8.9, you kick things off by creating a new `ScriptTagProxy` ❶ and pass a configuration object as the property `api`, which denotes URLs for each of the CRUD actions, with `read` being the request to load data. Instead of using the dummy successTrue.js file as a single controller, you'll use somewhat intelligent remote server-side code, where a controller exists for each CRUD action. `Writer` requires intelligent responses; thus remote server-side code was developed. Technically, you could use the same server-side script for all of the CRUD actions, but I find it easier to create one for each action.

You then move on to create the list of fields, which gets translated into, *what*? Correct! `Ext.data.Fields`. These `Fields` are the lowest supporting class for the, *what*? Yes! The `Ext.data.Record`. You're progressing in this framework nicely.

Next, you create a subclass of `Ext.data.DataWriter`, known as `JsonWriter` ❷, which has the ability to save a request to modify a single or batch (list) of `Records`. In the `JsonWriter` configuration object, you specify `writeAllFields` as `true`, which ensures that for each operation `Writer` returns all of the properties, which is great for development and debugging. Naturally, you want to set this to `false` in production, which will reduce overhead over the wire and at the server-side and database stack.

The last thing you do in this listing is reconfigure the `Store`. Note that everything is exactly the same except for a few property additions to enable `Writer` integration and some debugging capabilities.

The first addition is autoSave ❸, which you set to false but defaults to true. If left as true, the Store would automatically fire requests for CRUD operations, which isn't what you want just yet. I want to show you how *easy* it is to invoke CRUD requests with Writer now in the picture.

Next, you add the successProperty, which is used as an indication that the operation was a success or failure and is consumed by the JsonReader, which the JsonStore automatically instantiates for you. Remember, this is just like when you submitted data with the FormPanel, where you required at a minimum a return of { success : true } as the response from the web server. The same principle applies with the Store when using DataWriter. In your new remoteJsonStore, you're specifying the success-Property of 'success', which is common and self-documenting.

The last change you make is adding a global exception event listener to your JsonStore, which is needed if you want something to occur upon any exception that the Store raises. Here, you spit all of the arguments to the Firebug console, which I use when developing with Ext.data.DataWriter because it provides a wealth of information that's hard to find anywhere else during debugging. I highly suggest you doing the same. Trust me; it will save you time in the long run.

Cool! You've just re-created our ScriptTagProxy to work with your new instance of Ext.data.JsonWriter and reconfigured our Store to prevent autoSaves. Your next task is to modify the PagingToolbar and make the delete context menu handler leaner, as shown in the following listing.

Listing 8.10   Reconfiguring the PagingToolbar and delete handler

```
var pagingToolbar = {
    xtype       : 'paging',
    store       : remoteJsonStore,
    pageSize    : 50,
    displayInfo : true,
    items       : [
        '-',
        {
            text    : 'Save Changes',                   ❶ Save changes
            handler : function () {                         via Writer
                remoteJsonStore.save();
            }
        },
        '-',
        {
            text    : 'Reject Changes',                  ❷ Reject changes
            handler : function () {                          from our Store
                remoteJsonStore.rejectChanges();
            }
        },
        '-'
    ]
};

var onDelete = function() {                              ❸ Leaner onDelete
                                                           context menu handler
```

```
var grid          = Ext.getCmp('myEditorGrid');
var selected      = grid.getSelectionModel().getSelectedCell();
var recordToDelete = grid.store.getAt(selected[0]);

grid.store.remove(recordToDelete);
};
```

In listing 8.10, you reconfigure the `PagingToolbar`'s save button handler ❶ to call the `save` method of the data `Store`, which uses `Writer` to gather the data to save and eventually invoke a request to save changes. This effectively replaces the previous `onSave` handler, which is what was responsible for sending create and update `Ajax.requests`. This is where you start to see some of the code savings we discussed earlier. You also add an inline method to reject ❷ the `Store`'s changes.

Next, you refactor the `onDelete` ❸ context menu handler. You remove the typical confirmation dialog box to make it much leaner. You can choose to reject the changes from here, which means that the `Records` that are deleted from the UI are rolled back via the `rejectChanges` handler you created previously. You also remove the `Ajax.request` code, for more code savings.

Your changes to integrate `Writer` into your `EditorGridPanel` panel are now complete. The `EditorGridPanel` configuration code stays exactly the same as in listing 8.8. Let's see `Writer` in action.

8.5.3 *Using DataWriter*

The changes you made in the previous listings where you integrated `Writer` were designed so you could use the same interaction to invoke a request. Now let's see how you can reduce the amount of code when using `Writer` relative to creating your own `Ajax.requests` and handlers.

You'll start by modifying some `Records` and clicking Save Changes to inspect what `Writer` is sending to the server. Figure 8.14 illustrates the parameters being sent for an update request in Firebug's request inspection tool.

In figure 8.14 you see the result of a request being sent to the update URL as configured in the `Proxy` API. Along with the usual `_dc` (cache buster) and `callback` parameters, you see `id`, which is a list of IDs affected, and `records`, which is the list of

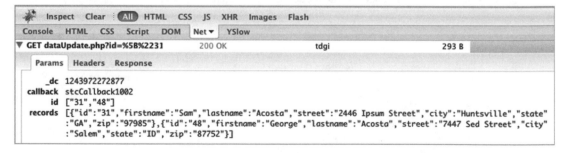

Figure 8.14 The result of our update request as shown in Firebug's request inspection tool

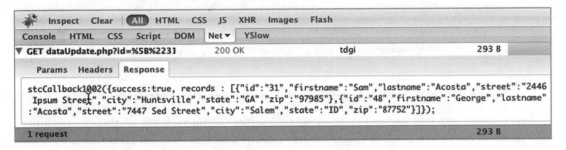

Figure 8.15   The server-side response from our update request with `Writer`

`Records` that were changed. You see the entire `Record` contents here because we set the `writeAllFields` configuration parameter to `true`.

Our server-side code then processes the list of records and returns the following JSON. The response looks like figure 8.15.

Notice that the `successProperty`, `success`, has a value of `true`, which is an indication that the server processed the data successfully. It also returned the list of records after it was processed. This is used to apply any changes that may be required by business logic. For instance, what if someone put a forbidden word as one of the values? The server could reject the change by quietly replacing that forbidden value with what was previously in that field. The UI would then update accordingly, thus completing an update cycle.

Next, you should perform an insert and see what happens. This is where things get interesting. Insert a `Record` via the context menu, add some values, and click the Save Changes `Button` in the `PagingToolbar`. You'll see that a request was made to the `create` URL that you defined in the `api` configuration object for the `ScriptTagProxy`, as shown in figure 8.16.

The most important item to note in the `records` parameter being sent to the server is the `id` property. Notice that the `id` is fictitious; its value is `"ext-record-1"`. Because the `create` server-side action is different than the update action, the `id` parameter is ignored when the record is inserted into the database. The server then gets the `id` for the newly inserted record and returns the database `id` in return, as illustrated in figure 8.17.

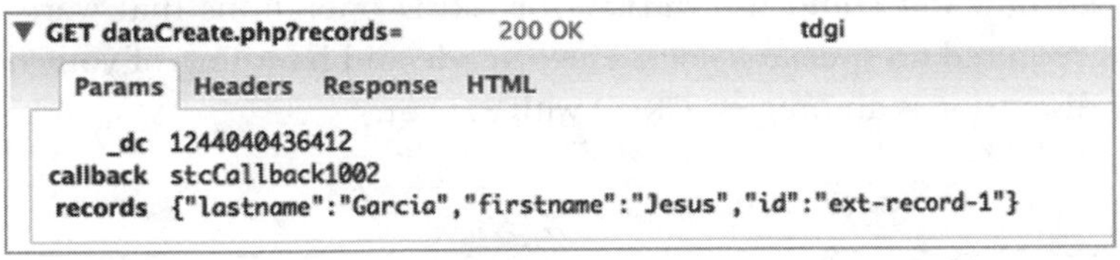

> ▼ **GET dataCreate.php?records=**   200 OK   tdgi
>
> ┌───┐
> │ **Params**   Headers   Response   HTML   │
> ├───┤
> │   _dc   1244040436412   │
> │   callback   stcCallback1002   │
> │   records   {"lastname":"Garcia","firstname":"Jesus","id":"ext-record-1"} │
> └───┘

Figure 8.16   Inserting a `Record` with `Writer`, as viewed in the Firebug request inspection tool

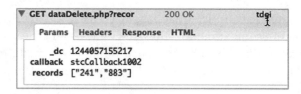

```
▼ GET dataCreate.php?records=        200 OK              tdgi              103 B

    Params  Headers  Response  HTML

    stcCallback1002({success:true, records : {"lastname":"Garcia","firstname":"Jesus","id":"1244040436"}
    });
```

Figure 8.17   Using Firebug to inspect the results of a `Record` insert using `Writer`

If an insert was successful, then the id value (along with all of the other values) returned to the browser will be applied to the recently inserted record. This ensures action requests for update and delete will submit the database id of the record moving forward. This is where you can see the added value of using `Writer`, because you don't have to manage this verification logic yourself.

In our test case, you inserted a single `Record`. If you insert multiple `Records`, they'll be submitted to the server, upon save, in an array. It's important to note that the server must return the records in the exact same order, or the database id to record mapping or association will fail.

The delete action is the simplest, where the delete request sends a list of IDs to the host for processing. To try this out, right-click a `Record`, and choose Delete from the context menu. Heck, do this for a few `Records`. Notice how they're removed from the store? Now click Save Changes and inspect the request in Firebug; our results are shown in figure 8.18.

```
▼ GET dataDelete.php?recor       200 OK              tdgi

    Params  Headers  Response  HTML

       _dc  1244057155217
    callback  stcCallback1002
    records  ["241","883"]
```

Figure 8.18   The JSON parameters for a delete action request

For the delete action requests, the records parameter is a list of IDs. Let's look at what the server side returns. Figure 8.19 shows the result from the server for the delete request.

The server-side code takes the list of IDs, removes the records from the database, and returns the list of IDs the store is to permanently remove. And that's all there is to delete operations.

You've seen how you could use `Writer` for CRUD operations that were invoked manually but required no special `Ajax.request` code and handling of your own. The last topic for discussion is automated CRUD with `Writer`.

```
▼ GET dataDelete.php?records=%5B%22241%22%;        200 OK

    Params  Headers  Response  HTML

    stcCallback1002({success:true, records :[{"id":"241"},{"id":"883"}]});
```

Figure 8.19   The result of our delete action request using `Writer`

8.5.4 *An automated writing store*

To set up `Writer` for automated CRUD actions, all you need to do is set the `autoSave` property for the data `Store` configuration object to `true`. That's it. You already set up all of the hard stuff, if you want to call it that. Now all you need to do is exercise CRUD operations, and the `Store` will automatically invoke requests based on your CRUD action.

The one thing to look out for with a Store that automatically writes is that there's *no undo for actions.* When data has been modified in the database, the `rejectChanges` method has no effect. The database reflects the latest changes. The same goes for delete and insert operations.

8.6 *Summary*

In this chapter you got your first exposure to the `EditableGrid` class and learned how it uses `Ext.form.Fields` to allow for editing of data on the fly. This gave you an opportunity to learn about the `CellSelectionModel` and some of its methods, such as `getSelectedCell`. You also learned how you could leverage keyboard and mouse gestures to navigate the `EditorGridPanel` to edit data relatively rapidly.

You learned how to manually code for CRUD operations with your own custom `Ajax.request` logic and used a mock controller while doing so. You added two menu items to the `PagingToolbar` and a context menu to the `EditableGrid` to allow you to insert and delete `Records` as well as reject changes. In doing this, you learned how to use `getModifiedRecords` from the `Store` for submission to the mock controller.

Finally, you learned how you could reduce the amount of code you need to generate by leveraging the `Ext.data.DataWriter` class for CRUD operations. We also discussed how to set up an automated `Store` with `Writer`.

In the next chapter, you'll learn about another data `Store`–consuming component, the `DataView` and its descendant the `ListView`.

DataView and ListView

This chapter covers

- Learning about `DataView`s
- Customizing the `DataView` rendering of data
- Implementing a custom `XTemplate`
- Exercising multicomponent event communication

Displaying lists of data in a web application is something that we've all had to deliver at one time or another in our careers. Whether it's a list of books, servers on a particular subnet, or a list of employees, the process is the same. Retrieve the data; format and display it. Although this process is simple from a high level, the burden of maintaining the under-the-hood JavaScript has prevented us from being able to focus all of our attention on getting the task done. Throw in the ability to select multiple items, and you find yourself spending more time on maintenance than further developing your application.

In this chapter, you'll learn that with the `DataView` you can achieve this goal easily, saving you time and allowing you to focus on the deliverables at hand. We'll begin by constructing a `DataView` and introduce a major supporting class, the `XTemplate`, along the way. You'll learn what it takes to properly configure the `DataView` for single or multiple `Record` selections.

Afterward, you'll learn how to create a `ListView` to display data in a tabular format, much like the `GridPanel`. You'll see what it takes to bind it to your implementation of the `DataView` to assist with the filtering of data from the `DataView`.

As icing on the cake, you'll learn how to make complex two-way bindings between the `DataView` and `FormPanel`, to allow users to update data. What you'll learn in the final exercise will help you in binding the `DataView` and `ListView` to other widgets in the framework.

9.1 What is the DataView?

The `DataView` class uses the data `Store` and `XTemplate` to provide the ability to paint data on the screen easily. It has all of the necessary plumbing on its DOM structure to provide for tracking the mouse and has single- or multiple-node selection models.

Figure 9.1 illustrates a `DataView` in action and highlights how the data `Store` and `XTemplate` support it.

As illustrated, the `DataView` consumes data from the data `Store` by means of event bindings. Because of these bindings, it's smart enough to know how to efficiently handle the DOM changes. For instance, if a single `Record` is deleted from a store, the element whose `index` matches the `Record index` is removed from the DOM. For added flexibility, pagination can also be applied to the `DataView` via binding a `Paging-Toolbar` to the `DataView`'s bound store.

> **NOTE** Unlike the `GridPanel` and `TreePanel`, `DataView` doesn't extend from `Panel`, which means that it can't be configured to use any of the `Panel` features, such as `Toolbars`. The good news is that the `DataView` does extend from `BoxComponent`, which means it can be used in layouts and can easily be wrapped by a `Panel`.

We talked about `Templates` earlier in this book, and you learned how you can stamp out HTML fragments easily with that tool. The `DataView` uses the `Template`'s more powerful cousin, the `XTemplate`, which adds the ability to have subtemplates, inline code execution, conditional processing, and much more.

Now that you know what a `DataView` is and does, it's time to start building one.

Figure 9.1 The `DataView` and various supporting classes

9.2   *Constructing a DataView*

You've been asked to develop a full-screen mini-application to allow members of the HR team to quickly list employees in the company. They want the records to be styled and have a background similar to a manila folder. For each Record, the view needs to be able to display the employee's full name, department, date hired, and email address. The requestor stated that this view would be part of a larger app, which you'll learn more about once you've completed this view. The backend is complete and ready to serve up JSON, which means that all you need to do is write the frontend code.

To fulfill this initial requirement, you'll have to create a DataView that will live in a ViewPort. But before you can start writing the JavaScript code, you need to construct the CSS for your HTML. This is because when implementing DataViews, as end developers you're *required* to configure the CSS to style the contents of the widget. If you didn't apply styling, the painted data would be unusable.

Figure 9.2 shows what our DataView would look like if it was not styled, versus styled.

It should be obvious that a styled DataView is better for both usability and the user's eyes. Each implementation of the DataView has its own styles. Perhaps when you implement this widget on your projects, you can create a base CSS set of rules that all of these widgets can leverage, giving a unified look to the application.

Having seen what it needs to look like, you can configure the CSS before you begin work on the JavaScript for the widget and its supporting classes, as shown in the following listing.

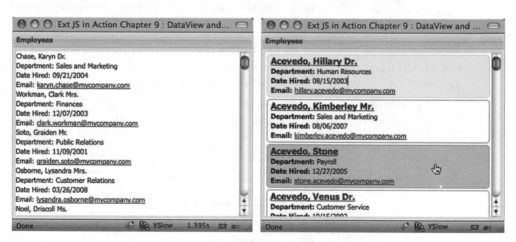

Figure 9.2   An unstyled (left) DataView compared to a styled (right) DataView

Listing 9.1   Setting the `DataView` styles

```css
<style type="text/css">
    .emplWrap {
        border: 1px #999999 solid;
        margin : 3px;
        -moz-border-radius: 5px;
        -webkit-border-radius: 5px;
        background-color: #ffffcc;
        padding-bottom: 3px;
    }

    .emplSelected {
        border: 1px #66ff66 solid;
        background-color: #ccffcc;
        cursor: pointer;
    }

    .emplOver {
        border: 1px #9999ff solid;
        background-color: #ccccff;
        cursor: pointer;
    }

    .emplName {
        font-weight: bold;
        margin-left: 5px;
        font-size: 14px;
        text-decoration: underline;
        color: #333333;
    }

    .title {
        margin-left: 5px;
        font-weight: bold;
    }
</style>
```

1 Color all Records yellow

2 Color selected Records green

3 Custom color on mouseover

4 Enlarge employee name

In listing 9.1, you configure all of the CSS that will be used by the `DataView`. The first rule, `emplWrap` **1**, will be used to style each `Record` with a light gray border and a yellowish background. The next rule, `emplSelected` **2**, will be used to color a `Record` green when a user has selected it. The third rule, `emplOver` **3**, will be applied to a `Record` when the mouse is hovering over it and will color it blue. The last two rules, `emplName` **4** and `title`, are additional rules to style the inner contents of each rendered `Record`.

Now that you have the CSS in place, you can begin with the construction of the store that will provide the data.

9.2.1   Building the Store and XTemplate

We're constructing the data `Store` first, in the following listing, because it will help you know what the mapped fields are when you configure the `XTemplate` for the `DataView`.

```
var employeeStoreProxy = new Ext.data.ScriptTagProxy({
    url : 'http://extjsinaction.com/getEmployees.php'
});

var employeeDvStore = {
    xtype    : 'jsonstore',
    root     : 'rows',
    autoLoad : true,
    storeId  : 'employeeDv',
    proxy    : employeeStoreProxy,
    fields   : [
        { name : 'datehired',  mapping : 'datehired'  },
        { name : 'department', mapping : 'department' },
        { name : 'email',      mapping : 'email'      },
        { name : 'firstname',  mapping : 'firstname'  },
        { name : 'id',         mapping : 'id'         },
        { name : 'lastname',   mapping : 'lastname'   },
        { name : 'middle',     mapping : 'middle'     },
        { name : 'title',      mapping : 'title'      }
    ]
};
```

❶ Create remote Proxy
❷ Configure JsonStore XType

You create the `JsonStore` for your `DataView` in listing 9.2, which leverages a remote `ScriptTagProxy` ❶ to perform the data request tasks. When creating the `JsonStore` ❷ XType, you set `autoLoad` to `true`, which will automatically cause the proxy to fire the request after instantiation. You also define the field mappings inline for all of the required data points. This will help you in constructing the `XTemplate`.

Because the `Store` is a nonvisual component, there's not much to see at this point. You'll begin by constructing the `XTemplate` in the next listing, and then we'll have a brief discussion about it because it's important to understand how the data that will be passed to the `XTemplate` is applied to construct the DOM fragments.

```
var employeeDVTpl = new Ext.XTemplate(
    '<tpl for=".">',
        '<div class="emplWrap" id="employee_{id}">',
            '<div class="emplName">{lastname}, {firstname} {title}</div>',
            '<div>',
                '<span class="title">Department:</span>'
                '{department}',
            '</div>',
            '<div>',
            '<span class="title">Email:</span>',
            '<a href="#">{email}</a>',
            '</div>',
        '</div>',
    '</tpl>'
);
```

❶ Template branch data point
❷ Record displaying HTML fragment

In order for a `DataView` to render data onscreen, it needs an Ext JS `Template`. This is why you instantiate an instance of `Ext.XTemplate` first ❶. Although we're not going to dive too deeply into the usage of XTemplates, I do feel that it's important to discuss what the XTemplate is doing. This is your first exposure to this Component, and many developers commonly overlook the tpl tag and the for attribute ❷. I want to make sure you're not one of them.

The first (and last) tags that are specified in the XTemplate list of arguments are tpl, and they help the XTemplate organize logical branches of HTML. In the first tpl tag, there is a for attribute, which specifies which data point the XTemplate is to use to fill in for that branch. To help you understand this, we'll quickly examine the data returned by the server and ponder how the Template would look if the data were different.

Each of the Records the XTemplate will use is constructed like the following plain JavaScript object:

```
{
    'id'        : '1',
    'firstname' : 'Karyn',
    'lastname'  : 'Chase',
    ...
}
```

By setting the for attribute of the tpl tag with a single period ".", the XTemplate knows that the branch below the tpl will use the root object to fill the data points as specified in the HTML fragment defined within.

Figure 9.3 shows what that Record looks like stamped out in the DOM with the XTemplate we just defined.

The HTML fragment illustrated in the figure shows the Template filled out with the data for a single Record. Notice that all of the data points that are defined in the XTemplate are replaced by the actual data from the *root* of the Record.

Okay, but what if the requirement was for phone numbers to be displayed in a flexible fashion—to display only what's in the record? For this, the data might be structured differently.

For instance, added to the following object is a phoneNumbers property, which is an array of objects containing the phone type and number:

```
▼ <div id="employee_1" class="emplWrap">
      <div class="emplName"> Chase, Karyn Dr. </div>
   ▼ <div>
         <span class="title"> Department: </span>
         Sales and Marketing
      </div>
   ▼ <div>
         <span class="title"> Date Hired: </span>
         09/21/2004
      </div>
   ▼ <div>
         <span class="title"> Email: </span>
         <a href="#"> karyn.chase@mycompany.com </a>
      </div>
   </div>
```

Figure 9.3 A rendered HTML fragment as viewed in Firebug's DOM inspection panel

```
{
    'id'           : '1',
    'firstname'    : 'Karyn',
    'lastname'     : 'Chase',
    ...
    'phoneNumbers' : [
        {
            'type' : 'Mobile',
            'num'  : '555-123-4567'
        },
        {
            'type' : 'Office',
            'num'  : '555-765-4321'
        }
    ]
};
```

In this case, the XTemplate to consume this data would look like the following:

```
var otherTemplate = new Ext.XTemplate(
    '<tpl for=".">',
        '<div class="emplWrap" id="employee_{id}">',
            '<div class="emplName">{lastname}, {firstname} {title}</div>',
            '<div>',
                <span class="title">Department:</span>',
                {department},
            '</div>',
            '<div>',
                '<span class="title">Date Hired:</span>',
                '{datehired}',
            '</div>',
            '<div>',
                '<span class="title">Email:</span> ',
                '<a href="#">{email}</a>',
            '</div>',
            '<tpl for="phoneNumbers">',
                '<div><span class="title">{type}:</span> {num}</div>',
            '</tpl>',
        '</div>',
    '</tpl>'
);
```

Notice the second `tpl` tag toward the end of the argument list. This denotes another branch of the HTML fragment, and the `for` attribute specifies that this branch is *for* the `"phoneNumbers"` property, which happens to be an array. For every object in that array, XTemplate will loop through and produce a copy of that branch of HTML. Figure 9.4 shows that HTML fragment.

Notice that there are two `div` elements for the `phoneNumber` objects, and the values for the mapped properties are populated within. You now

---

Learn more about `XTemplates`

Though we won't be touching on the `XTemplate`'s many capabilities, it's important to note that the Ext JS API has well-written examples of the `XTemplate` on the API documentation page: http://www.extjs.com/deploy/dev/docs/?class=Ext.XTemplate.

```
▼ <div id="employee_1" class="emplWrap">
      <div class="emplName">Chase, Karyn Dr. </div>
   ▼ <div>
         <span class="title">Department: </span>
         Sales and Marketing
      </div>
   ▼ <div>
         <span class="title">Date Hired: </span>
         09/21/2004
      </div>
   ▼ <div>
         <span class="title">Email: </span>
         <a href="#">karyn.chase@mycompany.com</a>
      </div>
   ▼ <div>
         <span class="title">Mobile: </span>
         555-123-4567
      </div>
   ▼ <div>
         <span class="title">Office: </span>
         555-765-4321
      </div>
   </div>
```

Figure 9.4 The exploded HTML fragment that can be produced by the XTemplate with a for loop

know how to flex some of the XTemplate's muscle, and you're better prepared for a similar situation.

You now have your XTemplate (employeeDvTpl) constructed and a basic understanding of what the tpl tag and for attribute arguments are and what they do. We can now move forward with constructing the DataView and placing it in a Viewport.

9.2.2 Building the DataView and Viewport

In the following listing, you'll construct the DataView that will display all of the employees in the company.

Listing 9.4 Constructing the DataView

```
var employeeDv = new Ext.DataView({
    tpl             : employeeDvTpl,                                     Instantiate new
    store           : employeeDvStore,                               ❶ DataView
    singleSelect    : true,
    itemSelector    : 'div.emplWrap',                                    Enable single-node
    selectedClass   : 'emplSelected',                                ❷ selection
    overClass       : 'emplOver',
    style           : 'overflow:auto; background-color: #FFFFFF;'
});
```

To construct the DataView ❶, not much configuration has to be applied. Most of the code to create a DataView occurs in the configuration or instantiation of the supporting data Store and XTemplate. But it's important to take a good look at the configuration options that have been supplied.

Other than the usage of the template and store, you set `singleSelect` ❷ to the Boolean value `true`. Setting this property as such will instruct the `DataView` to allow single or multiple (`multiSelect`) node selections when `DataView`'s element is clicked. This is important when you want a rendered `Record` to be selectable. We set this property to `true` because I have a strong feeling that the company will want to do something with this `DataView` in the future, such as update `Records` when an item is selected.

In order to help the `DataView` along with the selection of a node, when setting `singleSelect` or `multiSelect` properties to `true` you must set the `itemSelector` property, which must be filled in with a proper CSS selector. This property helps the `DataView` hone in on the element that you want to be displayed as selected. It also helps with managing the visual cues for mouseover. The selector that you set will help the `DataView` highlight the entire `Record`. In this case, you're using the `div` element with the CSS class `emplWrap` as the selector.

Next, you set `selectedClass` and `overClass` for the CSS classes that you defined earlier, and they'll be used to give the user visual cues as to when a `Record` is selected or when the mouse hovers over a `Record`.

In order to allow automatic scrolling of the `DataView`'s element, you need to manually set the CSS on the element. I elected to include it inline to help you see the CSS being applied for automatic scrolling; you can just as easily replace the style with `cls`, whose value is a CSS class to enable automatic scrolling.

This concludes the `DataView` construction. You need to give it a home. Because the client wants a full-screen view, you should place this in a `Viewport`, which is what you'll do in the next listing.

Listing 9.5   Constructing the `Viewport`

```
new Ext.Viewport({
    layout       : 'hbox',           ◁┐  Create the
    defaults     : {                  ❶  Viewport
          : 1
    },
    layoutConfig : {
        align : 'stretch'
    },
    items        : [
        {
            title  : 'Employees',    ◁┐  Panel to
            frame  : true,            ❷  manage DataView
            layout : 'fit',
            items  : employeeDv      ◁┐  Include
        }                             ❸  employee DataView
    ]
});
```

Here you instantiate an instance of `Viewport` ❶ to help render the `DataView` to take up the full browser view. You could instruct the `Viewport` to use the `FitLayout`, because there's a single child element, but to have room for future expansion, you'll use the `HBoxLayout`.

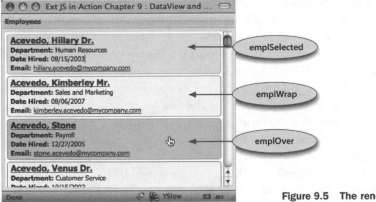

Figure 9.5 The rendered DataView

Also, notice that the first child item for the Viewport is a Panel ❷, whose layout is 'fit' and has its frame property set to true. Wrapping the DataView ❸ in a Panel will allow you to provide a nice blue frame around it, helping users understand what they're looking at.

This concludes the construction of the DataView. Let's see what this thing looks like and how it behaves onscreen (figure 9.5).

Our DataView renders onscreen, giving users the ability to view all of the employees in the company. You can see that the mouseover event is properly tracked and a single rendered Record can be selected. Great!

But something isn't right. The UI seems somewhat slow. The initial render of the data is slow, and when the browser is resized, the UI update lags significantly, as apparent in figure 9.6.

If you look at the Store, you'll see 2,000 Records onscreen. Surely this is impacting performance. Also, users would most likely complain if we bombarded them with that many rows at a time. We need to come up with a way to increase performance. We need to take a moment to ponder the possible solutions.

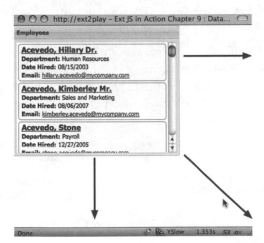

Figure 9.6 Because there are too many Records onscreen, the simple act of resizing the browser results in a visual delay of the Ext Viewport resize.

A quick fix would be to add a `PagingToolbar` to the `DataView`'s parent `Panel` and bind it to the `DataView`'s `Store`. Surely this would assist with the performance, but it wouldn't really make the `DataView` usable. Even if we split 2,000 `Records` into 100-`Record` pages, users would have to flip through 20 pages of data to get what they want. How can we increase performance and make it more usable?

What's that you say? Display the `Records` by department? Yes! I love that idea. Okay, but how? We could use a `ComboBox`, but the list of departments wouldn't be static. Also, it would require two clicks to select a department. I think users would want something that contained a static list of `Records`, allowing them to filter the list by means of a single click to select a department.

We could use another `DataView`, but I think it would be helpful to display the number of employees in each department, which means we need something that can easily manage the data in a column format. A `GridPanel` would be a nice choice, but it's overkill. It has features such as column drag and drop, which aren't needed and add costs to the UI. I think this is a perfect job for the `ListView`.

9.3   *Enter the ListView*

We just constructed a `DataView` that renders data about all of our company's employees onscreen at one time, and its performance is less than ideal. We determined that we should use the `ListView` to display the departments in our company and how many employees each department contains. But what's a `ListView`?

The `ListView` widget is a subclass of the `DataView` class that provides a means of displaying data in a tabular format and has a few of the features from the `DataView` and `GridPanel`. These features include resizable and sortable `Columns`, selectable `Records`, and the ability to have customized `Templates`.

> **NOTE** Even though the `ListView` presents a `GridPanel`-like UI, it's not designed to be used in place of the `GridPanel` where `GridPanel`-specific features are required. For instance, the `ListView` doesn't have the ability for horizontal scrolling and has no native support for editing the data inline like the `EditorGridPanel`. The `ListView` also doesn't have the ability to drag and drop `Columns`, nor does it include a `Column` menu.

The `ListView` also comes prepackaged with a `Template` and required CSS, which makes it a cinch to implement, as you'll see. Let's construct the `ListView` that you'll need. After all of the configuration required to use the `DataView`, you'll see that constructing a `ListView` is much easier. This code will have to be placed before the `Viewport`, because it will be rendered next to the `DataView`.

Listing 9.6   Constructing the `ListView`

```
var listViewStore = new Ext.data.ScriptTagProxy({          Create
    url : 'http://extjsinaction.com/getDepartments.php'  ❶ ScriptTagProxy
});

var departmentLvStore = {            ❷ Configure JsonStore
    xtype    : 'jsonstore',
```

```
    root     : 'records'
    autoLoad : true,
    storeId  : 'departmentDv',
    proxy    : listViewStore,
    fields   : [
        { name : 'department',   mapping : 'department'   },
        { name : 'numEmployees', mapping : 'numEmployees' }
    ]
};

var departmentLV = new Ext.ListView({          ◄──❸ Create ListView
    store          : departmentLvStore,
    singleSelect   : true,
    style          : 'background-color: #FFFFFF;',
    columns        : [                          ◄─┐  Configure
        {                                         │  ListView's
            header    : 'Department Name',      ❹  Columns
            dataIndex : 'department'
        },
        {
            header    : '# Emp,',
            dataIndex : 'numEmployees',
            width     : .20
        }
    ]
});
```

To construct the ListView, you begin with the creation of ScriptTagProxy ❶ to fetch and feed the data to the reader of the ListView-supporting JsonStore ❷. The Json-Store is pulling only the department name and number of employees per Record.

Next, you create the ListView ❸ to display the departments. In addition to the previously created JsonStore, the configuration properties contain singleSelect, to enable selection. Because the ListView ships with prebuilt CSS rules and a Template, you needn't specify the overCls, selectedCls, and itemSelector properties. But if you do want to use a custom Template for your own projects, you'll most likely have to set those properties accordingly to match your Template.

Next, you style the ListView with a white background. By default, the ListView element contains no background styling and would appear blue when it renders in the wrapped Panel because you set the Panel's frame property to true. Notice that you don't have to set the scroll CSS rule. This is because the ListView sets its element to automatically scroll for you.

Finally, you set a columns ❹ property, which is an array of objects that are used to configure the Columns that will vertically organize the data. The second Column is configured to display the number of employees for the departments. Notice that the width is .20, which is to express the percentage of the ListView width that column will take. Because there's no horizontal scrolling with this grid-like widget, the Column-sizing rules are a bit convoluted. Knowing these rules will help you understand why we've configured these Columns this way and in further implementations of this widget.

The first rule is that Column widths are always expressed as a percentage of the ListView's container. If no Column widths are configured, the ListView will automatically size each `Column` equally to fit the `ListView`'s element. This means that for any `Columns` that you wish to have some control over the widths, you must configure them. Otherwise, if left blank, they'll be automatically resized.

To translate these rules to listing 9.6, because the `'Department Name'` `Column` has no defined width property, it will be stretched to the remaining width of the `ListView` after 20 percent has been carved out for the `'# Emp'` `Column`. This gives the `'Department Name'` `Column` as much room as possible and makes the `'# Emp'` `Column` small enough to display the data without being truncated.

The `ListView` is now set up and ready to be rendered onscreen. Let's wrap the `ListView` in a `Panel` and place it in a `Viewport` to the left of the `DataView`. To do this, you'll have to modify the `Viewport`'s `items` array. Here's what the changes should look like:

```
items  :  [
    {
        title  : 'All Departments',
        frame  : true,
        layout : 'fit',
        items  : departmentLV,
        flex   : null,
        width  : 210
    },
    {
        title  : 'Employees',
        frame  : true,
        layout : 'fit',
        items  : employeeDv
    }
 ]
```

To add the `ListView` to the `Viewport`, you wrap it in a `Panel`. You inject it before the Employees `DataView` so it will be rendered to the left-most column and have a static width. Figure 9.7 shows what the `ListView` looks like rendered next to the `DataView`.

Cool! The `ListView` renders to the left of the `DataView`, and department `Records` can be selected. There are two problems with the current implementation of these two widgets. The first should be obvious—nothing happens when you select a `Record`. Also, the Employees `DataView` is still loading the 2,000 `Records`. In order to finish this, you'll need to bind the `DataView` to the `ListView` and prevent it from loading all of those `Records` automatically.

9.3.1   Binding the DataView to the ListView

We just solved the problem of displaying the departments and their total number of employees by implementing a `ListView` and rendering it to the left of the Employees `DataView`, but we didn't bind them to solve the performance problem. To do this, we'll first need to prevent the `DataView`'s store from automatically loading. This one is easy. Set the `autoLoad` property of the `employeeDvStore` as follows:

```
autoLoad : false
```

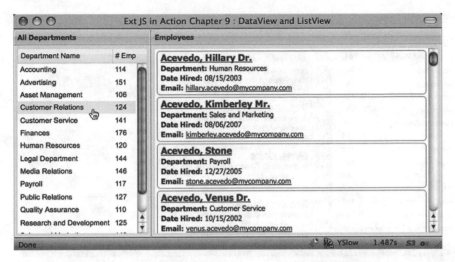

Figure 9.7 The ListView (left) rendered with the DataView (right)

Next comes the fun part: configuring a click listener for the ListView to call on the DataView's store to request the employees for the department that's selected. To do this, you'll need to add the following listeners configuration object to the List-View's config properties.

```
listeners : {
    click : function(thisView, index) {
        var record = thisView.store.getAt(index);
        if (record) {
            Ext.StoreMgr.get('employeeDv').load({
                params : {
                    department : record.get('department')
                }
            });
        }
    }
}
```

By adding this listener to the ListView, you ensure that the DataView is loaded with the Records that represent the department desired by the users. Here's how it works.

The click event generated by the DataView (remember, ListView is a descendant of DataView) passes the source view Component and the index of the Node that was clicked as located by the configured itemSelector. You attempt to create a reference of the Record selected to instruct the Employees DataView to load. If the Record is defined, then you use the Ext.StoreMgr.get method to obtain a reference to the Employees DataView store by its ID and call its load method. You pass in an object, which contains a params object. The params object contains the department name that was selected.

The load method call will instruct the Employees DataView store to call on the proxy to invoke a request for the employees of the selected department, as shown in figure 9.8. Let's examine how this changes the behavior thus far.

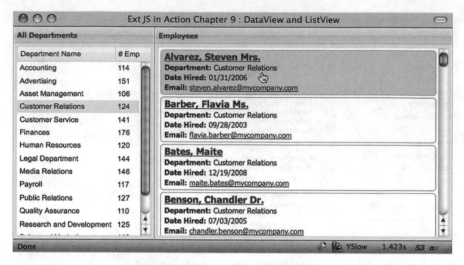

Figure 9.8   The `ListView`'s (left) `click` event now filters the `DataView` (right).

Excellent. The `ListView` now filters the `DataView` as you've configured it to. You can see that the changes result in a much more responsive UI for the user.

I've sent this over to the users, and they've responded expressing their appreciation but have one last request. They want the ability to modify the data for the employee selected. To do this you'll have to configure a `FormPanel` and add it to the `Viewport`. This gives you an excellent opportunity to learn how to bind a `FormPanel` to a `DataView` and observe the `DataView`'s ability to efficiently update data on HTML onscreen.

9.4   *Bringing it all together*

In order to allow users to edit the employee `Records`, you'll need to create a `Form-Panel` for them. The `FormPanel` needs to have a `Button` to allow them to commit the saved changes. In order to get all of this stuff to work together, you'll have to create a small event model. Here's how this stuff will work.

Figure 9.9 shows the proposed layout changes and proposed event handlers and their expected behavior.

To populate the `FormPanel` with the selected data, you'll have to reconfigure the `DataView` with a click handler to get the job done. Also, the `FormPanel`'s Save `Button` will be required to set the various properties on the `Record` to update the `DataView`. Last, the Departments `ListView` will have to clear the `FormPanel`'s values when it's clicked to avoid an exception. It sounds like a lot of work, but it's not. You've done most of it alsready.

Let's begin by creating the `FormPanel` and adding it to the `Viewport`. Then we'll circle back and work on the bindings.

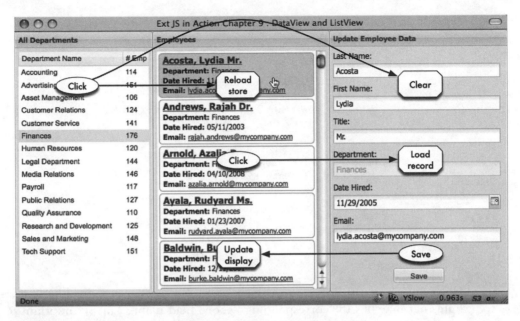

Figure 9.9 The addition of the `FormPanel` and the required event model

9.4.1 Configuring the FormPanel

The following listing is lengthy, but it's mainly due to the number of fields that need to be in the form. The following code needs to be placed just before the instance of `Viewport` is created.

Listing 9.7 Constructing the `FormPanel`

```
var updateForm = {
    frame       : true,
    id          : 'updateform',
    labelWidth  : 70,
    xtype       : 'form',
    defaultType : 'textfield',
    buttonAlign : 'center',
    title       : 'Update Employee Data',
    labelAlign  : 'top',
    defaults    : {
        anchor : '-5'
    },
    items       : [
        {
            name       : 'lastname',
            fieldLabel : 'Last Name'
        },
        {
            name       : 'firstname',
            fieldLabel : 'First Name'
        },
```

```
        {
            name        : 'title',
            fieldLabel  : 'Title'
        },
        {
            name        : 'department',
            fieldLabel  : 'Department',
            disabled    : true
        },
        {
            xtype       : 'datefield',
            name        : 'datehired',
            fieldLabel  : 'Date Hired'
        },
        {
            name        : 'email',
            fieldLabel  : 'Email'
        }
    ]
};
```

Here you create the `FormPanel` with six fields. Notice that each field has a `name` attribute that matches the corresponding `Record` field name. This is important to know because if you want to load the `Record`, the field name must match the `Record` that it will be configured to consume.

The Department field is disabled because the users have indicated that they don't want to use this tool to update departments. They want a drag-and-drop tool for that, which we'll be tasked to build later on.

Next, you'll place it in the `Viewport`. Here's what the modified `items` array will look like:

```
items           : [
    {
        title  : 'All Departments',
        frame  : true,
        layout : 'fit',
        items  : departmentLV,
        flex   : null,
        width  : 210
    },
    {
        title  : 'Employees',
        frame  : true,
        layout : 'fit',
        items  : employeeDv,
        flex   : 1
    },
    updateForm
]
```

Notice that all you're doing is adding the `updateForm` reference to the end of the list, which will make it appear to the right of the Employees `DataView`. Figure 9.10 shows what it will look like rendered.

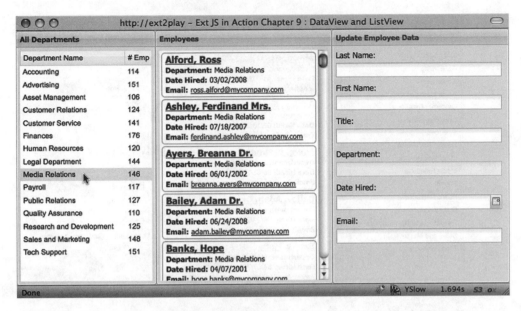

Figure 9.10 The `ListView` (left), `DataView` (center), and `FormPanel` (right)

The `FormPanel` renders perfectly, which means you're ready to begin the bindings. This is where the fun begins.

9.4.2 *Applying the final bindings*

You'll begin by binding the Employees `DataView` to the `FormPanel` by means of a click handler, which will retrieve the selected `Record` and call on the `FormPanel`'s Basic-Form to load the `Record`. To assist with the task of binding the `FormPanel` to the `Data-View`, you'll set a local reference to the selected `Record` on the `FormPanel` itself.

To add the click handler to the Employees `DataView`, you'll need to add the following `listeners` object to its configuration object:

```
listeners : {
    click : function(thisDv, index) {
        var record = thisDv.store.getAt(index);
        var formPanel = Ext.getCmp('updateform');
        formPanel.selectedRecord = record;
        formPanel.getForm().loadRecord(record);
    }
}
```

This code snippet works just like the click handler you assigned to the `ListView` a bit earlier. The difference is that you're setting the `Record` reference on the `FormPanel` and calling on its `BasicForm`'s `loadRecord` to set the values of the fields. Notice that the `Record` reference that's being set is `selectedRecord`. This will be key when you work on the round-trip binding.

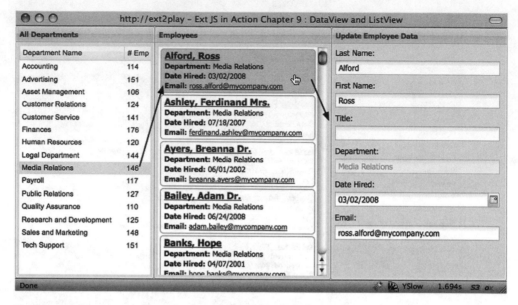

Figure 9.11   Testing the `DataView` to `FormPanel` binding

You can test this by refreshing the page, selecting a department, and then choosing an employee. The `Record` should load and the fields should be set with the data accordingly, as shown in figure 9.11.

Excellent! You have your one-way binding from the `DataView` to the `FormPanel` in place. In order to commit the changes, the users will need a Save `Button`. To do this, you'll have to add a `buttons` property to the `FormPanel`'s configuration object with a single `Button`, whose text is "Save." The handler will be responsible for leveraging the recently set `FormPanel`'s `selectedRecord` and setting its value according to the changes made on the `FormPanel`.

Add the following snippet to the `FormPanel`:

```
buttons : [
    {
        text    : 'Save',
        handler : function() {
            var formPanel = Ext.getCmp('updateform');
            if (formPanel.selectedRecord) {
                var vals  = formPanel.getForm().getValues();

                for (var valName in vals) {
                    formPanel.selectedRecord.set(valName, vals[valName]);
                }
                formPanel.selectedRecord.commit();
            }
        }
    }
]
```

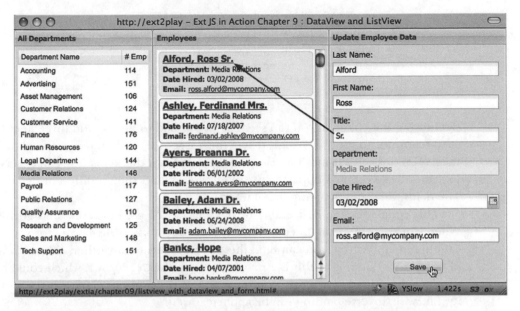

Figure 9.12   Testing the round-trip binding of the FormPanel to the DataView

When the newly configured Button is pressed, it will use Ext.getCmp to get a reference to the FormPanel. If it contains a selectedRecord property, it will loop through each value retrieved from the form and set the Record's corresponding property accordingly. Last, the Record's commit method is called, making the changes permanent and causing the DataView to repaint only the Node that was modified.

As illustrated in figure 9.12, clicking Media Relations and then Alford Ross will cause that employee's Record to populate the FormPanel. I added "Sr." to the Record, because the value was missing, and clicked the newly added Save Button. What you can immediately see is that the rendered Record is updated based on the data from the FormPanel, completing the two-way binding between the DataView and the FormPanel.

> **NOTE**   Because the exercises in this chapter leverage a remote data Store, we can't save data via Ajax because of the same-domain policy that the XHR object enforces. This is why this example doesn't invoke a form submission.

The last thing you need to do is code the clearing of the FormPanel when the Department ListView selection changes. This will help prevent exceptions that the user might cause if they attempt an update on a Record that might not be there because of a department selection change.

Replace the previously developed click handler with the following code:

```
click : function(thisView, index) {
    var record = thisView.store.getAt(index);
    if (record) {
        Ext.StoreMgr.get('employeeDv').load({
            params : {
```

```
                    department : record.get('department')
            }
        });
        var formPanel = Ext.getCmp('updateform');
        delete formPanel.selectedRecord;
        formPanel.getForm().reset();
    }
}
```

By studying the changes, you can see that all you had to do was add three lines to create a reference to the `FormPanel`, delete the `selectedRecord` reference, and then call the `BasicForm`'s `reset` method, clearing the data from the fields. You can observe this in action by selecting a department, an employee, and then a different department. The fields will clear, signaling that it works.

This concludes the deliverable of binding `DataView`, `ListView`, and `FormPanel`. When you encounter the need to implement a `DataView` or `ListView` for your application, remember that you can bind these two widgets to any other widgets by means of events. An example of this is a `rowclick` event of a `GridPanel`, which could trigger the data `Store` load of a `DataView` or `ListView` to provide a level of drill-down capability. Likewise, inverse binding can be applied as well.

9.5   *Summary*

In this chapter we explored two commonly used widgets, the `DataView` and its cousin the `ListView`. In doing so, we not only looked at how they work but also saw how to bind them together, applying advanced concepts that could be carried into any application.

We began by explaining what a `DataView` is and what it takes to configure one. While exploring the `DataView`, we took some time to discuss one of its supporting classes, the `XTemplate`. By an example, you saw that you're required to create the CSS to style the painted data onscreen.

Next, you learned about the `ListView` class and the features it provides. We discussed the rules of the column-sizing model, and you learned how to bind the `ListView` to a `DataView` by means of a `click` event.

Last, you learned how to create a two-way binding between a `FormPanel` and a `DataView` to allow your users to update the data for the employees. In doing so, you got to witness the efficiency of the `DataView` in updating only the DOM linked to the record that was updated.

Next, we'll tackle the use of `Charts`, and you'll learn how to configure them to respond to click gestures.

10

Charts

This chapter covers

- Learning the basics of Ext JS `Charts`
- Deconstructing the `Chart` class hierarchy
- Exploring the various `Charts` available in the framework
- Implementing each of the `Charts`
- Mixing a `Chart` series into a hybrid `Chart`
- Customizing the look and feel of your hybrid `Chart`

Many of the applications that I've developed in the past have required data visualization. Whether it was the amount of space used for a particular disk volume or the value of a stock over time, the problems were exactly the same and ultimately amounted to a couple of major factors: which charting package will be used, and how much is it going to cost to integrate and ultimately manage?

All of this introduces risk to the application and adds support costs, which dissatisfies customers. Thankfully, this is all now behind us. Ext JS 3.0 provides a charting package that handles the four most commonly used charts—line, bar, column, and pie—thus mitigating the risk of using and supporting a third-party charting package and reducing support costs.

In this chapter, you'll learn all about `Ext.charts`. We'll begin by exploring the anatomy of charts and discussing the various classes that compose the chart package. We'll also visually explore the different types of charts available to you.

Next, we'll take an exploratory approach when talking about the different charts in the framework. You'll begin by creating a basic `LineChart` and learn how to customize the colors used, create a custom `ToolTip` renderer method, and display legends.

Because the `LineChart`, `ColumnChart`, and `BarChart` are based on the same basic chart, you'll use your newly found knowledge to convert the `LineChart` to a `ColumnChart` and a `BarChart` by literally flipping the x- and y-axis configurations. You'll also learn how to create hybrid charts, such as `ColumnCharts` with embedded `LineSeries`.

In the final section, you'll learn all about the `PieChart` and how it differs from the three other basic charts. You'll also learn how to add context to the `PieChart` `ToolTip` by means of a custom tip-renderer function, making it much more useful.

10.1   *Defining the four charts*

Charts provide the ability to visualize statistical data in a graphic format. There are four basic types of charts: line, bar, column, and pie. `LineChart`, `BarChart`, and `ColumnChart` are similar because they're based on the same *Cartesian*-style chart, where points of data are plotted in a two-dimensional X-Y coordinate plane system.

This is why you can mix the `Bar` and `LineSeries` in the same chart. Likewise, you can mix the `LineSeries` with the `ColumnSeries` in a `Chart`. But `Column` and `BarSeries` can't exist in the same `Chart`.

The `PieChart` is kind of a black sheep of the chart classes. Because it isn't based on the `CartesianChart` system, it can only leverage the `PieSeries` and is designed to display data representing percentages.

What makes using charts in the framework so cool is that you need not have any Flash experience to get this stuff to work for you. As you'll see, everything will be done via JavaScript.

Let's look at a line chart in action and analyze it; see figure 10.1.

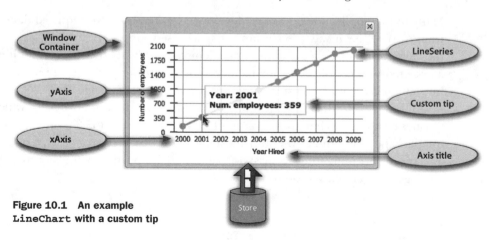

**Figure 10.1   An example
`LineChart` with a custom tip**

Extcharts are based on the YUI Charts library and are wired to consume data from a data Store, much like the GridPanel and DataView classes. Because Charts follow the same pattern as every other data Store consumer class, providing data for this widget requires no additional knowledge. This binding also provides the benefit of automatic Chart updates when data in the Store changes, which could be displayed with or without animation.

Users have the ability to interact with Charts with the mouse by means of mouseover and click gestures. A mouseover gesture can provide useful information by means of a ToolTip, which can be customized, as shown in figure 10.1.

The click gesture can provide powerful user interaction with your Charts, allowing users to click a point in the LineSeries, a bar in the BarSeries, a column in the ColumnSeries, or a slice in the PieSeries to make stuff happen in the UI, such as drilling down into that data point for a more fine-grained view of the data. This works by means of the Chart's itemclick event, which we'll explore and use when we start to build our first Charts.

Next, we'll look under the hood and peek at the Components that make Charts work.

10.2 Charts deconstructed

Like everything else UI, Charts can be rendered to any div on the page or configured as a child item of any parent Container widget. This is because the Chart classes are descendants of the BoxComponent class, which, if you recall, gives any Component the ability to take part in a layout.

Figure 10.2 shows a hierarchy diagram for the Chart classes.

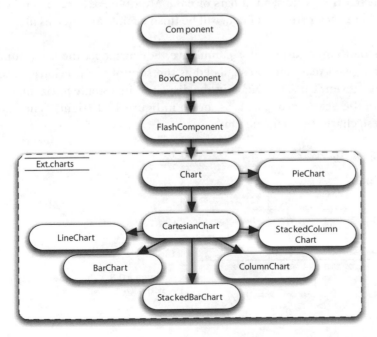

Figure 10.2   The Chart class hierarchy

Charts are Adobe Flash–based and require special handling when compared to generic HTML objects. For instance, if Flash is to be displayed on a page, logic needs to be in place to detect whether the browser has Flash and, if so, whether it's the correct version. If Flash isn't installed or if the version is less than what's required, a link to install Flash is rendered in the area where the Flash content is to be; otherwise, the Flash widget is rendered onscreen and all is well. Managing this type of logic, in addition to the cross-browser markup differences, can be quite a hassle on your own.

Luckily, the `FlashComponent` takes care of this for us and serves as the base class for the `Charts`. The `FlashComponent` is a special class because it leverages the `SWFObject` to handle just about all Flash-specific issues and can be extended to allow Ext JS to manage any Flash-based content. It's for this reason that the `Chart` class subclasses `FlashComponent`.

Focusing on the `Chart` class, which exists in the `Ext.charts` namespace, you can see that it has two descendants, `PieChart` and `CartesianChart`. The `Chart` class is what wraps the YUI Charts and is what binds the data `Store` and mouse gesture events to the framework. It's the most heavyweight class in the entire hierarchy. Most of the work is done in the YUI Chart's compiled SWF, which is beyond the scope of this book.

Looking at the descendants of `CartesianChart`, you can see three major categories of charts: `LineChart`, `BarChart`, and `ColumnChart`. This is important to know when deciding how to implement them, because they're the three main Cartesian chart options available.

The `LineChart` is used to plot dots of intersecting data on the X-Y plane, and a line is drawn connecting those dots. Figure 10.3 illustrates a `LineChart` implementation that contains two `LineSeries`.

The `BarChart` displays horizontal bars of data. Multiple `BarSeries` can be added to the chart, where each category of data will be flush against another, as illustrated in figure 10.4.

Sometimes data to be displayed is cumulative. For instance, the total number of employees for a given year can be calculated as the sum of the previously hired and newly hired for a given year. This data must be displayed in a single horizontal line but segmented with the `StackedBarChart`, as shown in figure 10.4 (right). The data used for both of these charts is exactly the same.

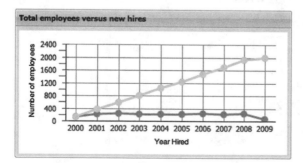

Figure 10.3 The `LineChart` with two `LineSeries`

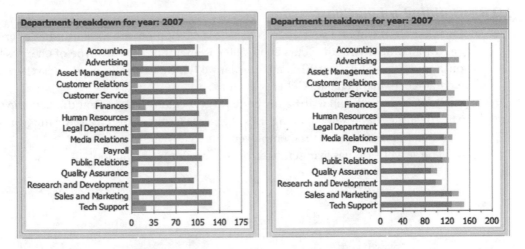

Figure 10.4 `BarChart` (left) and `StackedBarChart` (right) examples

The `ColumnChart` is used to plot the chart data in vertical bars. The columns can be stacked via the `StackedColumnChart`. Just like in figure 10.4, the data for figure 10.5 is the same in both charts.

In contrast to the Cartesian-style charts, the `PieChart` is used only to display percentages of data. Figure 10.6 is an illustration of a `PieChart` in action.

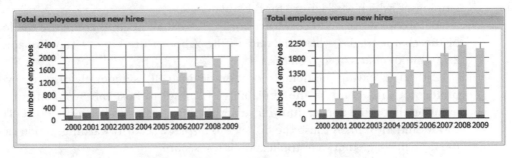

Figure 10.5 The `ColumnChart` (left) and `StackedColumnChart` (right)

Just as with the `LineChart`, `ColumnChart`, and `BarChart`, the `Series` for the `PieChart` (slices) can display a `ToolTip` when a mouseover gesture occurs. The `Series` can also be clicked, which will generate the useful `itemclick` event.

You now have a high-level understanding of which `Charts` are available and how they work, which means that we can begin the code exploration of the different `Charts`. We'll kick it off with the construction of a `LineChart`, where you'll learn the basics of `Chart` creation.

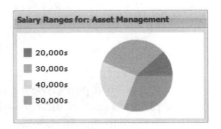

Figure 10.6 A `PieChart`

10.3 *Building a LineChart*

Our first chart will be a single-series `LineChart` that plots the total number of employees for a company for the years 2000–2009. Remember that this type of `Chart` is based on X and Y coordinates, which means that we'll have to configure the `Chart` to utilize a data `Store`–mapped data field for each `Axis`.

But before we begin writing the code for this `Chart`, let's look at the data the `Chart` will consume. Relatively speaking, this is an easy task, because we're dealing with only two data points: year and total employees for each year.

The server side has been crafted for us, and the JSON will look like this:

```
[
    {
        "newHires"  : 135,
        "year"      : 2000,
        "total"     : 136,
        "prevHired" : 1
    },
    ...
]
```

The JSON contains an array of objects representing records in the database. We can see the year and total attributes for each record. This means that we need to craft a `JsonStore` that will map these two fields. There are two other attributes per record that report the number of new hires (`newHires`) and previously hired (`prevHired`) employees, which we'll ignore for the time being.

Before we move on to construct our first chart, we need to configure the location of the charts.swf file, which defaults to the Yahoo! URL: http://yui.yahooapis.com/2.7.0/build/charts/assets/charts.swf.

Although leaving the default location of this URL is generally okay, many would prefer not to depend on the availability of Yahoo! to host the SWF content. Not to mention that if the application you're developing is going to be riding on HTTPS, this URL would most likely cause the browser to display a security warning, which can send the false message that your application is less secure.

Also, if your application is within a secured intranet, the client's browser may not have access to outside web servers, thus rendering `Charts` completely unusable. Configuring charts to require the SWF file from the local intranet server will help mitigate this issue.

To configure Ext JS to use a particular SWF for `Charts`, set the `CHART_URL` property on the `Chart` class as follows:

```
Ext.chart.Chart.CHART_URL = '<path to extjs>/resources/charts.swf';
```

You want to place this line of code just after the Ext JS base libraries. This will ensure that the property is set before your code begins to get parsed by the JavaScript interpreter. This is similar to setting the `BLANK_IMAGE_URL` (`'s.gif'`) configuration property earlier in this book.

With that out of the way, you can move on to create the `LineChart` that will plot this data onscreen, as follows.

Listing 10.1   Constructing a basic `LineChart`

```
var employeeStoreProxy = new Ext.data.ScriptTagProxy({
    url : 'http://extjsinaction.com/getNewHireData.php'
});

var remoteStore = {
    xtype    : 'jsonstore',
    root     : 'records',
    autoLoad : true,
    storeId  : 'employeeDv',
    proxy    : employeeStoreProxy,
    fields   : [
        { name : 'year',  mapping : 'year' },
        { name : 'total', mapping : 'total' }
    ]
};

var chart = {                                    ❶ Configure
    xtype      : 'linechart',                        LineChart XType
    store      : remoteStore,
    xField     : 'year',                             Set x- and
    yField     : 'total'                         ❷ y-axis fields
};

new Ext.Window({
    width  : 400,
    height : 400,
    layout : 'fit',
    items  : chart
}).show();
```

In listing 10.1, you create the data `Store` that maps the year and total fields that are provided by the server-side code and the line chart that lives in a `Window`. As you can see, creating a basic `Chart` is extremely simple to do. Here's how it works.

When creating the `LineChart` `XType` configuration object ❶, you set the mandatory xtype property and required JSON data `Store`. The next two properties, `xField` and `yField` ❷, are used to automatically create the x-axis and y-axis and map the data from the `Store`. That's pretty much it.

To display the `Chart`, you create a `Window` with the `FitLayout`, which hosts the `LineChart`. Figure 10.7 shows what our first `LineChart` looks like.

As illustrated in figure 10.7, our `LineChart` renders inside an `Ext.Window` plotting the statistical data. If you hover your mouse cursor over one of the points in the line, you'll see the two values for the point in a tip. But this presents a problem.

For this `Chart`, the data in the tip provides no context to the figures being presented, thus providing little value. Likewise, the x-axis and y-axis have the same dilemma. It's obvious that the number on the x-axis represents years. But you can't tell what the y-axis represents. This is precisely a situation where you'd want to customize the `Chart`.

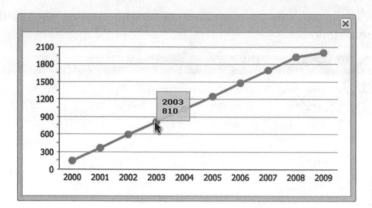

Figure 10.7
Our first `LineChart`

10.3.1 *Customizing the ToolTip*

The first problem we'll tackle is providing context for the `ToolTip`. To do this, you'll have to add a `tipRenderer` to your `LineChart` configuration object, as follows:

```
tipRenderer : function(chart, record, index, series){
    var yearInfo = 'Year: ' + record.data.year;
    var empInfo  = 'Num. employees: ' + record.data.total;

    return yearInfo + '\n' + empInfo ;
}
```

In this `tipRenderer` method, you create two strings, `yearInfo` and `empInfo`, which insert a meaningful label in front of the data. The method returns a concatenation of the `yearInfo` and `empInfo` with a newline character, `\n`, to introduce a line break between the two data fields. Why a newline character and not a standard <br />, you ask?

The `tipRenderer` function works similarly to the column renderer of the `Grid-Panel`, where the method is expected to return a string to be displayed onscreen; however, although the column renderer allows HTML, the `tipRenderer` doesn't. This is because the `ToolTip` is rendered inside Flash and doesn't support HTML. In order to introduce a line break between lines of data, the only way to do so is by means of the standard UNIX-style newline string (\n).

Figure 10.8 shows what the new `ToolTip` will render.

With the addition of the custom `tipRenderer`, `mouseover` events now provide context to the tips. Next, we'll work on customizing the x- and y-axes to add labels.

10.3.2 *Adding titles to the x- and y-axes*

To add labels to a Cartesian `Chart`, you must manually configure and create an axis. But you must use the correct axis for the type of data you're displaying. There are three possible axes to use: `CategoryAxis`, `NumericAxis`, and `TimeAxis`. Based on the `LineChart` we've created thus far, which axis would you choose for each x- and y-axis?

The values for each axis are numeric. The obvious choice is `NumericAxis` for both—right? Wrong. Here's why.

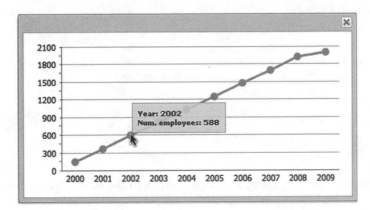

Figure 10.8
Our LineChart with our custom ToolTip

If you take a good look at how the CartesianCharts process data, you can tell that the Charts display two types of values: measurements and something that's being measured. The thing that's being measured in each Chart is known as the category.

Applying this to the LineChart, you can see that the measurement for our chart is the number of employees and the category is the year. The same logic can be applied to a Chart that measures how many sales car manufacturers have made, as shown in figure 10.9.

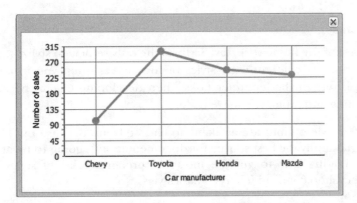

Figure 10.9 Categories of data are clearly defined in this car sales LineChart.

With this knowledge, you can see that the CategoryAxis is logically the only choice for the x-axis. This means you'll have to reconfigure the Chart to utilize new x- and y-axes, as shown here.

Listing 10.2 Reconfiguring the Chart to utilize new x- and y-axes

```
var chart =  {
    xtype       : 'linechart',
    store       : remoteStore,
    xField      : 'year',
    yField      : 'total',
    tipRenderer : function(chart, record, index, series){
        var yearInfo = 'Year: ' + record.data.year;
```

```
        var empInfo  = 'Num. employees: ' + record.data.total;
        return yearInfo + '\n' + empInfo ;
    },
    xAxis: new Ext.chart.CategoryAxis({          ◁──── Set the new x-axis
        title  : 'Year Hired'          ◁──── Title the x-axis
    }),

    yAxis: new
    Ext.chart.NumericAxis({
        title  : 'Number of employees'          ◁─┐ Use NumericAxis
    })                                             │ for y-axis
}
```

In listing 10.2, you add the xAxis and yAxis properties to the main Chart configuration object. The xAxis is set to an instance of CategoryAxis, whereas the yAxis property is set to an instance of NumericAxis. Each new axis is configured with a title parameter.

Let's see what it looks like after adding the newly overridden axis (figure 10.10).

If you look at the y-axis label, you can see that it's clearly wasting space. The only way to mitigate this issue this is to rotate the text, which can be done only through custom styling of this widget.

Next, you'll learn how to stylize the Chart body. Later on, you'll learn how to stylize the Series as well.

10.3.3 *Styling the Chart body*

In contrast to the rest of the framework, JavaScript is the only vehicle to stylize Charts. This means that you must configure the styles of the Charts when you instantiate them. To me, this is one of the lengthier tasks when developing Charts because it requires a lot of testing and ultimately more code.

> **NOTE** Quite a few style options are available to choose from. Because Ext JS uses YUI Charts, naturally the best source for documentation is going to be at YUI. Visit the following URL to get the most comprehensive list of styles: http://developer.yahoo.com/yui/charts/#basicstyles.

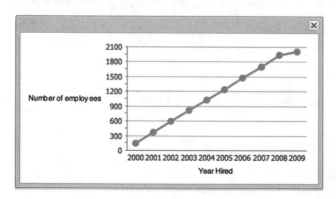

Figure 10.10   Adding y-axis titles without custom styling results in wasted screen space.

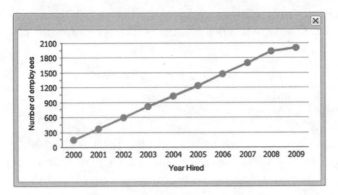

Figure 10.11 The `yAxis` is now rotated -90 degrees, which reduces wasted space.

In order to rotate the title, you need to include custom style configuration in your line `Chart`'s configuration object. This is done by means of setting the `extraStyle` property like so:

```
extraStyle : {
    yAxis: {
        titleRotation  : -90,
    }
}
```

In this code snippet, you create the `extraStyle` configuration object, which contains another configuration object for the y-axis. Inside the `yAxis` configuration object, the `titleRotation` property is set to `-90` (degrees).

Figure 10.11 shows what the newly styled `Chart` looks like.

You can see that by adding the `extraStyle` configuration property and its contents to our `LineChart`, it renders with the y-axis title rotated, thus reducing the amount of wasted space.

Thus far, you've created a single `LineChart` and have provided some light styling to improve its readability. There are a few more measurement figures to add to the `Chart`. To show these on the screen, you'll need to refactor the `Store` and `Chart` configuration completely.

10.4 Adding multiple Series

When you looked at the data being provided by the server side, you saw multiple data points that are related to the number of employees for a given year. If you peek at the data again, you can see that the other two figures are `newHires` and `prevHired`.

```
[
    {
        "newHires"  : 135,
        "year"      : 2000,
        "total"     : 136,
        "prevHired" : 1
    },
    ...
]
```

To make use of this data, you'll need to reconfigure the data Store to map the fields. Luckily, all you have to do is add the two fields to the mappings list for the data Store.

```
fields   : [
    { name : 'year',      mapping : 'year'       },
    { name : 'total',     mapping : 'total'      },
    { name : 'newHires',  mapping : 'newHires'   },
    { name : 'prevHired', mapping : 'prevHired'  }
]
```

Next comes the fun part: refactoring the Chart to add the extra Series. While you're at it, you'll apply custom styles to make the Chart much easier to read and more pleasing to look at. This is where you'll see that customizing Charts requires quite a bit of code, but it's easy once you understand it. This is why you'll break up the refactoring effort into smaller, more digestible chunks.

You'll begin with the configuration of the series, as follows.

Listing 10.3   Configuring the Series for our multiseries Chart

```
var series =  [
    {
        yField       : 'prevHired',                  ❶ Map data point
        displayName : 'Previously Hired',               to Series          ❷ Display name for
        style       : {                                                       tips and legends
            fillColor    : 0xFFAAAA,    ❹ Set point's fill color
            borderColor : 0xAA3333,                                 ❸ Custom style
            lineColor    : 0xAA3333                                     for each Series
        }                               Configure        Specify point's
    },                               ❻ line color     ❺ border color
    {
        yField       : 'total',
        displayName : 'Total',
        style        : {
            fillColor    : 0xAAAAFF,
            borderColor : 0x3333FF,
            lineColor    : 0x3333FF
        }
    },
    {
        yField       : 'newHires',
        displayName : 'New Hires',
        style        : {
            fillColor    : 0xAAFFAA,
            borderColor : 0x33AA33,
            lineColor    : 0x33AA33
        }
    }
];
```

In listing 10.3, you create an array of configuration objects that are used to configure the three different Series. Here's what all of these properties do.

In each Series configuration object, you map the data points by means of the yField ❶ property. Setting the yField property replaces the yField property in the main chart configuration object. It may be easier to think of it as mapping the dataIndex to GridPanel columns. You also set the displayName ❷, which is used in both the ToolTip and the legend, which you'll learn about in a bit.

Next, you set a custom style ❸ configuration object for each series, which sets the color for the point's fill ❹ and border ❺ as well as the color for the lines ❻. Setting these styles will clearly distinguish each Series, enhancing Chart readability.

With the Series in place, you can move on to construct a tipRenderer that's much more flexible and create the extraStyle configuration, as shown in the following listing.

Listing 10.4   Creating a flexible `tipRenderer` and `extraStyle`

```
var tipRenderer = function(chart, rec, index, series){
    var yearInfo = 'Year: ' + rec.get('year');
    var empInfo =  series.displayName + ': '          ❶ Generate label
        + rec.get(series.yField);                         with displayName
    return yearInfo + '\n' + empInfo ;
 };

 var extraStyle = {
    xAxis : {
        majorGridLines : {                            ❷ Add vertical lines
            color : 0x999999,                            to Chart
            size  : 1
        }
    },
    yAxis: {
        titleRotation  : -90
    }
 };
```

In listing 10.4, you create the custom tipRenderer, which is much more flexible than the previous one. This is because this tipRenderer leverages the Series's display-Name ❶ to create the custom label for the Series. It also uses the Series's yField property to pull the mapped data, resulting in a truly dynamic tipRenderer.

Next, you create a configuration object to contain the custom style parameters. Along with the yAxis's titleRotation, you add an xAxis configuration object, which contains majorGridLines ❷. This configuration property instructs the Chart to display a vertical line for each category data point, resulting in intersecting lines across the entire grid area.

You now have all you need to configure the chart. Let's do that next.

Listing 10.5   Refactoring the `Chart`

```
var chart = {
    xtype       : 'linechart',
    store       : remoteStore,
    xField      : 'year',
    tipRenderer : tipRenderer,
    extraStyle  : extraStyle,
    series      : series,
```

```
xAxis         : new Ext.chart.CategoryAxis({
    title : 'Year Hired'
}),
yAxis : new Ext.chart.NumericAxis({
    title : 'Number of employees'
})
};
```

To refactor the `Chart` configuration object, you remove the `yField` property. Remember that this is already present in each of the `Series` configuration objects and aren't needed in the `Chart` configuration. You also set the `tipRenderer`, `extraStyle`, and `series` properties to the variables that you created a bit earlier.

Figure 10.12 shows what the `Chart` now looks like rendered inside the `Window` you created earlier.

When looking at our multiseries `LineChart` you can see that each `Series` is colored differently and the vertical lines are now drawn at each x-axis data point. But you're left with a problem. In order to tell what figure each line represents, you have to mouse over a point on the graph, which isn't exactly user friendly.

The solution for this is to add a legend to the chart.

10.4.1 *Adding legends*

To add a legend to your `Chart`, you need only add the style configuration object to the `extraStyles` configuration object, like this:

```
legend : {
    display : 'bottom',
    padding : 5,
    spacing : 2,
    font    : { color : 0x000000,  family : 'Arial', size   : 12 },
    border  : { size : 1, color  : 0x999999 }
}
```

When you set the legend style configuration object, the property that controls whether the legend will display or not is `display`. This property defaults to `"none"`, which prevents it from displaying. In addition to `"bottom"`, it can be set to `"top"`, `"right"`, or `"left"`.

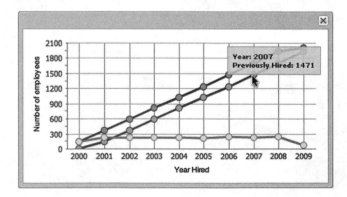

Figure 10.12   Our multiline `Chart` with much more custom styling

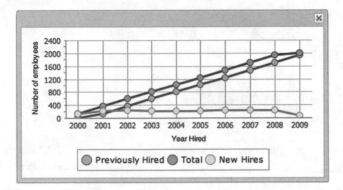

Figure 10.13 **The addition of the legend enhances readability for multiseries `Charts`.**

The `padding` property works much like the CSS padding style. The `spacing` property specifies how many pixels separate the `Series`. To configure the `font` and `border`, you have to create separate configuration properties for each. Remember that all of the possible styles are detailed in the YUI documentation.

The addition of the legend is shown in figure 10.13.

We've spent a lot of time on the `LineChart`, and you learned how to customize it quite a bit with the inclusion of a custom `tipRenderer`, multiple `Series`, and applicable styles. What about the `Column` and `Bar Charts`? How does the construction of each differ from the `LineChart`?

10.5 *Constructing ColumnCharts*

If you're comfortable with constructing `LineCharts`, then you'll be happy to learn that the construction of a `ColumnChart` is nearly identical. The biggest difference is that instead of setting the xtype to `'linechart'`, you set it to `'columnchart'`.

Here's the `LineChart` refactored into a `ColumnChart`.

Listing 10.6   Creating a `ColumnChart`

```
var chart = {
    xtype       : 'columnchart',
    store       : remoteStore,
    xField      : 'year',
    tipRenderer : tipRenderer,
    extraStyle  : extraStyle,
    series      : series,
    xAxis       : new Ext.chart.CategoryAxis({
        title : 'Year Hired'
    }),
    yAxis : new Ext.chart.NumericAxis({
        title  : 'Number of employees'
    })
};
```

It's that simple. Figure 10.14 shows what the `ColumnChart` looks like rendered onscreen.

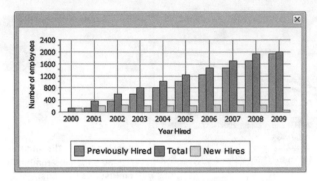

Figure 10.14
A multiseries `ColumnChart`

When looking at this `Chart`, it's hard to see that the number of newly hired plus previously hired employees equals the total number of employees. This is where the `StackedColumnChart` fits in.

10.5.1 *Stacking columns*

You just learned that the conversion from a `LineChart` to a `ColumnChart` is relatively simple. But to make this `Chart` much easier to read, you'll need to stack the columns. The conversion from a `ColumnChart` (or `LineChart` for that matter) is a bit more involved.

To make this conversion, you'll need to refactor the `series` array to remove the `Series` representing the total number of employees, because it's unnecessary:

```
var series = [
    {
        yField      : 'prevHired',
        displayName : 'Previously Hired',
        style       : {
            fillColor   : 0xFFAAAA,
            borderColor : 0xAA3333,
            lineColor   : 0xAA3333
        }
    },
    {
        yField      : 'newHires',
        displayName : 'New Hires',
        style       : {
            fillColor   : 0xAAFFAA,
            borderColor : 0x33AA33,
            lineColor   : 0x33AA33
        }
    }
];
```

Next you'll need to refactor the `Chart` configuration object a bit:

```
var chart = {
    xtype       : 'stackedcolumnchart',
    store       : remoteStore,
    xField      : 'year',
```

```
        tipRenderer : tipRenderer,
        extraStyle  : extraStyle,
        series      : series,
        xAxis       : new Ext.chart.CategoryAxis({
            title : 'Year Hired'
        }),
        yAxis : new Ext.chart.NumericAxis({
            stackingEnabled : true,
            title           : 'Number of employees'
        })
    };
```

In the newly refactored `Chart` configuration object, you set the `xtype` to `'stacked-columnchart'`. The only other change you'll make is the addition of the `stacking-Enabled` property to the y-axis, `NumericAxis`. These are the only changes necessary to construct a `StackedColumnChart`.

Here's what it looks like painted onscreen (figure 10.15).

When analyzing the results of the `StackedColumnChart`, you can see that the previously hired and newly hired employee figures appear stacked, amounting to the total number of employees for a given year. This is exactly what we wanted to do. But we introduced a problem. How do we find the total number of employees for a given year? Let's ponder the possibilities.

If we leave the total (`StackedColumn`) series in, then the sum of the columns will double, which is undesirable. Surely there has to be a way to allow the users to see the total.

One way to display the total is via the `ToolTip`. Although this would work, it's always best to keep the tip within the context of the `Series` being hovered over. We need something to tie the totals together.

A `LineSeries` would work perfectly for this situation.

10.5.2 *Mixing a line with columns*

Thus far, we've exercised the ability to leverage multiple `Series` in a `Chart`, but we haven't looked into configuring a hybrid `Chart`, that is, a chart with multiple types of `Series`. It's much easier than you'd think.

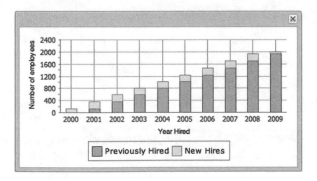

Figure 10.15
Our `StackedColumnChart`

To add a line `Series`, add the following `LineSeries`-style configuration object to the series array that you used to set up the `StackedColumnChart`:

```
{
    type        : 'line',
    yField      : 'total',
    displayName : 'Total',
    style       : {
        fillColor   : 0xAAAAFF,
        borderColor : 0x3333FF,
        lineColor   : 0x3333FF
    }
}
```

Notice that the configuration object for this newly added `Series` is almost identical to that of the total `Series` you removed when initially configuring the `StackedBarChart`. The item to key in on here is the `type` property, which is set to `'line'`.

Setting this property causes the framework to use a specific type of `Series` to display in a `Chart`. It's the XType equivalent for `Charts` and saves us time from having to directly instantiate an instance of `LineSeries`. To ensure that this line will render on top of the other `Series`, it's important that you add this `LineSeries` configuration as the last object of the `series` configuration object's array. How the `Series` are rendered onscreen is directly proportional to the order in which they're placed in the series array. To put this in context, think about z-order with CSS, and it will all make sense. The order of the `Series` also affects how they appear in the legend as well.

Look at the newly configured hybrid `LineChart` and `ColumnChart` in action in figure 10.16.

After adding the `LineSeries` to the `StackedColumnChart`, you can easily access the total figure data by hovering the mouse cursor over the points rendered by the newly added `LineSeries`.

We've explored the depths of the `ColumnChart` and `StackedColumnChart` by means of converting the previously constructed `LineChart`. Along the way, we customized the `StackedColumnChart` by adding a `LineSeries`.

Next, we look at creating a `BarChart` by converting our `StackedColumnChart`.

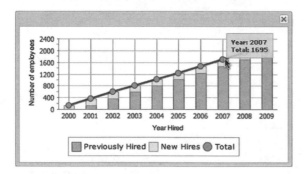

Figure 10.16   Our hybrid `LineChart` and `ColumnChart`

10.6 Constructing BarCharts

To construct a BarChart, you can use all of the same plumbing that you created before, with some tweaks. When thinking about BarCharts, you just have to think about swapping the LineChart or ColumnChart x-axis and y-axis. Why?

Remember that the LineChart and ColumnChart use the category data on the x-axis, whereas the measurement figures are to be on the y-axis. The BarChart expects the category data to be on the y-axis and the measurement data to be on the x-axis.

Using this logic, you can refactor the StackedColumnChart to a StackedBarChart quite easily. This means that all you need to do is refactor the Series to leverage data on the x-axis and modify the Chart configuration object slightly, as shown here.

Listing 10.7 Configuring the Series for the StackedBarChart

```
var series = [
    {
        xField      : 'prevHired',
        displayName : 'Previously Hired',      ←⌐ Configure data
        style       : {                        ❶ point for x-axis
            fillColor   : 0xFFAAAA,
            borderColor : 0xAA3333,
            lineColor   : 0xAA3333
        }
    },
    {
        xField      : 'newHires',
        displayName : 'New Hires',
        style       : {
            fillColor   : 0xAAFFAA,
            borderColor : 0x33AA33,
            lineColor   : 0x33AA33
        }
    },
    {
        type        : 'line',                  ←⌐ Embed
        xField      : 'total',                 ❷ LineSeries
        displayName : 'Total',
        style       : {
            fillColor   : 0xAAAAFF,
            borderColor : 0x3333FF,
            lineColor   : 0x3333FF
        }
    }
];
```

In this listing, the Series and styles remain the same. The difference is that instead of setting the yField property for the configuration objects, you set xField ❶. You also keep the LineSeries ❷ configuration object intact.

In order for the custom and dynamic tipRenderer to work, you'll need to modify it to read the xField property of the series configuration definitions:

```
var tipRenderer = function(chart, record, index, series){
    var yearInfo = 'Year: ' + record.get('year');
    var empInfo  =  series.displayName + ': '+ record.get(series.xField);
    return yearInfo + '\n' + empInfo ;
};
```

In this snippet, the `tipRenderer` method is nearly identical to the previous one with the replacement of `series.yField` with `series.xField`. Remember, you do this because of the series configuration changes you made.

Next, you'll refactor the `Chart` configuration object, completing the transformation.

Listing 10.8   Configuring the `StackedBarChart`

```
var chart =  {
    xtype        : 'stackedbarchart',        Set xtype to
    store        : remoteStore,           ❶ 'stackedbarchart'
    yField       : 'year',
    tipRenderer  : tipRenderer,
    extraStyle   : extraStyle,
    series       : series,
    xAxis        : new Ext.chart.NumericAxis({  ❷ Configure x-axis
        stackingEnabled : true,
        title           : 'Number of employees'  Enable stacking
    }),                                    ❸ on x-axis
    yAxis        : new Ext.chart.CategoryAxis({
        title : 'Year Hired'              Configure
    })                                     ❹ y-axis
};
```

To configure the configuration object for a `StackedBarChart`, you first set the `xtype` property ❶ to `'stackedbarchart'`. The next change is setting the `xAxis` property to ❷ to leverage the `NumericAxis`, with `stackingEnabled` set to `true` ❸. Last, you set the `yAxis` property to an instance of `CategoryAxis` ❹, removing the previously defined `stackingEnabled` property.

That's pretty much all that's needed to convert this `Chart`. Figure 10.17 shows what it looks like rendered in a browser.

Great, everything works as expected, including the dynamic `ToolTip`. How would you convert this to a generic `BarChart`? The steps are as simple as unraveling the configuration parameters to enable bar stacking.

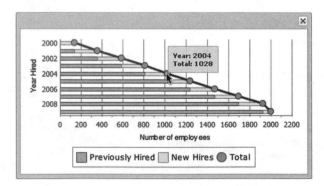

Figure 10.17
The `StackedBarChart`

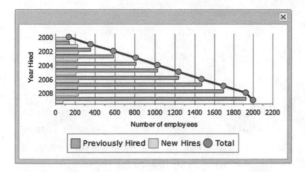

Figure 10.18 The BarChart with an integrated LineSeries

10.6.1 Configuring a BarChart

The steps to modify our StackedBarChart to a BarChart are short and simple. First, change the Chart configuration object xtype property to 'barchart', like this:

```
xtype : 'barchart',
```

Next, remove the stackingEnabled property from the x-axis (NumericAxis) configuration object:

```
xAxis : new Ext.chart.NumericAxis({
    title  : 'Number of employees'
}),
```

And that's it. Figure 10.18 shows what the BarChart looks like with the integrated LineSeries.

With the changes you've made, you can see that the newHires and prevHired columns sit side by side on the line. If you want to remove the LineSeries for the total measurement, all you need to do is remove the type attribute, and Ext JS will use that configuration object to create a BarSeries.

You've just seen the similarities between the LineChart, ColumnChart, and BarChart. The PieChart, however, is completely different because it's not a descendant of the Cartesian line of Charts.

Next, we'll explore this final Chart type, and you'll learn how to apply some customizations.

10.7 A slice of PieChart

As with all Charts, when considering the implementation of a PieChart, you must consider the data that the Chart will consume and display. The PieChart is relatively simple, because it works with only two pieces of information: the category and related numeric data. If you think of it in simplistic terms, the category is the name for the slice of pie, and the numeric data determines how large that slice will be relative to the other slices in the data set.

For the PieChart we're going to build, the data will look like this:

```
[
    {
        'total'  :  '42',
        'range'  :  '20,000s'
    }
    ...
]
```

We'll build a `PieChart` that will display data describing the number of employees for a particular salary range. In the JSON data, the category will be the salary range, and the data will be the `total` property of each record. To put this in plain English, in the example record, there are 42 employees within the 20,000s range.

With this knowledge at hand, constructing a data `Store` to consume this is trivial, as demonstrated here.

Listing 10.9   Creating the data `Store` for the `PieChart`

```
var remoteProxy = new Ext.data.ScriptTagProxy({
    url : 'http://extjsinaction.com/salaryRanges.php'
});

var pieStore = new Ext.data.JsonStore({
    autoLoad : true,
    proxy    : remoteProxy,
    id       : 'piestore',
    root     : 'records',
    fields   : [
        { name : 'total', mapping : 'total' },
        { name : 'range', mapping : 'range' }
    ]
});
```

Next, you can construct the `PieChart` to consume the data. You'll do so with some custom styling to depict the ranges with varying colors from green to red, as follows.

Listing 10.10   Creating the `PieChart` with a legend

```
var pieChart = {
    xtype           : 'piechart',
    store           : pieStore,
    dataField       : 'total',          ①  Set data field
    categoryField   : 'range',          ②  Set category field
    series          : [{
        style : {
            colors : [0xB5FF6B, 0xFFFF6B, 0xFFB56B, 0xFF6B6B]
        }                                    Apply custom
    }],                                      colors to Series ③
    extraStyle : {
        legend : {                      ④  Extra styles
            display : "bottom",             to show legend
            padding : 5,
            spacing : 2,
            font    : { size : 12, color : 0x000000, family : "Arial" },
            border  : { size : 1,  color : 0x999999                    }
        }
```

```
    }
};

new Ext.Window({
    width  : 400,
    height : 250,
    layout : 'fit',
    items  : pieChart
}).show();
```

To create the PieChart configuration, you first set the xtype property to 'piechart', which Ext JS uses to configure an instance of Ext.chart.PieChart. The next two properties, dataField ❶ and categoryField ❷, are crucial to the PieChart's operation. These are similar to the xField and yField properties of the basic Cartesian-style Chart you created earlier.

What makes these so important is that you can't configure a custom Series for the PieChart. Therefore, the only place to tell the Chart what Record Fields to map for the category and data is in the root configuration object for the PieChart.

You're probably wondering what the series property is doing in the PieChart configuration object if you can't configure the Series. It's there because the only way you can customize the colors used in the Series is by means of a nested colors array ❸, and it's completely optional. If you configure a PieChart without custom colors, the framework will use its own custom palette of colors for the Series.

In the last configuration area, you reuse the extraStyle configuration object you created earlier to display a legend on the bottom of the chart ❹. The PieChart doesn't display labels on the series, which means that a legend is important for users to decipher the data that the PieChart presents to them.

Finally, you place the PieChart inside an Ext.Window to be rendered on a resizable canvas.

Our PieChart looks like figure 10.19 when painted onscreen. Looking at the PieChart, you can see that the legend displays with the custom palette, ranging from green to red. If you hover the mouse cursor over the different Series, you see the out-of-the-box tip display, revealing the data that's used to draw the Chart. But just as in the other Charts, sometimes it doesn't provide much context to the data.

The only way to remedy this situation is to apply a custom tipRenderer, which is what we'll embark on next.

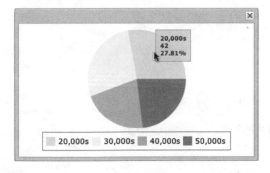

Figure 10.19 The PieChart rendered onscreen with custom colors and a generic ToolTip

10.7.1 *Custom tipRenderer*

When developing a custom `tipRenderer` for the `PieChart`, you're presented only the data used to draw the `Chart`. When a configured `tipRenderer` is called, the information for the category and data fields is all that's provided. This means that unless the percentage is provided by the web service for each record, you'll have to code the calculation manually.

The following listing offers a quick recipe for how to do just that.

Listing 10.11   Creating the `PieChart`

```
var tipRenderer = function(chart, record, index, series) {
    var seriesData = record.data;              ◁┐  Get reference
    var total = 0;                             ❶  to Series data

    Ext.each(series.data, function(obj) {      ◁┐  Calculate sum
        total += parseInt(obj.total);          ❷  of all data
    });

    var slicePct = (seriesData.total/total) * 100;   ◁┐  Calculate
    slicePct    = ' (' + slicePct.toFixed(2) + '%)';      percentage
                                                     ❸  for Series
    var rangeMsg = 'Salary Range : ' + seriesData.range;
    var empMsg = 'Num Emp. : ' + seriesData.total + slicePct;

    return rangeMsg + '\n' + empMsg;           ◁┐  Return
};                                             ❹  custom tip text
```

In the `tipRenderer` method, you first create a reference of the `Series` data by using the passed `Record`'s data object ❶. Next, you use `Ext.each` to loop through the `series.data` array to get the sum of all of the `records` ❷ and calculate the percentage for the tip ❸. Finally, you assemble the message for the `ToolTip` ❹.

Next, you have to configure the `PieChart` to use the custom `tipRenderer`:

```
tipRenderer : tipRenderer,
```

With the custom `tipRenderer` in place, let's see what the new `ToolTip` looks like on the chart (figure 10.20).

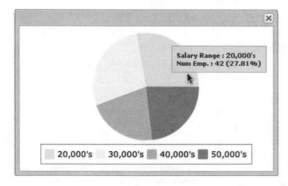

Figure 10.20   The `PieChart` with a custom `ToolTip`

As you can see, by taking some time to add a custom `tipRenderer` to a `pieChart`, you can add context to the information presented inside the `ToolTip`, making it more useful. One of the things to be careful of when developing custom `tipRenderers` is not to display too much information in that little tip balloon. Bombarding the user with too much information could reduce the usability of the `ToolTip`. I'd suggest using the `itemclick` event to display the data somewhere outside the `Chart`.

10.8 *Summary*

In this chapter, we took an in-depth look at the various charts provided by the framework, and you learned what it takes to configure the different kinds of charts. Along the way, you learned the basics of applying simple styling and a custom `ToolTip`.

We began by discussing the different `Charts` available to us in the framework. You learned that the `CartesianChart` is the base class for the `LineChart`, `ColumnChart`, and `BarChart` widgets. You also learned how the `PieChart` is different from the others, and we discussed the details while examining the `Chart` package class hierarchy.

Using an exploratory approach, we implemented each of the `Charts` available to us in the framework. While doing so, you saw what it takes to create a simple `LineChart`, customize it, and then modify it to create a `ColumnChart`. By flipping the x-axis and y-axis and modifying the configuration slightly, you were able to convert the `ColumnChart` to a `BarChart`. You also learned how to create hybrid `Charts` by adding a `LineSeries` to a `ColumnChart` and `BarChart`.

Finally, you learned how to create `PieCharts`, further noting their differences from the other `CartesianChart`-based `Charts`. Along the way, you learned how to add context and percentage data to the `ToolTip`, making it more useful.

In the next chapter, we'll explore how to leverage one of the more powerful `UI` widgets, the `TreePanel`, to display hierarchical data.

Taking root with trees

11

This chapter covers

- Dissecting the `TreePanel` widget
- Rendering in-memory data with `TreePanel`s
- Implementing a remote-loading data `TreePanel`
- Adding a custom `ContextMenu` to `TreePanel` nodes
- Exercising full CRUD lifecycle for nodes
- Using a `TreeEditor` to edit node data

I can recall the first time I was tasked to create an application with what was known then as a `TreeView`. I had to allow for the navigation directory in a filesystem, which required that I allow users to modify the filenames easily. I was lucky that I had Ext JS in my toolbox to aid me in my task. Using the framework not only made things easier, but it also sped up the development time of this task dramatically.

In this chapter, you'll learn about the Ext JS `TreePanel`, which is used to display hierarchical data, much like a typical filesystem. You'll learn how to set up both static and dynamic implementations of this widget. After getting comfortable with this `component`, you'll work to set up CRUD operations by use of a dynamically updating context menu and `Ajax.requests` to send data. This is going to be a fun chapter.

250

11.1 What is a tree (TreePanel)?

In the UI world, the word *tree* is meant to describe a widget or control that displays hierarchical data, which generally begins at some central point, known as a *root*. And like the botanical tree, trees in UIs have branches, which means that they contain other branches or leaves. Unlike botanical trees, computer trees have only one root.

In the computer world, this paradigm is ubiquitous and lives under our noses without much thought. Ever browse your computer's hard disk? The directory structure is a tree structure. It has a root (any drive letter in Windows), branches (directories), and leaves (files). Trees are used in application UIs as well and are known by a few other monikers.

In other UI libraries, other names for this type of widget include `TreeView`, `Tree UI`, or simply `Tree`, whereas in Ext JS it's known as the `TreePanel`. The reason it's called `TreePanel` is because it's a direct descendant of the `Panel` class. And much like the `GridPanel`, it isn't used to contain any children except those it was designed for. The reason `TreePanel` extends from `Panel` is simple—convenience. This gives us the flexibility to leverage all of the `Panel`'s UI goodness, which includes the top and bottom `ToolBars` and the footer button bar.

Like the `EditorGrid`, `TreePanels` can be configured to allow the edit data but don't have a `DataWriter` equivalent, which means that we must code our own `Ajax.requests` for CRUD actions. We'll explore how to make a `TreePanel` editable and how to code for CRUD actions.

Unlike the `GridPanel`, however, the number of the supporting classes is quite small, which makes the configuration of a `TreePanel` simple in contrast, as you'll see a little later on. On the flip side, many developers find that the server-side code and related SQL to support them are much more challenging due to the relational nature of the data.

Finally, the `Ext.data` classes don't apply to `TreePanels`; thus, `Proxies` and `Readers` are out of the picture. This means that the data for the `TreePanel` must come either from memory or remotely but is limited to the same domain. Before we get down to building our first `TreePanel`, we'll discuss how a `TreePanel` works.

11.1.1 Looking under the roots

`TreePanels` work by loading data via a `TreeLoader` class, which reads JSON-formatted data either from memory or remotely from the web server, or it can be a mixture of both. Each object in the JSON stream is converted to an instance of `tree.TreeNode`, which is a descendant of the `Ext.data.Node` class. This `data.Node` class is the core of all of the `TreePanel` data logic and includes many of the utilities such as `cascade`, `bubble`, and `appendChild`.

In order for the `TreePanel` to display the nodes visually, the `TreeNode` class uses the `TreeNodeUI` class. The root `Node` gets some special attention, because it's the source of the entire structure and has its own `RootTreeNodeUI` class. If you want to customize the look and feel of `Nodes`, you extend this class.

Cool! You now have a high-level understanding of what a `TreePanel` is and how it works. We can start constructing our first `TreePanel`, which will load data from memory.

11.2   *Planting our first TreePanel*

As I mentioned before, coding a `TreePanel`, relative to the `GridPanel`, is pretty simple. You'll start out by constructing the `TreePanel`, which loads its data from memory. This will give you more insight into what you learned some time ago.

The following listing shows how to construct a static `TreePanel`.

Listing 11.1   Building a static `TreePanel`

```
var rootNode = {
    text     : 'Root Node',                          ◁┐ JSON data for
    expanded : true,                                  ❶ TreeNodes
    children : [                                      ◁┐ Child Nodes
        {                                             ❷ for this branch
            text : 'Child 1',
            leaf : true                               ◁┐ Specify that a
        },                                            ❸ Node is a leaf
        {
            text : 'Child 2',
            leaf : true
        },
        {
            text     : 'Child 3',
            children : [
                {
                    text     : 'Grand Child 1',
                    children : [
                        {
                            text : 'Grand... you get the point',
                            leaf : true
                        }
                    ]
                }
            ]
        }
    ]
}

var tree = {
    xtype      : 'treepanel',                         ◁┐ Configure
    id         : 'treepanel',                         ❹ TreePanel
    autoScroll : true,
    root       : rootNode
}

new Ext.Window({
    height : 200,
    width  : 200,
    layout : 'fit',
    border : false,
    title  : 'Our first tree',
    items  : tree
}).show();
```

Yikes! Most of the code in listing 11.1 is the data to support the `TreePanel`. In walking through the `rootNode` ❶ JSON, you see that the root `Node` (object) has a `text` attribute. This is important because the `text` property is what the `TreeNodeUI` uses to display the `Node`'s label. When writing the server-side code to support this widget, be sure to keep this property in mind. If you don't set it, the `Nodes` may appear in the `TreePanel` but will have no labels.

You also see an `expanded` property, which is set to `true`. This ensures that, when rendered, the `Node` is expanded immediately, thus displaying its contents. You set this here so you can see the root's `childNodes` immediately upon the rendering of the `TreePanel`. This parameter is optional; leave it out to have the `Node` render initially collapsed.

A `children` property is set on the root node ❷, which is an array of objects. When a `Node` has a `children` array, the objects in that array will be converted to `tree.Tree-Nodes` and populated in the parent `Node`'s `childNodes` array. A similar paradigm can be found in the `Container` hierarchy, where a `Container` has children in its `item`'s `MixedCollection`.

If you walk through the `rootNode`'s `children`, you see that the first and second children have no `children` property but have a `leaf` ❸ property, which is set to `true`. Setting a `Node`'s `leaf` property to `true` ensures that this node will never contain other child `Nodes`, thus making it a leaf and not a branch. In this case, `'Child 1'` and `'Child 2'` are leaf `Nodes`, whereas `'Child 3'` is a branch because it doesn't have a `leaf` property set to `true`.

The `'Child 3'` `Node` contains one child `Node`, which is a `leaf` because—yes. It's a leaf because its `leaf` property is set to `true`. Wow! You learn quickly. This `Node` has a single child, which also has a single child.

After configuring the supporting data, you move on to configure the `TreePanel` using an `XType` ❹ configuration object. This is where you see the simplistic nature of the configuration of this widget. All of these properties should make sense to you but the `root`, which is what you use to configure the root `Node`. In this case, the topmost-level object of the `rootNode` JSON will be treated as the `TreePanel`'s root.

You can change your `TreeNode` icons by adding either an `icon` or `iconCls` property to the node's configuration object, where `icon` specifies a direct location for an image and `iconCls` is the name of a CSS class for an icon style. But the `iconCls` property for the `TreeNode` works like the `Panel`'s `iconCls` configuration object and is the preferred method for changing the icon.

The last thing you do in this listing is create an instance of `Ext.Window` to display your `TreePanel`. Figure 11.1 shows what our rendered `TreePanel` looks like.

After rendering your `TreePanel`, you can see the `TreeNodes` displayed as you laid them out in the JSON. You can expand `'Child 3'` and its child `Node` to display the rest of the hierarchy. It's easy to exercise the selection model by clicking a `Node`. If you want to hide the root `Node`, set `rootVisible` in the `TreePanel` configuration object to `false`, as depicted in figure 11.1 (left).

And there you have it, a static `TreePanel` in action. Simple stuff, huh? Now that we have this out of the way, we'll move on to creating a remote `TreePanel`.

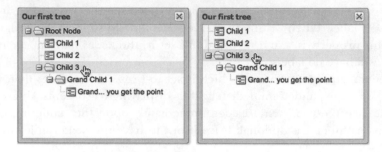

Figure 11.1   Our first (expanded) `TreePanel` with the root `Node` visible (left) and the root `Node` hidden (right)

11.3   *Dynamic TreePanels grow*

Because our previous `TreePanel` is static, there was no need to directly create a `Tree-Loader`. This changes with a remote-loading `TreePanel`. We're going to develop a `TreePanel` that will use the same data that we used for our `GridPanels` in chapter 7, where we displayed people. It just so happens that those people are employees for "My Company" and belong to different departments. Here you'll configure the `TreePanel` to utilize the server-side component to list employees by department.

Listing 11.2   Building a static `TreePanel`

```
var tree = {
    xtype      : 'treepanel',
    autoScroll : true,
    loader     : new Ext.tree.TreeLoader({          ❶ TreeLoader for
        url :  'getCompany.php'                        remote data calls
    }),
    root       : {                                   ❷ Configure root
        text     : 'My Company',                        Node inline
        id       : 'myCompany',                      ┐
        expanded : true                              │ ❸ Set ID
    }                                                    of root Node
}

new Ext.Window({
    height   : 300,
    width    : 300,
    layout   : 'fit',
    border   : false,
    title    : 'Our first remote tree',
    items    : tree
}).show();
```

As you can see in listing 11.2, you configure a `TreeLoader` ❶, which has a configuration object passed with a `url` property set to `'getCompany.php'`. When configuring your `TreePanel`, replace this PHP file with your controller of choice. Before you start coding your controller, however, please allow me to finish walking through the request-and-response cycle, which follows shortly after we look at the rendered version of this `TreePanel` implementation.

The next thing you do when configuring this `TreePanel` is configure the `root` ❷ inline. It's extremely important to notice that you added an `id` ❸ property to this

> **TreeLoaders can't talk across domains**
>
> Unlike the data `Store`, which backs the `GridPanel` and other views, the `Tree-Loader` doesn't have the capability out of the box to connect to a remote data source. This is because the `TreeLoader` doesn't have the same internal architecture as the data `Store`.

`Node`. As you'll see, this property will be used to request the child data from the server. Also notice that you set `expanded` to `true`. This will ensure that the root `Node` expands and *loads* its children as soon as it's rendered.

Last, you configure a bigger instance of `Ext.Window` to contain your `TreePanel`. Configuring the window a bit bigger for this demonstration will both increase the `TreePanel`'s viewing space and eliminate horizontal scrolling because of long names. Figure 11.2 shows what the rendered `TreePanel` looks like.

After rendering the `TreePanel`, you see the root `Node` (My Company) load immediately, as shown in figure 11.2 (left), displaying all of the departments in My Company. To view the employees in a particular department, click the expand icon (+), or double-click the label and you'll see the remote loading indicator appear in place of the folder icon, as shown in the center of figure 11.2. Once the employee nodes are loaded successfully, they'll appear below the department `Node`.

We went through this pretty fast. Let's recap a bit and look at the requests being fired. We'll discuss what the server-side controller is doing to support this implementation of the `TreePanel`.

11.3.1 Fertilizing the TreePanel

To analyze the client/server interaction model with the `TreePanel`, we'll start with the load request fired off by the automatic expansion of the root `Node`, as shown in figure 11.3. Remember that you set the root's `expanded` property to `true` and that this

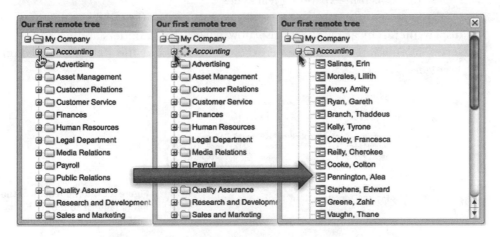

Figure 11.2 Our remote `TreePanel` displaying its ability to load data remotely

```
▼ POST http://ext2play/extia/chapter09/getCompany.php   200 OK 170ms

   Headers   Post   Response

   node  myCompany
```

Figure 11.3   The post parameter of the initial Node request

expands a Node when it's rendered, thus either rendering the children if they're in memory or firing a load request.

As you can see, the first request to the getCompany.php controller was made with a single parameter, node, which has a value of myCompany. Can you remember where you set that value and which property you set it to? If you said "the id property root node," you're correct! When an asynchronously loading Node is being expanded for the first time, the loader will use its id property to pass the child data to the controller.

The controller will accept this parameter and query the database for all nodes associated with that id and return a list of objects, as illustrated in figure 11.4. In this figure, you see an array of objects that define a list of departments. Each object has both text and id properties. How does the text property apply to the NodeUI? You're correct! The text applies to the label of the NodeUI. Notice that the departments lack the leaf and children properties. Are these leaf or branch Nodes? Correct again. They're branch Nodes. Because neither property is defined, they're treated as branch Nodes. This means that when they're initially expanded, the TreeLoader will invoke an Ajax.request, passing the department's ID as the node parameter. The controller will accept the node parameter and return a list of employees for that department.

Using what you just learned, you can safely predict that when you expand the Accounting department Node, a request to the getCompany.php controller will be made with a single parameter, node, passed with a value of 'Accounting'. Let's take a quick look at the results from the controller request, shown in figure 11.5.

As you look at the JSON results, you see that a list of objects is returned, each with id, text, and leaf properties. Remember, that because the leaf property is set, the Nodes appear as non-expanding leaf Nodes.

Congratulations! You've successfully constructed static and dynamic TreePanels to display hierarchical data. You also now have a basic understanding of the client/server interaction model between the TreePanel and the web service feeding the TreePanel data.

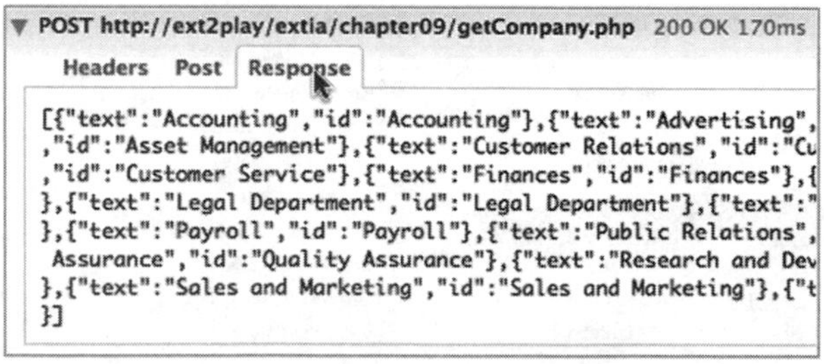

```
▼ POST http://ext2play/extia/chapter09/getCompany.php   200 OK 170ms

   Headers   Post   Response

[{"text":"Accounting","id":"Accounting"},{"text":"Advertising",
,"id":"Asset Management"},{"text":"Customer Relations","id":"Cu
,"id":"Customer Service"},{"text":"Finances","id":"Finances"},{
},{"text":"Legal Department","id":"Legal Department"},{"text":"
},{"text":"Payroll","id":"Payroll"},{"text":"Public Relations",
 Assurance","id":"Quality Assurance"},{"text":"Research and Dev
},{"text":"Sales and Marketing","id":"Sales and Marketing"},{"t
}]
```

Figure 11.4   The results of the initial request to the getCompany.php controller

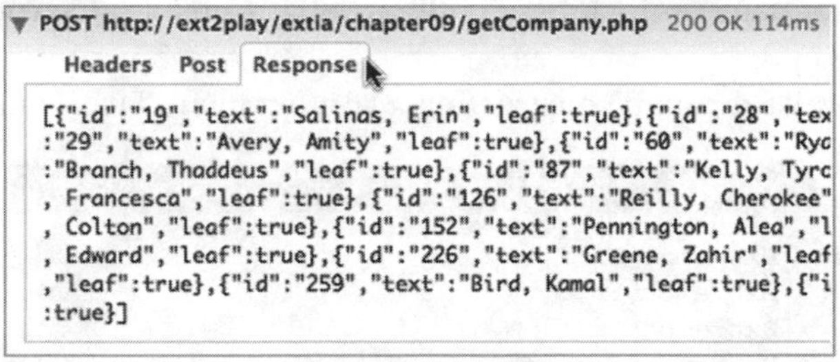

[{"id":"19","text":"Salinas, Erin","leaf":true},{"id":"28","tex
:"29","text":"Avery, Amity","leaf":true},{"id":"60","text":"Rya
:"Branch, Thaddeus","leaf":true},{"id":"87","text":"Kelly, Tyrc
, Francesca","leaf":true},{"id":"126","text":"Reilly, Cherokee"
, Colton","leaf":true},{"id":"152","text":"Pennington, Alea","l
, Edward","leaf":true},{"id":"226","text":"Greene, Zahir","leaf
,"leaf":true},{"id":"259","text":"Bird, Kamal","leaf":true},{"i
:true}]

POST http://ext2play/extla/chapter09/getCompany.php 200 OK 114ms
Headers Post **Response**

Figure 11.5   The results from the Accounting department Node request

Configuring a `TreePanel` for loading is just a small part of the job if you're tasked to build a UI that offers CRUD functionality for this type of widget. Next, we'll look at how to construct a `TreePanel` for these types of interactions.

11.4   CRUD on a TreePanel

To configure CRUD UI functionality, you'll need to add much more code to the mix. After all, the `TreePanel` doesn't support these features natively. Here's what you're going to do.

To enable CRUD actions, you'll modify your `TreePanel` by adding a `contextmenu` listener to it, which will call a method to select the `Node` that was right-clicked and create an instance of `Ext.menu.Menu` to be displayed at the mouse cursor's X and Y coordinates. This will be very similar to how you coded the `EditorGridPanel`'s context menu handler in the last chapter.

You'll create three menu items: add, edit, and delete. Because you can only add employees to a department, you'll dynamically change text for the menu items and enable and disable the various menu items based on the type of node that was clicked: root, branch, or leaf.

Each of the handlers will perform an `Ajaxrequest` to mock controllers for each CRUD action. Again, much of this will function like the CRUD for the `EditorGrid-Panel`, but it will be adapted to the `TreePanel` to deal with `Nodes` instead of rows.

Get ready. This will be the most complicated code yet. You'll start by creating the context menu handler and the context menu factory method.

11.4.1   Adding context menus to a TreePanel

To add a context menu to the `TreePanel`, you must register a listener for the `context-menu` event. This is super simple. Add a `listeners` configuration option to the `Tree-Panel` as follows:

```
listeners    : {
    contextmenu : onCtxMenu
}
```

Adding the previous code will ensure that the `onCtxMenu` handler will be called when the `contextmenu` (or right-click) event is fired.

Cool! Your `TreePanel` is now set up to call the `onCtxMenu` handler. Before you code it, you should construct a factory method to generate an instance of `Ext.menu.Menu`.

This will help simplify onCtxMenu quite a bit. You'll see what I mean once you've finished with the factory method.

The following listing walks through constructing a context menu factory method.

Listing 11.3 Configuring a context menu factory method

```
var onConfirmDelete = Ext.emptyFn;
var onDelete        = Ext.emptyFn;
var onCompleteEdit  = Ext.emptyFn;
var onEdit          = Ext.emptyFn;
var onCompleteAdd   = Ext.emptyFn;
var onAddNode       = Ext.emptyFn;

var buildCtxMenu = function() {
    return new Ext.menu.Menu({
        items: [
            {
                itemId  : 'add',
                handler : onAdd
            },
            {
                itemId  : 'edit',
                handler : onEdit,
                scope   : onEdit
            },
            {
                itemId  : 'delete',
                handler : onDelete
            }
        ]
    });
}
```

In listing 11.3, you first set up a bunch of placeholder methods that point to Ext.emptyFn, which is the same thing as instantiating a new instance of a function but is easier on the eyes. We're adding them now so that when we circle back and fill in these methods, you'll know exactly where to place them.

Next, you generate the buildCtxMenu factory method, which returns an instance of Ext.menu.Menu and will be used by the onCtxMenu handler that you'll generate next. If you've never seen or heard of a factory method, from a high level, it's a method that constructs (hence the name *factory*) something and returns what it constructed. That's all there is to it.

Notice that each of the menu items has no text property, but each has itemId specified. This is because the onCtxMenu will dynamically set the text for each menu item to provide feedback to the user that something may or may not be allowed. It will use the itemId property to locate a specific item in the menu's items MixedCollection.

The itemId configuration property is similar to the id property of Components except it's local to a child Component's Container. This means that unlike the Component's id property, itemId isn't registered with ComponentMgr; thus only the parent Component has the ability to look into its item's MixedCollection to find a child Component with a specific itemId.

Each `MenuItem` currently has a hardcoded handler to `Ext.emptyFn` as a place-holder so you can see your menu display in the UI without having to code the real handler. You'll go on to create each handler after you develop and review the `onCtx-Menu` handler, which is next.

Listing 11.4   Configuring a context menu factory method

```
var onCtxMenu = function(node, evtObj) {
    node.select();
    evtObj.stopEvent();

    if (! this.ctxMenu) {
        this.ctxMenu = buildCtxMenu();            ❶ Use context menu
    }                                                factory method

    var ctxMenu    = this.ctxMenu;
    var addItem    = ctxMenu.getComponent('add');
    var editItem   = ctxMenu.getComponent('edit');
    var deleteItem = ctxMenu.getComponent('delete');
                                                  ❷ Configure menu for
                                                    each type of Node
    if (node.id =='myCompany') {
        addItem.setText('Add Department');
        editItem.setText('Nope, not changing the name');
        deleteItem.setTex('Can\'t delete a company, silly');

        addItem.enable();
        deleteItem.disable();
        editItem.disable();
    }
    else if (! node.leaf) {
        addItem.setText('Add Employee');
        deleteItem.setText('Delete Department');
        editItem.setText('Edit Department');

        addItem.enable();
        editItem.enable();
        deleteItem.enable();
    }
    else {
        addItem.setText('Can\'t Add Employee');
        editItem.setText('Edit Employee');
        deleteItem.setText('Delete Employee');

        addItem.disable();
        editItem.enable();
        deleteItem.enable();
    }

    ctxMenu.showAt(evtObj.getXY() ;
}
```

In listing 11.4 you construct your `onCtxMenu` handler, which does quite a bit to enable your context menu to be dynamic. The first task that this handler accomplishes is selecting the `Node` in the UI by firing the `Node`'s `select` method. You select the `Node` because you're going to need to query the TreePanel for the selected Node further on, after Ajax calls are made.

Every time the TreePanel's contextmenu event fires, it passes two arguments: the node that the event occurred on and the instance of EventObject that was generated. If bells are ringing in your ears, it's probably because this is very similar to the Grid-Panel's contextmenu event, where the row in which the event occurred and an instance of EventObject are passed to the handler.

Next, you stop the browser's default context menu from showing up by calling evtObj.stopEvent. You'll see this pattern repeat anywhere you need to display your own context menu in place of the browser's.

The handler then constructs the context menu by calling the buildCtxMenu factory method you created a bit ago ❶. It stores the reference locally as this.ctxMenu so it doesn't have to reconstruct a menu for each subsequent handler call.

You then create a local reference to the context menu, ctxMenu, and each of the menu items. You're doing this for readability further on, where you manage the menu items.

After you create the local references, you move on to an if ❷ control block, where you detect the type of Node and modify the menu items accordingly. This is the bulk of the code for this handler. Here's how this logic breaks down.

If the node that was right-clicked is the root (node.id == 'myCompany'), you configure the menu items to allow the addition of departments but disallow the deletion and editing of the company text. You also disable those menu items so they can't be clicked. After all, you don't want anyone to destroy an entire company by a single mouse click, do you?

Moving on, you detect whether the Node is a leaf (department). You then modify the text to allow the addition of employees and deletion of the entire department. Remember, the company needs to be able to downsize by removing an entire department if need be. You also enable all menu items.

The code will encounter the else block if the Node that was right-clicked is a leaf item. In this case, the text for the add item is modified and disabled to reflect the inability to add an employee to an employee, which would be weird. Then you modify and enable the edit and delete menu item texts.

Last, you show the context menu at the coordinates of the mouse by calling the EventObject's getXY method. Figure 11.6 shows what the menu looks like customized for each node.

As illustrated in figure 11.6, our context menu displays and changes for each type of Node that is right-clicked, which demonstrates how you can use the same menu to perform similar tasks with some modifications. If you wanted to not show or hide the menu items instead of enabling and disabling them, you'd swap the MenuItem enable calls for show and disable for hide. We can now begin to wire up handlers for our context menus. We'll start with the easiest, edit.

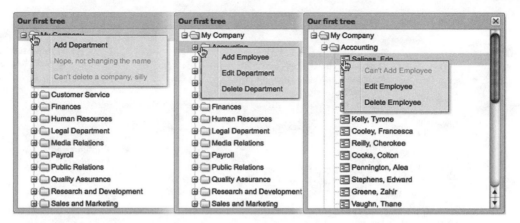

Figure 11.6 Displaying our dynamic context menu for the company (left), department (center), and employee (right) `Nodes`

11.4.2 Wiring up the Edit logic

You probably noticed that clicking a `MenuItem` resulted in nothing more than the menu disappearing. This is because you have your context menu set but no real handlers for it to call. You'll start by creating the `edit` handler, which is by far the easiest to code.

This is where you'll instantiate an instance of `TreeEditor` to allow for inline edits of `Node` names. In order to get the `TreeEditor` to invoke an `Ajax.request` to submit the modified `Node` name, you'll have to set up a listener for the `TreeEditor`'s published `complete` event, which indicates that an edit has completed and the value of the `Node` has been changed. You'll code for the `complete` handler first and then move on to create the `onEdit` handler, which you'll attach to the edit `MenuItem`.

Here's where you'll start filling in some of those placeholder methods.

Listing 11.5   Configuring a context menu factory method

```
var onCompleteEdit = function(treeEditor, newValue, oldValue) {
    var treePanel =  Ext.getCmp('treepanel')
    treePanel.el.mask('Saving...', 'x-mask-loading');          ◁─  TreeEditor complete
                                                                    event handler  ❶
    var editNode = treeEditor.editNode;
    var editNodeId = editNode.attributes.id;

    Ext.Ajax.request({                            ◁─   Invoke an
        url    : 'editNode.php',                    ❷  Ajax.request
        params : {
            id      : editNodeId,
            newName : newValue
        },                                                 Revert the change  ❸
        success : function (response, opts) {              { success : false }
            treePanel.el.unmask();
            var responseJson = Ext.decode(response.responseText);
            if (responseJson.success !== true) {           ◁─
```

```
                        editNode.setText(oldValue);
                        Ext.Msg.alert('An error occured with the server.');
                    }
                },
            failure : function (response, opts) {
                treePanel.el.unmask();
                editNode.setText(oldValue);
                Ext.Msg.alert('An error occured with the server.');
            }
        });
    }

var onEdit = function() {
    var treePanel = Ext.getCmp('treepanel');
    var selectedNode = treePanel.getSelectionModel().getSelectedNode();

    if (! this.treeEditor) {
        this.treeEditor = new Ext.tree.TreeEditor(treePanel, {}, {
            cancelOnEsc     :
true,
            completeOnEnter : true,
            selectOnFocus   : true,
            allowBlank      : false,
            listeners       : {
                complete : onCompleteEdit
            }
        });
    }

    this.treeEditor.editNode = selectedNode;
    this.treeEditor.startEdit(selectedNode.ui.textNode);
}
```

4 **If request fails, revert change**

5 **Configure edit MenuItem handler**

Create TreeEditor if it doesn't exist **6**

In listing 11.5, you create two methods that take care of the edit functionality. The first is the handler that will be called when the edit event of the TreeEditor is fired and is responsible for firing off an Ajax.request to the server to save the modification. The second is the handler that's fired when the edit MenuItem is clicked. Here's how they work.

When the TreeEditor fires the complete event, it passes three parameters to the listeners: a reference to the TreeEditor that fired the event, the new value, and the old value. Our onCompleteEdit ❶ event handler uses all three parameters to do its job. This method first sets a local reference to the TreePanel that's being edited and masks its element. It then sets two more local references to the Node being edited and its ID.

Next, it fires of an Ajax.request ❷ to save the data. Notice that in the parameters configuration object of the Ajax.request, it's passing the ID of the Node and its new name. This would be important if you had to modify a value in a database where an ID identifies Nodes.

If there are other application-specific values for that Node that you were looking to send as parameters to the server, you can find them in the attributes property of the node. Any properties that are part of the Node to create the tree are tucked away for use in the attributes property. For instance, employee Nodes could have employee-specific personal attributes, such as DOB or sex, on each Node. Obviously, this depends on the application you're developing for. Also, if you want to send an attribute from the Node's parent, you can access it by the Node's parentNode property and tack it on to the params configuration object for the Ajax.request.

In the request's success handler, the return JSON from the server is encoded and the success ❸ property is tested. If the server returns a false success property, the method reverts the value of the Node. This is helpful if an invalid value is placed per the business rules processed on the server. Likewise, if the request fails for some reason, the failure handler ❹ is triggered and the Node's text value will be reverted. Both handlers will unmask the TreePanel when they're triggered.

The second method in this listing, onEdit ❺, will be called when the edit Menu-Item is clicked. It first creates a local reference for the TreePanel and the selected Node. It then creates an instance of TreeEditor ❻ and sets a self (this) reference if it doesn't exist. Notice that it configures the onCompleteEdit listener for the complete event. Last, it will set the editNode property as the selectedNode on the TreeEditor and trigger the editing of that Node by calling startEdit and passing the selected-Node's ui.textNode reference, which will tell the TreeEditor where to render and position itself.

Triggering the edit in this manner will ensure that the TreeEditor doesn't scroll the Node to the top of the list if the TreePanel is scrollable, thus preventing this undesired effect from happening.

Great! You have your edit logic all in place, which means you can see it in action! Refresh your page, right-click a Node, and click the edit MenuItem. I'll follow along and show you what I see. Refer to figure 11.7.

In figure 11.7, I changed the Accounting department's name to Legal by right-clicking it, which selected the Node. I then clicked the edit MenuItem, which rendered the TreeEditor where the text of the Node is. Remember that the TreeEditor knows where to render and position itself because we passed the textNode reference of the TreeNode's ui. I then changed the name from Accounting to Legal and pressed Enter.

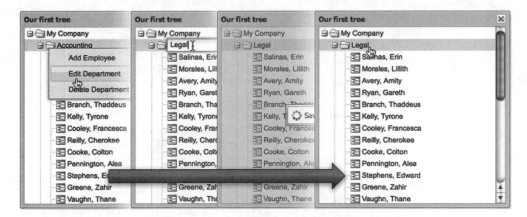

Figure 11.7   The results of editing a Node **in the** TreePanel **using the** TreeEditor **with an** Ajax.request **to save the data**

This caused the `Node` value to change and the `complete` event to fire, thus triggering the `onComplete` method. Because the server accepted the value, the `TreePanel`'s element was unmasked and the new value persisted in the UI. Remember that if the server had returned { `success : false` } or if the request had failed, the text value of the `Node` would have been reverted.

This wraps up the easiest of the CRUD functionality for our `TreePanel`. Editing names in this widget is a common task among web applications. Naturally, how you implement it depends on the business requirements. Using the `TreeEditor` results in a cleaner application flow by saving you from having to use an input dialog box, such as `MessageBox.prompt`.

Next, we're going to ratchet up the level of difficulty by tackling the deletion of `Nodes`. This will be far more complex than what we've done previously in this chapter.

11.4.3 *Tackling delete*

To set up the delete functionality of your `TreePanel`, you'll create a handler for the delete `MenuItem`. Naturally, requirements usually dictate that a confirmation dialog box be presented to the user, so you'll have to code for user confirmation. To make things a bit easier, you'll use the out-of-the-box `MessageBox.confirm` dialog box. This means that you'll have to construct a callback method for the confirmation dialog box. The dialog box callback will trigger the `Ajax.request` and ultimately delete the `Node` if the server returns a favorable result.

Now that you have an idea of what you need to do, you can get on with coding the handler methods, as shown in the following listing.

Listing 11.6   Adding deletion functionality to your `TreePanel`

```
var onConfirmDelete = function(btn) {                    Confirmation message
    if (btn == 'yes') {                               ❶ box callback
        var treePanel = Ext.getCmp('treepanel');
        treePanel.el.mask('Deleting...', 'x-mask-loading');

        var selNode = treePanel.getSelectionModel().getSelectedNode();

        Ext.Ajax.request({                            Ajax.request to
            url    : 'deleteNode.php',             ❷ delete selected Node
            params : {
                id : selNode.id
            },                                            Ajax.request
            success : function (response, opts) {  ❸ success handler
                treePanel.el.unmask();
                var responseJson = Ext.decode(response.responseText);

                if (responseJson.success === true) {  ❹ Remove
                    selNode.remove();                     selected Node
                }
                else {
                    Ext.Msg.alert('An error occurred with the server.');
                }
            }
```

```
        });
    }
}

var onDelete = function() {
    var treePanel =  Ext.getCmp('treepanel');
    var selNode = treePanel.getSelectionModel().getSelectedNode();

    if (selNode) {
        Ext.MessageBox.confirm(
            'Are you sure?',
            'Please confirm the deletion of ' + selNode.attributes.text,
            onConfirmDelete
        )
    }
}
```

⑤ The delete MenuItem handler

⑥ Confirm Node deletion

In listing 11.6, you create the two methods that take care of the delete operations of your CRUD functionality. The first method, onConfirmDelete ①, is the handler for the confirmation dialog box that you'll create a little later on. If the Yes Button is clicked in the confirmation dialog box, it will mask the TreePanel and invoke an Ajax.request ② to delete the selected Node. Notice that you're passing only the ID of the Node to the server.

In our fictitious mini-application, the server would take the value of the Node ID and perform a delete operation in the database or filesystem and return something like {success:true}, which fires the request's success ③ handler. This removes the TreePanel's element mask and updates the UI by removing the Node ④ from the TreePanel by using the Node's remove method.

To reduce complexity for this listing, I left out the Ajax.request failure handler, which would post a failure message to the user. Naturally, when you develop your applications, you'll want to include it. In this case, it should remove the TreePanel's element mask and alert the user that a failure occurred.

The second method you create, onDelete ⑤, is the handler for the delete Menu-Item. When this method is called, it presents a confirmation dialog box by using the out-of-the-box MessageBox.confirm ⑥ method and passes in three arguments: title, message body, and callback. This presents the user with a message and two options to proceed. Either Button will trigger the callback, but remember that to perform the deletion of the Node, the Yes Button has to be clicked.

Please refresh your UI and delete a Node. I'll do the same, and we'll discuss how things transpire. Figure 11.8 illustrates what happened when I refreshed my UI and deleted the Accounting department Node.

After I right-clicked the Accounting department Node, our customized context menu appeared. I then clicked the delete MenuItem, which triggered the onDelete handler. This immediately displayed the confirmation dialog box. I clicked Yes, which caused the TreePanel's element to mask, indicating that a request was being made to delete the Node. When the server returned a favorable result, the mask was removed and the Accounting department Node disappeared.

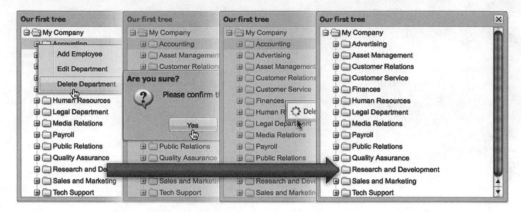

Figure 11.8   Deleting a `Node` with a confirmation box and an `Ajax.request` to the server

In a real-world application, deleting a branch `Node` would generally require the server to recursively gather a list of all of the child nodes and remove them from the database before removing the branch node itself. A clever way to do this could be to set up a trigger in the database to call a stored procedure to delete all associated child nodes when a delete operation is performed on a container node.

Deleting `Nodes` from our `TreePanel` required a bit more effort because of the typically required confirmation dialog box. Adding a `Node`, however, is equally difficult because the UI code needs to know what type of node is being added. Is it a branch or leaf `Node`? Next, you'll see how to code for this type of branch and have the UI react accordingly.

11.4.4   Creating nodes for our TreePanel

To create a `Node` using the `TreeEditor`, you're going to have to do a lot of work, which makes this the hardest listing in this chapter, but the results will be pretty sweet.

Because the `TreeEditor` needs to bind and display on top of a `Node`, you'll need to inject a `Node` into the `TreePanel` and trigger an edit operation on the `Node`. Once the edit of the new temporary `Node` is complete, an `Ajax.request` is fired off to the server with the name of the new `Node`. If the server returns favorably, the ID is set to the `Node`. This works similarly to the way rows are added to the `EditorGrid` we created last chapter.

Here's the code for the create `Node` functionally.

Listing 11.7   Adding create functionality to your `TreePanel`

```
var onCompleteAdd = function(treeEditor, newValue, oldValue) {
    var treePanel = Ext.getCmp('treepanel');

    if (newValue.length > 0) {
        Ext.Ajax.request({
            url    : 'createNode.php',
            params : {
```

TreeEditor complete event handler ❶

Invoke Ajax.request ❷ if new Node name

```
                    newName : newValue
                },
                success : function (response, opts) {
                    treePanel.el.unmask();
                    var responseJson = Ext.decode(response.responseText);

                    if (responseJson.success !== true) {
                        Ext.Msg.alert('An error occured with the server.');
                        treeEditor.editNode.remove();              ❸ Remove
                    }                                                 temporary Node
                    else {
                        treeEditor.editNode.setId(responseJson.node.id);
                    }
                }
            });
        }
        else {                                       ❹ Temporary Node
            treeEditor.editNode.remove();               is removed
        }
    }

var onAddNode = function() {                       ❺ The add
    var treePanel =  Ext.getCmp('treepanel');        MenuItem handler
    var selNode = treePanel.getSelectionModel().getSelectedNode();

    if (! this.treeEditor) {
        this.treeEditor = new Ext.tree.TreeEditor(treePanel, {}, {
            cancelOnEsc    : true,
            completeOnEnter : true,
            selectOnFocus  : true,
            allowBlank     : false,
            listeners      : {
                complete : onCompleteAdd
            }
        });
    }

    selNode.expand(null, null, function() {        ❻ Insert Node and
        var newNodeCfg = {                            trigger edit
            text : '',
            id   : 'tmpNode',
            leaf : (selNode.id != 'myCompany')
        }

        var newNode = selNode.insertBefore(newNodeCfg,
            selNode.firstChild);
        this.treeEditor.editNode = newNode;
        this.treeEditor.startEdit(newNode.ui.textNode);
    }, this);
}
```

You're doing quite a bit of work in listing 11.7 to get the create functionality to work smoothly. Just like the code for the edit operations, to reduce complexity for the listing, we omit the Ajax.request failure handler. Here's how all of this stuff works.

The first method in the listing is the `TreeEditor` complete event handler, `onCompleteAdd` ❶. This handler is arguably more complex than the edit `TreeEditor` complete event handler for a multitude of reasons. When this method is fired, if a new name has been entered for the `Node`, an `Ajax.request` will be fired ❷. If the server responds favorably, it will return the database ID of the newly inserted node. The code will set the new `Node`'s ID via its `setId` method. This is important because it will ensure that subsequent edits to this `Node` will occur against the proper database record. If the server returns unfavorably, the temporary `Node` is removed from the `TreePanel` ❸. This also occurs if `onCompleteAdd` is called without a new name ❹. Having the UI coded this way ensures that phantom `Nodes` can't exist in the `TreePanel`. If you plan on using this pattern to create `Nodes`, be sure to add a failure handler, which should alert the user of a failure and remove the temporary `Node`.

The second method, `onAddNode` ❺, is the handler for your add `MenuItem`. This method does quite a bit of work as well to provide the user with a temporary `Node` to add to the `TreePanel`. It does this by instantiating an instance of `TreeEditor` if it does not exist and binding the `onCompleteAdd` handler to its `complete` event. Next, it expands the selected `Node`. You expand ❻ the selected `Node` because the `TreeEditor` needs a home, which will be the soon-to-be-created `Node`.

Notice that you're passing `null`s as the first two parameters. You pass `null` because you don't need to set them. They're for deep expansion (to expand branches of branches) and to enable animation. You do pass the third and fourth parameters, however, a callback method and scope for which it's to be called, which is the `onAddNode` method. You use a callback because the Ajax load is asynchronous, and you need to make sure that the load is complete for a branch `Node` and all of its children to be rendered before you can inject a new `Node`.

The callback method creates a `Node` configuration object with an empty string for the text, an id of `'tmpNode'`, and uses JavaScript shorthand to set the `leaf` value if the selected `Node`'s id isn't `'myCompany'`. This ensures that if the department has been selected to have a `Node` added to it, it will set the `leaf` property to `true`, meaning a person; otherwise it's `false`, meaning a department `Node`. It then uses the new `Node` configuration to create a new `TreeNode` using the selected `Node`'s `insertBefore` method, passing the `newNode` configuration object and the selected `Node`'s `firstChild` reference to specify where to insert the new `Node`. Last, an edit operation is triggered on the newly created `Node`, giving users the ability to add a name to it.

Wow, that was a long one! Let's refresh the UI and see our code in action, as shown in figure 11.9. In this figure, you can see the how we can use the `TreeEditor` to add `Nodes` to the `TreePanel` in a way that mimics operating system behavior.

When I right-clicked the Accounting department `Node`, the dynamic context menu appeared as expected. I clicked the add `MenuItem`, which triggered our `onAdd` handler. This caused the Accounting `Node` to expand. After the child `Nodes` were loaded, a new `Node` was inserted and an edit operation was immediately triggered on that `Node` using the `TreeEditor`. I typed in a new employee name and pressed Enter. This caused the

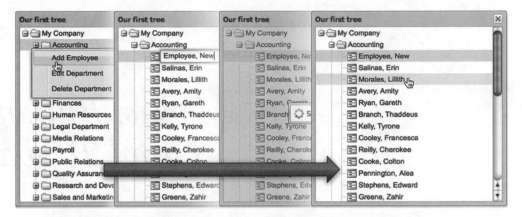

Figure 11.9   Adding a new `Node` to our `TreePanel` using the `TreeEditor`

complete event to be fired by the `TreeEditor`, thus invoking the `onCompleteAdd` handler, which masked the `TreePanel` and performed an XHR (XMLHttpRequest). The server returned favorably, so the new `Node` stayed in the UI, and the database ID of the newly inserted `Node` was applied to the `TreePanel`. You can also implement this code to add department `Nodes` to the tree and add employees to that.

Great work! You now know how to construct `TreePanels`, feed them data from the server, and apply CRUD workflows with them. You can now add these widgets to your applications.

11.5   Summary

In this chapter, we covered quite a bit of code when discussing `TreePanels` and how to set up really cool CRUD interaction for nodes.

We started by talking about the `TreePanel` and discussed supporting classes like the `TreeLoader`, `TreeNode`, and `TreeNodeUI`. Remember that the `TreePanel` is a direct descendant of `Panel` and can be configured as a child for any `Container`. You constructed a static `TreePanel`, where the `Nodes` were read by memory, and analyzed how the JSON should be formatted.

We then moved on to build a dynamic `TreePanel` that loaded data from a remote data source and spent lots of time enabling full CRUD operations. To enable CRUD, you learned how to dynamically modify, enable, and disable the reusable context menu. You saw what it took to set up adding and editing with the `TreeEditor` class, which gives the `TreePanel` the ability to edit node names inline.

Until now, we've only scratched the surface with some of the tools of the framework: the `Toolbar`, `Menus`, and `Buttons`. In the next chapter, we're going to dive deep, and you'll learn more about how they work and how you can better put them to work for your applications.

Menus, Buttons,
and Toolbars

12

This chapter covers

- Learning about `Menu`s and how they work
- Styling your `Menu`s with freely available 16 x 16 gif icons
- Dealing with complex `Menu Item`s
- Attaching a `Menu` to a `Button`
- Displaying and stylizing a custom `Item` in a submenu
- Grouping `Button`s together
- Implementing `Toolbar`s
- Using `Ext.Action` to configure `Button`s

In the chapters leading up to this one, we've configured and used `Menu`s, `Button`s and `Toolbar`s, but we never got to take a moment to really look at these widgets and learn more about them and what else they have to offer. You might ask, "Why are these three lumped into one chapter?" The answer is simple. Their use cases are related in one way or another. For instance, a `Button` can be configured to display a `Menu`, and a `Toolbar` can contain that `Button`.

For this reason we'll take an in-depth look at the `Ext.menu` and `Item` classes, where you'll learn how to display menu-specific `Items` in a `Menu`. We'll even dive into displaying non-`Menu` `Items`.

Afterward, we'll focus on the `Button` class and its cousin the `SplitButton`, where you'll learn about things such as how to change the inner `Button` layout and how to attach a `Menu` to it.

Once you become more familiar with the `Button` class, we'll create clusters of buttons, known as `ButtonGroups`. We'll even take a moment to create a `ButtonGroup` that emulates one from Microsoft Word 2007's famous ribbon toolbar.

Last we'll tie all of this together in a `Toolbar` and discuss how to abstract like functionality with the use of `Ext.Action` to save us time when developing `Buttons` and `Menus`.

12.1 *Menus at a glance*

For a moment, let's take a step back and ask ourselves, "What is a menu?" In the simplest definition, a *menu* is something that displays a list of items to choose from. Menus are all around us, including your local coffee shop, where you choose the blend of java to indulge in. This, by the way, is my favorite kind of menu, because I am a self-proclaimed coffee addict.

If we think about it, in the computer world we use menus all the time. The most common are the typical file, edit, and view menus on your application toolbar, where you choose a menu item to open a document or copy something to the clipboard. Another common type of menu is a context menu, which is displayed within the *context* of an item that has been either clicked or right-clicked. This context menu displays only options that are available for the item that the menu was summoned for. Right-clicking anything on your computer displays a context menu. In Ext JS, you can use and display menus the same way.

In Ext JS, `Menus` typically contain one or more `MenuItems` or descendants of `MenuItems`. Although in 2.0 it was possible to embed another widget inside a menu, it was rather laborious to do so. In version 3.0 of Ext JS, accomplishing this task is so much easier because the `Menu` widget extends `Container` and uses the `MenuLayout`. This means that you get the power of the `Container` model managing your `Menu`, affording you the flexibility to manage the `Menu`'s children much as you would any `Container`.

As in the desktop menu model, Ext JS `Menus` can be displayed a number of ways. In the previous `GridPanel` and `TreePanel` chapters, you learned how to configure an instance of `Menu` to display and replace the browser's context menu. Although this is a common use case for this `Menu` widget, it's not the only one.

You have complete flexibility when developing with `Menus`. For instance, `Menus` can be attached to a `Button` and displayed upon the click of that `Button`. Or they can be anchored to and shown by any element on demand. How you employ the `Menu` will be based on the requirements of your applications, which means that you can employ Ext JS Menus much like menus are deployed in the desktop model.

I'm itching to start writing some code—aren't you?

12.1.1 *Building a menu*

Even though we've built and displayed a context menu in the past, we've only scratched the surface of how to use the Menu widget. In the coming sections, we're going to explore the different Menu items and how to use them.

In the following listing you begin by creating a plain-Jane menu with a single Menu Item with a newDepartment handler that you'll reuse.

Listing 12.1   Building your base Menu

```
var genericHandler = function(menu.Item) {                                    ◁┐
    Ext.MessageBox.alert('', 'Your choice is ' + menu.Item.text);             │
}                                                                    Handler to provide
                                                                     visual feedback  ❶
var newDepartment = {                           ◁┐  XType configuration for
    text    : newDepartment Item',               ❷  Ext.menu.Menu.Item
    handler : genericHandler
}

var menuItems = [                  ◁──❸  List of menu items
    newDepartment
];

var menu = new Ext.menu.Menu({                  ◁┐  Create instance of
    items      : menuItems,                      ❹  Ext.menu.Menu
    listeners : {
        'beforehide' : function() {             ◁┐  Prevent menu from
            return false;                        ❺  hiding for testing
        }
    }

});

menu.showAt([100,100]);
```

In listing 12.1 you do a whole heck of a lot to set up your test bed, which contains a newDepartment handler and a base Menu with a single Item. You accomplish this with a few lines of code. Here's how it works.

The first thing you do is create a genericHandler ❶ method, which you'll use for just about every Menu Item that you create and use. When clicked, Menu Items call handlers with two arguments, the instance of Menu Item that was clicked and the instance of Ext.EventObject that was generated by the click action of the user. In our newDepartment handler, you only accept the Menu Item argument and use its text property to display a MessageBox alert window to provide you with feedback that the handler was called.

Next, you create a configuration object for a Menu Item, newDepartment ❷, which has a text property and a handler property, which is a reference to our generic-Handler. Notice that you're not specifying an xtype property for this configuration object. This is because the defaultType property for the Menu widget is 'menuitem' out of the box.

You then create an array referenced as menuItems ❸. You do this so you can abstract the list of Menu Items that you're creating for our test Menu. As you continue, you'll add items to this list.

Next you create an instance of Ext.menu.Menu ❹, which has two properties. The first is items, which is the reference to the menuItems array of items. Next is a listeners configuration object, which contains a beforehide event listener that you place here just for testing purposes ❺. If you recall our Component model conversation from eons ago, you may remember that certain events can be vetoed, causing the cancellation of a specific behavior. By the listener explicitly returning false, you prevent the Menu from hiding. This keeps the Menu frozen onscreen, which is perfect for testing.

Last, you show the Menu by calling its showAt method and pass a single argument, which is an array of coordinates, top and left.

Figure 12.1 shows this thing in action. When you render your code, you see the Menu with the single menu Item (figure 12.1, left) and when you click it, the Mes-sageBox appears (figure 12.1, right), pro-viding feedback that the handler was called. Cool! Something is missing, how-ever. The Menu seems, well, a bit plain to me. What do you think about adding some icon flare to the Menu? I like the idea too. Let's do it.

Figure 12.1 Our newDepartment Menu Item (left) and the Item handler (right) in action

12.1.2 Obtaining and using Icons

Early in the book, we discussed how to add icons to widgets by means of the iconCls configuration property. With so much material since then, I think it's relatively safe to say that a quick refresher is in order.

Most developers who use Ext JS use 16x16 icons in their applications. The pre-ferred method to specify icons is by means of CSS rules. Here's an example:

```
.icon-accept {
    background-image: url(icons/accept.png) !important;
}
```

The icon-accept CSS class contains a background-image rule with an !important directive. That's it, no magic. Per the Ext JS CSS (unwritten) standard, I typically pre-fix all CSS icon rules with icon-. This ensures that there's no cross-pollution with any other CSS namespace in the CSS domain. I highly recommend you do the same.

By now you're probably wondering where you can get these icons. Well, the most widely used icon set is the famfamfam Silk icon set, which has over 1,000 16x16 icons at your disposal and was developed by Mark James. It's licensed under the Creative Commons Attribution 2.5 License. To download it, visit http://famfamfam.com/lab/icons/silk/.

If that's not enough, then you can add over 460 icons from developer Damien Guard, known as the Silk Companion icon set and containing many useful derivatives of the famfamfam Silk icons. To download this set, visit http://damieng.com/creative/icons/silk-companion-1-icons. The Silk Companion set is licensed under both the Creative Commons Attribution 2.5 and 3.0 licenses.

NOTE   To read learn more about the Creative Commons Attribution 2.5 and 3.0 licenses, see http://creativecommons.org/licenses and click the 3.0 links.

If you've been doing your math, you've probably calculated over 1,460 icons from which to choose if you use both sets. This means 1,460 CSS rules to write. Let me tell you that there's absolutely no way I'd write those CSS rules by hand! How do we solve the problem of having to write all of those rules by hand?

12.1.3   *Taming the icon madness*

I solved this problem easily by downloading both icon sets, merging them into one directory, and writing a quick and dirty Bash shell script to compile a CSS file that contains a rule for each icon.

To use this compilation, you'll need to download the compiled set at http://extjsinaction.com/icons/icons.zip. When you extract the file, you'll find two CSS files, icons.css and icons.ie6.css, along with the directory icons, which contains the icon images.

The first CSS file is a compilation for all of the icons that are in their native PNG (Portable Network Graphics) format, which works well for Mozilla-based browsers as well as Internet Explorer 7 and 8. PNGs, however, don't get rendered properly in Internet Explorer 6 without some extensive JavaScript hacking, which I refuse to do.

To solve that problem, I created GIF versions (via a shell script) of the PNG icons to make them compatible with IE6 and compiled a list of the .gif files named icons.ie6.css.

To use any one of these, you must include the required CSS in the head of your browser, as follows:

```
<link rel="stylesheet" type="text/css" href="icons/icons.css" />
```

Next, you need to change the newDepartment configuration object to include the iconCls property:

```
var genericItem = {
    text    : 'Generic Item',
    handler : genericHandler,
    iconCls : 'icon-accept'
}
```

Refresh the page and see the result of your change. Mine is shown in figure 12.2.

As you can see, the `accept.png` icon image file now displays to the left of our `Menu Item` as instructed in the `iconCls` configuration property. Remember that you can use any of these icons in any widget that

Figure 12.2   The result of adding an `Icon` to a `Menu Item` via the `iconCls` configuration property

accepts the `iconCls` property, which includes `Buttons`, `TreeNodes`, and `Panels`, to name a few.

You'll be using this icon set for the rest of this chapter and every chapter moving forward. Please remember to include the icons when you generate new pages to work with.

Now that we have this out of the way, we can move on to the next typical Ext JS `Menu` problem, which is adding submenus to our `Menus`.

12.1.4   Adding a submenu

Developing submenus for `Menus` is something that's another pretty common task for Ext JS developers. They perform two useful functions at the same time. The first is the organization of like `Menu Items` and the second is a direct result of the grouping, which is cleanup of the parent `Menu`.

Let's add a submenu to our `Menu`. You'll want to add this code somewhere before the `menuItems` array you created earlier.

Listing 12.2   Adding a submenu to our base `Menu`

```
var newDepartment = {
    text   : 'New Department',                    ❶  Menu Item configuration
    iconCls : 'icon-group_add',                       object with submenu
    menu   : [                                     ❷  Menu shortcut list
        {                                              of configuration
            text    : 'Management',
            iconCls : 'icon-user_suit_black',
            handler : genericHandler
        },
        {
            text    : 'Accounting',
            iconCls : 'icon-user_green',
            handler : genericHandler
        },
        {
            text    : 'Sales',
            iconCls : 'icon-user_brown',
            handler : genericHandler
        }
    ]
}
```

In listing 12.2, you create another `newDepartment` Menu Item, `newDepartment` ❶, that contains the typical configuration properties such as `text` and `iconCls`. What's new is the `menu` property ❷, which contains a list of `Menu Item` configuration objects, each using our `genericHandler`. This *shortcut* method of adding a submenu to a `Menu Item` is common. In the spirit of Ext JS, there's more than one way to skin this cat. You could elect to set `menu` as an instance of `Ext.menu.Menu` or specify a `Menu XType` configuration object.

Here's what the code would look like if you specified an `xtype` instead of a shortcut array of `Menu Items`:

```
var newDepartment = {
    text    : 'New Department',
    iconCls : 'icon-group_add',
    menu    : {
        xtype : 'menu',
        /* menu specific properties here */
        items : [
            /* menu Items here */
        ]
    }
}
```

Choosing the implementation method is up to you. I suggest creating a separate configuration object for a submenu only if you need to set menu-specific properties. Obviously, if you have no menu-specific properties to apply to a submenu, you'll set the `menu` property to an array of menu `Items`.

Next, you need to add your menu to the `menuItems` array:

```
var menuItems = [
    genericMenuItem,
    newDepartment
];
```

To see the fruits of your labor, you'll have to refresh your page. Mine is shown in figure 12.3.

Cool, you can now see the New Department `Menu Item` displayed in your `Menu`. Hovering over the `MenuItem` reveals the submenu. Clicking any of the `Menu Items` in the submenu will result in the `MessageBox` `alert` dialog box displaying the text of the submenu.

Although this is usable, it can be improved somewhat. Next, we'll explore adding a `SeparatorItem` to the main `Menu` and a `TextItem` to the submenu, cleaning up the `Menu` UI a bit.

Figure 12.3   The addition of a Menu Item with a submenu

12.1.5   *Adding a Separator and TextItem*

Much like the `Toolbar Separator` widget is used to separate `Toolbar` items with a line, `menu.Separators` are used to physically separate menu `Items`. These are typically used to separate groups or clusters of like `Menu Items` from another group or cluster. Because all of the `Menu Items` moving forward will contain submenus, you should separate them with a `Separator`.

Modify the `menuItems` array as follows:

```
var menuItems = [
    genericMenuItem,
    '-',
    newDepartment
];
```

Add a string with a hyphen to the menu's items list, and it will get interpreted as `menu.Separator`. Figure 12.4 shows the change to our UI.

Figure 12.4 Adding a `menu.Separator` (horizontal line) to our `Menu`

You can see now that a horizontal line separates the first and the second `Menu Items`. Although the `Separator` is generally used to group like items, it's much more powerful than a simple line.

Here we used the shortcut to generate the `Separator`. Technically, it extends `menu.BaseItem`, which means that you can make it clickable and assign a handler to it. Although it's technically possible to do this, in terms of UI design, I don't advocate using it in this manner.

We've added the `Separator`, but I think we can dress up the department submenu a bit. In the following listing, you'll add a menu `TextItem`. To do this, you'll have to create a configuration object to add it to the department submenu.

Listing 12.3 Adding a text item to the department submenu

```
{
    xtype : 'menutextitem',              ◁⎤  Set xtype
    text  : 'Choose One',                 ❶  property
    style : {
        'border'           : '1px solid #999999',   ◁⎤  Set style
        'margin'           : "0px 0px 1px 0px",      ❷  of TextItem
        'display'          : 'block',
        'padding'          : '3px',
        'font-weight'      : 'bold',
        'font-size'        : '12px',
        'text-align'       : 'center'
        'background-color' : '#D6E3F2',

    }
},
```

In listing 12.3, you injected the new configuration object as the first element of the menu array for the `newDepartment` `Menu`. Remember that the `defaultType` for `Menu` is `'menuitem'`, so you have to override this setting by setting the `xtype` property to `'menutextitem'` ❶. You also set the `style` ❷ of this `TextItem` to ensure that it looks presentable. I'll show you in a bit what the unstyled `TextItem` looks like.

To see the `TextItem` in action, you need to refresh your page. My page is shown in figure 12.5.

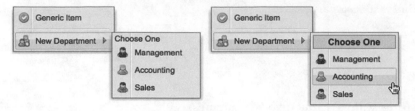

Figure 12.5   Choosing not to style a `TextItem` (left) will result in an incomplete look and feel for your `Menu`. Adding a touch of style (right) will clean up the `Menu`.

Looking at figure 12.5, it's easy to see the difference between the unstyled and styled `TextItems`. Obviously, the `style` of the item is left up to you and your requirements.

We've covered how to add the `menu.Separator` and `TextItem`, both of which aid in the visual styles of our `Menu`. There are two other types of `Menus` that I'd like you to become familiar with, `DateMenu` and `ColorMenu`.

12.1.6 *Picking a color and choosing a date*

As developers, we're often tasked to allow for the selection of a date or color, perhaps the start and end dates of an appointment or the color of text to be displayed. Ext JS provides two widgets that allow us to give this functionality to our users via `Menus`. They're the `ColorMenu` and `DateMenu`, which are both descendants of `Ext.menu.Menu`.

This means that you can create a direct instance of both and anchor and display them like their superclass. Unlike a traditional `Menu`, they don't manage any child items other than what they're designed for.

Instead of creating instances of these directly, let's add them to our test-bed `Menu`. But, in order to do that, you'll have to add `Menu Items` that you can anchor them to. Also, their handlers pass somewhat different arguments than `Menu Items`, so you'll need to create a generic handler specifically for these newly added `Menus`.

Here comes that itch to code again. Let's get started.

Listing 12.4   Using `ColorMenu` and `DateMenu`

```
var colorAndDateHandler = function(picker, choice) {          Color and
    Ext.MessageBox.alert('', 'Your choice is ' + choice);   ❶ date handler
}

var colorMenuItem = {                           Menu Item to
    text    : 'Choose Color',                 ❷ display the ColorMenu
    iconCls : 'icon-color_swatch',
    menu    : {
        xtype   : 'colormenu',                  ColorMenu
        handler : colorAndDateHandler         ❸ configuration Object
    }
}

var dateMenuItem = {
    text    : 'Choose Date',
    iconCls : 'icon-calendar',
```

```
    menu    : {
        xtype   : 'datemenu',
        handler : colorAndDateHandler
    }
}
var menuItems = [
   genericMenuItem,
   '-',
   genericWithSubMenu,
   colorMenuItem,
   dateMenuItem
];
```

DateMenu
4 configuration Object

Add ColorMenu and
5 DateMenu to array

In listing 12.4, you create a common handler ❶ for both the ColorMenu and Date-Menu, which is similar to the genericHandler that you created earlier but accepts a second argument, choice. Here's how this stuff works.

When an item is chosen from either the ColorMenu or DateMenu, the handler is fired with two arguments. The first is the picker from which the item was selected, and the second is the value of the item that was selected, which we aptly named choice. This works the way it does because the ColorMenu uses the ColorPalette widget and relays its select event. Likewise, the DateMenu uses the DatePicker widget in the exact same way.

The next task listing 12.4 accomplishes is to create the configuration objects ❷ for the Menu Items that will be used to display the ColorMenu ❸ and DateMenu ❹. Notice that you register the colorAndDateHandler with both the ColorMenu and DateMenu. Also, you choose appropriate icons for these Menu Items.

Last, you append the newly created colorMenuItem and dateMenuItem references to the menuItems array ❺. Let's refresh our UI and see the changes to our Menu, as shown in figure 12.6.

As illustrated in figure 12.6, our DateMenu and ColorMenu can be displayed via hovering over the respective Menu Item. Clicking a color or a date in the respective Menu will trigger the handler, resulting in a MessageBox alert displaying the value of the item selected.

The ColorPalette for the ColorMenu and DatePicker for the DateMenu can be customized by applying ColorPalette- or DatePicker-specific properties to their respective containers.

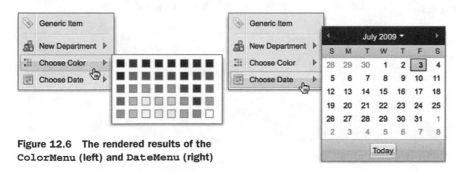

Figure 12.6 The rendered results of the
ColorMenu (left) and DateMenu (right)

For instance, to show only the colors red, green, and blue on the ColorMenu, set the colors property with an array of color hex values as follows:

```
colors  : ['FF0000', '00FF00', '0000FF']
```

Setting this property will result in the ColorMenu displaying three boxes, one for each of the colors we described in the array. To learn more about the ColorPalette- or DatePicker-specific properties to configure, check out their respective API documents.

We've just tackled using the ColorMenu and DateMenu widgets. We have yet one more Menu topic to discuss, and that's CheckItems, which allows you to configure a Menu Item that works like a Checkbox or RadioGroup.

12.1.7   *Put that menu Item in check*

In forms, Checkboxes and RadioGroups allow users to select an item, and the selection is visibly persisted in the UI. In Microsoft Word for Apple OS X, for instance, I can choose how to view a document by clicking View and selecting a view to activate, as shown in figure 12.7.

In this figure, I selected the Print Layout view, and the selection is persisted for each and every subsequent viewing of this menu. The same paradigm could exist in an Ext JS application. One such paradigm could be where a user chooses between a Grid-Panel and a DataView to display data from a single Store.

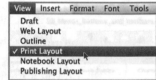

First, I want to show you exactly how to leverage a single menu CheckItem and multiple CheckItems in a checkGroup. Afterward, we'll discuss a possible use for this widget in the hope that it will spark ideas on how to leverage it.

In the following listing you'll create a single CheckItem and add it to our menuItems array.

Figure 12.7   A check view menu in OS X, where the user selection is persisted

---

Listing 12.5   Adding a single `CheckItem`

```
var singleCheckItem = {
    text          : 'Check me',
    checked       : false,
    checkHandler  : colorAndDateHandler
}

var menuItems = [
    genericMenuItem,
    '-',
    genericWithSubMenu,
    colorMenuItem,
    dateMenuItem,
    '-',
    singleCheckItem
];
```

❶ Create a CheckItem configuration

❷ Add checked Boolean value

❸ Specify checkHandler

❹ Add SeparatorItem and CheckItem to array

In listing 12.5 you create a single CheckItem ❶ using typical XType configuration. If you run down the list, you'll see only three properties, none of which is the xtype.

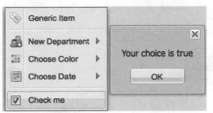

Figure 12.8 Clicking our
`CheckItem` (left) makes a
check icon appear and triggers
the `checkHandler` (right).

This is because you can be extremely lazy with this widget and specify whether the item is `checked` or not. Ext JS will conveniently handle the instantiation of the `menu.CheckItem` widget for you if the checked ❷ property is a Boolean and is present.

The next property of importance is `checkHandler` ❸, which is similar to the typical `Menu Item` handler property, except it passes whether the `CheckItem` has been *checked* or not, which is the second argument that's passed to this method. It's much like the arguments passed to the `ColorMenu` and `DateMenu` handlers. It's for this reason that we're reusing the `colorAndDateHandler`.

Finally, you add a menu `Separator` and our `singleCheckItem` to the `menuItems` array ❹. Figure 12.8 shows what the addition of the `CheckItem` looks like in our `Menu`.

Because you used the `menu.Separator`, you can see the physical separation of your menu `CheckItem`. Because you set the `checked` value to `false`, the `CheckItem` appears with an icon that's unchecked. Clicking it calls the `checkHandler`, which displays the `MessageBox` alert dialog box.

> **NOTE** We didn't set the `iconCls` for the `CheckItem`, but you technically can. Setting the `iconCls`, however, means that you're responsible for programmatically changing the `iconCls` upon call of the `checkHandler`, which can be done by using the `Item.setIconClass` method. See the `Menu.Item` API documentation page for details.

The use and configuration of a single `CheckItem` are obviously pretty easy. Remember that `CheckItems` can be grouped, which allows users to select a single `CheckItem` out of that group, much like the Microsoft Word View menu you saw previously. Next, we'll construct such a group.

12.1.8 *Select only one item at a time*

The configuration of a single `CheckItem` is relatively trivial compared to that of a group of `CheckItems`. This is mainly because you're configuring multiple `CheckItems` at the same time. In the following listing you'll construct a cluster of grouped `CheckItems`.

Listing 12.6 Adding a cluster of `CheckItems`

```
var setFlagColor = function(menuItem, checked) {
    if (checked === true) {
        var color = menuItem.text.toLowerCase();
        var iconCls = 'icon-flag_' + color;
```

Common
checkHandler
❶ for CheckItems

```
            Ext.getCmp('colorMenu').setIconClass(iconCls);
    }
}

var colorCheckMenuItem = {
    text    : 'Favorite Flag',          ◁──        Menu Item for
    id      : 'colorMenu',               ❷          CheckItems
    iconCls : 'icon-help',
    menu    : {                          ◁──        Menu configuration
        defaults : {                                object for
            checked       : false,       ❸          CheckItems
            group         : 'colorChkGroup',
            checkHandler  : setFlagColor
        },
        items : [
            { text : 'Red'   },
            { text : 'Green' },
            { text : 'Blue'  }
        ]
    }
}
```

In listing 12.6, you create a new common checkHandler, setFlagColor ❶, for the grouped CheckItems you'll create later. You do this because when CheckItems are grouped, they each call their respective checkHandler when any member in the group has been clicked, with each call passing the checked value of the respective CheckItem.

This shared checkHandler will test the value of the checked parameter. If it's true, it will call setIconCls on the parent Menu Item of the CheckItems Menu. This will effectively set the icon with a flag color that matches the selection of the grouped CheckItem. This is a fun way to provide visual feedback that something was selected and flex some of the Menu Item's muscle and flexibility.

You create the Menu Item colorCheckMenuItem ❷, which has a question mark icon as default. Notice that the menu configuration is an object ❸ instead of an array. This is precisely what we were talking about before, where you can use an Object to configure a Menu instead of an array of Menu Item configuration objects.

You do this because you want to set the default on all Menu Items that are checked to false, the common group that each CheckItem will belong to, and the check-Handler. This means that the items array of the Menu configuration object can be simple objects with just a text property for each Item.

Now that you have that complete, please refresh the page and see this in action. It should look similar to figure 12.9.

Refreshing this page reveals our recently configured Favorite Flag Menu Item in our test Menu with a question mark icon. Hover over that Item and it will reveal the submenu with the three grouped color CheckItems. Notice that none of the items bears the check mark. Remember, this is because all items are set to checked : false per the defaults configuration object. You could have easily set any one item as checked : true.

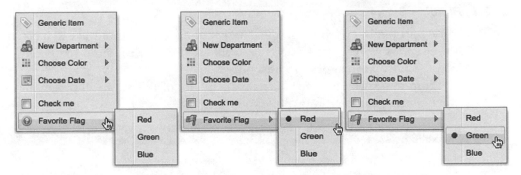

Figure 12.9 A group of `CheckItems` (left), where only one item can be selected (center and right)

Click a `CheckItem` and it will change the `iconCls` for the parent `Menu Item`. Revealing the `Menu` that contains the checked items again will result in a radio icon showing to the left of the selected item. Selecting a different `Item` will result in the relative changes occurring for that `CheckItem`.

This wraps up our long, detailed view into the world of the Ext JS `Menu`, where you learned about and exercised all of the `Menu Items` along with the color and date `Menus`. Next, we'll dive into the world of Ext `Buttons` and `SplitButtons`, where you'll learn how to configure them and associate `Menus` to them.

12.2 *Users know how to push your Buttons*

In this section, you'll learn how to implement `Buttons` and then learn about the `SplitButton`, which is a descendant of the `Button` widget.

`Buttons` in Ext JS 2.0 were rigid; they didn't scale well and the icon position couldn't be configured. It was also particularly difficult to have a `Button` take part in a layout as a managed child item.

Some of these limitations had to do with how the `Button` widget itself was constructed, where the `Button` class in 2.0 extended `Component`, which means that it's not meant to be used in a layout. Also, the `Button` sprite images were not designed to allow the `Button` to scale much larger than its intended size. In 3.0 of the framework, this changes for the better.

The `Buttons` in this version of the framework extend `BoxComponent`, which is where all of the child size-management methods are, meaning that `Buttons` are now fully capable of taking part in any layout. Likewise, the `Button` sprites were updated to allow for extremely large `Buttons`. You could have a single `Button` take one-half of the screen if you want to, though it would probably scare away your users.

As you transition to learning more about and constructing `Buttons`, you'll learn that `Buttons` have a lot in common with `Menu Items`.

12.2.1 *Building Buttons*

You'll start out by creating a simple handler and a Button that will call it, as shown in listing 12.7. Create a blank page that includes all of the required Ext JS files and the icon CSS file that you worked with a bit ago.

From our work with Menu Items earlier, a lot of this stuff will be familiar to you, which means that you can increase your pace a bit.

Listing 12.7   Building a simple `Button` with a generic handler

```
var btnHandler = function(btn) {             Generic Button
    btn.el.frame();                        ❶ handler
}

new Ext.Button({                        ❷ Generic Button
    renderTo : Ext.getBody(),
    text     : 'Plain Button',
    iconCls  : 'icon-control_power',
    handler  : btnHandler
});
```

In listing 12.7, you create a generic Button handler, btnHandler ❶, that will call the frame effect on the element of the Button that calls it. Next, you create an instance of an Ext Button ❷ and render it to the document.body by means of the Ext.getBody method call. You also set the text, iconCls, and handler properties, which are exactly like the menu Item configuration properties.

Load the page with this code and you'll see the Button in action, as shown in figure 12.10.

Our Button renders onscreen, seemingly just waiting to be pushed. Clicking it forces the handler to be called, which applies the frame effect to the Button's element, giving you visual indication that the handler fired properly. Simple, isn't it? Next, you'll attach a Menu to a Button, which is a common practice in Ext JS applications.

Figure 12.10   Our Button in action (left) and the frame effect (right), which is a visual indication that the handler was called

12.2.2 *Attaching a Menu to a Button*

You attach a Menu to a Button exactly the same way you attach a Menu to a Menu Item, which is specifying either a list of menu Item configuration objects or a complete Menu configuration object. For this exercise, shown in the following listing, you'll do the latter.

Listing 12.8   Attaching a `Menu` to a `Button`

```
var setFlagColor = function(menuItem, checked) {        Modified
    if (checked === true) {                           setFlagColor
        var color = menuItem.text.toLowerCase();     ❶ handler
        var iconCls = 'icon-flag_' + color;
        Ext.getCmp('flagButton').setIconClass(iconCls);
```

```
        }
    }
    new Ext.Button({
        renderTo : Ext.getBody(),
        text     : 'Favorite flag',
        iconCls  : 'icon-help',
        handler  : btnHandler,
        id       : 'flagButton',             ❷ Associate
        menu     : {                            menu to Button
            defaults : {
                checked      : false,
                group        : 'colorChkGroup',
                checkHandler : setFlagColor
            },
            items : [
                { text : 'Red'   },
                { text : 'Green' },
                { text : 'Blue'  }
            ]
        }
    });
```

In listing 12.8, you re-create the scenario for the previous CheckItems exercise but modify it to fit the Button. Here's how it works.

You first create the checkHandler, setFlagColor ❶, which works exactly like the one you constructed earlier, except it changes the iconCls of the Button.

Next, you create another Button that's similar to the first Button you created and is rendered to the document.body. The main difference between this Button and the other is that you configure ❷ a Menu with three grouped CheckItems, all registered to call the setFlagColor handler.

Figure 12.11 shows what our code additions and changes bring forth.

At first glance at our newly configured Button, you can see that a little black arrow now appears to the right of the text. This is the visual indication to the user that this Button contains a Menu to be revealed by a click of the Button. To display the Menu, click the Button. What happens?

You see that the Menu appears and that the Button frame effect is shown as well. Wait. What? How can this be? Well, that's because you didn't remove the handler property, which means when the Button is clicked, the Menu shows *and the handler is called.* In some cases, this is desirable behavior, but in most cases, it's not. If all this Button is to do is display a Menu, then you should remove the handler. But if you want a handler to be called separately from the display of the associated Menu, this is where the SplitButton can be useful.

Figure 12.11   Adding a Menu to a Button, which contains a few menu CheckItems

12.2.3 Do a split (SplitButton)

Use of a `SplitButton` is similar to that of a `Button`. The main difference is that the `SplitButton` has a second handler that it can call when clicked, which is known as the `arrowHandler`.

To implement the `SplitButton`, you'll slightly modify listing 12.8 to the following.

Listing 12.9   Building a simple `Button` with a generic handler

```
new Ext.SplitButton({
    renderTo : Ext.getBody(),                ◁─┐  Use SplitButton
    text     : 'Favorite flag',                │  instead of Button
    iconCls  : 'icon-help',
    handler  : btnHandler,
    id       : 'flagButton',
    menu     : {
        defaults : {
            checked      : false,
            group        : 'colorChkGroup',
            checkHandler : setFlagColor
        },
        items : [
            { text : 'Red'   },
            { text : 'Green' },
            { text : 'Blue'  }
        ]
    }
});
```

To exercise the `SplitButton`, you use the same `setFlagColor` handler you created in listing 12.8, and all of the code is the same except that you're instantiating an instance of `SplitButton` instead of `Button`. That's it. Let's render this onscreen so you can examine the visual and functional differences; see figure 12.12.

You can see that a `Separator` line has been added to the `Button`, which is the only visual difference between a regular `Button` and a `SplitButton`. But this visual difference depicts the functional difference between the `Button` and `SplitButton`.

This visual `Separator` between the arrow and the rest of the `Button` is an indication of two distinct zones for the `SplitButton`, whereas the `Button` has only one, which is why when you clicked the button, the handler was called and the `Menu` appeared.

Clicking what I like to call the "Button zone" in the `SplitButton` will call its registered `handler`. Likewise, clicking what I like to call its "Arrow zone" will display the menu and call an `arrowHandler` if it was registered.

As I said earlier, the 3.0 `Button` family is a lot more flexible in terms of layout and can scale well relative to its 2.0 ancestor. Next, we'll discuss how to modify the look of the button itself and examine some of the configuration options available to allow you to do just that.

Figure 12.12
Our `SplitButton` in action

12.2.4 *Customizing the layout of your Button*

Thus far, you've only configured `Buttons` and `SplitButtons` for use without altering the layout. With this version of the framework, you can elect to display the (Menu indication) arrow at the bottom of the button if you wish. You'd do this by configuring the `Button` via the `arrowAlign` property, which can have the value of `right` or `bottom`.

Likewise, the icons can be aligned at any side of the `Button`, but left is the default. Figure 12.13 demonstrates each of the `arrowAlign` and `iconAlign` options.

In this illustration, we used 16 x 16 icons, which fit perfectly in just about every portion of the framework where custom icons can be used. You can use larger icons if you wish. Also, even though you see the `SplitButton` being used in figure 12.13, remember that `Buttons` also can be configured in the same way.

The height of the `Buttons` and `SplitButtons` can be conveniently configured via the `scale` configuration property. This also controls the height of the icon that can be displayed in the `Button`. There are three possible values for this property: `small` (16 pixels high, the default), `medium` (24 pixels high), and `large` (32 pixels high). You'll see this configuration property in action when you work through `ButtonGroups` in a bit.

A great demonstration of larger icons in `Buttons` can be found in the examples in the SDK. You can see them by viewing the following page in your browser: `<your_ext_dir>/examples/button/buttons.html`.

You now have the necessary skills to employ `Buttons` and `SplitButtons` with any possible icon and arrow alignment. Now that you have those important skills, you can learn how to cluster buttons in what's known as a `ButtonGroup`.

12.3 *Grouping your Buttons*

New to Ext 3.0 is the `ButtonGroup` widget, which is an extension of `Panel` and has a sole purpose: grouping similar or like functionality into clusters for the user. Ext JS `ButtonGroups` do a pretty good job of emulating the button groups found in Microsoft Word 2007 for Windows.

Being an extension of `Panel` means that just about any layout can be employed to control the way the `ButtonGroup` looks. Please be aware that even though most layouts will work within the confines of the `ButtonGroup`, please heed to my advice and stay within the confines of well-known UI design patterns. Remember, we like to keep the users happy.

Here's a pop quiz. Ready?

What class does `Button` extend? Right! The `Button` widget extends `BoxComponent`. Next question. Why is this important? Right again! This is important because

Figure 12.13 Various implementations of the `SplitButton` with the possible icon and arrow alignments

BoxComponent contains the Component size-management methods that allow a Component to take part in a layout.

Next, you'll build your first ButtonGroup using the default layout. If you're following along and want to display the icons, please remember to include the icon CSS file.

Listing 12.10   Grouping Buttons with a ButtonGroup

```
new Ext.ButtonGroup({                                    ┌─  Construct a new
    renderTo : Ext.getBody(),                            ❶  ButtonGroup
    title    : 'Manage Emails',
    items    : [
        {
            text     : 'Paste as',                       ┌─  Use SplitButton
            iconCls  : 'icon-clipboard',                 ❷  instead of Button
            menu     : [
                {
                    text    : 'Plain Text',
                    iconCls : 'icon-paste_plain'
                },
                {
                    text    : 'Word',
                    iconCls : 'icon-paste_word'
                }
            ]
        },
        {
            text    : 'Copy',
            iconCls : 'icon-page_white_copy'
        },
        {
            text    : 'Cut',
            iconCls : 'icon-cut'
        },
        {
            text    : 'Clear',
            iconCls : 'icon-erase'
        }
    ]
});
```

In listing 12.10, you construct a new instance of ButtonGroup ❶ with four Buttons, one of which has an attached Menu ❷. Like the Buttons that you created earlier, you render the ButtonGroup to the document body. That's all there is to it. Figure 12.14 shows what our ButtonGroup looks like rendered onscreen.

Here you see our first ButtonGroup, which contains three Buttons, the first of which is a SplitButton, in action. By default, the ButtonGroup uses the TableLayout, which is why the Buttons are arranged in a single row.

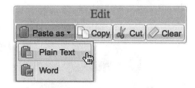

Figure 12.14   Our first ButtonGroup in action

Next, you'll use your `TableLayout` ninja skills to rear-
range these `Buttons` so they look a little more like the edit
button group in Word 2007 for Windows. If you're unfa-
miliar with the toolbars of Microsoft Word 2007, figure
12.15 is a snapshot of what you're trying to achieve in listing 12.11.

**Figure 12.15 The Clipboard
button group as found in MS
Word 2007 for Windows**

Now that you know what you're going to replicate, let's
get down to business.

Listing 12.11   Visually reorganizing our `ButtonGroup`

```
new Ext.ButtonGroup({
    renderTo : Ext.getBody(),          ①  Re-create the
    title    : 'Clipboard',                ButtonGroup
    columns  : 2,
    items    : [                        ②  Specify 2 columns for
        {                                   TableLayout config
            text       : 'Paste',
            iconCls    : 'icon-clipboard_24x24',   ③  Paste Button
            rowspan    : '3',                          spans 3 rows
            scale      : 'large',
            arrowAlign : 'bottom',      ④  Scale Button and
            iconAlign  : 'top',             icon as large
            width      : 50,
            menu       : [
                {
                    text    : 'Plain Text',
                    iconCls : 'icon-paste_plain'
                },
                {
                    text    : 'Word',
                    iconCls : 'icon-paste_word'
                }
            ]
        },
        {
            iconCls : 'icon-cut'
        },
        {
            iconCls : 'icon-page_white_copy'
        },
        {
            iconCls : 'icon-paintbrush'
        }
    ]
});
```

In listing 12.11, you use all of your acquired knowledge to leverage the default `Table-
Layout` that the `ButtonGroup` ① uses to create a Microsoft Word 2007–like button
group. Here's how it works.

When re-creating the `ButtonGroup`, you instruct the `TableLayout` to render only two columns ❷. This ensures that the `Buttons` within this group will be properly aligned.

You also modify how you create the first `Button` in the set. You set a `TableLayout` only-child configuration property, `rowspan` ❸ to 3, which ensures that this `Button` spans the first three rows of the table. You also set the `scale` ❹ to `large`, which ensures that the modified famfamfam clipboard icon that I stretched to fit the 24 x 24 form factor fits in the large `Button` nicely. Also notice that you set the `arrowAlign` to `bottom`, which helps you complete the look.

The rest of the `Buttons` have their `text` property removed, which means that their icon is the only visual representation of what the `Button` does. Let's see what our changes render, and compare the result to the Microsoft Word 2007 button group, as shown in figure 12.16.

Our latest implementation of the Ext `ButtonGroup` is similar, but obviously it's not a 100 percent match. It's close, though. And that's what is important to our users, right? The shallower the learning curve for the applications that you build for them, the happier they'll be.

The point of this exercise wasn't to exactly duplicate the Word 2007 button group but rather to show that you can, if you choose to, configure the Ext `ButtonGroup` to organize the buttons it contains however your application requires.

As you just learned, `ButtonGroups` are a good tool to leverage to group similarly functioning `Buttons`. The learning curve to using the `ButtonGroup` is relatively shallow because you already know how to use the various layouts and so on.

Now that you know how to use `Menus`, `Buttons`, and `ButtonGroups`, you can shift gears and learn how to apply them to `Toolbars`, where they're most commonly used.

Figure 12.16   Our modified `ButtonGroup` (left) versus the Microsoft Word 2007 `Button` group (right)

12.4   *Toolbars*

`Toolbars` are generally an area where you can lay out a cluster of items for the user to interact with. In Ext 3.0, `Toolbars` can easily manage just about anything you want to put in them. This is because of the recent enhancements to the `Toolbar` class and the introduction of the `ToolbarLayout`.

`Toolbars`, like any `Component`, can be `renderedTo` any element in the DOM but are most commonly used in `Panels` and any descendant thereof. This is where you'll keep your focus for this `Widget`.

In the next example, you'll create a `Window` that contains a `Toolbar` with quite a few items, including a `ComboBox`, as an exercise to show how easy it is to add `Components` other than `Buttons` to the `Toolbar`. The following listing is lengthy because of the number of child items that you're going to create for the `Toolbar`.

Listing 12.12 Building a `Toolbar` within a `Window`

```
var tbar = {                                    ◁┐  Create Toolbar
    items : [                                    ❶  configuration object
        {
            text        : 'Add',
            iconCls     : 'icon-add'
        },
        '-',                                     ◁┐  Shorthand for
        {                                        ❷  Toolbar Separator
            text        : 'Update',
            iconCls     : 'icon-update'
        },
        '-',
        {
            text        : 'Delete',              ❸  Shorthand for
            iconCls     : 'icon-delete'             Toolbar greedy
        },                                       ◁   spacer
        '->',
        'Select one of these: ',                        ◁┐  Shorthand
        {                                                   for Toolbar
            xtype     : 'combo',         ◁┐  Configuration ❹  TextItem
            width     : 100,             ❺  object for
            store     : [                    ComboBox
                'Toolbars',
                'Are',
                'Awesome'
            ]
        }
    ]
};

new Ext.Window({
    width  : 500,
    height : 200,                    ❻  Add toolbar
    tbar   : tbar                  ◁    to Window
}).show();
```

In listing 12.12, you create a `Toolbar` configuration object ❶. This object has a single property, `items`, which is a list of configuration objects and some strings. Notice that you don't have to specify an `xtype` for the `Toolbar` configuration object. This is because when you associate it to the `Window` via the `tbar` or `bbar` property, Ext will automatically *assume* that the configuration object is for a `Toolbar`.

The `items` array contains quite a few, well, items that we should discuss. The first you've seen, which is a typical `Button` configuration with a `text` property and `iconCls`. The reason you don't see an `xtype` property for `Buttons` is that the `defaultType` for toolbars is `button`.

After the first `Button` is defined, you use the shorthand for the `Toolbar.Separator` class ❷, which provides a vertical line dividing items in the `Toolbar`. Although you *could* write out the configuration of the `Separator`, I typically use the shorthand. If you wanted to have granular control over the `Separator`, you'd need to write out the complete configuration object for it, including the `xtype` property, which is `tbseparator`.

Moving on, you create two more buttons with another `Separator` between them. After that, you'll find this funny-looking string, `'->'`, which is shorthand for the `Toolbar.Fill` ❸ widget. This little widget will instruct the `Toolbar` widget to place any item(s) defined thereafter on the right side of the toolbar. This effectively pushes the items to the right of the `Toolbar`.

> **NOTE** Only one `Fill` item can be placed in the `Toolbar`. Think of it as an absolute divider, between the left side of the `Toolbar` and the right. Once you place that divider, any items following it will be placed to the right. Any other `Fill` definitions after the first will be ignored.

Next, you use the shorthand for the `Toolbar.TextItem` ❹ widget. Like the other shorthand strings, the `TextItem` can be configured via a configuration object, which will give you greater control over it, including styling. I honestly only configure a `TextItem` via an object if I need this control. Otherwise, I use the string shorthand.

After the `TextItem` configuration, you set up a quick and dirty `ComboBox` ❺ configuration object. You do this to demonstrate how easy it is to embed items other than `Buttons` in the `Toolbar`.

Last, you render a new instance of `Window` and affix our `Toolbar` configuration object to the top `Toolbar` position by referencing it via the `tbar` ❻ property. Let's render it onscreen and see what it looks like (figure 12.17).

When you look at your rendered `Toolbar`, you'll see that the three `Buttons` appear with `Separators` between them, all of which are left aligned. Right aligned are the `TextItem` and `ComboBox`.

The placement of `Buttons` in a `Toolbar` is relatively common practice, but a `Toolbar` can quickly get overcrowded. Using `ButtonGroups` helps alleviate this situation. Adding `ButtonGroups` to a `Toolbar` is as simple as referencing it as a child item of the `Toolbar`.

Figure 12.18 is a great example of `ButtonGroups` being used in the experimental Ext Surf chat application.

As you've learned, using `Toolbars` is relatively straightforward, and you can add all types of stuff to the `Toolbar` to give your users the ability to effectively interact with your applications.

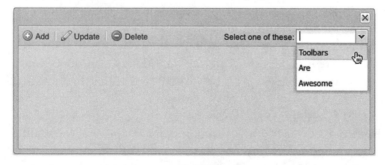

Figure 12.17 Our `Toolbar` rendered inside a `Window`

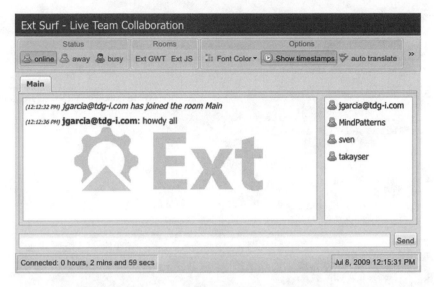

Figure 12.18 ButtonGroups used in a Toolbar as seen in the Ext Surf live chat application

> ### The dangers of using a different layout
> Remember that the `Toolbar` uses the `ToolbarLayout`. This layout is what gives the `Toolbar` a lot of its power, including responsiveness to the `Toolbar.Fill` widget. You need to exercise some caution when thinking about using another layout with a `Toolbar`. Although you *technically* can leverage another layout, you'll lose features like the `Toolbar Fill` and automatic overflow protection, which are part of what make the `Toolbar` what it is.

This wraps up our discussion of `Toolbar`s. We can now focus on the last topic, `Ext.Action`, which ties together everything you've learned and practiced thus far.

12.5 Read, set, Ext.Action!

Often, as developers, we're tasked to provide a means for the same functionality to be accessed by different methods. For instance, we may be asked to create an edit menu that contains the typical cut, copy, and paste `Menu Items` along with adding them directly to a `Toolbar`.

With that request, we have two options: either create instances of `Button` and `Menu Item` each with similar configurations or abstract them to an `Ext.Action`. I vote for the latter, because it's much easier.

You'll build out a couple of actions in the next listing, and we'll go into further detail about how this all works.

Listing 12.13   Using Ext.Actions

```
var genericHandler = function(menuItem) {
    Ext.MessageBox.alert('', 'Your choice is ' + menuItem.text);
}
var copyAction = new Ext.Action({
    text    : 'Copy',
    iconCls : 'icon-page_white_copy',
    handler : genericHandler
});

var cutAction = new Ext.Action({
    text    : 'Cut',
    iconCls : 'icon-cut',
    handler : genericHandler
});

var pasteAction = new Ext.Action({
    text    : 'Paste',
    iconCls : 'icon-paste_plain',
    handler : genericHandler
});

var editMenuBtn = {
    text : 'Edit',
    menu : [
        cutAction,
        copyAction,
        pasteAction
    ]
}
new Ext.Window({
    width       : 300,
    height      : 200,
    tbar        : [
        editMenuBtn,
        '->',
        cutAction,
        copyAction,
        pasteAction
    ]
}).show();
```

Create generic handler for actions ❶

Create first Ext.Action ❷

Add actions as menu Items ❸

Add actions as toolbar buttons ❹

In listing 12.13 you do quite a lot to leverage Ext.Action to build out the hypothetically required UI. First you re-create the genericHandler ❶ that you used earlier in this chapter.

Next, you create three Actions ❷ for the copy, cut, and paste functionality that you desire. Notice that the properties set on each action are syntactically the same as those of the Button and Menu Items you've created in the past. This is part of the key to understanding what Actions are and how they work, which is why we're going to digress a little.

Action is a class that does nothing more than encapsulate the common configuration of a Button or MenuItem. That's it. When you create an instance of an Ext.Action and inspect it in Firebug, you'll see a bunch of methods and properties. When you (or Ext JS) go to instantiate an instance of Button or MenuItem using Action, the properties and methods of the Action that you're using are applied to the Button or MenuItem during the constructor call of either class.

Ext.Action is a configuration wrapper for either the Button or MenuItem, where many instances of each of those classes can share the Action configuration. Now that you know exactly what Actions are, understanding the rest of this listing will be a breeze.

After you create the Actions, you create a Button ❸ configuration object and set a menu property, which is an array of each of the Actions. Next, you create and show an instance of Ext.Window, where you specify a tbar property, which is a list containing the Button with a Menu, a Separator, and the three Actions ❹. This is where you can see the usability of Actions.

Without rendering this onscreen, you can predict what the code will construct. Go ahead and display the page and see if you're right; my page is shown in figure 12.19.

Ah-ha! The rendered UI from listing 12.13 is as we expected. You see three menu Items appear under the Edit Button when clicked and three Buttons that are right-aligned in the Toolbar.

Unfortunately, Action is one of those classes that are commonly overlooked by developers. I have to admit that I'm guilty of this myself. When developing Buttons and Menus for your UI, try to remember that if the functionality is the same for two or more Buttons or Menu Items, use Actions. Trust me, it will save you time in the long run.

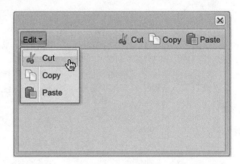

Figure 12.19 The results of listing 12.13, where Actions are being used to configure Buttons and Menu Items

12.6 Summary

In this chapter we covered quite a few topics, which revolve around Menus, Buttons, Toolbars, and Actions.

We started by exploring the ins and outs of Menus and all of the Menu Items that can be used. In doing so, we digressed a little to show you more about where to get free 16 x 16 icons that lots of web 2.0 applications are using. You also learned how to nest Menus and even affix Color and Date menus to Menu Items.

You also took time to learn about the Ext Button and SplitButton, where you learned how to configure how they look and feel by setting the iconAlign and arrow-Align properties. Next, you learned how to leverage the ButtonGroup to cluster similar Buttons together and took the time to leverage the TableLayout to organize your

Buttons in a special way. Remember to set the scale property to medium or large if you're using an icon that's larger than 16 x 16.

Last, you began to tie together what you learned about Menus and Buttons when we discussed the Toolbar. You also learned about timesaving with the Ext.Action configuration wrapper class.

In the next chapter, we're going to tackle the challenge of implementing drag and drop with DOM nodes.

Part 4

Advanced Ext

The goal of this part is to take you up to the level of the Ext JS experts, where we'll take on the many ways to empower our applications with drag and drop. We'll also tackle how to extend Ext JS by creating extensions and plug-ins.

Chapter 13 is the introduction to the world of drag and drop with the framework, where we'll peek under the hood and learn about the various classes that make this user interaction possible. Along the way, we'll implement simple drag and drop with generic HTML `div`s.

Chapter 14 will springboard from chapter 13, as you learn how to implement drag and drop with the `DataView`, `GridPanel`, and `TreePanel` widgets.

This section ends in chapter 15 with an in-depth look at the world of creating Ext JS extensions and plug-ins, paving the way for you to create an application.

By the end of this section, you will have learned many of the secrets to implementing advanced features in the framework.

Drag-and-drop basics

This chapter covers

- Understanding the drag-and-drop workflow
- Dissecting the Ext JS drag-and-drop classes
- Implementing drag-and-drop override methods
- Exercising the full drag-and-drop lifecycle

One of the greatest advantages of using a graphical user interface is the ability to easily move items around the screen with simple mouse gestures. This interaction is known as *drag and drop*. We use drag and drop just about every time we use a modern computer without giving it a second thought. If you step back and think about it, you'll realize how this makes our lives a lot easier.

Want to delete a file? Click and drag the file icon and drop it on the trash or recycle bin icon. Easy, right? What if you didn't have drag and drop? How would you move a file from one location to the recycle bin? Let's quickly ponder the possibilities. You'd first click the file to provide it focus. You could then use a keyboard key combination to "cut" the file. You'd then have to find and focus the recycle bin window and use the keyboard key combination to "paste" it in. Another option would be to click to select the file to focus it and press Delete on your keyboard, but if you're right handed, this would require you to take your hand off your mouse. In contrast, drag and drop is much simpler, isn't it? Now put yourself in the world of the RIA user. What if you could use drag and drop to simplify their experience?

Fortunately, Ext JS provides a means for you to do that. In this chapter, you'll see that with a bit of elbow grease and determination, you can achieve the goal of adding drag and drop to your applications. You'll start off by learning to apply drag and drop to basic DOM elements, which will give you the foundation for applying these behaviors to widgets such as the `DataView`, `GridPanel`, and `TreePanel`, which you'll learn about in the chapter following this.

13.1   Taking a good look at drag and drop

Before drag and drop can take place, the computer must decide what can and can't be dragged and what can or can't be dropped upon. For instance, icons on your desktop can generally be dragged around, but other items, such as the clock on your taskbar (Windows) or menu bar (OS X) can't. This level of control is necessary to allow the enforcement of certain workflows, as we'll discuss in a bit.

In order to really understand drag and drop, we need to discuss the entire workflow. We'll do this by dividing the workflow into what I like to call the drag-and-drop lifecycle, which can be broken up into three major categories: start of drag, the drag operation, and drop.

13.1.1   The drag-and-drop lifecycle

Using the desktop paradigm, any icon on the desktop can be dragged around, but only a select few can be dropped on (generally disk or folder icons) the trash or recycle bin, or icons for executables (applications). In Ext JS, the same registrations must occur for drag and drop to be possible. Any element that can participate in drag and drop must be initialized as such. For elements in the DOM to participate in drag and drop, they must, at the least, be registered as drag items and as drop targets. Once the items are registered, drag and drop can take place.

Drag operations are initiated by clicking and holding a mouse button over a UI element followed by mouse movement while the mouse button is being held. The computer decides, based on the registration described previously, whether the item that's being clicked is draggable. If it isn't, then nothing happens. The user can click and attempt a drag operation but with no results. But if an element is allowed to be dragged, the UI generally creates a lightweight duplicate of that object, known as a drag proxy, that's anchored to the movements of the mouse cursor. This gives the user the feeling that they're physically moving or dragging that item onscreen.

During each tick, or X-Y coordinate change, of the mouse cursor during the drag operation, the computer determines whether you can drop the item at that given position. If drop is possible, then some sort of visual invitation for a drop operation is displayed. In figure 13.1, you see a form of drop invitation where a file icon proxy is dragged over a folder icon on the desktop.

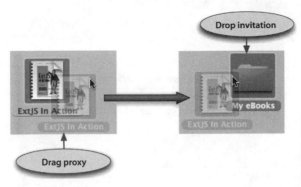

Figure 13.1 Desktop drag-and-drop interaction as seen in Mac OS X, where a drag proxy (left) is created upon an item drag event and a drop invitation is being displayed (right)

The drag-and-drop lifecycle ends when a drop operation occurs. A drop operation occurs when the mouse button is released after a drag operation has occurred. At this time the computer must decide what to do with the drop operation. Did the drop event occur on a valid drop target? If so, is the drop target part of the same drag-and-drop group as the drag element? Does it copy or move the item that was dragged? This decision is generally left to the application logic to decide and where you'll be doing most of your coding.

Although it's relatively easy to describe how drag and drop should behave, it's orders of magnitude more difficult to implement—but not impossible. One of the keys to being able to effectively implement drag and drop is a basic understanding of the class hierarchy and the jobs that each class performs. This holds true from implementing drag and drop from the basic DOM level, as you'll see in a bit, all the way to implementing it on Ext JS UI widgets.

Throttle up. We're going to climb up to 30,000 feet and take a bird's-eye view of the drag-and-drop class hierarchy.

13.1.2 A top-down view of the drag-and-drop classes

At first glance, the list of drag-and-drop classes can be a bit overwhelming. I know that when I first glanced at the list of classes in the API, I was taken aback by the options. With 14 classes, it can be considered a framework within a framework that provides functionality from the basic, such as the ability to make any DOM element draggable, to more complex features, such as the ability to drag and drop multiple nodes using what is called a *proxy*. The cool thing is that once you take a high-level look at the classes, it isn't that difficult to organize the supporting classes and understand their roles.

This is where we'll start our exploration. Figure 13.2 shows what the class hierarchy looks like. In this figure, you see the 11 drag-and-drop classes. All of the drag-and-drop functionality for the entire framework starts with the `DragDrop` class, which provides the base methods for everything drag and drop and is *meant* to be overridden. It provides only the basic tools for you to implement this behavior. It's up to you to write the code for the entire spectrum of the implementation.

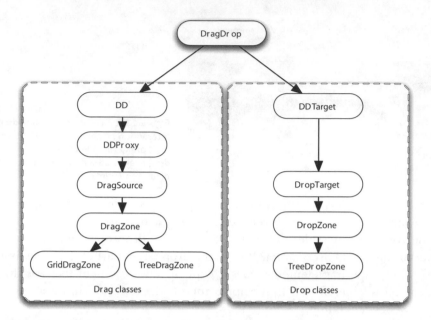

Figure 13.2   The drag-and-drop class hierarchy can be broken up into two major sections, drag (left) and drop (right).

This is the fundamental key to understanding how drag and drop works because this code design pattern is repeated throughout the drag-and-drop class hierarchy. This concept is extremely powerful because by having the basic tools to add this behavior to your application, you can easily ensure that drag and drop works for your application's needs.

As you look down the chain of inheritance, you can see that a split, which starts with DD (left) and DDTarget (right). DD is the base class for all drag operations, whereas DDTarget is the base class for all drop operations. Both provide the base functionality for their respective behaviors. Having this split in functionality allows you to focus on specific behaviors. You'll see this in action when we look at implementing drag and drop with DOM nodes a little later on.

As you move down the chain, you can see that Ext JS adds features progressively for the intended behavior. Table 13.1 enumerates the classes and provides a brief description of their designated task.

There you have it, each of the drag-and-drop classes and what they're designed to do. A drag item (DD class or subclasses) can be a drop target, but a drop target (DDTarget or subclasses) can't be a drag item. It's important to know this because if you ever decide on having an element being a drag item *and* a drop target, you must use one of the drag classes.

If you're implementing drag and drop with generic DOM nodes, where you need to allow for one drag node at a time, you'd use DD or DDProxy, as you'll see later in this chapter. If you're looking to drag more than one element, you'll want to use either

Table 13.1 Drag-and-drop classes

Drag classes		Drop classes	
Name	**Purpose**	**Name**	**Purpose**
DD	A base drag implementation where an element can be dragged around and dropped anywhere. This is where most DOM-level drag implementations take place.	DDTarget	The basic class to allow any element to participate in a drag-and-drop group, but it can't be dragged around, meaning it can only have items dropped on it.
DDProxy	A basic drag implementation where a lightweight copy of the drag element, known as a *drag proxy*, is dragged around instead of the source element. It's common practice to use this class for drag operations where a drag proxy is desired.	DropTarget	A base class that provides the empty plumbing for an element to take action when a draggable element is dropped onto this one. It's left up to the developer to finish the implementation by overriding the notify methods.
DragSource	Provides a base implementation for drag and drop using status proxies and is the base class for DragZone. This can be used directly, but it's more common to use the DragZone class (see below).	DropZone	A class that provides the means for multiple nodes to be dropped onto this element; it works best with the DragZone class. There is a TreePanel-specific implementation of this known as the TreeDropZone.
DragZone	This class allows for the drag of multiple DOM elements at a time and is commonly used with the DataView or ListView widget. To provide drag and drop with the GridPanel and TreePanel, each has its own implementations of this class known as the GridDragZone and TreeDragZone.		

the DragSource or DragZone classes. This is why the TreePanel and GridPanel have their own respective extensions or implementations of the DragZone class.

Likewise, if you're looking to drop a single node, the DDTarget will be your drop class of choice. For multiple-node drops, the DropTarget or DropZone is required because they have the necessary plumbing to interact with the DragSource, DragZone, and their descendant classes.

Knowing what the classes are is just one piece of the puzzle. The next piece that you'll need to know is what methods are to be overridden, which is the biggest key to successful deployment.

13.1.3 *It's all in the overrides!*

As we discussed earlier, the various drag-and-drop classes were designed to provide a base framework for various drag or drop behaviors and are only part of what's needed to make drag and drop useful. Each of the drag-and-drop classes contains a set of abstract methods that are meant to be overridden by you, the end developer.

Table 13.2 **Commonly used abstract methods for drag and drop**

Method	Description
onDrag	Called for each `onMouseMove` event while the element is being dragged. If you plan to do something before an item is dragged, you may elect to override the `b4Drag` or `startDrag` methods.
onDragEnter	Called when a drag element first intersects another drag/drop element within the same drag/drop group. This is where you can code for drop invitation.
onDragOver	Called while a drag element is being dragged over.
onDragOut	Called when a drag element leaves the physical space of an associated drag or drop element.
onInvalidDrop	Called when a drag element is dropped on anything other than an associated drag or drop element. It's a great place to inject notification to the user that they dropped a drag element in the wrong place.
onDragDrop	Called when a drag element is dropped on another drag/drop element within the same drag/drop group.

Although all of these methods are listed in the framework API for each drag/drop class, it's a good idea to at least briefly discuss a few of the more commonly used abstract methods that are to be overridden for the `Ext.dd.DD` class. This way you get a sense of what to look for in the API. Table 13.2 provides an overview of these methods.

Remember that `Ext.dd.DD` is the base class for all drag-specific elements, and as you move down the hierarchy, more features get added. The features added by the subclasses progressively override these methods for you.

For instance, there are a few "b4" (before) methods that `Ext.dd.DD` provides that allow you to code a behavior before something happens, such as before the `mousedown` event fires (b4MouseDown) and before the drag of an element occurs (b4StartDrag). `Ext.dd.DDProxy`, the first subclass of `Ext.dd.DD`, overrides these methods to create a draggable proxy just before the drag code begins to execute.

To figure out which methods you need to override to achieve a specific implementation, you'll need to consult the API for that specific drag or drop class. Because Ext JS has a more aggressive release cycle, obviously some methods may be added, renamed, or removed, so looking at the API regularly will help you stay fresh with the current changes.

The last bit of drag-and-drop theory we need to discuss is the use of drag-and-drop groups and what they mean for implementing this behavior in your application.

13.1.4 *Drag and drop always work in groups*

Drag-and-drop elements are associated with groups, which is the basic constraint that governs whether a drag element can be dropped on another element. A group is a label that helps the drag-and-drop framework decide whether a registered drag element should interact with another registered drag or drop element.

Drag or drop elements must be associated with at least one group but can be associated with more than one. They're generally associated with a group upon instantiation and can be associated with more via the addToGroup method. Likewise, they can be unassociated via the removeFromGroup method.

This is the last piece of the puzzle to understanding the basics of drag and drop with Ext JS. It's time to start using and reinforcing what you've learned. We'll start out simple by implementing drag and drop with DOM elements.

13.2 *Starting out simple*

We'll begin our exploration with a plot that mimics a swimming pool setting, complete with locker rooms, a swimming pool, and a hot tub. There are constraints that we must follow. For instance, men and women nodes can only be in their respective locker rooms. All can go in the swimming pool, but only a few like to go into the hot tub. Now that you understand what we must create, we can begin coding.

As you'll see, it's extremely simple to configure an element to be dragged around the screen. But before we can do that, we must create a workspace to manipulate. We'll do this by creating some CSS styles that govern how a specific set of DOM elements look and then apply drag logic to them. We'll keep things as simple as possible to focus on the subject matter.

13.2.1 *Creating a small workspace*

Let's create the markup to represent the locker rooms and people inside them. This listing is rather lengthy because of the HTML required to achieve the desired style and layout.

Listing 13.1 Creating our simple drag-and-drop workspace

```
<style type="text/css">
    body  {
        padding: 10px;
    }

    .lockerRoom {
        width:               150px;
        border:              1px solid;
        padding:             10px;
        background-color:    #ECECEC;
    }

    .lockerRoom div {
        border:              1px solid #FF0000;
        background-color:    #FFFFFF;
        padding:             2px;
        margin:              5px;
        cursor:              move;
    }
</style>

<table>
```

① Drag element container styles

② Child nodes look different

```
<tr>
    <td align='center'>
        Male Locker Room
    </td>
    <td align='center'>
        Female Locker Room
    </td>
</tr>
<tr>                                          ❸ HTML markup for
    <td>                                        our drag items
        <div id="maleLockerRoom" class="lockerRoom">
            <div>Jack</div>
            <div>Aaron</div>
            <div>Abe</div>
        </div>

    </td>
    <td>
        <div id="femaleLockers" class="lockerRoom">
            <div>Sara</div>
            <div>Jill</div>
            <div>Betsy</div>
        </div>
    </td>
</tr>
</table>
```

In listing 13.1, you create the CSS styles and markup to set the stage for your exploration of basic DOM drag and drop. We begin by defining the CSS that will control the styles for the `lockerRoom` ❶ element containers and their (people) child nodes ❷. Last, we set up the markup ❸ to utilize the CSS.

Figure 13.3 shows what our locker HTML looks like rendered. In this figure, you see the HTML rendered onscreen. If you notice, when you hover the mouse cursor over a child node of a locker room element, the arrow will change into a hand. This is due to the CSS styling that we configured previously, and it provides a nice means of inviting a drag operation.

Next, we'll configure the JavaScript to allow these elements to be dragged around.

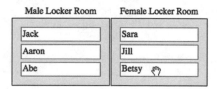

Figure 13.3   The locker room HTML rendered

13.2.2 *Configuring items to be draggable*

In the following listing, you'll configure the locker room child items to be draggable. You'll see exactly how easy it is to do this.

Listing 13.2 Enabling drag for our elements

```
var maleElements = Ext.get('maleLockerRoom').select('div');

Ext.each(maleElements.elements, function(el) {
    new Ext.dd.DD(el);
});

var femaleElements = Ext.get('femaleLockerRoom').select('div');

Ext.each(femaleElements.elements, function(el) {
    new Ext.dd.DD(el);
});
```

1 Gather list of child items

2 Make child items draggable

In listing 13.2, you configure the locker room child items to be dragged around the screen. To accomplish this, you gather a list of child elements in the `maleLockerRoom` element by chaining a `select` call (DOM query) to the results of the `Ext.get` call **1**. You then utilize `Ext.each` to loop through the list of child nodes and create a new instance of `Ext.dd.DD` **2**, passing the element reference, which enables that element to be dragged around the screen. You do the exact same thing for the elements in the `femaleLockerRoom`.

After refreshing the page, you can easily drag and drop the elements around the screen. As you can see in figure 13.4, you can drag any of the child `div`s around the screen, without constraints.

Let's examine how `Ext.dd.DD` works and what it does to our DOM elements. To do this, we'll need to refresh the page again and open up Firebug's live HTML inspection tool. We'll focus on Jack.

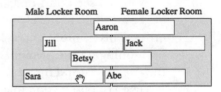

Figure 13.4 Drag enabled on the locker room elements without constraints

13.2.3 *Analyzing the Ext.dd.DD DOM changes*

Figure 13.5 shows the HTML of our drag elements just after a page refresh along with the DOM inspection view in Firebug.

When looking at the Jack element (highlighted), the first thing you might notice is that it's assigned a unique ID of `"ext-gen3"`. Recall that in our markup, we didn't assign an ID to this element. If the element already had its own unique ID, `Ext.dd.DD` would use it. But instead, in order to track this element by ID, it's assigned one by the `Ext.dd.DD`'s superclass, `Ext.dd.DragDrop`.

> **WARNING** If the `id` of the element is changed after it has been registered for drag, the drag configuration for that element will cease to function. If you plan to change the `id` for a particular element, it's best to call the destroy method on the instance of `Ext.dd.DD` for that element and create a new instance of `Ext.dd.DD`, passing the new element ID as the first parameter.

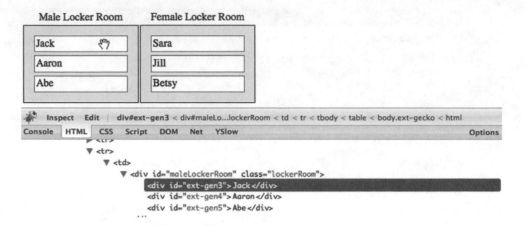

Figure 13.5   **Inspecting the DOM for the Jack element (highlighted) before a drag operation takes place**

Another thing that you'll notice from looking at the HTML inspection is that no other attributes are assigned to that element. Now, let's drag the element a little and observe the changes, as shown in figure 13.6.

You can see that I dragged the Jack element a little. `Ext.dd.DD`, in turn, added a `style` attribute to the element, which changes the `position`, `top`, and `left` CSS properties. This is important to know because using `Ext.dd.DD` will result in a change of positioning for the element onscreen and is one of the key differences between using the `Ext.dd.DD` and the `Ext.dd.DDProxy`, which we'll explore later on.

The last observation that we'll discuss is the ability for the dragged elements to be seemingly dropped anywhere. At first, this may seem cool, and it is! But it's hardly of use. In order to make this useful, we'll have to apply constraints.

To do this, we'll need to create some containers to drop them onto. This is where we'll generate the pool and hot tub for these people to enjoy.

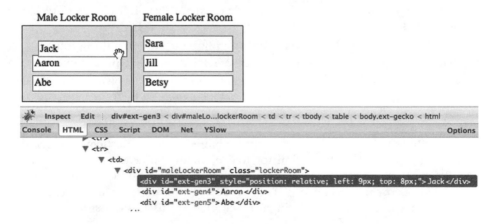

Figure 13.6   **Observing the changes that the drag operation makes on the Jack element**

13.2.4 *Adding the pool and hot tub drop targets*

As before, we'll add some CSS to stylize the HTML. Please insert the following CSS inside the `style` tags of your document. They'll set the background color of the pool and hot tub to blue and red, respectively.

```
.pool {
    background-color: #CCCCFF;
}

.hotTub {
    background-color: #FFCCCC;
}
```

Now we'll need to add the HTML to the document body. Append the following HTML markup below the locker room HTML table:

```
<table>
    <tr>
        <td align='center'>
            Pool
        </td>
        <td align='center'>
            Hot Tub
        </td>
    </tr>
     <tr>
        <td>
            <div id="pool" class="lockerRoom pool"/>
        </td>
        <td>
            <div id="hotTub" class="lockerRoom hotTub"/>
        </td>
    </tr>
</table>
```

This will give us the elements we'll need to set up drop targets. Figure 13.7 shows what the HTML now renders to.

We've added all of the HTML that we need for now. Next you must set up the `Pool` and `Hot Tub` elements as `DropTargets`, which will enable them to participate in the drop portion of the drag and drop. You'll add this code just after the JavaScript in listing 13.2.

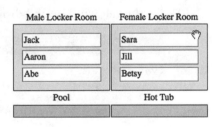

Figure 13.7 The `Pool` and `Hot Tub` HTML rendered onscreen

```
var poolDDTarget   = new Ext.dd.DDTarget('pool', 'males');

var hotTubDDTarget = new Ext.dd.DDTarget('hotTub', 'females');
```

Here you set up an instance of `Ext.dd.DDTarget` each for the `'pool'` and `'hotTub'` elements. The first parameter for the `DDTarget` constructor is the ID of the element (or DOM reference). The second parameter is the group the `DDTarget` is to participate in.

Now, refresh your page, and drag and drop a male node onto the pool node or a female node onto the hot tub node. What happens when you drop the item onto the target? Yes—nothing. Why is that? Well, you set up drag items and the drop targets, which set the stage for complete drag and drop, but remember that it's left up to you to follow through with the rest of the implementation. You must develop the code for the drop invitation and for valid and invalid drops. As you'll see, this is precisely where most of the drag-and-drop implementation code will take place and is what we'll do next.

13.3 *Finishing our drag-and-drop implementation*

As you just saw, setting up an element to be dragged around is simple, as is setting up a drop target. But unless you connect the dots, you're left with a source and destination but no way to get there.

In order to add the drop invitation and valid and invalid behaviors, you need to refactor how you configure the elements to be dragged around. We'll begin by adding one last CSS class, which you'll use to turn the drop target green for the drop invitation.

```
.dropZoneOver {
    background-color: #99FF99;
}
```

As you can see, this CSS is simple. Whatever element has this class will have a green background. Next, we'll work on refactoring the way you set up the male and female elements to be dragged around by setting up an `overrides` object that gets applied to each instance of `Ext.dd.DD`.

13.3.1 *Adding the drop invitation*

To add the drop invitation, you'll have to completely replace how you initialized the drop targets before. The following listing shows what you'll use and will set the stage for the valid and invalid drop behaviors.

Listing 13.3   Refactoring our implementation of `Ext.dd.DD`

```
var overrides = {
    onDragEnter : function(evtObj, targetElId) {          ➊ Create
        var targetEl =  Ext.get(targetElId);                overrides
        targetEl.addClass('dropZoneOver');        ➋ Add drop    object
    },                                               initiation
    onDragOut : function(evtObj, targetElId) {
        var targetEl =  Ext.get(targetElId);        ➌ Remove drop
        targetEl.removeClass('dropZoneOver');          invitation
    },
    b4StartDrag   : Ext.emptyFn,
    onInvalidDrop : Ext.emptyFn,
    onDragDrop    : Ext.emptyFn,
    endDrag       : Ext.emptyFn
};

var maleElements = Ext.get('maleLockerRoom').select('div');
```

```
Ext.each(maleElements.elements, function(el) {          ④  Male elements to
    var dd = new Ext.dd.DD(el, 'males', {                   be drag items
        isTarget  : false              ◁┐  These won't be
    });                                ⑤  drop targets
    Ext.apply(dd, overrides);                           ◁┐  Override methods
});                                                     ⑥  to the DD instance

var femaleElements = Ext.get('femaleLockerRoom').select('div');
Ext.each(femaleElements.elements, function(el) {
    var dd = new Ext.dd.DD(el, 'females', {
        isTarget  : false
    });
    Ext.apply(dd, overrides);
});
```

In listing 13.3, you create an object, overrides, which will be *applied* to the instances of Ext.DD that will be created. You'll override a total of five methods to achieve the desired results, but for now you'll override only onDragEnter ❶ and onDragout ❷.

Remember that onDragEnter will be called only when a drag element first intersects a drag or drop element with the same associated group. Your implementation of this method will add the 'dropZoneOver' CSS class, which changes the background color of the drop element to green and provides the drop invitation that you want.

Likewise, the onDragOut method gets called when the drag element first leaves a drag-and-drop object with the same associated group. You use this method to remove the invitation from the background of the drop element ❸.

You then stub four methods, b4StartDrag, onInvalidDrop, onDragDrop, and end-Drag, which we'll fill in later on. We don't do these now because I want you to be able to focus on the behaviors and constraints that we add in layers. But, in case you're curious, we'll use b4StartDrag to get the original X and Y coordinates of the drag element. These coordinates will be used in the onInvalidDrop method, which will set a local property to indicate that this method was fired. The onDragDrop method will be used to move the drag node from its original container to the dropped container. Last, the endDrag method will reset the position of the drag element if the invalid-Drop property is set to true.

In order to use this overrides object, you have to refactor how you're initializing the drag objects ❹, for both male and female elements.

You do this because you need to prevent the drag element from being a drop target, which is why you add a third argument to the DD constructor, which is meant to be a somewhat limited configuration object. You'll see what I mean by *limited* in a bit. In that configuration parameter, you set isTarget ❺ to false, which sets the controlling behavior for this drag item to not be a drop target.

Finally, you apply the overrides object to the newly created instance of Ext.DD ❻. Earlier, I said that the configuration object is used only to set a limited number of properties. I said this because the drag-and-drop code that exists in Ext JS today was written back in the early Ext JS 1.0 days, before most constructors applied configuration properties to themselves. This is why you have to use Ext.apply to inject the

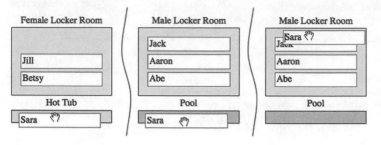

Figure 13.8 Conditional drop invitation for the male nodes

override methods instead of setting them on the configuration object as you would for most constructors in the framework.

We've just added the code for the invitation. Let's see what happens when we try to drag a male node over the pool or hot tub (figure 13.8).

As your knowledge of drag and drop and code dictates, dragging a male node over a drop target (think `onDragEnter`) with the same associated group will result in a drop invitation, which is the background of the drop target turning green, as shown in figure 13.8. When you drag the element out of the same drop target (think `onDragOut`), the background will return to its original state, removing the drop invitation.

Conversely, dragging a male element over any other drop target, such as the hot tub, will result in no invitation. Why does this happen? There's no drop invitation on the hot tub element because the hot tub is not associated with the `males` drop group.

Another thing you'll notice is that dragging a female element over the hot tub results in a drop invitation on the hot tub element but not the pool, as shown in figure 13.9. That's because the hot tub is associated only with `females`.

Although this demonstrates the drop invitation well, you still have the issue of the pool and the hot tub needing to be able to receive both male and female nodes. To do this, you must register them with an additional group. You need to call the `addToGroup` method, passing in an alternate group. Here's what the pool and hot tub element `DDTarget` registration looks like with the addition of `addToGroup` calls:

```
var poolDDTarget = new Ext.dd.DDTarget('pool', 'males');
poolDDTarget.addToGroup('females');

var hotTubDDTarget = new Ext.dd.DDTarget('hotTub', 'females');
hotTubDDTarget.addToGroup('males');
```

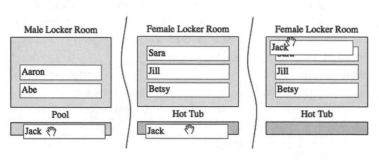

Figure 13.9 The conditional drop invitation for the female nodes

After injecting this into your example, refresh the page. You can see that the pool and the hot tub drop elements now invite the drop, but what happens when you drop a drag element onto a valid drop target? Absolutely nothing. That's because you didn't code for the valid drop operation.

You'll do this next.

13.3.2 Adding valid drop

To add the valid drop behavior to your drag-and-drop implementation, you must replace the onDragDrop method in your overrides object, as follows.

Listing 13.4   Adding valid drop to your overrides

```
onDragDrop : function(evtObj, targetElId) {
    var dragEL = Ext.get(this.getEl());
    var dropEl = Ext.get(targetElId);               ❶ Is drag parent
                                                        element same as
    if (dragEl.dom.parentNode.id != targetElId) {  ◁── drop target?

        dropEl.appendChild(dragEl);                        ◁── Move node to
        this.onDragOut(evtObj, targetElId);           ◁──  ❷ new container
        dragEl.dom.style.position ='';
                                                ❸ Clear drop
    }                                              invitation
    else {
        this.onInvalidDrop();        ◁── Move drag
    }                                  ❹ node back
}
```

In your onDragDrop method, you set up the code for a successful or valid drop operation. To do this, you first need to create local references for the drag and the drop elements.

Next, you hit a conditional if statement ❶, where you test to see if the drag element's parent node's ID is the same as the drop target id and exercises the control where you don't want to perform a drop operation on a drop target where the drag element is already a child. If the drop target element is not the same as the drag element's parent, then you allow the drop operation to occur; otherwise, you call the onInvalidDrop method, which you'll code shortly.

The code to physically move the drag element from one parent container to another is simple. Call the drop element's appendChild ❷ method, passing in the drop element. Remember that even though Ext.dd.DD allows you to move the drag element onscreen, it only changes the X and Y coordinates. If you don't move the drag element to another parent node, it will still be a child of its original container element.

Next, you call the onDragOut override ❸, which will clear the drop invitation. Notice that you're passing the eventObj and targetElId arguments to the onDragOut method. This is so the onDragOut method can do its job as designed.

Last, you clear the element's style.position attribute. Recall that DD sets the position to relative, which isn't needed after the node has been moved from one parent container to another.

This ends the override of the onDragDrop
➍ method. Figure 13.10 shows what this does
to our page. As illustrated in this figure, we
can successfully drop male and female elements onto both the pool and hot tub drop
elements, which successfully demonstrates our
onDragDrop method in action.

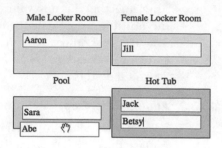

**Figure 13.10   Male and female nodes can
now be dropped onto the pool and hot tub
drop targets.**

Although it's nice that males and females
can now be dropped into the pool or hot tub,
you can't let them stay in there forever or
they'll prune. You need to be able to pull them
out and put them back in the locker room.
What happens if you try to drag them over their respective locker room? No invitation. Why? Correct. It's because you haven't registered the locker room elements as
DDTargets. Let's do that now.

```
var mlrDDTarget = new Ext.dd.DDTarget('maleLockerRoom', 'males');

var flrDDTarget = new Ext.dd.DDTarget('femaleLockerRoom', 'females');
```

Adding this code to the bottom of your drag/drop implementation allows the male
drag elements to be invited and dropped on every drop target except for the female
locker room. Likewise, female drag elements can be dropped on any drop target
except the male locker room. This follows the paradigm where most public places
don't have coed locker rooms. We now have the drop operations completely developed. The last piece to this implementation is the invalid drop behavior set, which is
what we'll work on next.

13.3.3   *Implementing invalid drop*

We've implemented drop invitation and valid drop to our example set. I'm sure by now
you've noticed that when you drop a node anywhere onscreen other than a valid drop
point, the element stays stuck where it was dropped. This is because you need to set up
the invalid drop behavior that will place the element back in its original position.

We'll do this with style using the Ext.fx class. The following listing replaces the
b4StartDrag and onInvalidDrop methods in the overrides object.

Listing 13.5   Cleaning up after invalid drop

```
b4StartDrag : function() {
    var dragEl = Ext.get(this.getEl());          ◁── Override
    this.originalXY = dragEl.getXY();                  b4StartDrag
},                              ◁── Store original   ➊ method
                                ➋ coordinates
onInvalidDrop : function() {
    this.invalidDrop = true;    ◁── Set this.invalidDrop
},                              ➌ to true
endDrag : function() {
    if (this.invalidDrop === true) {     ◁── Animate drag
        var dragEl = Ext.get(this.getEl());  ➍ element return
```

```
        var animCfgObj = {                                  Create
            easing   : 'elasticOut',              5      animation config
            duration : 1,
            callback : function() {
                dragEl.dom.style.position = '';             Reset drag
            }                                     6      element's position
        };
        dragEl.moveTo(this.originalXY[0], this.originalXY[1], animCfgObj)
        delete this.invalidDrop;                            Animate reset
    }                                                    of drag element  7
},
```

In listing 13.5, you first override the `b4StartDrag` ❶ method, which is called the moment a drag element is dragged. At this juncture you can store the drag element's original X and Y coordinates ❷, which will be used for the repair operation. To *repair* an invalid drop means to reset the position of the drag element or proxy (as you'll see in a bit) to its position before the drag operation took place.

Next, you override `onInvalidDrop` ❸, which is called when the drag item is dropped on anything other than a valid drop point, which is associated with the same group. In that method, all you do is set the local `invalidDrop` property to `true`, which will be used in the next method, `endDrag`.

Last, you override the `endDrag` method, which will perform the repair operation if the local `invalidDrop` property is set to `true` ❹. It also uses the local `originalXY` property set by the `b4StartDrag` method. This method creates a configuration object for the animation ❺.

In the configuration object, you set the `easing` to `'elasticOut'`, which will give the element a nice springy or elastic end to the animation, and set the `duration` to one second. This ensures the animation is smooth and not jerky. You also create a callback method to reset the drag element's `style.position` attribute ❻, which ensures that the drag element fits exactly where it needs to go.

> **NOTE** If you wanted to forgo the animation and just reset the position of the drag element, all `onInvalidDrop` has to do is set the `style.position` to an empty string, like so: `dragEl.dom.style.position = '';`.

Next, you call the drag element's `moveTo` method, passing in the X and Y coordinates as the first and second parameters and the animation configuration object as the third. This invokes the animation on your drag element.

Last, you delete the local `invalidDrop` reference, because it's no longer needed. You'll need to refresh the page to see these three override methods at work.

When you drag an element and drop it anywhere other than an associated drop element, you see that it slides back to its original position and has a cool springy effect when it gets to its target X and Y coordinates ❼.

You've now seen what it takes to implement drag and drop with the `Ext.dd.DD` and `Ext.DD.DDTarget` classes. Next, you'll see how to implement the `DDProxy` class, which is similar.

13.4   Using the DDProxy

The use of drag proxies in drag-and-drop implementation is common and is worth going over because the implementation is similar to DD but not quite the same. This is because the DDProxy allows you to drag around a lightweight version of the drag element, which is known as the *drag proxy*. Using the DDProxy could result in huge performance savings if the drag element is complex. Part of the performance savings comes from the fact that every instance of DDProxy uses the same proxy div element in the DOM. Remembering that the drag proxy is the element being moved around onscreen will help you understand our implementation code.

In this exercise, we'll use the same HTML and CSS that we used before, and we'll provide the pattern that you'll need to use if you plan on using drag proxies in your drag-and-drop implementations.

The first thing you'll need to do is add one more CSS rule to your page, which will style the drag proxy with a yellow background:

```
.ddProxy {
    background-color: #FFFF00;
}
```

We'll follow the exact same flow as we did with implementing the DD class. In doing this, you'll see that implementing the DDProxy takes a bit more code than the DD class.

13.4.1   Implementing DDProxy and drop invitation

The DDProxy class is responsible for creating and managing the X and Y coordinates of the reusable proxy element, but it's up to you to style it and fill it with content. You'll do this by means of overriding the startDrag method instead of the b4Drag method as you did with the DD implementation.

In the following listing, you'll create the overrides object along with the instance of DDProxy. This listing is rather long, but you're accomplishing quite a bit.

Listing 13.6   Implementing the drop invitation

```
var overrides = {                                          ❶ Override
    startDrag : function() {                                  startDrag method
        var dragProxy = Ext.get(this.getDragEl());
        var dragEl = Ext.get(this.getEl());

        dragProxy.addClass('lockerRoomChildren');         ❷ Stylize DragProxy
        dragProxy.addClass('ddProxy');
        dragProxy.setOpacity(.70);
        dragProxy.update(dragEl.dom.innerHTML);
        dragProxy.setSize(dragEl.getSize())
        this.originalXY = dragEl.getXY();
    },

    onDragEnter : function(evtObj, targetElId) {          ❸ Add drop invitation
        var targetEl = Ext.get(targetElId);
        targetEl.addClass('dropzoneOver');
    },
```

```
        onDragOut : function(evtObj, targetElId) {
            var targetEl =  Ext.get(targetElId);
            targetEl.removeClass('dropzoneOver');
        },

        onInvalidDrop : function() {
            this.invalidDrop = true;
        },

        onDragDrop : Ext.emptyFn
};

var maleElements = Ext.get('maleLockerRoom').select('div');
Ext.each(maleElements.elements, function(el) {
        var dd = new Ext.dd.DDProxy(el, 'males', {
            isTarget  : false
        });
        Ext.apply(dd, overrides);
});

var femaleElements = Ext.get('femaleLockerRoom').select('div');
Ext.each(femaleElements.elements, function(el) {
        var dd = new Ext.dd.DDProxy(el, 'females', {
            isTarget  : false
        });
        Ext.apply(dd, overrides);
});
```

❹ **Add onDragDrop stub**

In listing 13.6, you accomplish the tasks of stylizing the proxy, adding the drop invitation, and instantiating the instances of Ext.dd.DDProxy for each of the elements. Here's how this all works.

The startDrag method ❶ takes care of stylizing the drag element by first adding the lockerRoomChildren and ddProxy CSS classes ❷ to the DragProxy element. Next, it sets the proxy's opacity to 70 percent and duplicates the HTML contents of the drag element. It then sets the size of the DragProxy to the size of the drag element. Then the originalXY property is set, which will be used for an invalid-drop repair operation down the road.

Next, you add the drop invitation by means of overriding the onDragEnter and onDragOut methods ❸. This is exactly the same as the prior implementation. The onInvalidDrop override is the same as before as well. The last override is a stub for the onDragDrop method ❹, which you'll fill out in just a bit.

Before you can use the drop invitation, you have to set up the drop targets for the pool, hot tub, and locker room elements:

```
var poolDDTarget = new Ext.dd.DDTarget('pool', 'males');
poolDDTarget.addToGroup('females');

var hotTubDDTarget = new Ext.dd.DDTarget('hotTub', 'females');
hotTubDDTarget.addToGroup('males');

var mlrDDTarget = new Ext.dd.DDTarget('maleLockerRoom', 'males');
var flrDDTarget = new Ext.dd.DDTarget('femaleLockerRoom', 'females');
```

Now that you have those set up, let's try out the DDProxy implementation we've cooked up thus far. Refresh your page and drag around a drag element.

Figure 13.11 illustrates what the drag proxy looks like in action.

As you can see, performing a drag gesture on a draggable element produces the Drag-Proxy, which is dragged around while the drag element itself remains stationary. You can also see that the drop invitation works. What happens when you drop the drag element on a valid or invalid drop target?

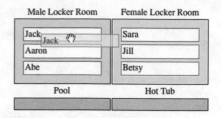

Figure 13.11   The DDProxy in action with one of our male drag elements

In both cases, the drag element is moved to the DragProxy's last known coordinates, which mimics the behavior of the DD class without the valid and invalid drop behavior constraints.

Let's add those next. The following listing wraps up our DDProxy implementation.

Listing 13.7   Adding the valid and invalid drop behaviors

```
onDragDrop : function(evtObj, targetElId) {                    Override
    var dragEl = Ext.get(this.getEl());                       onDragDrop
    var dropEl = Ext.get(targetElId);                      ❶ method

    if (dragEl.dom.parentNode.id != targetElId) {

        dropEl.appendChild(dragEl);
        this.onDragOut(evtObj, targetElId);
        dragEl.dom.style.position ='';
    }
    else {
        this.onInvalidDrop();
    }
},

b4EndDrag : Ext.emptyFn,                             ❷ Prevent proxy from
                                                       hiding before drag ends

endDrag : function() {                                  Override
    var dragProxy = Ext.get(this.getDragEl());       ❸ endDrag method

    if (this.invalidDrop === true) {                   Execute repair
        var dragEl = Ext.get(this.getEl());          ❹ animation

        var animCfgObj = {
            easing    : 'easeOut',
            duration : .25,
            callback : function() {
                dragProxy.hide();
                dragEl.highlight();
            }
        };
        dragProxy.moveTo(this.originalXY[0],
                this.originalXY[1], animCfgObj);
    }
    else {                                           ❺ Hide drag proxy
        dragProxy.hide();                                if valid drop
    }
    delete this.invalidDrop;
}
```

In listing 13.7 you finish up the rest of our DDProxy implementation by adding the onDragDrop, b4EndDrag, and endDrag overrides.

The onDragDrop ❶ method is exactly the same as the DD implementation, where if the drop element is not the same as the drag element's parent, you allow the drop to occur, moving the node to the drop element. Otherwise, you call the onInvalidDrop method, which sets the invalidDrop property to true.

The b4EndDrag ❷ method is an intentional override using the Ext.emptyFn (empty function) reference. You do this because the DDProxy's b4EndDrag method will hide the DragProxy before the endDrag method is called, which conflicts with the animation that you want to perform. And because it would be wasteful to allow the Drag-Proxy to be hidden and then show it, you prevent it from hiding by overriding b4EndDrag with a function that does nothing.

As in the DD implementation earlier, the endDrag ❸ method is tasked with doing the repair if the invalidDrop property is set to true ❹. But instead of animating the drag element itself, it animates the DragProxy. The animation uses the easeOut easing to allow for a smoother animation finish. The callback will hide the DragProxy and then call the highlight effect method of the drag element, animating the background from yellow to white.

Last, if the endDrag was called with the invalidDrop property not set, it hides ❺ the proxy element from view, completing your DDProxy implementation.

As you've seen, implementing the full gamut of drag and drop with generic DOM elements requires some work and understanding of basics of the drag-and-drop class hierarchy. The reward is a cool way to drag and drop elements across the screen, adding that extra bit of functionality for your users.

13.5 Summary

In this chapter we explored the basics of drag and drop and implemented two types of drag behaviors with DOM nodes, which pave the way for you to learn to implement this behavior with the UI widgets.

Along the way, we explored the basics of drag and drop and took some time to discuss its behavior model. We took a good look at the drag-and-drop mini-framework, and you learned that the classes can be grouped into two major categories: drag and drop. While discussing the class hierarchy you learned what each class is designed for.

Afterward, you learned what it takes to implement drag and drop with DOM nodes with constraints using drag groups. We discussed some of the common methods that need to be overridden to make this possible. You got to play with the cool "elastic" easing when developing the repair of the drag element.

In the last stretch, we took our basic drag-and-drop implementation and modified it to use drag proxies. You learned how to properly code a repair operation, which differs from the repair for the DD.

Next, we'll exercise our basic knowledge of drag and drop, and you'll learn to implement drag and drop with three UI widgets, DataView, GridPanel, and TreePanel, where you'll learn of the different vectors for implementing this behavior.

14

Drag and drop with widgets

This chapter covers

- Learning drag and drop with Ext JS widgets
- Implementing drag and drop with the `DataView`
- Exercising drag and drop between `GridPanel`s
- Creating two drag-and-drop `GridPanels`
- Tackling drag and drop with the `TreePanel`
- Applying `TreePanel` drag-and-drop restrictions

When developing your projects, it's easy to produce context `Menu`s and `Button`s to perform certain actions, such as moving a `Record` from one grid to another. But users always crave an easier way to perform those actions. Providing drag and drop behavior to your applications will allow your users to accomplish these tasks much more effectively. The less mouse clicking users have to do, the happier they ultimately are.

In this chapter we'll explore applying this behavior to the three widgets that drag and drop is commonly used with: `DataView`, `GridPanel`, and `TreePanel`. As we do that, we'll descend farther into the DragDrop class hierarchy and touch on the DragZone and DropZone classes and their descendants.

You'll learn about the different implementation patterns that are required to get drag and drop working with each of these widgets, and we'll discuss some of the hidden tricks and inner workings of the drag-and-drop classes.

Because the nature of this behavior is complex, this will be a code-heavy chapter.

14.1 A quick review of the drag-and-drop classes

Before we get down to implementing drag and drop with widgets, we'll do a quick review of the DragDrop class hierarchy, shown in figure 14.1. This will give you a good picture of the road ahead and help you understand what classes to use and why.

In the last chapter, we covered the DD and DDProxy drag classes and the DDTarget drop class. Recall that we utilized those classes because they were designed for single-node drag-and-drop applications, which met our requirements at that time.

Each of the widgets we'll use to employ drag and drop has selection models that allow for multiple node selections. This means that we'll leverage the classes designed for handling that. The DragSource and DropTarget classes are technically designed to handle this type of drag-and-drop behavior. But we're going to start with the DragZone and DropZone classes. Here's why.

Although the DragSource has all of the necessary mechanics to handle multinode drag operations, the DragZone class goes a few steps further and adds useful features like managing the scroll bar of a container if the container is scrollable. You'll see this in action when we employ drag and drop with DataViews in just a bit.

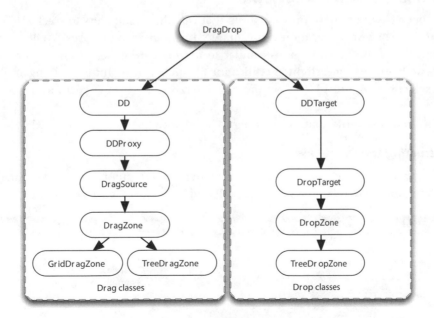

Figure 14.1　The DragDrop class hierarchy

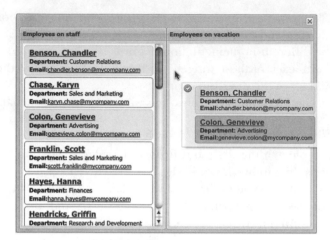

Figure 14.2   The outcome of our `DataView` construction

The `DropZone` class adds features to the `DropTarget` class, such as being able to track the nodes that the drag element is currently hovering over, which makes it easy to allow for precision drop operations of a drag node to specific indexes. You'll get a chance to exercise this when we learn how to employ drag and drop with `GridPanels` a little later on.

You now know more about our starting point. Because the application of drag and drop with `DataViews` provides essential information for the `GridPanel` and `TreePanel` implementations, we'll begin with it.

14.2   Drag and drop with DataViews

We've been tasked to develop something that will allow managers to track employees who are on staff or on vacation using simple drag-and-drop gestures. We'll construct two `DataViews`, both of which are similar to the ones we constructed earlier. To use them, we'll make some slight modifications, which will include enabling multiple-node selection. Figure 14.2 shows the two `DataViews` encapsulated in an instance of `Ext.Window`.

Now that you know what we're going to build, let's begin.

14.2.1   Constructing the DataViews

You'll start by creating the CSS required to style the elements within the `DataView`. The drag-and-drop–related CSS will be included, so let's get it out of the way.

Listing 14.1   Setting up the CSS for our `DataViews`

```
<style type="text/css">
    .emplWrap {
        border: 1px #999999 solid;
        -moz-border-radius: 5px;
        -webkit-border-radius: 5px;
        margin : 3px;
        padding : 3px;
```

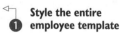 **Style the entire employee template**

```
        background-color: #ffffcc;
    }

    .emplOver {
        border: 1px #9999ff solid;
        background-color: #ccccff;
        cursor: pointer;
    }

    .emplSelected {
        border: 1px #66ff66 solid;
        background-color: #ccffcc;
        cursor: pointer;
    }

    .emplName {
        font-weight: bold;
        margin-left: 5px;
        font-size: 14px;
        text-decoration: underline;
        color: #333333;
    }

    .emplAddress {
        margin-left: 20px;
    }
</style>
```

2 Style on mouseover

3 Set the selected employee style

In the CSS in listing 14.1, you style how each employee div will look in the DataViews. An unselected employee element will have a yellow background **1**, similar to that of a manila folder. When the mouse hovers over the name of an employee, it will use the emplOver **2** CSS class to style it blue. When selected, the employee will be colored green using the emplSelected **3** CSS class.

You now have the CSS in place for your future DataViews to use. Next, you'll configure the two stores that will be consumed by the different DataViews.

Listing 14.2 Configuring the stores for the DataViews

```
var storeFields =  [
    { name : "id",          mapping : "id" },
    { name : "department",  mapping : "department" },
    { name : "email",       mapping : "email" },
    { name : "firstname",   mapping : "firstname" },
    { name : "lastname",    mapping : "lastname" }
];

var onStaffStore = {
    xtype    : 'jsonstore',
    autoLoad : true,
    proxy    : new Ext.data.ScriptTagProxy({
        url : 'http://extjsinaction.com/examples/chapter12/getEmployees.php'
    }),
    fields   : storeFields,
```

1 Create list of Store Fields

2 Configure remote JsonStore

```
        sortInfo : {
            field     : 'lastname',
            direction : 'ASC'
        }
    };

    var onVactaionStore = {                              ③ A local
        xtype     : 'jsonstore',                            JsonStore
        fields    : storeFields,
        autoLoad  : false,
        sortInfo  : {
            field     : 'lastname',
            direction : 'ASC'
        }
    };
```

In listing 14.2, you create a list of fields ❶ and two configuration objects for Json-Stores. The first JsonStore ❷ uses a ScriptTagProxy to fetch the list of employees, whereas the second JsonStore ❸ sits quietly, waiting for Records to be inserted upon a drop gesture.

Now that you have the data Stores configured, you can create the DataViews, as shown in the following listing.

Listing 14.3 Constructing the two DataViews

```
var dvTpl = new Ext.XTemplate(
    '<tpl for=".">',                                     ① The XTemplate
      '<div class="emplWrap" id="employee_{id}">',          for the DataViews
         '<div class="emplName">{lastname}, {firstname}</div>',
         '<div><span class="title">Department:</span> {department}</div>',
           '<div>',
              '<span class="title">Email:</span><a href="#">{email}</a>',
           '</div>',
         '</div>',
      '</tpl>'
);

var onStaffDV = new Ext.DataView({                       ② The on-staff
    tpl           : dvTpl,                                   DataView
    store         : onStaffStore,
    loadingText   : 'loading..',
    multiSelect   : true,
    overClass     : 'emplOver',
    selectedClass : 'emplSelected',
    itemSelector  : 'div.emplWrap',
    emptyText     : 'No employees on staff.',
    style         : 'overflow:auto; background-color: #FFFFFF;'
});
                                                         ③ The on-vacation
var onVactionDV = new Ext.DataView({                        DataView
    tpl           : dvTpl,
    store         : onVactaionStore,
    loadingText   : 'loading..',
    multiSelect   : true,
```

```
    overClass       : 'emplOver',
    selectedClass : 'emplSelected',
    itemSelector    : 'div.emplWrap',
    emptyText       : 'No employees on vacation',
    style           : 'overflow:auto; background-color: #FFFFFF;'
});
```

In listing 14.3, you configure and construct the two DataViews starting with a common XTemplate instance **1**. The onStaffDV **2** will consume the data from the onStaff-Store to load the list of employees currently on staff, whereas the onVacationDV **3** will use the unpopulated onVacationStore.

We could render the DataViews onscreen, but I think they'd look better inside a Window and standing side by side with an HBoxLayout, as in the following listing.

Listing 14.4   Placing the DataViews inside a Window

```
new Ext.Window({                              Instantiate a Window
    layout         : 'hbox',                  1 for DataViews
    height         : 400,
    width          : 550,
    border         : false,
    layoutConfig : { align : 'stretch'},
    items          : [
        {
            title  : 'Employees on staff',
            frame  : true,
            layout : 'fit',                   2 Place DataViews
            items  : onStaffDV,                 inside Panels
            flex   : 1
        },
        {
            title  : 'Employees on vacation',
            frame  : true,
            layout : 'fit',
            id     : "test",
            items  : onVactionDV,
            flex   : 1
        }
    ]
}).show();
```

In listing 14.4 you create an instance of Ext.Window **1** that utilizes the HBoxLayout to place two panels side by side with an equal width and their height stretched to fit the Window's body. The panel on the left will contain the on-staff DataView **2**, whereas the panel on the right will contain the DataView for vacationers, as shown in figure 14.3.

You can see that our DataViews have rendered properly, with the on-staff employees appearing on the left and no one currently on vacation. With that, we've set the stage for applying drag and drop.

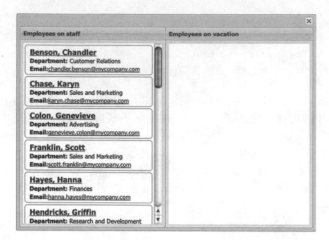

Figure 14.3   Our rendered
`DataViews` inside an
`Ext.Window`

14.2.2   Adding drag gestures

The application of drag and drop with `DataViews` arguably requires the most effort when compared to the `GridPanel` and `TreePanel`. This is because, unlike those widgets, the `DataView` class doesn't have its own `DragZone` implementation subclass for us to build upon, which means that we'll have to craft our own implementation of `DragZone`. Likewise, we'll have to develop an implementation of `DropZone` to manage the drop gestures.

The `DragZone` class uses a special proxy known as a `StatusProxy`, which will use icons to indicate whether a successful drop is possible. Figure 14.4 shows what they typically look like.

The `StatusProxy` by default is extremely lightweight and efficient but somewhat boring. Although it provides useful information, it's far from fun to use. We'll take advantage of the ability to customize the `StatusProxy` look to spice up the drag gestures and make them much more enjoyable and informational. Another feature that `DragZone` adds is automated repair of an invalid drop scenario, which reduces the amount of code that we need to generate to get this stuff working.

We'll begin by creating the overrides that will be applied to the instance of `DragZone` that we'll create afterwards. Because the `DataViews` *must* be rendered in order to have drag and drop applied, you'll need to insert the following code below that of listing 14.4.

Figure 14.4   The `StatusProxy`,
indicating that a drop is possible
(left) or not (right)

Listing 14.5   Creating the `DragZone` overrides

```
var dragZoneOverrides = {
    containerScroll : true,              ❶  Automatically scroll
                                             destination container
    scroll          : false,             ❷  Prevent document.body
                                             from scrolling
    getDragData     : function(evtObj){  ❸  Override getDragData method
```

```
        var dataView = this.dataView;
        var sourceEl = evtObj.getTarget(dataView.itemSelector, 10);
                                                                           Cache drag
                                                                            gesture
        if (sourceEl) {                                                    element    4
            var selectedNodes = dataView.getSelectedNodes();
            var dragDropEl = document.createElement('div');

            if (selectedNodes.length < 1) {                 Create and return
                selectedNodes.push(sourceEl);             5 drag data object
            }

            Ext.each(selectedNodes, function(node) {
                dragDropEl.appendChild(node.cloneNode(true));
            });                                                    Loop through
            return {                                            selectedNodes list  6
                ddel          : dragDropEl,
                repairXY      : Ext.fly(sourceEl).getXY(),
                dragRecords   : dataView.getSelectedRecords(),
                sourceDataView : dataView
            };
        }
    },
    getRepairXY: function() {
        return this.dragData.repairXY;
    }
};
```

In listing 14.5, you create the override properties and methods that will be applied to the future instances of DragZone. Even though the amount of code is relatively small, there's a lot going on that you need to be aware of. Here's how all of this works.

Initially, you set two configuration properties that help manage scrolling when a drag operation is under way. The first is containerScroll ❶, which is set to true. Setting this property to true instructs the DragZone to call Ext.dd.ScrollManager. register, which will help manage the scrolling of a DataView when scrolling operations are in effect. We'll examine this in detail when we look at the DataView after the application of DragZone.

The next property, scroll ❷, is set to false. Setting this to false prevents the document.body element from scrolling when the drag proxy is moved out of the browser's viewport. Keeping the browser canvas fixed during drag-and-drop operations will increase its effectiveness.

Next, you override getDragData ❸, which is an extremely important method to the multinode drag-and-drop application. The purpose of getDragData is to construct what's known as the *drag data object* that you'll see returned toward the end of this method. It's important to note that the drag data object that will be generated and returned by the getDragData method will be cached on the instance of the dropZone and can be accessed via the this.dragData reference. You'll see this in action in the getRepairXY method later on.

In this method, you first set a reference to the element that the drag gesture was initiated with ❹ sourceEl. You'll use it later to update the StatusProxy if the number of selected nodes the DataView thinks it has is wrong. You also create a container element, dragDropEl, that will be used to contain copies of the selected nodes during drag, and it will be placed in the StatusProxy.

> **NOTE**   The presence of sourceEl is tested in order for the rest of the method to continue. getDragData is called upon the mouse-down event of the element that's registered with the DragZone. This means that getDragData will be called even if the DataView element itself is clicked instead of a record element, which would cause the method to fail.

Next, you interrogate the number of items the DataView thinks it has selected during the drag operation. If the number of selectedNodes ❺ is less than 1, you append the element that the drag gesture was started with. You do this because sometimes a drag gesture is initiated before the DataView can register an element as visually selected. This is a quick fix to this odd behavior.

You then use Ext.each ❻ to loop through the selectedNodes list, appending it to the dragDropEl. This will help customize the StatusProxy and give the appearance that the user is dragging over a copy of the selected node(s).

In the last chunk of this override, you return an object that will be used to update the StatusProxy and any drop operations. The only required property that's to be passed in this object is ddel, which will be placed inside the StatusProxy.

For this implementation, you add a few other useful properties to the custom drag data object. First is repairXY, which is an array of the X and Y coordinates of the element that the drag gesture was initiated on. This will be used later on to help the invalid drop repair operation.

Also included is dragRecords, which contains a list of instances of Ext.data.Record for each of the nodes selected and being dragged. Last, you set sourceDataView as the reference of the DataView for which this DragZone is being used. Both dragRecords and sourceDataView properties will help the application of DropZone to remove the dropped records from the source DataView.

The last method in the list of overrides is getRepairXY, which returns the locally cached data object's repairXY property and helps the repair operation know where to animate the StatusProxy on an invalid drop.

You've now set your overrides, so it's time to instantiate instances of DragZone and apply them to the DataViews, as shown in the following code.

Listing 14.6   Applying DragZone to the DataViews

```
var onStaffDragZoneCfg = Ext.apply({}, {
    ddGroup     : 'employeeDD',
    dataView    : onStaffDV
}, dragZoneOverrides);

new Ext.dd.DragZone(onStaffDV.getEl(), onStaffDragZoneCfg);

var vacationDragZoneCfg = Ext.apply({}, {
```

❶ Custom copy of dragZoneOverrides

```
    ddGroup     : 'employeeDD',
    dataView    : onVactionDV
}, dragZoneOverrides);
```

```
new Ext.dd.DragZone(onVactionDV.getEl(), vacationDragZoneCfg);
```

In listing 14.6, you use `Ext.apply` to create a custom copy of the `dragZoneOverrides` object for the employment of `DragZone` targeted at the on-staff `DataView` ❶. The custom copy of the overrides will include a `ddGroup` property. Both `DragZone` implementations will share this. What makes each copy special is the `dataView` property, which references the `DataView` that's attached to the `DragZone` and is used by the `getDragData` method you created earlier. The same pattern is used to set up the `DragZone` for the vacation `DataView`.

One thing you may notice is that unlike the implementation of `DDTarget` in the last chapter, you don't apply the overrides to the instance of `DragZone`. This is because `DragZone`'s superclass, `DragSource`, takes care of that for you automatically, as `Ext.Component` does.

Refreshing your project page will allow you to exercise drag operations. You can also see your customized `StatusProxy` in action. Mine is shown in figure 14.5.

You can see that selecting and dragging one or more `Records` in the on-staff `DataView` reveals the `StatusProxy` with the copies of the selected nodes, which makes the drag operation nicer and much more fun to use.

You can also see the `getRepairXY` method in action by dropping the drag proxy anywhere on the page. The animation will make the drag proxy slide toward the X-Y coordinates of the element where the drag operation was initiated.

To exercise the `ScrollMgr`'s scroll-management capabilities, you'll need to initiate a drag gesture and hover the mouse over what I like to call the auto-scroll zones, as illustrated in figure 14.6.

As you can see in this figure, hovering the mouse in the zones highlighted by the boxes will result in the `DataView` automatically scrolling until it can no longer move.

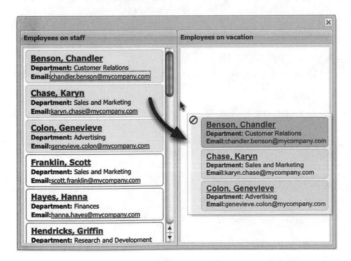

**Figure 14.5   `DragZone`
with a custom `DragProxy`**

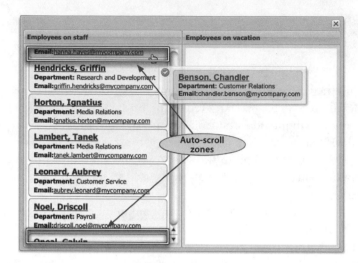

Figure 14.6   The areas where automatic scrolling will take place

You've probably already noticed that when you drag the nodes above the vacation `DataView`, the `StatusProxy` shows an icon indicating that the drop won't be successful. This is because we haven't employed a `DropZone`, which is what we'll do next.

14.2.3   Applying drop

Just like for our previous drag-and-drop applications, we must register a drop target of sorts for the drag classes to interact with. As we discussed before, we'll use the `Drop-Zone` class. Following the pattern for this, you'll create in the following listing an `over-rides` object, which will handle the drop gestures and is much easier to implement relative to drag gestures.

Listing 14.7   Creating the `DropZone` overrides

```
var dropZoneOverrides = {
    onContainerOver : function() {                           ❶ Update
      return this.dropAllowed;                                 StatusProxy
    },
    onContainerDrop : function(dropZone, evtObj, dragData) {

        var dragRecords = dragData.dragRecords;
        var store = this.dataView.store;

        var dupFound = false;                               ❷ Search for
                                                              duplicate records
        Ext.each(dragRecords, function(record) {

            var found = store.findBy(function(r) {
               return r.data.id === record.data.id;
            });

            if (found > -1 ) {
                dupFound = true;
            }
        });
```

```
        if (dupFound !== true) {                         ③  Remove all records
            Ext.each(dragRecords, function(record) {  ◁─┘     from source
                dragData.sourceDataView.store.remove(record);
            });
            this.dataView.store.add(dragRecords);              ┌─◁  Add
            this.dataView.store.sort('lastname', 'ASC'); ◁─┐   │     records to
        }                                            Sort records  ④  destination
        return true;      ◁─┐  Indicate          by last name ⑤
    }                        └  ⑥ successful drop
};
```

In listing 14.7, you create an override object with two methods, to enable drop gestures to successfully occur with the two DataViews. The first is onContainerOver ①, which is used to determine whether the drop should be allowed. In this application, no processing is needed, but you need to at least return the this.droppedAllowed reference, which is a reference to the CSS class x-dd-drop-ok that provides the green check icon. If you wanted to use a custom icon, this is where you'd return a custom CSS class.

The next method, onContainerDrop, is where you'll process the dropped nodes, and it will be called by the instance of DragZone when the mouseup event fires. Remember that DragZone won't interact with the DropZone if both aren't participating in the same drag/drop group.

In this method, you use the dragData object that you created in your DragZone getDragData override. A local reference to the selected records (dragRecords) and the destination DataView's Store (store) are created for later utilization.

Next, onContainerDrop searches for duplicate Records ②. This is useful if you're attempting a copy instead of a move. If no duplicates are found, Ext.each is used to loop through the drag Records to remove them from the sourceDataView's Store ③. The records are then added ④ to the destination DataView's Store and sorted ⑤ by last name in ascending order.

After all of the Record management has taken place, the onContainerDrop returns the Boolean value true. By returning true, you convince the DragZone that the drop was successful ⑥, and it doesn't initiate a repair animation. Any other value would indicate that the drop was unsuccessful, and a repair would occur.

Now that the overrides are in place, it's time to apply them to the DataViews, as shown in the following listing.

Listing 14.8 Creating the DropZone overrides

```
var onStaffDropZoneCfg = Ext.apply({}, {
    ddGroup         : 'employeeDD',
    dataView        : onStaffDV
}, dropZoneOverrides);

new Ext.dd.DropZone(onStaffDV.ownerCt.el, onStaffDropZoneCfg);

var onVacationDropZoneCfg = Ext.apply({}, {
    ddGroup         : 'employeeDD',
```

```
    dataView        : onVactionDV
}, dropZoneOverrides);

new Ext.dd.DropZone(onVactionDV.ownerCt.el,   onVacationDropZoneCfg);
```

In listing 14.8, you create custom copies of the `dropZoneOverrides` object for the implementation of `DropZone` for each of the `DataViews` and follow the same pattern that you used in listing 14.6, where you created instances of `DragZone`.

You can now see your end-to-end drag/drop application in action. Refresh your page and attempt a drag operation from the on-staff `DataView` to the vacation `Data-View`, as shown in figure 14.7.

Dragging nodes from the employee `DataView` to the vacation `DataView` produces a `StatusProxy` that contains a green checkmark to indicate a drop invitation. Dropping the nodes invokes the `onContainerDrop` method, moving the `Records` from left to right, as shown in figure 14.8.

There you have it, drag and drop from one `DataView` to another with a good-looking `StatusProxy`. Because each `DataView` has its own attached instance of `DragZone` and `DropZone`, you can drag and drop items from one to the other, and the `Records` will automatically be sorted by last name.

You've learned how to apply drag and drop to two `DataViews` and that you're responsible for employing the full end-to-end code for both gestures. Next, we'll dive into the world of drag and drop with `GridPanels`, where you'll learn that the implementation pattern is different from that of the `DataView`.

14.3   *Drag and drop with GridPanels*

We've been approached by management to create something that will allow them to track whether departments need computer upgrades. They want to be able to somehow flag the departments that require an upgrade and change the order in which the departments will get upgraded.

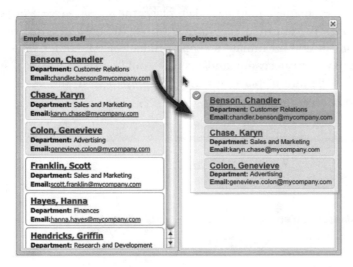

Figure 14.7
The `StatusProxy` now shows that a drop gesture can occur on the drop zone.

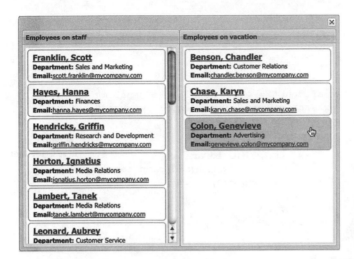

Figure 14.8
We've successfully dragged and dropped three `Records` from the left `DataView` to the right.

To get the job done, we'll use two GridPanels side by side, just like we did with the DataViews a short time ago. We'll put drag and drop into practice from GridPanel to GridPanel and allow for the reordering of departments in the list.

In this exercise, you'll learn that the application of drag and drop between two GridPanels is much simpler than for the DataView. This is mainly because GridPanels have their own DragZone subclass called GridDragZone, which takes care of half of the work for us. We're left to apply a DropZone and attach it to a good target element within the GridPanel.

In addition to exploring how to set up a DropZone with the GridPanel, we'll tackle one of the largest challenges that developers face, which is how to properly allow for drop gestures with the ability to select the index for the item to be dropped. This includes the ability for the GridPanel to allow for reordering self-drag-and-drop gestures.

We'll start by constructing two GridPanels that will live in a Window. The Window will manage the GridPanel dimensions by means of the HBoxLayout and is the same paradigm as the exercise we completed a short time ago.

14.3.1 Constructing the GridPanels

By now you should be comfortable with creating GridPanels and configuring their supported classes. In order to keep things moving, we'll pick up the pace a little. In the following listing you'll create the first GridPanel.

Listing 14.9 Creating the first `GridPanel`

```
var remoteProxy = new Ext.data.ScriptTagProxy({
    url : 'http://extjsinaction.com/examples/chapter12/getPCStats.php'
});                                                                          Creating remote
                                                                            ScriptTagProxy ❶

var remoteJsonStore = {                          Configuring
    xtype       : 'jsonstore',        ❷ remote JSON store
```

```
        proxy         : remoteProxy,
        id            : 'ourRemoteStore',
        root          : '',
        autoLoad      : true,
        totalProperty : 'totalCount',
        fields        : [
            { name : 'department',         mapping : 'department' },
            { name : 'workstationCount',   mapping : 'workstationCount'}
        ]
};

var depsComputersOK = new Ext.grid.GridPanel({          ❸ Instantiating
        title             : 'Departments with good computers',  first GridPanel
        store             : remoteJsonStore,
        loadMask          : true,
        stripeRows        : true,
        autoExpandColumn  : 'department',
        columns           : [
            {
                header    : 'Department Name',
                dataIndex : 'department',
                id        : 'department'
            },
            {
                header    : '# PCs',
                dataIndex : 'workstationCount',
                width     : 40
            }
        ]
});
```

In listing 14.9, you create a remote ScriptTagProxy ❶, which is utilized by the Json-Store ❷ and will fetch the data from extjsinaction.com. Next, you instantiate a Grid-Panel ❸, which will use the previously created remoteJsonStore to display the departments.

In the next listing, you'll create the second GridPanel, which will be used to list the departments in need of an upgrade.

Listing 14.10 Creating the second GridPanel

```
var needUpgradeStore = Ext.apply({}, {              ◁┐ Copy of
        proxy    : null,                              ❶ remoteJsonStore
        autoLoad : false
}, remoteJsonStore);

var needUpgradeGrid = new Ext.grid.GridPanel({        ◁┐ Configure
        title             : 'Departments that need upgrades',  ❷ second GridPanel
        store             : needUpgradeStore,
        loadMask          : true,
        stripeRows        : true,
        autoExpandColumn  : 'department',
        columns           : [
            {
                header    : 'Department Name',
```

```
            dataIndex : 'department',
            id        : 'department'
        },
        {
            header    : '# PCs',
            dataIndex : 'workstationCount',
            width     : 40
        }
    ]
});
```

In listing 14.10, you use `Ext.apply` ❶ to create a modified copy of the `remoteJson-Store`, which overrides the `proxy` parameter and sets `autoLoad` to `false`. This allows you to create a near duplicate of the `remoteJsonStore` but reuse most of the same properties, such as the fields.

Then you create the second instance of `GridPanel` ❷ for the departments that need to be upgraded. These `GridPanel`s need a home. Next you'll create an Ext `Window` to display these in.

Listing 14.11   Giving the `GridPanel`s a home

```
new Ext.Window({
    width       : 500,
    height      : 300,
    layout      : 'hbox',
    border      : false,
    defaults : {
        frame : true,
        flex  : 1
    },
    layoutConfig : {
        align : 'stretch'
    },
    items        : [
        depsComputersOK,
        needUpgradeGrid
    ]
}).show();
```

In listing 14.11 you create an Ext `Window`, which leverages the `HBoxLayout` to manage the two `GridPanel`s that you configured earlier. Let's take them out for a test drive. The results are shown in figure 14.9.

The two `GridPanel`s render perfectly in the `Window` as configured. Our next task is to configure them to enable drag and drop.

14.3.2 Enabling drag

To configure a `GridPanel` to enable drag gestures, all we need to do is add two properties to both of the `GridPanel` configuration objects, as follows:

```
enableDragDrop : true,
ddGroup        : 'depGridDD',
```

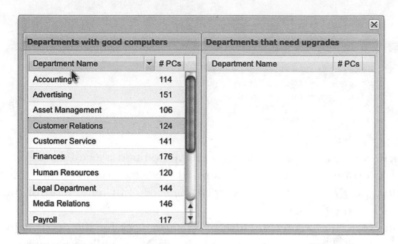

Figure 14.9
The two department
GridPanels
side by side

We can easily enable drag gestures with GridPanel because the GridView tests for the presence of the enableDragDrop (or enableDrag) in the GridPanel when it renders its UI. If the property is set, it will create an instance of GridDragZone and use the grid's ddGroup (drag/drop group) if present or a generic GridDD group.

When configuring drag and drop with GridPanels, I always like to specify a drag/drop group specific to the GridPanels that are to interact. If I don't, then all Grid-Panels with drag enabled would interact with one another, which could cause undesired effects and possibly lead to headaches down the road.

Refresh the GridPanel and see the drag gestures in action, as shown in figure 14.10. When attempting a drag gesture with the GridPanel on the left, you can see the StatusProxy appear with the number of rows selected. This is how the GridDragZone uses the getDragData method, where it displays the number of selected rows for the ddel property of the drag data object. Sound familiar?

You can see that the status proxy displays an unfavorable drop icon. This is because we haven't created a DropZone for the DragZone to interact with. Before we do that, we'll add some CSS styles that the DropZone will use to provide a better drop invitation.

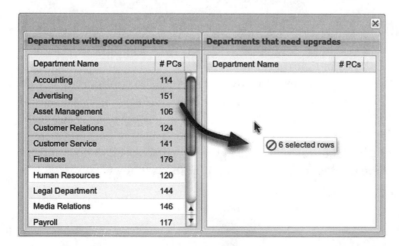

Figure 14.10
Drag gestures
enabled in the
GridPanel

14.3.3 Better drop invitation

Although the `StatusProxy` provides enough information to inform the user that a successful drop is possible, it doesn't provide feedback as to what index the drop operation will use, which is crucial to allow for the reordering of records.

We'll need some CSS rules to help us with this. Please add the styles in the following listing to the head of the page.

Listing 14.12   Adding some CSS styles to provide better drop invitation information

```
<style type="text/css">
    .gridBodyNotifyOver {
        border-color: #00cc33 !important;
    }
    .gridRowInsertBottomLine {
        border-bottom:1px dashed #00cc33;
    }
    .gridRowInsertTopLine {
        border-top:1px dashed #00cc33;
    }
</style>
```

Adding this CSS to the head of the document will enable you to provide a much better drop invitation to the user, which will allow them to accurately pinpoint which `Grid-Panel` they're going to be dropping on and in which row index they'll be inserting `Records`.

Now that we have that out of the way, we can begin the construction of the custom `DropZone` for our `GridPanels`.

14.3.4 Adding drop

Similar to the `DataView` drag-and-drop application, we can only instantiate instances of `DropZone` for the `GridPanels` after they're rendered. To simplify this process, add the code in listing 14.13 after the instantiation of `Ext.Window`.

You'll start by overriding the `onContainerOver` method, which will handle the necessary mouse movements to track what row the dragged `Records` are to be inserted on. The code to get the job done is pretty intense, but the results are well worth the effort.

Listing 14.13   Creating the `Overrides` object

```
var dropZoneOverrides = {
    ddGroup         : 'depGridDD',
    onContainerOver : function(ddSrc, evtObj, ddData) {
        var destGrid = this.grid;
        var tgtEl    = evtObj.getTarget();
        var tgtIndex = destGrid.getView()
                .findRowIndex(tgtEl);
        this.clearDDStyles();

        if (typeof tgtIndex === 'number') {
            var tgtRow       = destGrid.getView().getRow(tgtIndex);
            var tgtRowEl     = Ext.get(tgtRow);
```

1 Get index of element on hover-over

2 Is this a row?

```
            var tgtRowHeight = tgtRowEl.getHeight();
            var tgtRowTop    = tgtRowEl.getY();
            var tgtRowCtr    = tgtRowTop + Math.floor(tgtRowHeight / 2);
            var mouseY       = evtObj.getXY()[1];

            if (mouseY >= tgtRowCtr) {
                this.point = 'below';
                tgtIndex ++;
                tgtRowEl.addClass('gridRowInsertBottomLine');
                tgtRowEl.removeClass('gridRowInsertTopLine');
            }
            else if (mouseY < tgtRowCtr) {
                this.point = 'above';
                tgtRowEl.addClass('gridRowInsertTopLine');
                tgtRowEl.removeClass('gridRowInsertBottomLine')
            }
            this.overRow = tgtRowEl;
        }
        else {
            tgtIndex = destGrid.store.getCount();
        }
        this.tgtIndex = tgtIndex;

        destGrid.body.addClass('gridBodyNotifyOver');

        return this.dropAllowed;
    },
    notifyOut        : function() {},
    clearDDStyles    : function() {},
    onContainerDrop : function() {}
};
```

◁┐ **3** Is mouse above the row?

◁┐ **4** Is it below the row?

◁┐ **5** Append to the Store

◁┐ **6** Add green border to GridPanel

In listing 14.13, you create a `dropZoneOverrides` configuration object that contains the `ddGroup` property, `onContainerOver` implementation, and three stub methods that you'll fill in later. For now, we'll focus on the `onContainerOver` method. Here's how it works.

When the `DragZone` detects that the drag gesture is hovering over a like-group participating `DropZone`, it calls the `DropZone`'s `notifyOver` method, which calls `onContainerOver`. This occurs for each X and Y movement of the mouse while the mouse hovers over the `DropZone` element, which makes it perfect for detecting whether the drop gesture will result in an append, insert, or reorder operation.

In the `onContainerOver` implementation, you get the element that the mouse is hovering over (`tgtDiv`) and ask the `GridView` to find its index **1**. If `findRowIndex` returns a number, then you know that the mouse is hovering over a row that the `GridView` knows of, so the calculations to determine the insertion index can begin **2**.

To determine the exact coordinate of the target row, you must first get a reference to the row and wrap it with `Ext.Element`. From there, you use the helper methods to get the height and current coordinate. Next, you determine the center of the row and compare it to the mouse's Y position.

If the mouse's Y position is greater than or equal to the exact center of the target row's height, you know that the `Record` will be inserted *after* the target row **3**. You set a local this.point property, increase the targetIndex value by one, and add the 'gridRowInsertBottomLine' CSS class to the target row, providing the proper drop invitation to the user.

If the mouse's Y position is less than the target row's center, you know that the drop gesture will be an insert *above* the row ❹. You set the this.point property accordingly and add the 'gridRowInsertTopLine' CSS class to the row, which makes the top border green and dashed, providing the proper insertion index drop invitation.

When you drag over the DropZone element, the target index is set to the destination GridPanel's Record count ❺, which ensures that anything dropped is appended to the store.

Next, the target index is cached locally and the destination GridPanel's body element has its border colored green, which assists with the drop invitation ❻. Last, as for the DataView DropZone application, you return the this.dropAllowed reference to ensure the StatusProxy provides the correct drop invitation icon.

The last bit of this listing consists of three method stubs, notifyOut, clearDD-Styles, and onContainerDrop, which will handle the clearing of the added drop invitation and handle the drop gesture. Let's fill in those method stubs with some functionality.

Listing 14.14   Creating the Overrides object

```
notifyOut : function() {                        ⟵  Clear drop invitation
    this.clearDDStyles();                       ❶  upon drag out
},
clearDDStyles : function() {                              ⟵  Remove all drop
    this.grid.body.removeClass('gridBodyNotifyOver');     ❷  invitation CSS
    if (this.overRow) {
        this.overRow.removeClass('gridRowInsertBottomLine');
        this.overRow.removeClass('gridRowInsertTopLine');
    }
},
onContainerDrop : function(ddSrc, evtObj, ddData){   ⟵  Complete
    var grid      = this.grid;                       ❸  the drop logic
    var srcGrid   = ddSrc.view.grid;
    var destStore = grid.store;
    var tgtIndex  = this.tgtIndex;
    var records   = ddSrc.dragData.selections;

    this.clearDDStyles();

    var srcGridStore = srcGrid.store;                        ❹  Remove
    Ext.each(records, srcGridStore.remove, srcGridStore);    ⟵  all Records

    if (tgtIndex > destStore.getCount()) {
        tgtIndex = destStore.getCount();
    }                                          ❺  Insert
    destStore.insert(tgtIndex, records);       ⟵  dropped Records

    return true;
}
```

In finalizing the `dropZoneOverrides` object, you add the clearing of the drop invitation that will appear on the destination `GridPanel` and rows (if applicable) and complete the code to move the `Records` from the source `GridPanel` to the destination. Here's how all of this works.

The `notifyOut` ❶ override is extremely simplistic and calls the `clearDDStyles` method defined underneath it. Remember that `notifyOut` is called when the dragged object is pulled away from the `DropZone`, which means you need to remove the drop invitation.

Next is the `clearDDStyles` ❷ method, which is custom and not a template method that's required to get drag and drop working. You add it because the `onContainerOver` method will add styles to the target row and target `GridPanel` body, which means you need a way to clear them, and it's always best to move commonly reused code to a separate method. You just saw that this method is being called by `notifyOut`, and it will be called by `onContainerDrop` as well.

The last method, `onContainerDrop` ❸, works similarly to the employment of that method when you used `DropZones` for the `DataView`, where it's responsible for moving `Records` from one `Store` to another. Before it moves the `Records`, it calls `clearDD-Styles` to remove any added drop invitation CSS rules. Next, it removes the dropped `Records` from the source `GridPanel` ❹. Finally, it inserts the dropped `Records` into the destination `GridPanel` at the predetermined target index ❺ and returns `true` to signal to the `DragZone` that the drop was successful.

Our `dropZoneOverrides` object is finished. In order to complete this picture, you need to employ instances of `DropZone` for the `GridPanels`, as shown in the following listing.

Listing 14.15 Employing `DropZone` for the `GridPanels`

```
var leftGridDroptgtCfg = Ext.apply({}, dropZoneOverrides, {          ←┐
    grid : depsComputersOK                                     Copy of
});                                                       dropZoneOverrides ❶
new Ext.dd.DropZone(depsComputersOK.el, leftGridDroptgtCfg);   ←┐ New
                                                                 instance
var needdUpgradesDZCfg = Ext.apply({},dropZoneOverrides, {      ❷ of DropZone
    grid : needUpgradeGrid
});
new Ext.dd.DropZone(needUpgradeGrid.el, needdUpgradesDZCfg);
```

In listing 14.15, you copy the `dropZoneOverrides` object ❶, customizing it for each of the `GridPanels`, and then create instances of `DropZone` for each ❷. If it looks familiar, that's because you instantiated instances of `DropZone` for the `DataViews` in the same way.

Our drag-and-drop implementation with `GridPanels` is now properly configured and ready to rock. Refresh the page and see how the drop invitations react, per the `onContainerOver` code, as shown in figure 14.11.

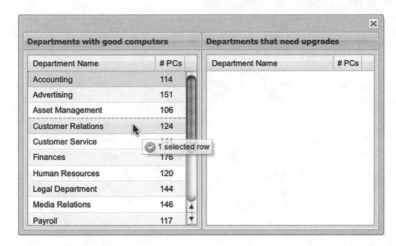

**Figure 14.11
The drop invitation
with mouseover row-
tracking drop index**

When you drag a `Record` above a `Record` in either of the two `GridPanels`, you see that the mouse movements are tracked properly, and when the mouse hovers over the top half of a row, that row's top border turns green and appears dashed.

Likewise, hovering the mouse below the bottom half of a row will make the row's bottom border appear green and dashed, indicating that a drop of the dragged `Record` will insert it below the row that you're currently hovering over, as demonstrated in figure 14.12.

And dropping the `Record` at the indicated position results in the `Record` being moved to that position. Likewise, dropping a `Record` from one grid to another results in the `Record` being moved as commanded, which concludes our `GridPanel` to `GridPanel` drag and drop. Notice that if a drop occurs on anything other than a row, the `Record` is appended to the destination `Store`.

You've learned that in order to make drag and drop between `GridPanels` possible, you don't have to instantiate a `DragZone` but instead only need to set `enableDragDrop`

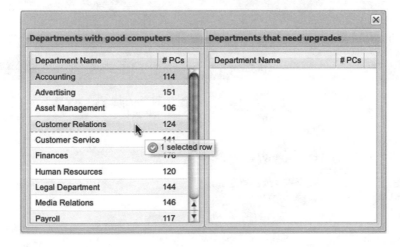

**Figure 14.12
The below-row drop
invitation**

on the `GridPanel`'s configuration object to `true`. Remember that setting that property instructs the `GridView` to instantiate an instance of `GridDragZone` when its UI renders. What you did have to implement, however, was the `DropZone`, and you did so with the ability to track the index of the record(s) to be dropped.

Next up is `TreePanel` to `TreePanel` drag and drop, where the implementation pattern changes somewhat again.

14.4   *Drag and drop with TreePanels*

Our company has purchased another company, and our management needs a way to track how to absorb employees from the purchased company's various departments. They requested that we develop something that will allow them to track the reassignment of employees using `TreePanels` and drag and drop.

The most important requirement is the ability to allow associates to be relocated to a specified set of similar departments. For instance, any associate from Accounting, Finances, or Payroll can be reassigned to any of those departments. Likewise, associates from Customer Relations, Media Relations, Customer Service, or Public Relations can be reassigned to any of those. Instead of building a valid drop matrix in JavaScript, the node list returned from the server will report a list of valid departments for each node. It will be up to us to somehow use that data to make the requirement a reality.

In this section, you'll not only learn how to enable drag and drop between trees, but you'll also tackle one of the most common challenges, which is to constrain the dropping of nodes. We'll begin by constructing the `TreePanels` and the `Window` that they'll live in.

14.4.1   *Constructing the TreePanels*

As with the `DataView` and `GridPanel` exercises before this, we'll configure two `TreePanels`, both of which will be managed by an instance of `Ext.Window` utilizing the `HBoxLayout`.

Because we've built a few `TreePanels` already, we're going to move through this pretty fast. The following listing sets the stage.

Listing 14.16   Setting the stage for `TreePanel` drag and drop

```
Ext.QuickTips.init();

var leftTree = {
    xtype      : 'treepanel',
    autoScroll : true,
    title      : 'Their Company',
    animate    : false,
    loader     : new Ext.tree.TreeLoader({
        url : 'theirCompany.php'
    }),
    root       : {
        text     : 'Their Company',
```

❶ Their company's TreePanel

```
          id        : 'theirCompany',
          expanded : true
      }
  };

  var rightTree = {
      xtype      : 'treepanel',
      title      : 'Our Company',
      autoScroll : true,
      animate    : false,
      loader     : new Ext.tree.TreeLoader({
          url :  'ourCompany.php'
      }),
      root       : {
          text     : 'Our Company',
          id       : 'ourCompany',
          expanded : true
      }
  };

  new Ext.Window({
      height      : 350,
      width       : 450,
      layout      : 'hbox',
      border      : false,
      layoutConfig : {
          align : 'stretch'
      },
      defaults    : {
          flex : 1
      },
      items       : [
            leftTree,
            rightTree
      ]
  }).show();
```

❷ Our company's
   TreePanel

❸ Window to contain
   the TreePanels

In listing 14.16, you create two TreePanels and an Ext Window, which will contain them and manage their sizes using the HBoxLayout. The left TreePanel ❶ will load a list of departments for the other company. Each department will have to be expanded to reveal the child items.

The right TreePanel ❷ will load up a list of departments for our company, which, lucky for us, aligns with the company being sold. For simplicity, we won't display the employees currently in our company's departments.

Last, the Ext Window is created ❸ to manage the two TreePanels side by side. Figure 14.13 shows our TreePanels rendered onscreen.

We have the two TreePanels rendered within the Ext Window. It's time to get the party started with drag and drop.

14.4.2 *Enabling drag and drop*

When exploring how to employ drag and drop with DataViews, we were required to implement both the DragZone and DropZone classes. When applying this feature to

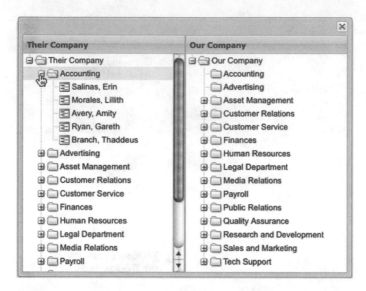

Figure 14.13
The two `TreePanels`

`GridPanels`, you learned that you were required to implement only `DropZone` because the `GridView` automatically creates `GridDragZone` if the `GridPanel` has the `enable-DragDrop` property set.

With the `TreePanel`, drag and drop is much easier. All we have to do is set the following property on both of the `TreePanel` configuration objects:

```
enableDD : true
```

The `TreePanel` takes care of instantiating the `TreeDragZone` and `TreeDropZone` classes for us. To specify the drag/drop group that the `TreePanel` is to participate in, set the `ddGroup` configuration parameter as follows:

```
ddGroup   : 'myTreeDDGroup'
```

Figure 14.14 shows what drag and drop with the two `TreePanels` looks like in action. As you can see, enabling drag and drop on `TreePanels` is simple to do. But wait a minute. Everything can be dragged and dropped, which can be useful for, let's say, a filesystem management tool, but for what we need, it just won't cut it.

Out of the proverbial box, the `TreeNode` class allows for some constraints to be applied to the dragging and dropping of nodes when drag and drop is applied to their owner `TreePanel`. The two parameters that help control these behaviors are `allowDrag` and `allowDrop`, both of which are configured on each node of the tree and default to `true` even if the properties don't exist. We could have the returning JSON include these properties, but they're rigid. With these two properties, you can either allow drag or not, or allow drop or not. Clearly this won't help us fulfill the requirement to allow any associate from a set group of departments to be dropped on those departments. For this, we'll need to craft something much more flexible.

We'll tackle this intense procedure next. Are you ready?

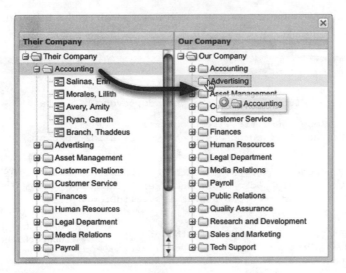

Figure 14.14 Drag and drop enabled on `TreePanels`

14.4.3 *Employing flexible constraints*

Thus far, when implementing drag and drop, we created objects to override the required template methods, which gave us the control we desired for the drag-and-drop classes. With the `TreePanel`, we can apply template overrides by specifying `drag-Config` or `dropConfig` objects in the `TreePanel`'s configuration object.

To have better control of what nodes can be dragged around, we'll create a `drag-Config` object, which overrides the `onBeforeDrag` template method. You'll need to place this code *before* the `TreePanel` configurations:

```
var dragConfig = {
    onBeforeDrag : function(dragData, eventObj) {
        return dragData.node.attributes.leaf;
    }
};
```

In this snippet, we create a `dragConfig` object that contains the `onBeforeDrag` override method. All it does is return the dragged node's `leaf` attribute. This will prevent all branch nodes from being dragged around the screen. To apply the drag constraint, set the `dragConfig` object on both `TreePanels` as follows:

```
dragConfig : dragConfig,
```

Refresh the page and you'll see that the department nodes can no longer be dragged around. This completes half of the requirement. As of now, any employee nodes can be dragged to any department, which means we need to work on the code to provide better drop point constraints.

Listing 14.17 is rather large because many tests need to take place in order to ensure that the desired drop operation is completely correct. Any slipup and nodes can be dropped where they don't belong. Please don't be alarmed; we'll go into an in-depth discussion about it.

As with the `dragConfig` object creation, you'll need to place the following code *before* the `TreePanel` configuration.

Listing 14.17   Applying better drop constraints

```
var dropConfig = {
    isValidDropPoint : function(nodeData, pt, dd, eventObj, data) {

        var treeDropZone = Ext.tree.TreeDropZone;
        var isVldDrpPnt  = treeDropZone.prototype.isValidDropPoint;

        var drpNd           = data.node;                                    ①  Gather
        var drpNdPrntDept   = drpNd.parentNode.attributes.text;                 drop node
        var drpNdOwnerTreeId = drpNd.getOwnerTree().id;                         references
        var validDropPoints = drpNd.attributes.validDropPoints || [];

        var tgtNd           = nodeData.node;                                 Gather target
        var tgtNdPrnt       = tgtNd.parentNode;                             ②  node references
        var tgtNdOwnerTree  = tgtNd.getOwnerTree();
        var tgtNdOwnerTreeId = tgtNdOwnerTree.id;

        var isSameTree = drpNdOwnerTreeId === tgtNdOwnerTreeId;

        if (!tgtNdPrnt || isSameTree) {            ③  Return false if
            return false;                              not droppable
        }
                                                                        ④  Create more
        var tgtNdPrntDept = tgtNdPrnt.attributes.text;                      target node
        var tgtNdTxt      = tgtNd.attributes.text;                          references

        if (drpNdPrntDept === tgtNdPrntDept) {          ⑤  Return true
            return isVldDrpPnt.apply(tgtNdOwnerTree.dropZone, arguments);      if droppable
        }
        else if (Ext.isArray(validDropPoints)) {        ⑥  Does node have valid
            var isVldDept = false;                          DropPoints array?

            var drpPoint = tree.dropZone.getDropPoint(
                            eventObj, nodeData, dd);

            Ext.each(validDropPoints, function(dpName) {    Loop through
                if (tgtNdTxt === dpName) {                   valid drop
                    isVldDept = dpName;                    ⑦  points
                }
            });
                                                        ⑧  Allow drop
            if (isVldDept && drpPoint === 'append') {
                return isVldDrpPnt.apply(tgtNdOwnerTree.dropZone, arguments);
            }
        }

        return false;
    }
};
```

In listing 14.17, you create a `dropConfig` object and work hard to constrain what nodes can be dropped where. You utilize the `TreeDropZone.prototype.isValid-DropPoint` method to finish the processing when you deem that the drop point is valid. Here's how all of this stuff works.

First, you create a reference to the `TreeDropZone.prototype.isValidDropPoint`. You do this because even though this `isValidDropPoint` method will *override* the targeted `TreeDropZone` instance, you still need the processing that's provided by the original `TreeDropZone isValidDropPoint` method. You need it because it's responsible for appending some important properties to the drag data object that the `TreeDragZone` creates. In order not to duplicate the code, you call it when you're comfortable with the current mouseover situation.

Next, you create quite a few drop node–related references ❶, such as the drop node's parent (department) text, the drop node's owner tree, and its id. Similarly, you gather references for the target node ❷. These references will be the backbone to help determine whether the target node is a valid drop target.

Moving on, you reach your first test, where you determine whether the drop target is a root node by detecting the absence of the target's parent node. If the target node has no parent, then it's a root node. You also try to see if the drop node's owner tree is the same as the target node's. If either test case is true, then you return `false` ❸.

Looking ahead, you create references for the target node's parent (department) text and the target node text ❹. You'll use both to determine whether the drop node is a valid drop point based on the possible drop scenarios.

You then reach your first major test, where you look to see if the drop node's parent text matches that of the target node ❺. This test is useful in the scenario where you're dropping a node on another leaf element that exists within a similar parent. For example, you drag "Salinas, Erin" from Accounting from their company and drop Erin on another associate node that exists within Accounting in our company. If this condition is true, you call on the `TreeDragZone`'s `isValidDropPoint` to properly process the drop and return the results, which ultimately results in a favorable possible drop condition.

If that test fails, you then determine whether the target node is a branch node and matches any of the drop points in the `validDropPoints` array ❻. You do this by testing the return of the utility method `Ext.isArray` to verify that the drop node's `validDropPoints` array is valid ❼.

If the test is favorable, then you get the drop point. The `TreeDropZone` performs similar calculations to the ones you did when determining whether the drag operation was occurring above or below a row, except it's concerned with nodes. Because drop nodes can be *appended* ❽ to a target branch as well as dropped *above* or *below* a target node, the `TreeDropZone getDropPoint` method returns any one of the values just mentioned.

This is important to know because when the drag node is hovering over a branch element, the drop point could be above or below, which means that the drop node could be dropped below or above a branch node. If you allowed this to occur, you'd have associates that would be placed *outside* a department, which is unfavorable.

Moving on, you loop through the `validDropPoints` array and test to see if any of the drop points in the array match the target (department) node text. If so, then you return the value of the `TreeDragZone`'s `isValidDropPoint` call to indicate that a successful drop is possible.

If none of these tests pass, then a `false` value is returned, and the `TreeDragZone` knows to update the `StatusProxy` indicating that a favorable drop isn't possible.

You've done a lot of work to get these constraints configured. In order to take advantage of this code, you need to reconfigure the `TreePanels` with the `dropConfig` object as follows:

```
dropConfig : dropConfig
```

Adding this configuration parameter to your `TreePanels` will ensure that an instance of `TreeDropZone` is created and bound to the `TreePanels`. Refresh your page and see the constraints in action; mine are shown in figure 14.15.

You can test your constraint logic by attempting to drag a department branch node. You'll see that it's impossible. This tells you that the `onBeforeDrag` override method is working as designed.

Next, to determine where the associate can be dragged, hover over it and you'll see a `ToolTip` appear with the values that are in the `validDropPoints` array. In hovering over Erin, we found that she can be dropped on Accounting but not Advertising. When we drag Erin over Accounting on the right-hand `TreePanel`, the `StatusProxy` displays a valid drop icon (figure 14.15). But if we hover her over Advertising, we see

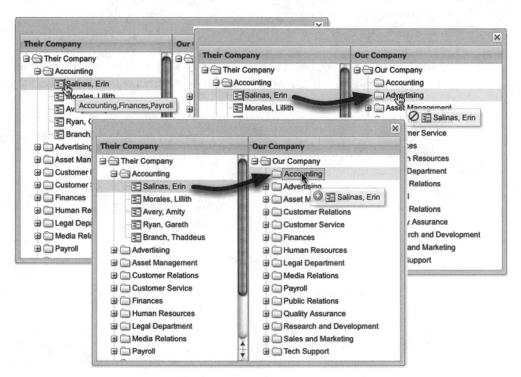

Figure 14.15   Testing our drop target constraint logic

an invalid drop icon in the `StatusProxy`. As extra credit, you can try to hover Erin over Finances and Payroll, and you'll see a valid drop icon there too.

The last test you can perform is to drop an associate or two onto a valid department. You can test the ability to drop leaf nodes above or below other leaf nodes within a valid department as well.

There you have it: drag and drop with two tree panels with a complex but somewhat flexible drop constraint system. I'm sure our managers will be pleased that we delivered what they were asking for.

14.5 Summary

We spent a lot of time in this chapter looking at different ways to implement drag and drop with the three most commonly used widgets within the framework, and you learned a lot while doing it.

We started with implementing this behavior with `DataViews`, where you learned that you're responsible for configuring both the `DragZone` and `DropZone` classes. While employing this behavior, we developed a custom and more useful way to display the `Record`s being dragged around.

Next, you learned how to employ this behavior with two `GridPanels` and learned that you're mainly responsible for implementing a `DropZone` to handle the drops. In doing so, you tackled the hard problem of detecting the index of a node drop to allow `Record`s to be inserted in any desired index.

Finally, we explored drag and drop with `TreePanels`. In this implementation, you discovered that enabling this behavior with `TreePanels` is the easiest task, and the application of somewhat complex constraints on the drop gestures is the most difficult task.

In the next chapter, you'll learn about plug-ins and extensions and how they work. You'll start to use object-oriented techniques with JavaScript and will have a lot of fun.

Extensions and plug-ins

Every Ext JS developer faces the challenge where reusability becomes an issue. Oftentimes, a component of an application is required to appear more than once within the application's usage lifetime. In much larger applications, reusability of components is paramount to performance as well as maintainability of the code itself. This is why we'll focus on the concept of reusability with the use of framework extensions and plug-ins.

In the first section of this chapter, you'll learn the basics of extending (subclassing) with Ext JS. You'll begin by learning how to create subclasses with JavaScript, where you'll get to see what it takes to get the job done with the native language tools. This will give you the necessary foundation to refactor your newly created subclass to leverage `Ext.extend`, implementing two different popular design patterns.

Once you've gotten familiar with creating basic subclasses, we'll focus our attention on extending Ext JS `Components`. This is where you'll get to have fun learning about the basics of framework extensions and solve a real-world problem by extending the `GridPanel` widget and seeing it in action.

When we finish the extension, you'll learn how extensions solve problems but can create inheritance issues where similar functionality is desired across multiple widgets. Once you understand the basic limitations of extensions, you'll convert your extension into a plug-in, where its functionality can easily be shared across the `GridPanel` and any descendant thereof.

15.1 Inheritance with Ext JS

JavaScript provides all of the necessary tools for class inheritance, but we as developers must take many manual steps in order to achieve this. The net result is wordy code. Ext JS makes inheritance much easier with its `Ext.extend` utility method. To begin learning about inheritance, you'll create a base class.

To help you along, envision we're working for an automobile dealership that sells two types of car. First is the base car, which serves as a foundation to construct the premium model. Instead of using 3-D models to describe the two car models, we'll use JavaScript classes.

> **NOTE** If you're new to object-oriented JavaScript or are feeling a bit rusty, the Mozilla foundation has an excellent article to bring you up to speed or polish your skills. You can find it at the following URL: https://developer.mozilla.org/en/Introduction_to_Object-Oriented_JavaScript.

We'll begin by constructing a class to describe the base car, as shown in the following listing.

Listing 15.1 Constructing our base class

```
var BaseCar = function(config) {                    Create
    this.octaneRequired = 86;                   ❶  constructor

    this.shiftTo = function(gear) {
        this.gear = gear;
    };

    this.shiftTo('park');
};

BaseCar.prototype = {                               Assign
    engine    : 'I4',                           ❷  prototype object
    turbo     : false,
    wheels    : 'basic',
    getEngine : function() {
        return this.engine;
    },
    drive     : function() {
        return 'Vrrrrooooooom - I'm driving!';
    }
};
```

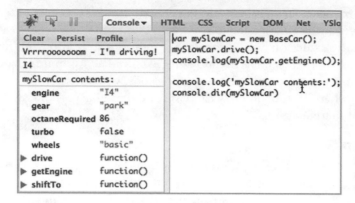

Figure 15.1   Instantiating an instance of `BaseCar` and exercising two of its methods

In listing 15.1, you create the `BaseCar` class constructor ❶, which when instantiated sets the instance's local `this.octaneRequired` property, adds a `this.shiftTo` method, and calls it, setting the local `this.gear` property to `'park'`. Next, you configure the `BaseCar`'s `prototype` object ❷, which contains three properties that describe the `BaseCar` and two methods.

You could use the following code to instantiate an instance of `BaseCar` and inspect its contents with Firebug:

```
var mySlowCar = new BaseCar();
mySlowCar.drive();
console.log(mySlowCar.getEngine());

console.log('mySlowCar contents:');
console.dir(mySlowCar)
```

Figure 15.1 shows what the output of this code looks like in the Firebug multiline editor and console.

With our `BaseCar` class set, we can now focus on subclassing the `BaseCar` class. We'll first do it the traditional way. This will give you a better understanding of what's going on under the hood when we use `Ext.extend` later on.

15.1.1 Inheritance with JavaScript

Creating a subclass using native JavaScript is achievable with multiple steps. Rather than simply describing them, we'll walk through the steps together. The following listing creates `PremiumCar`, a subclass of the `BaseCar` class.

Listing 15.2   Creating a subclass the old-school way

```
var PremiumCar = function() {
    PremiumCar.superclass.constructor.call(this);        Call superclass
    this.octaneRequired = 93;                            constructor  ❷

                                                         Configure
};                                                       subclass
                                                         constructor  ❶
PremiumCar.prototype   = new BaseCar();
PremiumCar.superclass  = BaseCar.prototype;              Set subclass
                                                         prototype  ❸
PremiumCar.prototype.turbo  = true;                      Set subclass's
                                                         superclass
                                                         reference  ❹
```

```
PremiumCar.prototype.wheels = 'premium';

PremiumCar.prototype.drive = function() {
    this.shiftTo('drive');
    PremiumCar.superclass.drive.call(this);
};

PremiumCar.prototype.getEngine = function() {
    return 'Turbo ' + this.engine;
};
```

To create a subclass, you begin by creating a new constructor, which is assigned to the reference PremiumCar ❶. Within this constructor is a call to the constructor method of the PremiumCar.superclass within the scope of the instance of PremiumCar ❷ being created (this).

You do this because, unlike other object-oriented languages, JavaScript subclasses don't natively call their superclass constructor ❷. Calling the superclass constructor gives it a chance to execute and perform any constructor-specific functions that the subclass might need. In our case, the shiftTo method is being added and called in the BaseCar constructor. Not calling the superclass constructor would mean that our subclass wouldn't get the benefits provided by the base class constructor.

Next, you set the prototype of PremiumCar to the result of a new instance of Base-Car ❸. Performing this step allows PremiumCar.prototype to inherit all of the properties and methods from BaseCar. This is known as *inheritance through prototyping* and is the most common and robust method of creating class hierarchies in JavaScript.

In the next line, you set the PremiumCar's superclass reference to the prototype of the BaseCar class ❹. You then can use this superclass reference to do things like create so-called extension methods, such as PremiumCar.prototype.drive. This method is known as an extension method because it *calls* the like-named method from the superclass prototype but from the scope of the instance of the subclass it's attached to.

> **TIP** All JavaScript functions (JavaScript 1.3 and later) have two methods that force the scope execution: call and apply. To learn more about call and apply visit the following URL: http://www.webreference.com/js/column26/apply.html.

With the subclass now created, you can test things out by instantiating an instance of PremiumCar with the following code entered into the Firebug editor:

```
var myFastCar = new PremiumCar();
myFastCar.drive();

console.log('myFastCar contents:');
console.dir(myFastCar);
```

Figure 15.2 shows what the output would look like in the Firebug multiline editor and console.

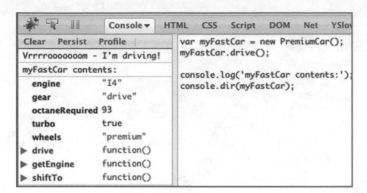

Figure 15.2
Our `PremiumCar`
subclass in action

This output shows that our subclass performed as desired. From the `console.dir` output, you can see that the subclass constructor set the `octaneRequired` property to 93 and the `drive` extension method even set the `gear` method as `"drive"`.

This exercise shows that you're responsible for all of the crucial steps in order to achieve prototypal inheritance with native JavaScript. First, you had to create the constructor of the subclass. Then, you had to set the prototype of the subclass to a new instance of the base class. Next, for convenience, you set the subclass's `superclass` reference. Last, you added members to the prototype one by one.

You can see that quite a few steps need to be followed in order to create subclasses with the native language constructs. Next, we'll show how `Ext.extend` makes creating subclasses much easier.

15.1.2 *Extending with Ext JS*

There are two common patterns in using `Ext.extend`. The first is an older method, whose roots stem from the 1.0 days of the framework, and involves first creating the subclass constructor and then calling on `Ext.extend` to finish the work. The second is a more modern method, stemming from the 2.0 days of the framework, and involves having `Ext.extend` do all of the work.

We'll begin by exploring the older pattern of `Ext.extend`. Knowing both patterns will benefit you when reading extension code from other Ext JS developers, because the usage between the two patterns varies from developer to developer. We'll be using the previously created `BaseCar` class for this exercise, shown in the following listing.

Listing 15.3 Creating our first extension

```
var PremiumCar = function() {
    PremiumCar.superclass.constructor.call(this);      ◁── Scope call of superclass constructor ❷
    this.octaneRequired = 93;
};

Ext.extend(PremiumCar, BaseCar, {
    turbo       : true,
    wheels      : 'premium',
    getEngine   : function() {
```

◁── Create **PremiumCar** ❶ constructor

◁── Extend ❸ **BaseCar**

```
            return this.engine + ' Turbo';
    },
    drive        : function() {
        this.shiftTo('drive');
        PremiumCar.superclass.drive.call(this);
    }
});
```

In listing 15.3, you create the PremiumCar class, which is an extension (subclass) of the BaseCar class using the Ext.extend tool. Here's how this works.

First, you create a constructor for the PremiumCar ❶. This constructor is an exact duplicate of the previously created PremiumCar constructor.

When thinking about extending classes, you must consider whether prototypal methods in the subclass will share the same name as prototypal methods in the base class. If they will share the same symbolic reference name, you must consider whether they'll be extension methods or overrides.

An extension method is a method in a subclass that shares the same reference name as another method in a base class. What makes this an extension method is the fact that it includes the execution of the base class method within itself. The Premium-Car constructor ❷ is an extension of the BaseCar constructor because of the included execution of the BaseCar constructor method. The reason you'd want to extend a method would be to reduce code duplication, reusing the code in the base class method.

An override method is a method in a subclass that shares the same reference name as another method in a base class but doesn't execute the same-named method from the base class. You override a method if you wish to completely discard the code that's in the like-named method in the base class.

To complete the extension process, you call on Ext.extend ❸, for which you're passing three parameters: subclass, base class, and what's known in the community as an *overrides object*. Here's how this works.

Ext.extend first sets the subclass's prototype to the result of a new instance of the base class, which is like what we did when creating our subclass manually. Ext.extend then applies the symbolic references of the overrides object to the prototype of the subclass. The symbolic references in the overrides object take precedence over those in the base class's prototype. This is similar to us manually adding the members when we created our subclass earlier.

You can see that it took only two steps to extend the BaseCar class: create the constructor for the subclass and use Ext.extend to tie everything else together. It not only took less work on your part, but the amount of code you had to write was much smaller and easier to digest, which is one of the lesser-known benefits of using Ext.extend to subclass.

Now that you have your PremiumCar configured using Ext.extend, you can see it in action using Firebug. You can do so using the exact same code you used when exercising your manually created subclass:

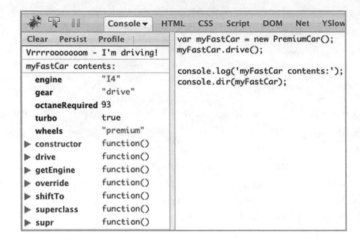

Figure 15.3 The results of the instantiation of the PremiumCar class

```
var myFastCar = new PremiumCar();
myFastCar.drive();

console.log('myFastCar contents:');
console.dir(myFastCar);
```

Figure 15.3 shows what it looks like in the Firebug console. Looking at that figure, you can see that Ext.extend adds some convenience references to the subclass. These can be useful from within the instance of the class. They're references to the constructor and superclass methods. The override method is useful if you want to change members for the instance of the class that you've instantiated.

You've just successfully extended a class using what's known as an old-fashioned method, which consists of creating a constructor and then calling on Ext.extend to copy the prototype from the base class to the subclass and apply the overrides object to the subclass's prototype. This pattern of extending works perfectly fine and many use it, but there's a much more modern pattern that we'll be using, which allows us to reduce the extension to a single step and provide the constructor inside the overrides object.

The following listing shows the exact same extension with the modern Ext.extend implementation pattern.

Listing 15.4 Implementing Ext.extend with the modern pattern

```
var PremiumCar = Ext.extend(BaseCar, {
    turbo      : true,
    wheels     : 'premium',
    constructor : function() {                    ❶ Include constructor
        PremiumCar.superclass.constructor.call(this);    in overrides
        this.octaneRequired = 93;
    },
    drive      : function() {
        this.shiftTo('drive');
```

```
        PremiumCar.superclass.drive.call(this);
    },
    getEngine   : function() {
        return this.engine + ' Turbo';
    }
});
```

In this implementation of `Ext.extend`, you pass two arguments. The first is a reference to the base class, and the second is the overrides object to be applied to the subclass's `prototype`. That's it. The biggest difference between the first implementation
and this one is that you're including the `constructor` ❶ method inside the overrides
object. Ext JS is smart enough to know to use this method to create a constructor for
you. Last, notice that the `PremiumCar` reference is the result of the `Ext.extend`
method call.

By now, you're probably wondering what makes this pattern better than the first.
The single and most compelling reason is code readability. For many, it's easier to
digest and read code formatted in this way. For this reason, many developers have created classes from scratch by means of extending `Object`, instead of creating a constructor and then a prototype object.

Here's how you create a simple class using this newer pattern:

```
var NewClass = Ext.extend(Object, {
    someProperty : 'Some property',
    constructor  : function() {
        NewClass.superclass.constructor.call(this);
    },
    aMethod      : function() {
        console.info("A method has executed.");
    }
});
```

By now, you understand how to use the utility method `Ext.extend` to create subclasses. You learned that `Ext.extend` provides a means for creating subclasses with
fewer steps compared to the traditional JavaScript method. You also got a chance to
explore the two most common `Ext.extend` patterns used by Ext JS developers. For the
rest of this book, we'll be using the modern pattern.

Next, you'll use your newly gain knowledge and learn how to extend `Components`.

15.2 *Extending Ext JS Components*

Extensions to the framework are developed to introduce additional functionality to
existing classes in the name of reusability. The concept of reusability drives the framework, and when utilized properly it can enhance the development of your applications.

Some developers create preconfigured classes, which are constructed mainly as a
means of reducing the amount of application-level code by stuffing configuration
parameters into the class itself. Having such extensions alleviates the application-level
code from having to manage much of the configuration, requiring only the simple
instantiation of such classes. This type of class is great, but only if you're expecting to
stamp out more than one instance of this class.

Other extensions add features such as utility methods or embed behavioral logic inside the class itself. An example of this would be a `FormPanel` that automatically pops up a `MessageBox` whenever a save operation failure occurs. I often create extensions for applications for this very reason, where the widget contains some built-in business logic.

My favorite kind of extension is what I like to call a *composite* widget, which combines one or more widgets into one class. An example of this would be a `Window` that has an embedded `GridPanel` or a `FormPanel` that embeds a `TabPanel` to spread its fields over multiple panels.

This is the type of extension that we'll focus on now, where we'll merge a `GridPanel` with a `Menu`.

15.2.1 *Thinking about what we're building*

When I work to construct an extension, I often take a step back and try to analyze the problem from all facets, as I do with puzzles. I do this because I view the creation of extensions as a way to solve issues. Sometimes these problems can be extremely complex, such as the creation of a dynamic wizard-like widget that has numerous workflow rules that must be controlled by the UI. Oftentimes I use extensions to solve the problem of reusability. This will be our focus for the rest of the chapter.

When thinking about common tasks during application development, I often wonder how such tasks can be made easier through an extension. One task that comes to mind is that end developers must code for the destruction of loosely coupled widgets, such as `Menus` or `Windows`, when their parent component is destroyed.

You experienced this when we explored the creation of a `GridPanel`, where you attached a `Menu` and configured it to display when the grid's `contextmenu` event fires. Recall that you had to manually configure the `Menu` to destruct upon the `GridPanel`'s destruction. If you extrapolate this task over the span of an application where many `GridPanels` coupled with `Menus` are to be rendered onscreen, you can easily visualize the amount of code duplication required to make this work. Before you start coding, let's take a moment to analyze the problem and come up with the best possible solution.

In order to mitigate this code-duplication risk, we'll have to create an extension to the `GridPanel` that will automatically handle the instantiation and destruction of the `Menu`. But what other features can we add to this extension to make it more robust?

The first thing that comes to mind is the differences in the selection getter and setter methods for `RowSelectionModel` and `CellSelectionModel`. `RowSelectionModel` has `selectRow` and `getSelected` whereas `CellSelectionModel` has `selectCell` and `getSelectedCell`. It would be great if our extension could handle this variation in the `GridPanel`'s selection models. Such a feature would reduce the amount of code in the application layer.

With a clear picture of the issues we're going to solve, we can begin the construction of our first Ext JS extension.

15.2.2 *Extending GridPanel*

To extend the GridPanel class, we'll leverage the Ext.extend method, using the modern pattern. To give you an overview of our extension, the following listing contains the template for the extension that we'll create.

Listing 15.5 The template for our GridPanel extension

```
var CtxMenuGridPanel = Ext.extend(Ext.grid.GridPanel, {
    constructor : function() {                     Constructor
                                                 ❶ extension
    },

    onCellCtxMenu : function(grid, rowInx,
                             cellIndx, evtObj) {    Custom contextmenu
                                                 ❷ event handler
    },

    getSelectedRecord : function() {          Convenience selection
                                           ❸ retrieval method
    },

    onDestroy : function() {            Extend onDestroy to do
                                     ❹ cleanup
    }

});
```

Listing 15.5 contains the template for our extension and provides four methods that will be applied to the subclass's prototype. The first is the constructor ❶, which will be our vector to extend the GridPanel. Let's take a moment to analyze why we're extending via the constructor method. Because this is such an important topic, we'll discuss the differences in the hope that you can make an educated choice when you decide to create extensions in your projects.

Earlier in this book when we discussed the Component lifecycle, you learned of the initComponent method, which is meant to augment the constructor and is intended to be a place for developers to extend components. You learned that initComponent is executed inside the Component class's constructor, but only after a few crucial setup tasks for the Component have taken place. These tasks include the caching and application of the configuration object properties to the instance of the class, the setup of base events, and the registration of the instance of Component with the ComponentMgr class.

Knowing this, you can make an educated decision as to where to extend an Ext JS Component. To make this decision, you must figure out if configured instances of the subclass will ever need to be cloned via the cloneConfig utility method. If so, then extending via the constructor is the best choice. Otherwise, extending via the init-Component method will work. If you're unsure, then default to extending via the constructor. Also, it's important to point out that all non-Component classes don't have an initComponent method; extending via constructor is the only option.

If you look at the rest of the extension template, you'll see three other methods in the overrides configuration object. The first, onCellContextMenu ❷, is the method that will respond to the `cellcontextmenu` events and will ultimately display the menu. The reason for choosing the `cellcontextmenu` event over the `rowcontextmenu` event is that with the `cellcontextmenu` event, you get the row and column coordinates for which the event occurred, which will help your extension understand how to select the row or cell. The `rowcontextmenu` event provides only the row where the event occurred and is unusable when taking the `CellSelectionModel` into consideration.

> **TIP** The arguments passed to the `onCellContextMenu` utility method can be found in the `Ext.grid.GridPanel` API documentation, under the `cellcontextmenu` events section.

The next template method, `getSelectedRecord` ❸, is a utility for getting the selected record despite the cell or row selected. This method takes into account the selection model and leverages the correct selection model getter method. Last, the `onDestroy` ❹ method extends the `GridPanel`'s own `onDestroy` method. This is where you'll code the automatic destruction of the `Menu`.

Your template class is now set and ready to be filled in. You'll start with the constructor in the following listing.

Listing 15.6 Adding the constructor to our extension

```
constructor : function() {
    CtxMenuGridPanel.superclass.constructor.apply(this, arguments);  ◁─

    if (this.menu) {                                        Call superclass constructor ❶
        if (! (this.menu instanceof Ext.menu.Menu)) {    ◁─
            this.menu = new Ext.menu.Menu(this.menu);         Intelligently
        }                                                     create
        this.on({                                             instance of
            scope            : this,                        ❷ Menu
            cellcontextmenu : this.onCellCtxMenu
        });                                                 ◁─  Register
    }                                                           cellcontextmenu
},                                                          ❸  event handler
```

Our `constructor` extension method takes care of automatically creating the instance of the `Menu` widget for us, but in an intelligent manner. The very first task is executing the superclass (`GridPanel`) constructor ❶ method within the scope of the instance of this subclass.

Next, in order to facilitate the automatic instantiation of the `Menu` widget, the method needs to know whether the local menu reference is present and if it's already an instance of `Ext.menu.Menu` ❷ or not. This simple test allows for three different implementation possibilities for this subclass.

You can pass either a `Menu` configuration object

```
new CtxMenuGridPanel({
    // ... (other configuration options)
    menu : {
        items : [
```

```
                { text : 'menu item 1' },
                { text : 'menu item 2' }
            ]
        }
});
```

or an array of `MenuItem` configuration objects

```
new CtxMenuGridPanel({
    // ... (other configuration options)
    menu :[
            { text : 'menu item 1' },
            { text : 'menu item 2' }
        ]
});
```

or an instance of `Ext.menu.Menu` as the `menu` configuration

```
var myMenu = new Ext.menu.Menu({
items : [
    { text : 'menu item 1' },
    { text : 'menu item 2' }
    ]
});

new CtxMenuGridPanel({
    menu : myMenu
});
```

Having this type of flexibility for the implementation of the subclass plays into the framework's culture. Truth be told, part of this flexibility comes from the `Menu` widget itself, whose constructor will accept a configuration object or array of `MenuItem` configuration objects. Also notice that the local `this.menu` reference is overwritten if an instance of `Ext.menu.Menu` is created.

At the end of this `constructor`, you configure the local `this.onCellContextMenu` method as the `cellcontextmenu` event handler ❸. Notice that the `scope` for the event handler is set to `this`, or the instance of your `GridPanel` subclass. Therefore, `onCell-ContextMenu` will need the local `this.menu` reference to manage the display of the `Menu` widget itself.

Next you'll construct an event handler method.

Listing 15.7 Constructing the `onCellContextMenu` event handler method

```
onCellContextMenu : function(grid, rowIndex, cellIndex, evtObj) {

    evtObj.stopEvent();

    if (this.selModel instanceof                              ❶ Selection model
              Ext.grid.RowSelectionModel) {                       method calls

            this.selModel.selectRow(rowIndex);
    }
    else if (this.selModel instanceof Ext.grid.CellSelectionModel) {
        this.selModel.select(rowIndex, cellIndex);
```

```
        }
    this.menu.showAt(evtObj.getXY());
},
```

In order to properly select the cell or row being right-clicked, the event handler method needs to determine which selection model the GridPanel is using. You can determine this by using the generic JavaScript instanceof operator. If the selection model is a RowSelectionModel ❶, the selectRow method is being used; if it's a CellSelectionModel, the select method is being used.

Having such logic in the contextmenu event handler brings another level of flexibility to this extension. You can also use the same logic to determine what selection getter method to use, which is what you'll do in the following listing.

Listing 15.8   Creating the getSelectedRecord utility method

```
getSelectedRecord : function() {
    if (this.selModel instanceof Ext.grid.RowSelectionModel) {
        return this.selModel.getSelected();
    }
    else if (this.selModel instanceof Ext.grid.CellSelectionModel) {
        var selectedCell = this.selModel.getSelectedCell();
        return this.store.getAt(selectedCell[0]);
    }
},
```

In this getSelectedRecord utility method, the Record related to the currently selected cell or row will be returned. Again, you're using the instanceof operator to determine what type of selection model is being used and to return result of the proper getter method call.

At this point, you have all but one method filled in. The last method, onDestroy, will handle the automatic cleanup for your extension, calling for the destruction of the menu if it exists.

```
onDestroy : function() {
    if (this.menu && this.menu.destroy) {
        this.menu.destroy();
    }

    CtxMenuGridPanel.superclass.onDestroy.apply(this, arguments);
}
```

In this extension method, you inspect for the presence of a local this.menu reference and check to see if that reference contains a destroy reference. If both of these conditions are true, then you execute its destroy method. Recall that the destroy method initiates the destruction phase of a Component's lifecycle, purging any DOM nodes that the loosely coupled Menu might have created. Last, you execute the superclass onDestroy method within the scope of this instance of your subclass, completing the extension.

Like all of the Ext JS widgets, you should register the extension with Ext.Component-Mgr to allow for the lazy instantiation of our extension with XTypes. To perform this registration, you'll execute `Ext.reg` and pass the XType string to identify your subclass and the reference to your subclass itself. These statements are placed at the very end of a class's creation:

```
Ext.reg('contextMenuGridPanel', CtxMenuGridPanel);
```

With our extension completed, we can next create an implementation of it and see it in action.

15.2.3 Our extension in action

When discussing the constructor to our `GridPanel` extension, we talked about the three different patterns for implementation, where the `menu` reference for the configuration object can be set to an array of `MenuItem` configuration objects, an instance of `Menu`, or a configuration object designed for an instance of `Menu`. For this implementation, we'll choose the first pattern, which is an array of `MenuItem` configuration objects. This will give us an opportunity to see an automatic instantiation of `Menu` as coded in our extension's `constructor`.

We'll start with the creation of the remote `JsonStore` in the following listing.

Listing 15.9 Creating the remote `JsonStore` for our extension implementation

```
var remoteProxy = new Ext.data.ScriptTagProxy({
    url : 'http://extjsinaction.com/dataQuery.php'
});

var recordFields = ['firstname','lastname'];

var remoteJsonStore = new Ext.data.JsonStore({
    proxy         : remoteProxy,
    id            : 'ourRemoteStore',
    root          : 'records',
    autoLoad      : true,
    totalProperty : 'totalCount',
    remoteSort    : true,
    fields        : recordFields
});


var columnModel = [
    {
        header    : 'Last Name',
        dataIndex : 'lastname'
    },
    {
        header    : 'First Name',
        dataIndex : 'firstname'
    }
];
```

Next, you'll create a generic handler for the `MenuItems` and the implementation of our extension.

Listing 15.10   Implementing our extension

```
var onMenuItemClick = function(menuItem) {                    ❶ Use
    var ctxMenuGrid = Ext.getCmp('ctxMenuGrid');                getSelectedRecord
    var selRecord = ctxMenuGrid.getSelectedRecord();   ◁──      utility
    var msg = String.format(
        '{0} : {1}, {2}',
        menuItem.text,
        selRecord.get('lastname'),
        selRecord.get('firstname')
    );

    Ext.MessageBox.alert('Feedback', msg);
};

var grid = {                                           ❷ Use extension's
    xtype       : 'contextMenuGridPanel',       ◁──      XType
    columns     : columnModel,
    store       : remoteJsonStore,
    loadMask    : true,
    id          : 'ctxMenuGrid',
    selModel    : new Ext.grid.CellSelectionModel(),
    viewConfig  : { forceFit : true },
    menu        : [
        {
            text    : 'Add Record',
            handler : onMenuItemClick
        },
        {
            text    : 'Update Record',
            handler : onMenuItemClick
        },
        {
            text    : 'Delete Record',
            handler : onMenuItemClick
        }
    ]
};
```

In listing 15.10, you first create a generic handler for the MenuItems that you'll configure later. This will provide visual feedback that you've successfully clicked a MenuItem. Notice that it leverages the extension's getSelectedRecord ❶ utility method to gain a reference to the record selected by the right-click event.

Next, you create an XType configuration object for the extension by setting the generic object's xtype ❷ property to 'contextMenuGridPanel', which is the string you registered with ComponentMgr. All of the configuration options are common to the GridPanel. Notice that you're using the CellSelectionModel instead of the default RowSelectionModel. This gives you an opportunity to test both the onCellContext-Menu event handler and the getSelectedRecord utility method to see if they can leverage the correct selection getter and setter methods.

The very last configuration item, menu, is an array of objects. Recall that your extension's constructor will automatically create an instance of Ext.menu.Menu for you if configured. This is the first time you get to see how taking the trouble to generate such an extension can save time.

To render this onscreen, let's wrap the extension in a `Window`:

```
new Ext.Window({
    height : 200,
    width  : 300,
    border : false,
    layout : 'fit',
    items  : grid,
    center : true
}).show();
```

To implement your extension, all you need to do is right-click any cell. This will invoke the display of the automatically instantiated `Menu` widget and select the cell that was right-clicked, using the `onCellContextMenu` event handler method. Next, click any of the `MenuItems`, which will invoke the generic `onMenuItemClick` hander. This will exercise the extension's `getSelectedRecord` utility method.

The contents of the selected `Record` will be displayed in the `MessageBox` as coded in the `onMenuItemClick` handler method. See figure 15.4.

With this implementation of our extension, you didn't have to create an instance of `Menu` and set up an event handler to display the `Menu`. You didn't have to configure the destruction of the `Menu`, either. Our extension takes care of all of the dirty work for us, requiring only the configuration an array of `MenuItem` configuration objects.

You've just seen our extension in action. Clearly, we solved a problem where code duplication would occur often in a large application. The extension solves this problem and automates a few of our actions. Although our extension solved the problem of code duplication, it does have some limitations that may not be apparent but are important to understand.

15.2.4 Identifying the limitations of extensions

For a moment, put yourself into this situation: You're building an application that requires the `GridPanel`, `EditorGridPanel`, and `PropertyGridPanel`. You're required to attach context menus to each of these types of widgets. You already made an extension to `GridPanel` to make the task of attaching menus easier.

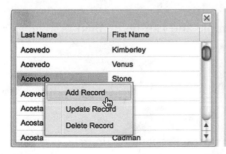

Figure 15.4   Our extension

So here's the question: How do you get the same easy menu functionality across the other types of grids? To put this into context, figure 15.5 illustrates the GridPanel class hierarchy, including our Context-MenuGridPanel extension.

This diagram illustrates that the Editor-GridPanel and ContextMenuGridPanel both extend GridPanel. How can we solve this problem? One solution would be to extend EditorGridPanel and Property-GridPanel to carry over this functionality. That would make the class hierarchy look like that shown in figure 15.6.

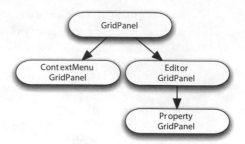

Figure 15.5 The GridPanel class hierarchy with our ContextMenuGridPanel extension

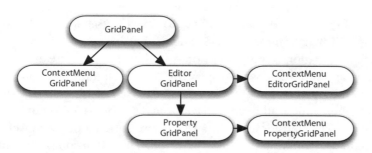

Figure 15.6 A proposed class hierarchy, where code duplication is possible

To achieve this solution, you could either elect to duplicate code or perhaps even stitch together some type of cross-inheritance model. No matter what the solution, it's not going to be elegant or useful.

The only real solution to this problem is a plug-in.

15.3 Plug-ins to the rescue

Plug-ins solve this exact problem by allowing developers to distribute functionality across widgets without having to create extensions; they were introduced in Ext JS version 2.0. What also makes plug-ins powerful is the fact that you can have any number of them attached to a Component.

The basic anatomy of a plug-in is simple and can be defined as a generic object with an init method:

```
var plugin = {
    init : function(parent) {

    }
}
```

If you can recall the initialization phase of the Component lifecycle, you'll remember that at the end of the Component constructor execution, any configured plug-ins are brought to life. The `Component` executes each plug-in's `init` method and passes itself (`this`) as the only argument.

From a plug-in's perspective, I like to think of the `Component` that a plug-in is attached to as the plug-in's parent. When a plug-in's `init` method is executed the first time, it's aware of its parent `Component`, and this is a crucial time for the plug-in to perform any work that may be required before a `Component` is rendered. An example of this is the attaching of event handlers.

Before we convert our extension to a plug-in, I want to show you a much more flexible and powerful plug-in design pattern.

15.3.1 A robust plug-in design pattern

When I develop plug-ins, I use a more complex but thorough pattern compared to the simple example shown previously. I do so because there are times where it's necessary to add methods to the parent `Component` itself. Also, it's our responsibility to code any cleanup actions, such as the destruction of any loosely coupled widgets.

Before we implement this pattern on a large scale, we should look at a skeleton and discuss it; see the following listing.

Listing 15.11 A thorough plug-in design pattern

```
var plugin = Ext.extend(Object, {
    constructor : function(config) {
        config = config || {};                ❶ Apply any passed
        Ext.apply(this, config);                  configuration
    },
    init : function(parent) {                 ❷ Set up
        parent.on('destroy', this.onDestroy, this);   automatic cleanup
        Ext.apply(parent, this.parentOverrides);
    },
    onDestroy : function() {
                                              ❸ Apply overrides
    },                                            to parent
    parentOverrides : {

    }
});

Ext.preg('myPlugin', plugin);
```

As you can see, this plug-in pattern is a bit more involved than the first but is much more robust. You start out with the extension of `Object` and have a full constructor, where the configuration properties passed are applied to the instance of the class ❶. This works *exactly* like most of the classes in the framework.

Next is the `init` method, which automatically registers the local `onDestroyMethod` as a handler ❷ for the parent `Component`'s `destroy` event. `onDestroy` is where you'd want to place your plug-in's cleanup code. Also, notice that you're applying the local `parentOverrides` ❸ object to the parent `Component`. Having this capability means that you can extend on the fly, or add methods and properties to the parent

Component. Not all plug-ins add members to the parent Component, but this mechanism provides a means to do so if you need to.

> **NOTE**   All methods *applied* to the parent Component will execute with the scope of the parent Component.

In the last bit, you execute Ext.preg, which registers the plug-in with Ext.ComponentMgr as what's known as a *PType*, or plug-in type, and is exactly like an XType. Although this last step isn't necessary for a plug-in to be used, it allows for lazy instantiation by the framework.

Now that you know the basics of plug-ins, we can begin work to convert our extension to a plug-in.

15.3.2 *Developing a plug-in*

Our plugin needs to be able to do exactly what the extension was capable of. This includes the instantiation of a Menu and attaching the cellcontextmenu to the parent Component to be able to display the Menu. It also needs to manage the destruction of the Menu when the parent Component is destroyed. We can't leave out the getSelectedRecord utility method, which means we'll get to exercise the application of the parentOverrides object of our plug-in design pattern.

A lot of the code we'll assemble will come from the extension we created earlier. This means that we can move a bit faster, focusing on how the plug-in works. The following listing is the template for our plug-in.

Listing 15.12   The template for our plug-in

```
var GridCtxMenuPlugin = Ext.extend(Object, {
    constructor : function(config) {

    },
    init : function(parent) {

    },
    onCellContextMenu : function(grid, rowIndex, cellIndex, evtObj) {

    },
    onDestroy : function() {

    },
    parentOverrides : {
        getSelectedRecord : function() {

        }
    }
});

Ext.preg('gridCtxMenuPlugin', GridCtxMenuPlugin);
```

In the plug-in template in listing 15.12, you add the onCellContextMenu handler method, which, just like in our extension, will handle the display of the menu and proper selection. You also add the getSelectedRecord utility method to the parentOverrides object. This will give you an opportunity to exercise adding a method to a parent Component on the fly.

Our template is set. We can begin filling in the methods. We'll start with the constructor and the init methods, shown in the following listing.

Listing 15.13 Adding the constructor and init methods to our plug-in

```
constructor : function(config) {
    config = config || {};
    Ext.apply(this, config);
},
init : function(parent) {
    this.parent = parent;                                    ❶ Cache parent
                                                                 reference
    if (parent instanceof Ext.grid.GridPanel) {
        if (! (this.menu instanceof Ext.menu.Menu)) {        ❷ Ensure plug-in
            this.menu = new Ext.menu.Menu(this.menu);            with all GridPanels
        }
        parent.on({
            scope          : this,                           ❸ Attach applicable
            cellcontextmenu : this.onCellContextMenu,           event handlers
            destroy        : this.onDestroy
        });

        Ext.apply(parent, this.parentOverrides);
    }
},
```

For the constructor method, you use the constructor from the pattern where you apply the passed configuration object to the instance of the plug-in. This will be useful because when you implement this plug-in, you'll be configuring the menu on the plug-in itself.

In the init method, you set a local this.parent ❶ reference to the parent Component. This is useful for methods on the plug-in itself that need to do something to or with the parent Component.

Next, an if block tests to see if the parent Component is an instance of the Grid-Panel widget ❷. This type of test allows this plug-in to work only with GridPanels or any descendant thereof and is the type of control pattern to use to prevent the accidental use of plug-ins for widgets that they aren't designed for.

Inside this block, the creation of a Menu widget and registration of related event handlers ❸ will occur just like for our extension. The difference is that a destroy handler is added to allow the plug-in to destroy the Menu widget.

The first two methods are filled in. In the next listing, you'll fill in the last three.

Listing 15.14 Adding the last three methods to our plug-in

```
onCellContextMenu : function(grid, rowIndex, cellIndex, evtObj) {
    evtObj.stopEvent();

    if (grid.selModel instanceof Ext.grid.RowSelectionModel) {
        grid.selModel.selectRow(rowIndex);
    }
```

```
        else if (grid.selModel instanceof Ext.grid.CellSelectionModel) {
            grid.selModel.select(rowIndex, cellIndex);
        }
        this.menu.stopEvent(evtObj.getXY());
    },
    onDestroy : function() {
        if (this.menu && this.menu.destroy) {
            this.menu.destroy();
        }
    },
    parentOverrides : {
        getSelectedRecord : function() {
            if (this.selModel instanceof Ext.grid.RowSelectionModel) {
                return this.selModel.getSelected();
            }
            else if (this.selModel instanceof Ext.grid.CellSelectionModel) {
                var selectedCell = this.selModel.getSelectedCell();
                return this.store.getAt(selectedCell[0]);
            }
        }

    }
}
```

The first of the last three methods, `onCellContextMenu`, will be called within the scope of the instance of the plug-in as registered in the `init` method. It works almost exactly like the similarly named method on our extension, except it references the parent `Component` via the first argument.

The `onDestroy` method too will execute within the scope of the instance of the plug-in and will destroy the menu accordingly. The `parentOverrides` object contains the `getSelectedRecord` utility method that's applied to the parent `Component` by the plug-in's `init` method. Remember that this method will execute within the scope of the parent `Component`.

The construction of the plug-in is now complete. It's time to put it into action.

15.3.3 *Our plug-in in action*

To exercise our plug-in, we'll construct a `GridPanel` that will use a lot of the same code from the previous `GridPanel` implementation. The difference is that we'll configure the plug-in, which will contain the `Menu` configuration. Replacing the `Menu` configuration on the `GridPanel` will be the `plugin`.

We'll begin by creating the data `Store`. A lot of this is repeat code, so we'll be moving relatively fast.

> **Listing 15.15   Constructing the data `Store`**

```
var remoteProxy = new Ext.data.scriptTagProxy({
    url : 'http://tdgi/dataQuery.php'
});

var recordFields = ['firstname','lastname'];

var remoteJsonStore = new Ext.data.JsonStore({
    proxy        : remoteProxy,
```

```
      id             : 'ourRemoteStore',
      root           : 'records',
      autoLoad       : true,
      totalProperty  : 'totalCount',
      remoteSort     : true,
      fields         : recordFields
});
```

In the next listing, we'll create the generic `MenuItem` handler and configure a plug-in.

Listing 15.16 `MenuItem` handler and plug-in

```
var onMenuItemClick = function(menuItem) {
    var ctxMenuGrid = Ext.getCmp('ctxMenuGrid');
    var selRecord = ctxMenuGrid.getSelectedRecord();
    var msg = String.format(
        '{0} : {1}, {2}',
        menuItem.text,
        selRecord.get('lastname'),
        selRecord.get('firstname')
    );

    Ext.MessageBox.alert('Feedback', msg);
};

var ctxMenuPlugin = {
    ptype : 'gridCtxMenuPlugin',
     menu : [
        {
            text     : 'Add Record',
            handler  : onMenuItemClick
        },
        {
            text     : 'Update Record',
            handler  : onMenuItemClick
        },
        {
            text     : 'Delete Record',
            handler  : onMenuItemClick
        }
     ]
};
```

Along with the creation of the generic `MenuItem` handler, we configure the plug-in using a PType configuration object. Ext JS will use this to lazy-instantiate an instance of the plug-in we created and registered with the string "`gridCtxMenuPlugin`". Again, this is just like XTypes for `Components`.

Last, we'll create the `GridPanel` that will use the plug-in and display it onscreen.

Listing 15.17 Configuring and showing the `GridPanel`

```
var columnModel = [
    {
        header    : 'Last Name',
        dataIndex : 'lastname'
    },
```

```
    {
        header    : 'First Name',
        dataIndex : 'firstname'
    }
];

var grid = {
    xtype       : 'grid',
    columns     : columnModel,
    store       : remoteJsonStore,
    loadMask    : true,
    id          : 'ctxMenuGrid',
    viewConfig  : { forceFit : true },
    plugins     : ctxMenuPlugin
};

new Ext.Window({
    height : 200,
    width  : 300,
    border : false,
    layout : 'fit',
    items  : grid,
    center : true
}).show();
```

In listing 15.17, we configure a `GridPanel` XType object that uses the `ctxMenuPlugin` that we configured earlier and display it via an `Ext.Window`. In this implementation, we configured only one plug-in via the `plugins` reference. If we had more than one, we'd configure an array of plug-ins such as `plugins : [ plugin1, plugin2, etc]`.

Rendering this onscreen, you can see that we have the exact same functionality as our `GridPanel` extension, as shown in figure 15.7.

If you want to read the source code for other plug-ins, you can look at the Ext JS SDK examples/ux directory, which has a few examples of plug-ins. Using the pattern that we just implemented, I contributed two plug-ins.

The first, shown in figure 15.8, is known as the `TabScrollerMenu` (TabScroller-Menu.js), which adds a `Menu` to scrolling `TabPanels`, allowing users to select and focus a `TabPanel` much easier than having to scroll. To see this plug-in in action, navigate to the <your extjs dir>/examples/tabs/tab-scroller-menu.html URL in your browser.

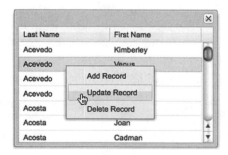

Figure 15.7   Our first plug-in

Figure 15.8 The `TabScrollerMenu`

The second, shown in figure 15.9, is known as the `ProgressBar PagingToolbar` (ProgressBarPager.js), which adds an animated `ProgressBar` to the `PagingToolbar` widget, making the `PagingToolbar` much nicer to look at. To view this plug-in in action, point your browser to <your extjs dir>/examples/grid/progress-bar-pager.html.

This concludes the exploration of plug-ins. By now, you have the necessary basics to create plug-ins that can enhance functionality in your projects. If you have an idea for a plug-in and aren't too sure if it's been done before, visit us at the Ext JS forums via http://extjs.com/forum. An entire section is dedicated to user extensions and plug-ins, where fellow community members have posted their work, some of which is completely free to use.

15.4 Summary

In this chapter, you learned how to implement the prototypal inheritance model using the basic JavaScript tools. During that exercise you got to see how this inheritance model is constructed step by step. Using that foundational knowledge, we

Sliding Pager				
Company	Price ▲	Change	% Change	Last Updated
Intel Corporation	$19.88	0.31	1.58%	09/01/2009
Microsoft Corporation	$25.84	0.14	0.54%	09/01/2009
Pfizer Inc	$27.96	0.4	1.45%	09/01/2009
Alcoa Inc	$29.01	0.42	1.47%	09/01/2009
General Motors Corporation	$30.27	1.09	3.74%	09/01/2009
AT&T Inc.	$31.61	-0.48	-1.54%	09/01/2009
General Electric Company	$34.14	-0.08	-0.23%	09/01/2009
The Home Depot, Inc.	$34.64	0.35	1.02%	09/01/2009
Verizon Communications	$35.57	0.39	1.11%	09/01/2009
Hewlett-Packard Co.	$36.53	-0.03	-0.08%	09/01/2009

Page 1 of 3 Displaying 1 - 10 of 29

Figure 15.9 A plug-in that adds an animated `ProgressBar` to the `PagingToolbar`

refactored our subclass using the `Ext.extend` utility method and implemented the two most popular extend patterns.

Next, we took all of our foundational knowledge and applied it to the extension of an Ext JS `GridPanel` and created a composite `GridPanel` and `Menu` component. This gave us an opportunity to discuss which vector to extend from, `constructor` or `initComponent`, and you learned how extensions can assist with reusability in your applications.

Last, we analyzed how extensions can be limited when reusability needs to span multiple widgets. You got to see this in action when we studied how the added features found in our newly created `GridPanel` extension could not be easily applied to descendants of the `GridPanel`, such as the `EditorGridPanel`. In order to mitigate this problem, we converted the code in our `GridPanel` extension into a plug-in that could be applied to a `GridPanel` or any descendant thereof.

Next, you'll learn how to use all of the knowledge we've gathered thus far in this book and learn the trade secrets of building complex applications.

Part 5

Building applications

The final part of *Ext JS in Action* is dedicated to developing applications with the framework. It not only covers key topics like reusability and code organization but also walks through some of the thought processes required to program effectively.

In chapter 16, you'll learn about the importance of developing applications with reusability in mind and put this concept into practice. We'll also walk through the requirements of programming an application, including discussions of workflows.

Chapter 17 will focus on implementing the widgets that you created and tying them together to create the structure of your application.

By the end of this section, you'll know the fundamentals of creating an extensible and maintainable Ext JS application.

16

Developing for reusability

This chapter covers

- Learning to develop with reusability in mind
- Organizing your code via namespace
- Discovering how to layer code
- Reviewing basic application requirements
- Developing reusable components

To me, developing an application is more of an art than a science. The methods and patterns chosen for application construction vary based on many factors, some of which may be completely out of your control.

For example, what if the requirements dictate that the server-side controller either includes or excludes one or more JavaScript modules or files based on security rules? Such a requirement isn't uncommon in larger role- or permission-based applications. The implications of this type of requirement are rather large because the view changes based on the user role. Knowing how to build extensible applications that can be easily changed over time can be a rewarding experience for the developer and customers alike.

In this chapter, we'll take on the challenge of developing a relatively large application using a pattern that allows it to be easily extended or modified in the future.

You'll be learning about the JavaScript namespace and a segmented pattern that will give this application room to grow.

Before we get down to coding, we'll take an extensive look at the requirements and analyze each bit of the wireframes presented to us. I'll walk you through the decision process of constructing the application namespace for the reusable components that you'll construct.

After you've digested the requirements, we'll begin constructing the reusable components, some of which will be implemented in this chapter. In constructing these classes, we'll work to abstract any reusable methods to reduce code complexity and duplication.

This chapter is the longest thus far, with listings longer than any other you've encountered here. Let's get started with some of the basic concepts behind developing extensible applications with Ext JS. Instead of spending a lot of time copying the code in the following listings, you can download the entire application by pointing your browser to http://app.extjsinaction.com/app.zip.

16.1   *Developing for the future*

When developing applications with Ext JS, I strive to continue the spirit of reusability that the framework promotes. No matter what the size of the application, I employ the module pattern, which is popular among other veteran Ext JS developers. The basis for the module pattern is simple—organize components using namespace. That's it.

Reusability

Developing reusable code is something that's taught in universities and talked about often, but not practiced by many. Developing without reusability in mind will ensure that you create a brittle and frail application, where the slightest change can cause catastrophic failure, costing you time and frustration. Ultimately, it will also cost your customers more for the extra time spent on simple changes. For these reasons this chapter will heavily emphasize reusability.

Because the concept of *namespace* is new to some JavaScript developers, we'll take a moment for you to understand what it is and how it can benefit your application development.

16.1.1 *Namespaces*

Because JavaScript is a "globals" language, you use namespaces to reduce the likelihood of a collision with other code. With the rising use of code developed by other parties, if namespaces were not used, there could be a bunch of function- or variable-naming collisions that could break your code.

You might not realize it, but Ext JS itself is organized in this way. For instance, almost all of the framework's classes are contained within the Ext namespace. The only exceptions to this rule are the additions to the JavaScript language itself, such as

> **Namespaces**
>
> Namespaces in JavaScript are merely a way of grouping classes into one or more logical containers. In simplest terms, a namespace is an object whose keys point to references of classes or other objects, known as packages.

`String.format`. Some of the classes are further organized and grouped by their similarity of functionality. For instance, all classes that are dedicated to the presentation of charts are located in the `Ext.chart` namespace. Likewise, form widgets are located in the `Ext.form` namespace, and so on.

When developing applications, it's important to create at least one namespace for your application. You can elect to use this namespace for the entire application if you wish. To create a namespace, I use the `Ext.ns` method, which is shorthand for `Ext.Namespace` and takes care of concerns such as namespace collisions automatically.

To create a namespace, use the following syntax:

```
Ext.ns('MyApp');
```

Then you can add classes via

```
MyApp.MyWindow    = Ext.extend(Ext.Panel, { /*...*/ });
MyApp.MyGridPanel = Ext.extend(Ext.grid.GridPanel, { /*...*/ }); // etc...
```

Then you can instantiate them via

```
var myWindow = new MyApp.MyWindow({/*config params*/});
myWindow.show();
```

Placing your classes inside a uniquely named namespace will reduce the chance of conflict. If you were developing a relative small app, keeping all of the classes inside the `MyApp` namespace would be easy. But you can readily envision a scenario where it could get rather difficult to manage on medium-to-large applications, where it may be cumbersome to keep all of your classes inside one namespace. Although there's no technical disadvantage to having lots of classes inside a single namespace, there is an organizational toll that's placed on the developer(s) working on the project.

This is where proper namespace segmentation can aid in class organization and even development.

16.1.2 *Namespace segmentation*

For medium-size applications I advise segmenting the namespace at least by the type of widget extension. For instance, let's say you have an application that requires at least two `GridPanel`, `FormPanel`, or `Panel` extensions and is expected to grow after the first release.

To meet this requirement, you could lay out the namespace as shown in figure 16.1. Following the namespace segmentation, I organize the JavaScript files in my project and computer's filesystem accordingly. For instance, to create the two `GridPanel`

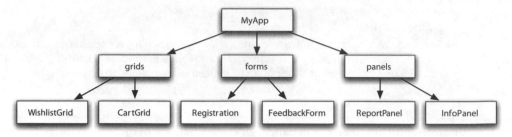

Figure 16.1   An example namespace with little segmentation

extensions shown, I'd create a directory in my project space called MyApp and then a subdirectory named *grids*. Inside the grids subdirectory, I'd create the files Wishlist-Grid.js and CartGrid.js.

Arranging your JavaScript in this manner is an organizational practice that's common with backend languages such as Java. Even though the location of the JavaScript *technically* doesn't matter to the browser's interpreter, it's something that I practice and encourage nonetheless.

To create a namespace like this, I add an Ext.ns declaration at the top of each file that contains a class. This ensures that the namespace for each class is properly defined before the class is constructed.

For example, inside WishlistGrid.js I'd insert the following:

```
Ext.ns("MyApp.grids");
MyApp.grids.WishlistGrid = Ext.extend(Ext.grid.GridPanel, { /*...*/});
```

By passing the string "MyApp.grids" to Ext.ns, the MyApp and MyApp.grid namespaces are created. This is because the utility is smart enough to split the string and create the necessary namespace objects in the global pool.

To create the fictitious CartGrid class, I'd add the following inside the CartGrid.js file:

```
Ext.ns("MyApp.grids");
MyApp.grids.CartGrid = Ext.extend(Ext.grid.GridPanel, { /*...*/});
```

We can use Ext.ns and pass a redundant namespace specification because it's smart enough to prevent the overwriting of any preexisting namespace objects.

This method of namespace segmentation works well for small- to medium-size applications, where application-specific code (business and workflow logic) can coexist with the extension classes. But I find that it's cumbersome for larger applications, where the separation of reusability from application-specific logic is necessary for ease of development and organization.

This is where further segmentation of code can be beneficial to larger application development efforts.

16.1.3 Namespace segmentation for large applications

For larger applications I divide the application code into two layers, logically separated by a root-level namespace. Figure 16.2 shows how I envision the JavaScript code stack.

Everything uses Ext JS, so it sits at the bottom and isn't aware of any of the code stacks above that implement it. This layer would also include your base framework of choice (Ext JS, YUI, jQuery, Prototype, and Scriptaculous) and any global overrides that you may want to put in place to fix any framework-related bugs or alter the way it operates.

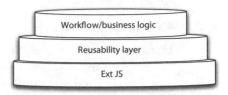

Figure 16.2 The different layers of a larger application

The middle layer is a layer of reusability that you develop, and it contains custom widgets that extend Ext JS classes and `Components`. It can also contain plug-ins that can be used by either the top or middle layer to enhance application functionality or usability. This layer contains little to no application-specific code and has no visibility into the application logic layer above. All of the extensions that this layer contains should provide events whenever things occur, such as a `Button` press.

The application logic is the top of the stack and implements the bottom two layers. It contains everything from the application bootstrap code (think `Ext.onReady()`) to all of the workflow-specific logic.

I favor this method of code separation and organization because I believe that it offers the greatest flexibility. Because the code is separated in this way, you can focus on a particular piece relatively easily.

For instance, whenever I have to add a screen or custom widget to an application, I generally work on the custom component outside the application on a vanilla HTML page. This lets me work outside the clutter of the application and keep my attention on what I'm working on. Once I've completed all of the necessary logic for the reusable component, I add it to the application and then stitch it into the application/business logic layer.

Another added benefit of this approach is smaller overall JavaScript file size. If you were to embed application and workflow logic inside the code while you're building components, the number of lines in your class files could easily exceed 1,000, which can be difficult to debug and digest.

For these reasons we'll develop our application using this method. We'll begin by analyzing the requirements and then move on to developing the middle layer.

16.2 Analyzing the application requirements

For the remainder of this chapter, you'll need to use a little imagination. Pretend we're working together on a project, where we're tasked to work on only the frontend of a new application. Lucky for us, the backend API has already been completed. Requirements have been provided along with application mockup screens. Also, the designer is aware of the framework's capabilities and can provide mockups that will mimic how the Ext JS Components will be rendered onscreen.

Before we begin developing, we'll quickly review the requirements so we can figure out where we can construct and implement reusable components.

16.2.1 Abstracting reusability

The application we're going to develop will service a small company whose initials are TKE, so all of the reusable components will live in this namespace. The goal of this application is to allow the company to manage full CRUD on departments and employees. According to the available documentation, the application will be presented using 100 percent of the available browser's canvas. It will contain three main screens, each with an instance of Ext.Window.

Figure 16.3   The application login screen window

Management has stated that they'll be extending this application after its initial production drop, so whatever can be abstracted to the middle layer should be. In order to do this properly, we need to review the screens that the design team has provided.

When the application launches, the user will be greeted with a login screen, shown in figure 16.3.

We'll call this class UserLoginWindow. Because it's so small, we won't spend time constructing and reviewing its code. This will allow us to focus on the more intense classes later on. The fully documented code is available in the downloadable source code.

Because this widget will live in the reusability layer, we'll add it the TKE namespace, encapsulated in a window package, shown in figure 16.4.

Next, we'll look at the Dashboard screen.

16.2.2 The Dashboard screen

After a successful login, the login window will disappear, revealing the application screen underneath. This is where the user will be able to access each of the three main application screens. The first of these is a dashboard containing two graphs and is shown in figure 16.5.

Before we discuss the Charts, we should talk about the way the application screen is laid out and configured.

Recall that the application will be required to take 100 percent of the viewable space in the browser. With this requirement, the first thought that's probably running through your mind is that we need to use a Viewport, which is correct.

Instead of using a typical widget like the TabPanel to allow users to switch between screens, the designer has elected to use the toolbar buttons as the main navigational

Figure 16.4
The UserLoginWindow inside the TKE namespace

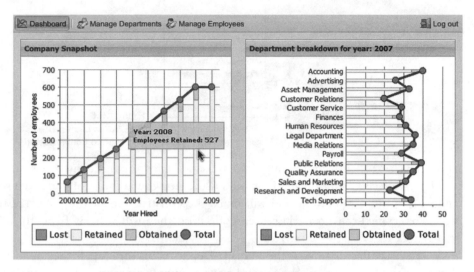

Figure 16.5 Analyzing the application layout and Dashboard screen

component. This decision is made based on the fact that the requirements dictated that a logout button must be present and visible at all times. The designer didn't want to waste the space of an entire toolbar for one button because implementing this type of CardLayout-based navigation doesn't require much work.

Because the Viewport is a Container that uses 100 percent of the browser's canvas and doesn't have luxuries such as Toolbars, we'll have to wrap the entire visible portion of the application in a Panel and embed it inside the Viewport, which leverages the FitLayout. Each of the screens will be a child of this Panel.

Focusing on the Dashboard screen, you can see that we have two Panels, each of which has a single chart. This screen is designed to give management a historical view of the company's growth based on the number of employees obtained, retained, and lost.

The Company Snapshot Chart (left) will plot the entire lifespan of the company from creation to the present. The requirements dictate that when the Company Snapshot Chart is clicked, the Department Breakdown Chart (right) will load, providing the user with a drill-down view of the statistics for the year, organized by department.

Looking at both of these charts, you can see a few reusable aspects. The first obviously is styles, and given the inherent nature of how styles are defined with Charts, we certainly need to have a base class that will contain the reusable factory and utility methods for these two Charts. Given all of this, we can modify the TKE namespace to contain a chartpanel object, which will contain our three Chart classes.

Figure 16.6 illustrates how it will be laid out.

The ChartPanelBaseCls will abstract all of the construction of the instances of Ext.chart.Chart and embed them into a Panel leveraging the FitLayout. Having the base class wrap the Chart into a Panel alleviates the application layer from having to configure the Panel, thus reducing the amount of code in that layer.

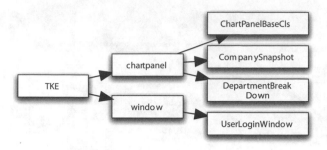

**Figure 16.6
The `TKE.chartpanel`
namespace configuration**

This base class will also contain all of the reusable styles and utility methods. Configuring the `Chart` classes in this manner will ensure that the amount of code that's duplicated is kept to a minimum and will make the construction of the `TotalEmployees` and `DepartmentBreakDown` classes easy, because they will inherit from the `ChartPanelBaseCls`.

When users decide to view the Manage Departments screen, all they need to do is click the associated `Button`. Let's spend a few moments discussing this screen, because it's the busiest in the entire application.

16.2.3   *The Manage Departments screen*

Refer to figure 16.7 as we discuss the Manage Departments screen.

The designer has generated a rather complex layout. This design allows for easy CRUD operations on departments and employees. The screen is split into two major sections. The `ListView` sits on the left (west region), displaying departments and a

Employee				
Last Name ▲	First Name	Email	Date Hired	Rate
Austin	Fleur	neque.non@nasceturr	06/18/2002	$126.00
Barrera	Germane	pede.Cras@bibendum	08/23/2000	$104.00
Baxter	Zelenia	ante@commodoaucto	10/06/2006	$69.00
Berger	Nevada	Phasellus.nulla@Aliqu	06/28/2007	$41.00
Booth	Porter	quis@Cras.edu	06/30/2002	$105.00
Boyer	Summer	Suspendisse@Nuncm	07/06/2006	$54.00
Brady	Kalia	Duis.dignissim@dispa	07/12/2004	$88.00
Brewer	Branden	eleifend.vitae@estMau	09/02/2002	$109.00
Burnett	Blaze	Phasellus.nulla@ipsur	08/06/2005	$122.00
Clarke	Quon	Donec.sollicitudin@es	01/15/2008	$83.00
Francis	Amal	risus.In.mi@luctusetui	12/09/2001	$21.00

Department Name: Accounting, Asset Management, Customer Relations, Customer Service, Finances, Human Resources, Legal Department, Media Relations, Payroll, Public Relations, Quality Assurance, **Research and Development**, Sales and Marketing, Tech Support, asdf, asdfasdfasdf, fdsafsfasdf

Dashboard | Manage Departments | Manage Employees | Log out
New Department | Save | Reset | Deactivate Department
Name: Research and Development   Description:
New Employee | Delete employee | Associate Employee(s)

Figure 16.7   The Manage Departments screen

FormPanel, and a GridPanel sits on the right (center region), displaying the details for the selected department.

The form input items in the top part of the center Panel allow users to modify a selected department, such as the department's name, activation date, and any details or notes. The GridPanel that's neatly embedded underneath the form lists all of the employees for the department selected on the left ListView Panel. Its purpose is to allow for full CRUD operations on employees along with the ability to associate (move) existing employees from other departments.

To make this screen possible, we'll create three separate components, which will all live in the reusability layer. They are the departments ListView, employees Grid-Panel, and a composite component, DepartmentForm, that will contain the department form input elements and the employees GridPanel.

Figure 16.8 illustrates how I'd envision the TKE namespace looking with the added ListView, GridPanel, and FormPanel extension classes.

To accommodate the reusable components in the Manage Departments screen, I've added three new namespace objects: listpanel, grid, and form. Looking at the listpanel object, you can see that there are two classes in that namespace, List-PanelBaseCls and DepartmentsListView. We're creating the ListPanelBaseCls for all of the same reasons as the ChartPanelBaseCls and will reap the same benefits.

The grid and form namespaces are areas where those related reusable components will be tucked away. The EmployeeGridPanel will extend from Ext.grid.Grid-Panel, whereas the DepartmentForm will extend from Ext.form.FormPanel and will implement the EmployeeGridPanel component.

Examining the last two areas of functionality for this screen, you can see that to add or edit employees for a particular department, the user is expected either to click the New Employee Button or double-click a Record in the EmployeeGridPanel,

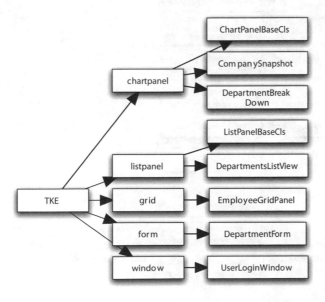

Figure 16.8   Adding the listpanel, grid, and form namespace objects to the TKE namespace

Edit Chen, Rashad						
Last:	Chen	Middle:	Roary	First:	Rashad	Title:
Email:	Sed.congue.elit@pedeNuncsed.org		DOB:	12/22/1975		
Office:	776-998-1060	Home:	947-905-4900	Mobile:	692-260-2578	
Dept:	Customer Service	Date Hired:	04/27/2001	Rate/hr:	130	
Street:	Ap #720-1827 Nunc Av.					
City:	Burlington	State:	AL	Zip:	60223	

X Cancel   Save

Figure 16.9   The Edit employee form embedded and displayed in a `Window`

which will display a modal `Ext.Window` containing the Edit employee form, as shown in figure 16.9.

Once this `Window` is displayed, the user can click the Cancel or Save `Button` to cancel or accept any changes. Given this requirement, we need to add a reusable `Form-Panel` component to our namespace. The `Window` class, however, will require a lot of application-specific logic and thus will stay in the application logic layer.

I like to add reusable utility methods to my `FormPanel` classes, so we'll have to add a base class that the `DepartmentForm` and `EmployeeForm` can extend from. Figure 16.10 shows TKE namespace with the added `FormPanelBaseCls` and `EmployeeForm` classes.

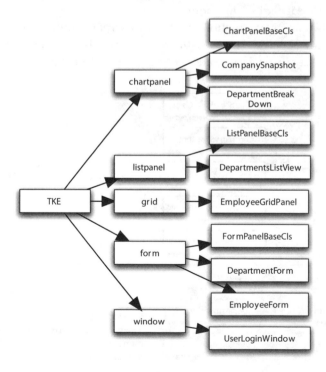

Figure 16.10   The `TKE` namespace with the added `EmployeeForm` and `FormPanelBaseCls` classes

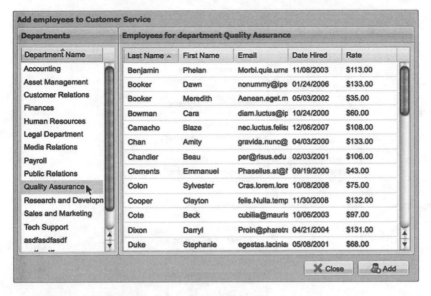

Figure 16.11 The employee association `Window`

The last Manage Departments requirement dictates that employees are to be associated with a selected department. When the Associate Employee(s) `Toolbar` `Button` is clicked, a `Window` will appear, as shown in figure 16.11.

If you examine the layout of the employee association `Window`, you'll see that the previously created `DepartmentsListView` and `EmployeeGridPanel` are reused. Because the `EmployeeAssociationWindow` class doesn't require application-specific rules, such as form-validation messages, it will live in the reusability layer and can be implemented by the `EmployeeGridPanel` located in the Manage Departments screen.

Figure 16.12 shows what our `TKE` namespace looks like with the added window object and `EmployeeAssociationWindow` class.

This wraps up our coverage of the Manage Departments screen. Next, we'll look at the Manage Employees screen and see if there are any reusable components that can be abstracted.

16.2.4 *The Manage Employees screen*

The Manage Employees screen is meant to allow fast and easy CRUD operations for employees. But unlike the Manage Departments screen, users won't be able to directly modify departments. Instead, they'll only be able to modify Employee data.

Figure 16.13 shows what it looks like rendered onscreen.

The workflow requirements for this screen are simple relative to the Manage Departments screen before it. Users will interact with this panel in a left-to-right fashion, clicking a department to set the context of the Employees list. To load the `EmployeeForm` on the right, they will click an employee `Record`.

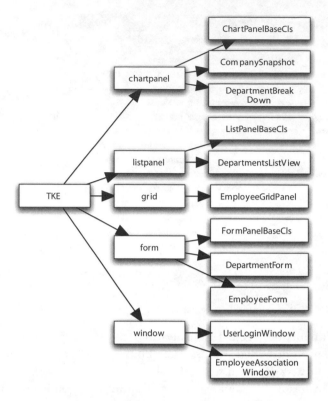

Figure 16.12
The TKE namespace with the added window namespace object and `EmployeeAssociationWindow` class

If you examine the layout, you'll see that all but one of the components for this screen are already developed. The layout contains the DepartmentsListView (left) and the EmployeeForm Panel (right). This means that we still need to create a ListView for the Employees Panel (center).

Figure 16.14 shows the TKE namespace with the newly added EmployeeList extension.

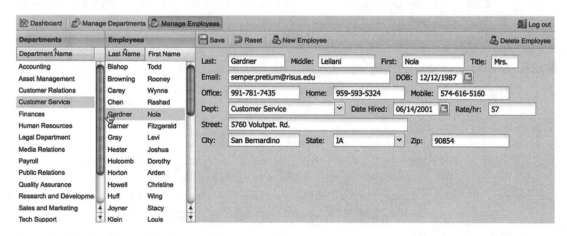

Figure 16.13   The Manage Employees screen

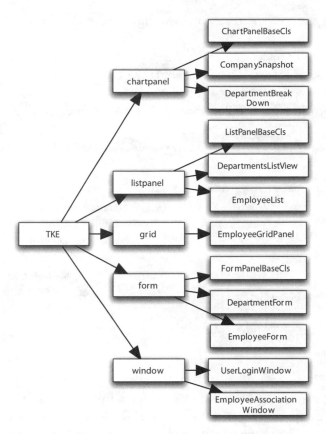

Figure 16.14 The `TKE` namespace modified to include the `EmployeeList` class

NOTE The classes for this application are designed to use the icon CSS file that we leveraged in chapter 12 of this book. You'll want to include it when constructing the HTML body for this application.

We've just completed a comprehensive review of the requirements for our application, which means we can get to work developing classes that will belong in the TKE namespace. We'll begin with the chart namespace.

16.3 *Constructing the ChartPanel components*

Recall that the Dashboard screen requires two `Charts`, wrapped by `Panels`, sharing the same styles and factory methods. This means that we'll need to create a base class to hold all of these shared items.

16.3.1 *The ChartPanelBaseCls*

In order to fulfill its role as a base class, the `ChartPanelBaseCls` must allow for the easy creation of extensions, with minimal configuration. In order to ensure easy extensibility, this base class will require the following features:

- Stub or template methods to create the `Chart` and `Store` along with so-called accessor methods
- All of the styles for the `Chart`
- The ability to relay the internal `Chart`'s `itemclick` event
- A reusable tip renderer method
- Our first listing provides the template for the class we'll create.

Listing 16.1   Constructing the `ChartPanelBaseCls`

```
Ext.ns('TKE.chartpanel');

TKE.chartpanel.ChartPanelBaseCls = Ext.extend(Ext.Panel, {
    frame          : false,
    layout         : 'fit',

    chartExtraStyles : {},
    seriesStyles     : {},

    initComponent     : function() {},
    buildChart        : function() {},
    buildSeries       : function() {},
    buildStore        : function() {},
    getChart          : function() {},
    getStore          : function() {},
    loadStoreByParams : function() {},
    tipRenderer       : function() {}
});
```

❶ Static Panel configuration

❷ Stub out Chart style configuration

❸ Methods for this class

The `ChartPanelBaseCls` extends `Ext.Panel`. You place all of the static `Panel`-specific configurations in the prototype of the extension ❶ along with the chart-specific styles ❷. You do this because the prototype is shared among all instances of this class, subclasses, and any instances of any subclasses. Under the `initComponent` extension method are the necessary factory and utility methods ❸ to make extending this class simple.

In the following listing, we'll focus on filling in the chart-style configuration objects and all methods for this base class.

Listing 16.2   Adding the styles to the `ChartPanelBaseCls`

```
chartExtraStyles : {
    xAxis : {
        majorGridLines : {color: 0x999999,  size  : 1}
    },
    yAxis: {
        titleRotation  : -90
    },
    legend : {
        display : "bottom",
        padding : 5,
        spacing : 2,
        font    : { color : 0x000000,  family : "Arial", size   : 12 },
        border  : { size : 1, color  : 0x999999 }
    }
```

❶ Chart extra styles object

```
    },
    seriesStyles : {
        red : {
            fillColor    : 0xFFAAAA,
            borderColor  : 0xAA3333,
            lineColor    : 0xAA3333
        },
        yellow : {
            fillColor    : 0xFFFFAA,
            borderColor  : 0xFFAA33,
            lineColor    : 0x33AA33
        },
        green : {
            fillColor    : 0xAAFFAA,
            borderColor  : 0x33AA33,
            lineColor    : 0x33AA33
        },
        blue : {
            fillColor    : 0xAAAAFF,
            borderColor  : 0x3333FF,
            lineColor    : 0x3333FF
        }
    },
```

◁┐ **Style Series**
❷ **in Charts**

The extra chart styles configuration object ❶ and the chart series style configuration object ❷ will be used when the instances of `Chart` are created. Because this is an abstract base class, you'll have to wait for the extensions of this class to see the style usage.

In the next listing, we'll add the `initComponent` extension method as well as the template and utility methods.

Listing 16.3 Adding the methods to the `ChartPanelBaseCls`

```
initComponent : function() {
    this.items = this.buildChart();
    TKE.chartpanel.ChartPanelBaseCls.superclass.initComponent.call(this);
    this.relayEvents(this.getChart(), ['itemclick']);
},                                                          ◁┐ Relay the Chart
buildChart : function() {                                   ❶ itemclick event
    return {};
},
buildSeries : function() {
    return [];
},
buildStore : function() {
    return {};
},
getChart : function() {
    return this.items.items[0];
},
getStore : function() {
    return this.getChart().store;
},                                                          ❷ A Store loader
loadStoreByParams : function(params) {                      ◁┘ utility method
```

```
        params = params || {};
        this.getStore().load({
            params : params
        });
    },
    tipRenderer :  function(chart, record, index, series){
        var yearInfo = "Year: " + record.get('year');
        var empInfo  =  'Employees ' + series.displayName + ': '
                + record.get(series.yField);
        return yearInfo + '\n' + empInfo ;
    }
```

❸ **The reusable tip renderer**

In listing 16.3, a lot is going on. First is the initComponent method, which sets the this.items reference to the results of the this.buildChart stub method. It also relays the internal Chart component's itemclick event ❶, which means for any application logic that decides to implement this or any subclass, this class can set up an itemclick ❷ event listener as if it was originating from the ChartPanelBaseCls itself. You won't see this used until we build the application logic.

The buildChart template method returns an empty object. It does so to allow this class to be instantiated if a developer decided to do so. Even though no instance of Ext.chart.Chart will exist when this class is implemented, it will at least be rendered as an empty Panel onscreen and not throw any exceptions. Even though this base class doesn't call the buildSeries and buildStore methods, they're there to remind developers that these are stub methods to be implemented. The rest of the methods are meant for utility methods, with the exception of the reusable tipRenderer method ❸, which will be implemented by subclasses.

You can test to see if it works by inserting the following code into a vanilla page:

```
new Ext.Window({
    width  : 100,
    height : 100,
    layout : 'fit',
    items  : new TKE.chartpanel.ChartPanelBaseCls()
}).show();
```

This code will result in a Window being rendered onscreen with a blank Panel inside its body and no exceptions thrown. This is a clear indication that our abstract base class works as designed and is ready to be extended, which is what we'll do next.

16.3.2 *The CompanySnapshot class*

We've just completed our ChartPanelBaseCls, which contains quite a bit to make extending this class extremely simple. In this section, we'll create an extension to the ChartPanelBaseCls, which will be used to easily configure a Chart to display all of the company's obtained, retained, and lost employees since it was created. We'll name it TotalCompany.

Here's the template for our class:

```
Ext.ns('TKE.chartpanel');
TKE.chartpanel.CompanySnapshot =
        Ext.extend(TKE.chartpanel.ChartPanelBaseCls, {
```

```
        url : 'stats/getYearlyStats,
        buildChart  : function() {},
        buildStore  : function() {},
        buildSeries : function() {}
    });
```

```
Ext.reg('total_employees_chart', TKE.chartpanel.CompanySnapshot);
```

Because the `ChartPanelBaseCls` does all of the heavy lifting, the `CompanySnapshot`
extension consists of only three overrides to the stub methods to create the internal
`Chart`. Let's fill those in.

First, we'll configure `buildChart`, as shown in the following listing.

Listing 16.4   The `CompanySnapshot` class template

```
buildChart : function() {
    return {
        xtype       : 'stackedcolumnchart',
        store       : this.buildStore(),
        xField      : 'year',
        tipRenderer : this.tipRenderer,
        series      : this.buildSeries(),
        extraStyle  : this.chartExtraStyles,
        xAxis       : new Ext.chart.CategoryAxis({
            title : 'Year Hired'
        }),
        yAxis : new Ext.chart.NumericAxis({
            stackingEnabled : true,
            title           : 'Number of employees'
        })
    };
},
```

The `buildChart` method returns an `Ext.chart.Chart` configuration object, which is
called and used by the `ChartPanelBaseCls` `initComponent` method. To reduce the
complexity of this method, it uses the `this.buildStore` and `this.buildSeries` factory
methods to generate the data `Store` and series configurations. It also configures the
`Chart` to leverage the `tipRenderer` method provided by the `ChartPanelBaseCls` as
well as the `chartExtraStyles`.

In the next listing, we'll complete the `buildStore` and `buildSeries` factory methods.

Listing 16.5   Completing the `buildStore` and `buildSeries` factory methods

```
buildStore : function() {
    return {
        xtype    : 'jsonstore',
        autoLoad : true,
        url      : this.url,
        fields   : [
            'year','numFired', 'prevHired', 'total', 'newHires'
        ]
    };
},
buildSeries : function() {
```

```
        var seriesStyles = this.seriesStyles;

        return [
            {
                yField      : 'numFired',
                displayName : 'Lost',
                style       : seriesStyles.red
            },
            {
                yField      : 'prevHired',
                displayName : 'Retained',
                style       : seriesStyles.yellow
            },
            {
                yField      : 'newHires',
                displayName : 'Obtained',
                style       : seriesStyles.green
            },
            {
                type        : 'line',
                yField      : 'total',
                displayName : 'Total',
                style       : seriesStyles.blue
            }
        ];
    }
```

The `buildStore` method returns an `Ext.data.JsonStore` XType configuration object that will be used by the internal instance of `Ext.chart.Chart`. Because this component will serve only one purpose in the application, I decided that it was okay to statically configure the `Store`'s URL and series configuration. Doing this will reduce the code in the application layer that will instantiate instances of this class.

With this class complete, we can work on the other `ChartPanelBaseCls` extension.

16.3.3 *The DepartmentBreakdown class*

The construction of the second `ChartPanelBaseCls` extension will be nearly identical to its cousin, the `CompanySnapshot` extension class. Instead of providing you with a template and then filling it in later, I'll show you the entire class in one fell swoop.

Listing 16.6   The `DepartmentBreakdown` class

```
Ext.ns('TKE.chartpanel');
TKE.chartpanel.DepartmentBreakdown =
        Ext.extend(TKE.chartpanel.ChartPanelBaseCls, {

    url : 'stats/getDeptBreakdown,
    buildChart : function() {
        return {
            xtype       : 'stackedbarchart',
            store       : this.buildStore(),
            yField      : 'name',
            series      : this.buildSeries(),
            extraStyle  : this.chartExtraStyles,
```

```
        xAxis        : new Ext.chart.NumericAxis({
            xField            : 'newHires',
            stackingEnabled : true
        }),
        yAxis        :   new Ext.chart.CategoryAxis({
            xField : 'newHires',
            yField : 'name'
        })
    };
},
buildStore : function() {
    return {
        xtype     : 'jsonstore',
        autoLoad : false,
        url       : this.url,
        fields    : [
            'name','numFired', 'prevHired', 'total', 'newHires'
        ]
    };
},
buildSeries : function() {
    var seriesStyles = this.seriesStyles;

    return [
        {
            xField        : 'numFired',
            displayName : 'Lost',
            style         : seriesStyles.red
        },
        {
            xField        : 'prevHired',
            displayName : 'Retained',
            style         : seriesStyles.yellow
        },
        {
            xField        : 'newHires',
            displayName : 'Obtained',
            style         : seriesStyles.green
        },
        {
            type          : 'line',
            xField        : 'total',
            displayName : 'Total',
            style         : seriesStyles.blue
        }
    ];
    }
}
});

Ext.reg('department_breakdown_chart', TKE.chartpanel.DepartmentBreakdown);
```

This concludes the construction of the Chart classes. With this exercise, you've seen what it takes to create a base class that can contain lots of reusable configuration parameters and do the heavy lifting for intended extensions.

Following the same base class pattern, we'll create the components that belong in the listpanel namespace.

16.4   *Constructing the listpanel components*

When reviewing our application requirements, you learned that at least two instances of Ext.list.ListView are to be implemented and are to live inside an instance of Ext.Panel. Because these are similar requirements to the Charts in the application, we'll use the same base class approach.

16.4.1   *The ListPanelBaseCls*

The purpose of this base class is to allow the easy creation of Ext.list.ListView instances that are wrapped in a Panel. It will relay the click event from the internal ListView class and the load event from the internally created Ext.data.Store class. Recall that the purpose of relaying these events is to make implementation of this class or any subclass leveraging these events as easy as possible.

Because we've been through this exercise before, I'll show you the entire base class. In this listing you'll find many similarities to the ChartPanelBaseCls, such as the construction of the view and the relaying of events from child components.

Listing 16.7   Constructing the ListPanelBaseCls

```
Ext.ns('TKE.listpanel');

TKE.listpanel.ListPanelBaseCls = Ext.extend(Ext.Panel, {
    layout   : 'fit',
    initComponent : function() {
        this.items = this.buildListView();

        TKE.listpanel.ListPanelBaseCls.superclass.initComponent.call(this);

        this.relayEvents(this.getView(), ['click']);
        this.relayEvents(this.getStore(), ['load']);
    },
    buildListView : function() {
        return {};
    },
    buildStore : function() {
        return {};
    },
    clearView : function() {
        this.getStore().removeAll();
    },
    createAndSelectRecord : function(o) {
        var view = this.getView();

        var record = new view.store.recordType(o);
        view.store.addSorted(record);
        var index = view.store.indexOf(record);
        view.select(index);
        return record;
    },
    clearSelections : function() {
        return this.getView().clearSelections();
    },
    getView : function() {
        return this.items.items[0];
```

```
        },
        getStore : function() {
            return this.getView().store;
        },
        getSelectedRecords : function() {
            return this.getView().getSelectedRecords();
        },
        getSelected : function() {
            return this.getSelectedRecords()[0];
        },
        loadStoreByParams : function(params) {
            params = params || {};

            this.getStore().load({params:params});
        },
        refreshView : function() {
            this.getView().store.reload();
        },
        selectById : function(id) {
            var view = this.getView();
            id = id || false;
            if (id) {
                var ind = view.store.find('id', id);
                view.select(ind);
            }
        }
    }
});
```

Just as the `ChartPanelBaseCls` does a lot of the heavy lifting for the `chartpanel` classes, the `ListPanelBaseCls` does the hard work for the `listpanel` classes, where there are many reusable utility methods.

Most of these utility methods revolve around managing the selection, loading the view, or clearing and even requesting the selection of a `Record` by ID. Some of them help get a reference to an underlying component, such as the `getView` and `getStore` methods. Having such utility methods can reduce the amount of code in your application layer significantly.

You can appreciate how much work this base class does by creating the first extension, which will be known as `DepartmentsListView`, because there are only two factory methods that the subclasses are meant to implement: `buildListView` and `buildStore`.

16.4.2 *The DepartmentsListView and EmployeeList classes*

The `DepartmentsListView` class is meant to extend from the `ListPanelBaseCls` and display the departments in the company. The following listing shows the `Departments-ListView` class in its entirety.

Listing 16.8 The `DepartmentsListView` class

```
Ext.ns("TKE.listpanel");

TKE.listpanel.DepartmentsListView =
  Ext.extend(TKE.listpanel.ListPanelBaseCls, {
    url : 'departments/getList',
```

```
     buildListView : function() {
        return {
            xtype           : 'listview',
            singleSelect  : true,
            store             : this.buildStore(),
            style             : 'background-color: #FFFFFF;',
            columns         : [
                {
                    header      : 'Department Name',
                    dataIndex : 'name'
                }
            ]
        };
     },
     buildStore : function() {
        return  {
            xtype    : 'jsonstore',
            autoLoad : this.autoLoadStore,
            url      : this.url,
            fields   : [ 'name', 'id' ],
            sortInfo : {
                field : 'name',
                dir   : 'ASC'
            }
        };
     }
});
Ext.reg('departmentlist', TKE.listpanel.DepartmentList);
```

As you can see, extending the ListPanelBaseCls to create the DepartmentsListView class is extremely easy, because all we needed to do was override the buildListView and buildStore factory methods, which each return their intended configuration objects.

In the next listing, we'll construct the EmployeeList class, which will follow the exact same pattern as the DepartmentsListView class we just created.

Listing 16.9   The EmployeeList class

```
Ext.ns("TKE.listpanel");

TKE.listpanel.EmployeeList = Ext.extend(TKE.listpanel.ListPanelBaseCls, {
    url : 'employees/listForDepartment',
    buildListView : function() {
        return {
            xtype           : 'listview',
            singleSelect  : true,
            store             : this.buildStore(),
            style             : 'background-color: #FFFFFF;',
            columns         : [
                {
                    header      : 'Last Name',
                    dataIndex : 'lastName'
                },
```

```
                   {
                       header    : 'First Name',
                       dataIndex : 'firstName'
                   }
               ]
           };
       },
       buildStore : function() {
           return {
               xtype    : 'jsonstore',
               autoLoad : this.autoLoadStore || false,
               url      : this.url,
               fields   : [ 'lastName', 'firstName', 'id'],
               sortInfo :  {
                   field     : 'lastName',
                   direction : 'ASC'
               }
           };
       }
   });
   Ext.reg('employeelist', TKE.listpanel.EmployeeList);
```

We've just created all three of the classes that compose the listpanel namespace using the same base class pattern that we used when constructing the chartpanel namespace classes. In using this pattern, you got a chance to see how architecting a namespace that has a common abstract base class can reduce the effort required when creating classes that are meant to be instantiated.

Looking ahead, we're going to create the EmployeeGridPanel class, which the department form and employee association window need.

16.5 *Constructing the EmployeeGridPanel class*

The EmployeeGridPanel component will be the only GridPanel extension to live in the application. This means that there's no real need to create a base class at this time, so it will have to contain all of the methods and configuration parameters. But it's constructed in such a way as to allow for easy abstraction of common methods and configuration properties in the future.

Because this class is rather lengthy, first I'll show you the template, and then we'll fill in the portions step by step later on.

Listing 16.10   The EmployeeGridPanel class

```
Ext.ns('TKE.grid');

TKE.grid.EmployeeGridPanel = Ext.extend(Ext.grid.GridPanel, {
    url           : 'employees/listForDepartment',
    viewConfig    : { forceFit : true },
    columns       : [],
    initComponent : function() {},
    buildStore    : function() {},
    add           : function() {},
    loadData      : function() {},
```

```
        load          : function() {},
        removeAll     : function() {},
        remove        : function() {},
        getSelected   : function() {}
});

Ext.reg('employeesgridpanel', TKE.grid.EmployeeGridPanel)
```

In the next listing, we'll fill in the columns array, which will be used by the Ext.grid.ColumnModel automatically instantiated by the Ext.grid.GridPanel class.

Listing 16.11   columns array

```
columns       : [
    {
        header    : 'Last Name',
        dataIndex : 'lastName',
        sortable  : true
    },
    {
        header    : 'First Name',
        dataIndex : 'firstName',
        sortable  : true
    },
    {
        header    : 'Email',
        dataIndex : 'email',
        sortable  : true
    },
    {
        header    : 'Date Hired',
        dataIndex : 'dateHired',
        sortable  : true
    },
    {
        header    : 'Rate',
        dataIndex : 'rate',
        sortable  : true,
        renderer  : Ext.util.Format.usMoney
    }
],
```

Next, we'll fill in the rest of the methods for the class.

Listing 16.12   EmployeeGridPanel class methods

```
initComponent : function() {
    this.store = this.buildStore();
    TKE.grid.EmployeeGridPanel.superclass.initComponent.call(this);
},
buildStore : function() {
    return {
        xtype    : 'jsonstore',
        url      : this.url,
        autoLoad : false,
        fields   : [
```

```
                    'id', 'lastName', 'firstName', 'email',
                    'dateHired', 'rate', 'departmentId'
                ],
                sortInfo : {
                    field : 'lastName',
                    dir   : 'ASC'
                }
            };
        },
        add : function(rec) {
            var store = this.store;
            var sortInfo = store.sortInfo;

            if (Ext.isArray(rec)) {
                Ext.each(rec, function(rObj, ind) {
                    if (! (rObj instanceof Ext.data.Record)) {
                        rec[ind] = new this.store.recordType(rObj);
                    }
                });
            }
            else if (Ext.isObject(rec) && ! (rec instanceof Ext.data.Record)) {
                rec = new this.store.recordType(rec);
            }

            store.add(rec);
            store.sort(sortInfo.field, sortInfo.direction);
        },
        loadData : function(d) {
            return this.store.loadData(d);
        },
        load : function(o) {
            return this.store.load(o);
        },
        removeAll : function() {
            return this.store.removeAll();
        },
        remove    : function(r) {
            return this.store.remove(r);
        },
        getSelected : function() {
            return this.selModel.getSelections();
        }
    }
```

Because this is a `GridPanel` extension, any of the native `GridPanel` events, such as `rowdblclick`, will be available upon instantiation of this class. But we'll work to make things easier for the application layer by adding a few convenience methods, such as `getSelected`, `removeAll`, and `load`.

The `add` method, which allows for the easy addition of one or more `Record`s to the `Store`, is a bit more involved. It's relatively flexible, because it'll accept an array or a single object. If it detects an array, it'll perform a check on each element, converting each to an instance of a `Ext.data.Record`, to be inserted into the `Store`. Likewise, if it detects a plain object being passed to this method, it'll use it to instantiate a new instance of `Ext.data.Record` and add it to the `Store`. The `Store`'s `sort` method will be manually called to ensure the `Record` is visually placed properly onscreen.

NOTE   The `Ext.data.Store`'s `addSorted` method works with only a single record at a time. Because our `add` utility method can accept multiple items, it's much faster to add the record and then manually call the `Store`'s `sort` method.

Next, we'll create the `EmployeeAssociationWindow` class, which implements the `EmployeeGridPanel` and the `DepartmentsListView` classes.

16.6   *The EmployeeAssociationWindow class*

Recall that the `EmployeeAssociationWindow` composite widget is designed to allow the user to move employees from one department to another. It does this by means of a layout, which displays the `DepartmentsListView` on the left side and the `Employee-GridPanel` on the right side of the `Window` body. Because the `EmployeeGridPanel` class is context sensitive to the department that's selected in the `DepartmentsListView` class, we'll have to set up some rudimentary event handling.

This class is rather lengthy, so we'll start with the template in the following listing and then fill in the methods later.

> **Listing 16.13   The `EmployeeAssociationWindow` class**

```
Ext.ns("TKE.window");
  TKE.window.EmployeeAssociationWindow = Ext.extend(Ext.Window, {
      width         : 600,
      height        : 400,
      maxWidth      : 600,
      maxHeight     : 500,
      modal         : true,
      border        : false,
      closable      : false,
      center        : true,
      constrain     : true,
      resizable     : true,
      departmentName : '',
      departmentId   : null,
      layout         : {
          type  : 'hbox',
          align : 'stretch'
      },
      initComponent            : function() {},

      buildButtons             : function() {},
      buildListViewPanel       : function() {},
      buildGridPanel           : function() {},
      onClose                  : function() {},
      onAddToDepartment        : function() {},
      onDepartmentListClick    : function() {},
      onDepartmentStoreLoad    : function() {}
  });
```

① **Custom configuration parameters**

The `EmployeeAssociationWindow` class template shown in listing 16.13 contains a lot of configuration parameters for its base class, `Ext.Window`. It's worth noting that there are two configuration properties, departmentName ❶ and departmentId, that are specific to this class.

The departmentName configuration property will be used to automatically set the Window title. Also, this entire window is context sensitive to the selected department in the application's Manage Departments screen. This means that once this window renders and its own DepartmentsListView class loads, we'll use the departmentId to automatically remove the Record for the selected department from the Department-Manager screen. This will ensure that the source department and destination department for the employee move operation are not the same.

In the following listing, we'll fill in the details for the initComponent method along with the three factory methods, each designed to construct the Buttons for the Window DepartmentsListView and EmployeeGridPanel.

Listing 16.14 The initComponent and factory methods

```
initComponent  : function() {

    Ext.apply(this, {
        title   : 'Add employees to ' + this.departmentName,
        buttons : this.buildButtons(),
        items   : [
            this.buildListViewPanel(),
            this.buildGridPanel()
        ]
    });

    TKE.window.EmployeeAssociationWindow.superclass.initComponent.call(this);

    this.addEvents({
        assocemployees : true                    ⊲—❶ Add custom event
    });
},
buildButtons : function() {
    return [
        {
            text    : 'Close',
            iconCls : 'icon-cross',
            scope   : this,
            handler : this.onClose
        },
        {
            text    : 'Add',
            iconCls : 'icon-user_add',
            scope   : this,
            handler : this.onAddToDepartment
        }
    ];
},
buildListViewPanel : function() {
    return {
        xtype           : 'departmentlist',
        itemId          : 'departmentList',
```

```
            title        : 'Departments',
            frame        : true,
            width        : 150,
            autoLoadStore : true,
            listeners    : {
                scope : this,
                click : this.onDepartmentListClick,
                load  : this.onDepartmentStoreLoad
            }
        };
    },
    buildGridPanel : function() {
        return {
            xtype    : 'employeegridpanel',
            itemId   : 'employeeGrid',
            loadMask : true,
            frame    : true,
            title    : 'Employees',
            flex     : 1
        };
    },
```

In listing 16.14, we create the contents for the initComponent and related factory methods. Before we continue, there are some things I should highlight and elaborate on, so that you're aware of what was running through my mind when I designed this.

The Buttons are configured to call two of our so-called on methods, which, if you can recall, are so named because they're generally called when a user-driven or system-driven event occurs. The onClose method will destroy the instance of this class, whereas the onAddToDepartment method will fire the custom assocemployees ❶ event that was configured in initComponent.

The class in the application layer that's responsible for instantiating this component will be listening for this event. When the event is fired, it will send the selected Records from the EmployeeGridPanel, allowing the class in the application layer to make the web service call and remove the Records from the EmployeeGridPanel if the employee move operation is successful. The removal of the Records from the EmployeeGridPanel upon successful reassignment of employees from one department to another provides visual feedback to the user that the move request was successful.

Finally, the code buildListViewPanel method configures the instance of DepartmentsListView to call upon this.onDepartmentListClick and this.onDepartmentStoreLoad when it relays its click and load events. These event bindings will allow the EmployeeAssociationWindow class to load the EmployeeGridPanel when a department in the DepartmentsListView class is selected as well as remove the Record department that the employees are being moved to using the this.departmentId configuration parameter.

Let's go ahead and construct the rest of the class.

Listing 16.15 The event listener methods

```
onClose : function() {
    this.close();
},
onAddToDepartment : function() {
    var employeeGrid = this.getComponent('employeeGrid');
    var selectedRecords = employeeGrid.getSelected();

    if (selectedRecords.length > 0) {
        this.fireEvent(
            'assocemployees',
            selectedRecords,
            employeeGrid,
            this
        );
    }
},
onDepartmentListClick : function(listView) {
    var record = listView.getSelectedRecords()[0];
    var employeeGrid = this.getComponent('employeeGrid');
    employeeGrid.load({
        params : {
            id : record.get('id')
        }
    });

    employeeGrid.setTitle('Employees for department ' +
        record.get('name')
    );
},
onDepartmentStoreLoad : function(store) {
    var deptRecInd = store.find('id', this.departmentId);
    store.remove(store.getAt(deptRecInd));
}
```

The four on methods will react to various events. onClose will be executed when the EmployeeAssociationWindow's close Button is clicked and will call the inherited this.close method, which will destroy the Window instance and all contained child Components. The onAddToDepartment method will gather the selected Records from the internal instance of EmployeeGridPanel and will fire the custom assocemployees event when one or more employee Records are selected.

The onDepartmentListClick will be executed when a department record from the internal instance of DepartmentsListView is selected by the user and will request that the EmployeeGridPanel's Store load using the selected department's ID to fetch the employees for that department. It will also dynamically set the title for the instance of EmployeeGridPanel based on the department selected by the user. Giving the user this type of feedback isn't necessary, but it's nice to have and something I recommend doing wherever possible.

Last, the onDepartmentStoreLoad method is responsible for removing the record for the department that's currently selected in the DepartmentManager screen. Recall that this is to prevent the user from trying to associate one or more employees to and from the same department.

The `EmployeeAssociationWindow` class is now fully configured. Next, we'll work on the last two components and their base class, which belong in the `form` namespace.

16.7   *The form namespace*

Inside the `form` namespace are two classes that extend from `FormPanelBaseCls`: `DepartmentForm` and `EmployeeForm`. `DepartmentForm` will implement an instance of `EmployeeGridPanel` in the center of its layout, whereas `EmployeeForm` will employ a bunch of form elements and a `Toolbar`. Both classes are lengthy because of the amount of configuration parameters required for the form elements.

We'll begin with `FormPanelBaseCls`, which will add a few reusable utility methods and reduce code duplication.

16.7.1   *The FormPanelBaseCls class*

The `FormPanelBaseCls` template shown in listing 16.16 will help us reduce the amount of duplicate code that will exist in the `DepartmentForm` and `EmployeeForm` subclasses that we'll produce after this. It will do this by allowing us to place static reusable methods in an abstract class that's not to be implemented directly, just extended.

> **Listing 16.16   The `FormPanelBaseCls` template**

```
Ext.ns('TKE.form');
TKE.form.FormPanelBaseCls = Ext.extend(Ext.form.FormPanel, {
    constructor : function(config) {
        config = config || {};
        Ext.applyIf(config, {
            trackResetOnLoad : true
        });
        TKE.form.FormPanelBaseCls.superclass
                        .constructor.call(this, config)
    },

    getValues : function() {
        return this.getForm().getValues();
    },
    isValid : function() {
        return this.getForm().isValid();
    },
    clearForm : function() {
        var vals   = this.getForm().getValues();
        var clrVals = {};

        for (var vName in vals)  {
            clrVals[vName] = '';
        }

        this.getForm().setValues(clrVals);
        this.data = null;
    },
```

① Add **trackResetOnLoad** to config object

```
        loadData : function(data) {
            if (data) {
                this.data = data;
                this.getForm().setValues(data);
            }
            else {
                this.clearForm();
            }
        },
        setValues : function(o) {
            return this.getForm().setValues(o || {});
        }
    });
```

When constructing the base class in listing 16.16, we extend from `Ext.form.Form-Panel`, create an extension to the constructor, and add four methods that will make implementation in the application layer a little more flexible. These utility methods are designed, like the classes we constructed previously, to allow the implementation code to not have to worry about interacting with the internal `BasicForm` instance.

> ### One of those hidden traps
> We're applying `trackResetOnLoad` to the `config` object ❶ for the constructor because `Ext.form.BasicForm` depends on this property to know how to handle calls to its `reset` method. This dependency is one of those not-well-known pitfalls of extending `FormPanel`.

The `clearForm` and `loadData` methods are designed to manually manage data on the form, much more so than the framework does. Because the form's data can be changed on the fly, we need that granular control. The `this.data` reference will be set whenever the `loadData` method is called and will be used in the extension classes to know whether the form is being used for a new `Record` or to modify an existing one. The `clearForm` method will manually purge the values in the form and set the `this.data` reference to `null`.

This base class is simple, as you can tell. Because we're just adding methods, we needn't configure a constructor. Remember, `Ext.extend` takes care of that for us when extending in this way.

Now that we have that out of the way, we can move on to the `DepartmentForm` class, which will extend this class.

16.7.2 The DepartmentForm class

Recall that the `DepartmentForm` will allow users to edit department information as well as display the employees for the department being displayed. They will be given the opportunity to perform full CRUD operations on employees via `Button`s in this widget and also associate employees with the department loaded. All of the employee-related actions will be driven by an implementation `EmployeeGridPanel` with a top `Toolbar`.

Each of the `Buttons` will fire custom events so that the application-layer code can react accordingly.

Because this is a large class, we'll begin with the template in the following listing and circle around, filling in the methods.

Listing 16.17   The `DepartmentForm` class template

```
Ext.ns("TKE.form");

TKE.form.DepartmentForm = Ext.extend(TKE.form.FormPanelBaseCls, {
    style  : 'border-top: 0px;',
    layout : {
        type  : 'vbox',
        align : 'stretch'
    },
    initComponent : function() {},
    buildGeneralInfoForm         : function() {},        ◄── ❶ Factory methods
    buildTbar                    : function() {},
    buildGeneralInfoFormLeftHalf : function() {},
    buildEmployeeGrid            : function() {},

    onGridRowDblClick            : function() {},        ◄── ❷ Event listener
    onSave                       : function() {},           methods
    onReset                      : function() {},
    onNewEmployee                : function() {},
    onEditEmployee               : function() {},
    onAssociateEmployees         : function() {},
    onDeleteEmployees            : function() {},
    onDeleteDepartment           : function() {},

    loadData                     : function() {},        ◄── ❸ Utility methods
    loadEmployeeGrid             : function() {},
    addRecordsToEmployeeGrid     : function() {},
    getEmployeeGridSelections    : function() {},
    reset                        : function() {}
});

Ext.reg('dept_form', TKE.form.DepartmentForm);
```

To reduce the size of the `initComponent` method, we use four factory methods ❶. In addition to those factory methods, there are eight event-driven methods ❷ and five utility methods ❸, all of which will make this composite widget easier to use and implement in the application.

Because this class is large, we'll construct the methods in small and digestible chunks, beginning with the `initComponent` and `buildGeneralInfoForm` factory methods.

Listing 16.18   The `initComponent` and `buildGeneralInfoForm` methods

```
initComponent : function() {
    this.items =  [
        this.buidGeneralInfoForm(),
        this.buildEmployeeGrid()
    ];

    TKE.form.DepartmentForm.superclass.initComponent.call(this);
```

```
        this.addEvents({
            save               : true,
            newemployee        : true,
            editemployee       : true,
            deleteemployee     : true,
            deletedepartment   : true
        });
    },

buidGeneralInfoForm : function() {
    var leftHalf = this.buildGeneralInfoFormLeftHalf();

    var rightHalf = {
        xtype      : 'container',
        title      : 'Description',
        flex       : 1,
        bodyStyle  : 'padding: 1px; margin: 0px;',
        layout     : 'form',
        labelWidth : 70,
        items      : {
            xtype      : 'textarea',
            fieldLabel : 'Description',
            name       : 'description',
            anchor     : '100% 100%'
        }
    };

    return {
        tbar         : this.buildTbar(),
        layout       : 'hbox',
        height       : 100,
        bodyStyle    : 'background-color: #DFE8F6; padding: 10px',
        layoutConfig : { align : 'stretch' },
        border       : false,
        items        : [
            leftHalf,
            rightHalf
        ]
    };
},
```

In the initComponent method, we set the this.items property as an array containing the results of the this.buildGeneralInfoForm and this.buildEmployeeGrid methods as well as configure five custom events for this class. The save, newemployee, delete-employee, and deletedepartment events will be fired when the user clicks a Button in a Toolbar. The editemployee event will be fired when a row is doubleclicked in the EmployeeGridPanel instance.

The this.buildGeneralInfoForm method will construct the form input elements as well as the containers and layout implementations to display them side by side, as illustrated earlier. Because the amount of configuration is rather large, I broke up the construction of the form and Toolbar items into separate factory methods for easier consumption.

In the next listing, we'll construct those form elements and the Toolbar configuration.

Listing 16.19   The `buildTbar` and factory methods

```
buildTbar : function() {
    return [
        {
            text    : 'Save',
            iconCls : 'icon-disk',
            scope   : this,
            handler : this.onSave
        },
        {
            text    : 'Reset',
            iconCls : 'icon-arrow_undo',
            scope   : this,
            handler : this.onReset

        },
        '->',
        {
            text    : 'Deactivate Department',
            iconCls : 'icon-delete',
            scope   : this,
            handler : this.onDeleteDepartment
        }
    ];
},

buildGeneralInfoFormLeftHalf : function() {
    return {
        xtype       : 'container',
        layout      : 'form',
        flex        : 1,
        labelWidth  : 60,
        defaultType : 'textfield',
        defaults    : { anchor: '-10' },
        items       : [
            {
                xtype       : 'hidden',
                name        : 'id'
            },
            {
                fieldLabel : 'Name',
                name       : 'name',
                allowBLank : false,
                maxLength  : 255
            },
            {
                xtype      : 'datefield',
                fieldLabel : 'Activated',
                name       : 'dateActive'
            }
        ]
    };
},
```

The `buildTbar` method returns an array of configuration items that will be resolved into instances of `Ext.Toolbar.Button` and a single `Ext.Toolbar.Fill`. Notice that each of the `Buttons` has its handler set to local methods. The `buildGeneralInfoForm-LeftHalf` method constructs a container with three fields, one of which is hidden.

Now that the form is configured, we can move on to code the grid factory method in the next listing.

Listing 16.20 The `buildEmployeeGrid` factory method

```
buildEmployeeGrid : function() {
    var tbar = [
        '<b>Employees</b>',
        '->',
        {
            text     : 'New Employee',
            iconCls  : 'icon-user_add',
            scope    : this,
            handler  : this.onNewEmployee
        },
        '-',
        {
            text     : 'Edit Employee',
            iconCls  : 'icon-user_edit',
            scope    : this,
            handler  : this.onEditEmployee
        },
        '-',
        {
            text     : 'Delete employee',
            iconCls  : 'icon-user_delete',
            scope    : this,
            handler  : this.onDeleteEmployee
        },
        '-',
        {
            text     : 'Associate Employee(s)',
            iconCls  : 'icon-link_add',
            scope    : this,
            handler  : this.onAssociateEmployee
        }
    ];

    return {
        xtype    : 'employeegridpanel',
        itemId   : 'employeeGrid',
        flex     : 1,
        loadMask : true,
        tbar     : tbar,
        style    : 'background-color: #DFE8F6; padding: 10px',
        listeners : {
            scope        : this,
            rowdblclick  : this.onGridRowDblClick
        }
    };
},
```

This method will return a configuration object for the implementation of the `EmployeeGridPanel` class we created earlier. It adds a `TopToolbar` with a `TextItem` and `Buttons` to allow the user to interact with the `EmployeeGridPanel` widget but within the scope of this class. Each of the `Buttons` has its handlers set to a local method, which will fire the event.

We've just completed the factory methods, which means that we can move on to construct the on methods. We'll begin in this listing with the first four.

Listing 16.21   The first four `on` methods

```
onGridRowDblClick : function(grid, rowIndex) {
    var record = grid.store.getAt(rowIndex);
    this.fireEvent('editemployee', this, grid, record);
},
onSave : function() {
    if (this.getForm().isValid()) {
        this.fireEvent('save', this, this.getValues());
    }
},
onReset : function() {
    this.reset();
},
onNewEmployee : function() {
    var employeeGrid = this.getComponent('employeegrid');
    if (this.data) {
        this.fireEvent('newemployee', this, employeeGrid);
    }
},
```

In listing 16.21, we complete four of the on methods. The `onGridRowDblClick` method will be called when the `EmployeeGridPanel`'s own `rowdblclick` event is fired, and it'll obtain a reference to the `Record` that the event occurred on and fire the custom `editemployee` event.

> **NOTE**   We could have chosen to relay the grid's `rowdblclick` event, but by firing a custom event we describe the requested action by the user, making it more meaningful to the implementation layer. This is why we implement custom events for simple user-driven actions, such as the click of a `Button` in a `Toolbar`.

Looking at the rest of the methods, `onSave` and `onNewEmployee` will fire events of their own, whereas `onReset` will reset the state of the form. Recall that we set the `trackResetOnLoad` property in the `FormPanelBaseCls` constructor, which enables `BasicForm`'s reset method to restore the form to its original state after being modified by a user.

There are four more on methods to finish developing, which we'll cover in the next listing.

Listing 16.22   The last four on methods

```
onEditEmployee : function() {
    var employeeGrid = this.getComponent('employeeGrid');
    var selectedEmployeeRec = employeeGrid.getSelected()[0];
    if (selectedEmployeeRec) {
        this.fireEvent('editemployee', this,
                employeeGrid, selectedEmployeeRec);
    }
},
onAssociateEmployees : function() {
    var selectedRecords = this.getEmployeeGridSelections();

    if (this.data && this.data.id) {
        var empSelectionWindow =
          new TKE.window.EmployeeAssociationWindow({
            departmentId   : this.data.id,
            departmentName : this.data.name
        });

        this.relayEvents(empSelectionWindow, ['assocemployees']);
        empSelectionWindow.show();
        empSelectionWindow = null;
    }
},
onDeleteEmployees : function(btn) {
    var selectedRecs = this.getEmployeeGridSelections();
    var employeeGrid = this.getComponent('employeegrid');
    if (selectedRecs.length > 0) {
        this.fireEvent(
            'deleteEmployees',
            selectedRecs,
            employeeGrid,
            this
        );
    }
},
onDeleteDepartment : function() {
    if (this.data) {
        this.fireEvent('deletedepartment', this.data.id);
    }
},
```

In listing 16.22, we tackle the last four event handler methods, starting with onEdit-Employee. This method is bound to the Edit Employee Button, which is located on the top Toolbar of the EmployeeGridPanel. When invoked, onEditEmployee will fire the custom editemployee if at least one Record in the EmployeeGrid is selected. If more than one Record is selected, only the first will be modified.

onAssociateEmployees will be called when the related Toolbar Button is clicked. This method instantiates a new instance of EmployeeAssociationWindow and passes the departmentId and departmentName as configuration parameters of the currently loaded department. It will do so only if this class's form is properly loaded via the inherited loadData method. Before the new EmployeeAssociationWindow is shown, we relay its `assocemployees` event. Relaying this event will give any implementation logic an opportunity to perform the Ajax request to allow employees to be associated with the department that's currently loaded.

The last two methods, `onDeleteEmployees` and `onDeleteDepartment`, will both fire related events, each sending required data along with the event. `onDeleteEmployees` will fire its event only if there are selected `Records` in the grid. `onDeleteDepartment` will fire its event when the Delete Department `Button` is clicked.

In the next listing, we'll look at the utility methods, starting with the ones responsible for data management for this class.

Listing 16.23 The data management utility methods

```
loadData : function(data) {
    TKE.form.DepartmentForm.superclass.loadData.apply(this, arguments);
    this.loadEmployeeGrid();
},
loadEmployeeGrid : function(data) {
    if (this.data && this.data.id) {
        this.getComponent('employeegrid').load({
            params : {
                id : this.data.id
            }
        });
    }
},
addRecordsToEmployeeGrid : function(records) {
    this.getComponent('employeegrid').add(records);
},
getEmployeeGridSelections: function() {
    return this.getComponent('employeegrid').getSelections();
},
reset : function() {
    this.getForm().reset();
}
```

In listing 16.23, we complete the rest of the methods for this class. The `loadData` extension method will be called when the implementing code in the application layer detects that a user has selected a department from the `DepartmentsListView` class. In addition to calling the `superclass.loadData` method, it will perform a load of the `EmployeeGridPanel`.

The `loadEmployeeGrid` method will call the `EmployeeGridPanel`'s `load` utility method. Recall that we added the `load` method to the `EmployeeGridPanel` extension to prevent any implementing code from having to directly call methods on its `Store` instance.

Similarly, the `getEmployeeGridSelections` is a utility method for this class that uses the `EmployeeGridPanel` `getSelections` utility method. Having this type of utility method prevents any implementations of this class from having to call methods directly on the `EmployeeGridPanel`.

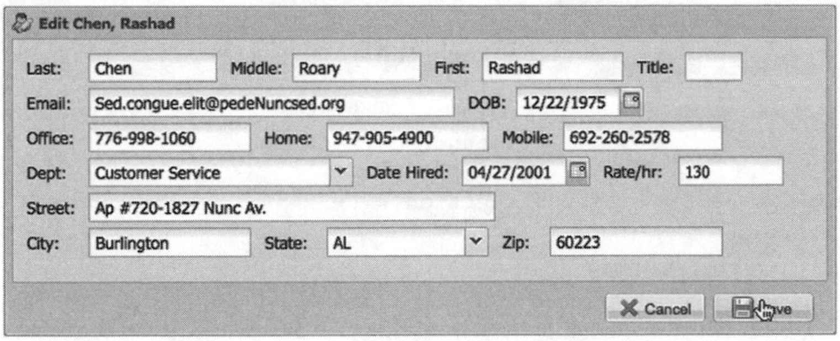

Figure 16.15 The Edit employee form embedded and displayed in a `Window`

This concludes the construction of the `DepartmentForm` composite widget. During this exercise, we explored how to construct a composite widget and both wire up event handlers and create utility methods to make implementing this widget easier. Next, we'll look at the last class, `EmployeeForm`, which will require a lot more configuration than any of the other custom widgets thus far.

16.7.3 *The EmployeeForm class*

The `EmployeeForm` consists mostly of form input configuration code. This is because of the number of fields that the requirements dictate and the field arrangement desired by the designer. To refresh your memory, figure 16.15 shows a snapshot of the `EmployeeForm` class implemented inside a `Window` that we'll create in the next chapter, when we work on the application layer logic.

Because this is another large class, we'll begin by analyzing the class template.

Listing 16.24 The `EmployeeForm` class template

```
Ext.ns("TKE.form");

TKE.form.EmployeeForm = Ext.extend(TKE.form.FormPanelBaseCls, {
    border        : true,
    autoScroll    : true,
    bodyStyle     : 'background-color: #DFE8F6; padding: 10px',
    labelWidth    : 40,
    defaultType   : 'textfield',
    defaults      : {
        width     : 200,
        maxLength : 255,
        allowBlank : false
    },
    initComponent                : function() {},

    buildTbar                    : function() {},
    buildFormItems               : function() {},
    buildNameContainer           : function() {},
    buildDepartmentInfoContainer : function() {},
    buildEmailDobContainer       : function() {},
    buildCityStateZipContainer   : function() {},
```

```
    buildPhoneNumbersContainer    : function() {},

    onNew                         : function() {},
    onSave                        : function() {},
    onReset                       : function() {},
    onDelete                      : function() {},

    loadFormAfterRender           : function() {}
});
```

```
Ext.reg('employee_form', TKE.form.EmployeeForm);
```

If you look at the `EmployeeForm` class template, you'll see that there are seven factory
methods in addition to the four event handlers and a single utility method. Each of
the factory methods is designed to construct a different row of the form; these methods are the bulk of this class. Designing the class like this ensures that you have code
that's segmented in such a way that it's easy for humans to digest and easy to modify.

For instance, let's say that in the future we get a change request to swap the First
and Last name fields in the top row of this form. All we'll need to do is focus our editor on the `buildNameContainer` method and modify the returned object accordingly.

Too often, you'll find developers who create massive configuration objects, which
can span many printed pages (even when using a small font). I highly discourage developing in such a way as this, because it makes code maintenance much more difficult
and troubleshooting the layout of the widgets orders of magnitude more time inten-
sive: you'll find yourself scrolling up and down the pages to figure out what's wrong.
For these reasons I encourage you to consider developing using factory methods.

We'll begin the construction of this class by working through the `initComponent`
and `buildTbar` methods.

Listing 16.25   The `initComponent` and `buildTbar` methods

```
initComponent : function() {
    Ext.applyIf(this, {
        tbar  : this.buildTbar(),
        items : this.buildFormItems()
    });

    TKE.form.EmployeeForm.superclass.initComponent.call(this);

    this.addEvents({
        newemp    : true,
        saveemp   : true,
        delemp    : true
    });

    if (this.record) {
        this.on({
            scope  : this,
            render : {
                single : true,
                fn     : this.loadFormAfterRender
            }
```

```
            });
        }
    },

    buildTbar : function() {
        return [
            {
                text    : 'Save',
                iconCls : 'icon-disk',
                scope   : this,
                handler : this.onSave
            },
            '-',
            {
                text    : 'Reset',
                iconCls : 'icon-arrow_undo',
                scope   : this,
                handler : this.onReset
            },
            '-',
            {
                text    : 'New Employee',
                iconCls : 'icon-user_add',
                scope   : this,
                handler : this.onNew
            },
            '->',
            {
                text    : 'Delete Employee',
                iconCls : 'icon-user_delete',
                scope   : this,
                handler : this.onDelete
            }
        ];
    },
```

The initComponent method does a lot to prepare the class for use. It uses Ext.applyIf to apply the items and tbar parameters *only* if the class doesn't have them configured. This allows us to implement the class and modify its behavior by implementing it either with items or via the Toolbar. Although we'd most likely implement this class without altering its items, we'll need to instantiate it without a top Toolbar, as illustrated a few pages ago.

After calling the superclass initComponent method, it adds four new events, each fired by a Button event handler method. Finally, if a Record property is set, it'll register an event handler, this.loadFormAfterRender, for the internal render event. This method will ensure that the internal BasicForm is loaded after the form is rendered.

In the next listing, we'll look at the buildFormItems method, which will leverage some of the other factory methods.

Listing 16.26   The `buildFormItems` method

```
buildFormItems : function() {
    var nameContainer              = this.buildNameContainer(),
        departmentSalaryContainer  = this.buildDepartmentInfoContainer(),
        emailDobContainer          = this.buildEmailDobContainer(),
        cityStateZip               = this.buildCityStateZipContainer(),
        phoneNumbers               = this.buildPhoneNumbersContainer();

    return [
        {
            xtype : 'hidden',
            name  : 'id'
        },
        {
            xtype : 'hidden',
            name  : 'departmentId'
        },
        nameContainer,
        emailDobContainer,
        phoneNumbers,
        departmentSalaryContainer,
        {
            fieldLabel : 'Street',
            name       : 'street',
            width      : 300
        },
        cityStateZip
    ];
},
```

This method will return an array of items, which will be rendered into the form. Because the `FormPanel` uses the `FormLayout` by default, each element of this array will be rendered into its own row, with the exception of the `hidden` input widget, which is injected into the DOM but not visible to the user.

Next, we'll fill out the rest of the form factory methods. These are all rather large, so we're going to move through them one at a time and somewhat quickly, because all they do is configure a container with rows of form input elements.

We'll begin with the `buildNameContainer` method.

Listing 16.27   The `buildNameContainer` method

```
buildNameContainer : function() {
    return {
        xtype       : 'container',
        layout      : 'column',
        anchor      : '-10',
        defaultType : 'container',
        defaults    : {
            width      : 150,
            labelWidth : 40,
            layout     : 'form'
        },
```

```
        items           : [
        {
            items       : {
                xtype       : 'textfield',
                fieldLabel : 'Last',
                name        : 'lastName',
                anchor      : '-10',
                allowBlank : false,
                maxLength  : 50
            }
        },
        {
            items       : {
                xtype       : 'textfield',
                fieldLabel : 'Middle',
                name        : 'middle',
                anchor      : '-10',
                maxLength  : 50
            }
        },
        {
            labelWidth : 30,
            items       : {
                xtype       : 'textfield',
                fieldLabel : 'First',
                name        : 'firstName',
                anchor      : '-10',
                allowBlank : false,
                maxLength  : 50
            }
        },
        {
            labelWidth : 30,
            width       : 90,
            items       : {
                xtype       : 'textfield',
                fieldLabel : 'Title',
                name        : 'title',
                anchor      : '-10',
                maxLength  : 5
            }
        }
    ]
    };
},
```

Because of the nature of the framework, in order to configure form input elements into columns, you need to encapsulate them in containers, which use the FormLayout. This will ensure the fieldLabel is rendered alongside the form input element, ensuring the proper association of the label element to the input element. You'll see this pattern used in the rest of the factory methods for this class.

We'll construct the buildDepartmentInfoContainer method in the next listing.

Listing 16.28   The buildDepartmentInfoContainer method

```
buildDepartmentInfoContainer : function() {
    return {
        xtype          : 'container',
        layout         : 'column',
        anchor         : '-10',
        defaultType : 'container',
        defaults       : {
            width  : 200,
            layout : 'form'
        },
        items          : [
            {
                labelWidth : 40,
                width      : 250,
                items      : {
                    xtype         : 'combo',
                    fieldLabel    : 'Dept',
                    hiddenName    : 'departmentId',
                    displayField  : 'name',
                    valueField    : 'id',
                    triggerAction : 'all',
                    editable      : false,
                    anchor        : '-10',
                    store         : {
                        xtype  : 'jsonstore',
                        url    : 'departments/getList',
                        fields : [ 'name', 'id' ]
                    }
                }
            },
            {
                labelWidth : 65,
                width      : 175,
                items      : {
                    xtype      : 'datefield',
                    fieldLabel : 'Date Hired',
                    anchor     : '-10',
                    name       : 'dateHired'
                }
            },
            {
                labelWidth : 50,
                width      : 145,
                items      : {
                    xtype           : 'numberfield',
                    fieldLabel      : 'Rate/hr',
                    name            : 'rate',
                    allowDecimals   : true,
                    anchor          : '-10',
                    decimalPrecision : 2
                }
            }
        ]
    };
},
```

In listing 16.28, we create a factory method, like the one prior, where we construct a Container that contains a row of Containers, which implement a form input field using the FormLayout. We have three more of these factory methods left to construct.

Next is the buildEmailDobContainer method.

Listing 16.29   The buildEmailDobContainer method

```
buildEmailDobContainer : function() {
    return {
        xtype       : 'container',
        layout      : 'column',
        defaultType : 'container',
        anchor      : '-10',
        defaults    : {
            layout : 'form'
        },
        items   : [
            {
                labelWidth : 40,
                width      : 325,
                items      : {
                    xtype      : 'textfield',
                    fieldLabel : 'Email',
                    name       : 'email',
                    anchor     : '-10',
                    maxLength  : 50
                }
            },
            {
                width      : 140,
                labelWidth : 30,
                items      : {
                    xtype      : 'datefield',
                    fieldLabel : 'DOB',
                    name       : 'dob',
                    allowBlank : true,
                    anchor     : '-10'
                }
            }

        ]
    };
},
```

By now, you should be able to see the pattern emerging from these factory methods, where we create a Container that represents a single horizontal row. Inside these Containers are other Containers that use the FormLayout to display a field element.

We use such deeply nested Containers because the FormLayout takes care of creating the Field element for us and linking its click to focus the associated form element. Also, in laying out the form in this way, we benefit from an automatic tab index, where the user can press the Tab key, and the browser will focus all of the fields from left to right in the order in which they're defined.

The next listing shows the buildCityStateZip method.

Listing 16.30   The buildCityStateZip method

```
buildCityStateZipContainer : function() {
    return {
        xtype        : 'container',
        layout       : 'column',
        defaultType  : 'container',
        anchor       : '-10',
        defaults     : {
            width       : 175,
            labelWidth  : 40,
            layout      : 'form'
        },
        items     : [
            {
                items : {
                    xtype      : 'textfield',
                    fieldLabel : 'City',
                    anchor     : '-10',
                    name       : 'city'
                }
            },
            {
                items    : {
                    xtype        : 'combo',
                    fieldLabel   : 'State',
                    name         : 'state',
                    displayField : 'state',
                    editable     : false,
                    valueField   : 'state',
                    triggerAction : 'all',
                    anchor       : '-10',
                    store        : {
                        xtype  : 'jsonstore',
                        url    : 'states/getList',
                        fields : ['state']
                    }
                }
            },
            {
                labelWidth : 30,
                items      : {
                    xtype      : 'numberfield',
                    fieldLabel : 'Zip',
                    name       : 'zip',
                    anchor     : '-10',
                    minLength  : 4,
                    maxLength  : 5
                }
            }
        ]
    };
},
```

Last, we'll construct the buildPhoneNumbersContainer method.

Listing 16.31 The buildPhoneNumbersContainer method

```
buildPhoneNumbersContainer : function() {
    return {
        xtype       : 'container',
        layout      : 'column',
        anchor      : '-10',
        defaultType : 'container',
        defaults    : {
            width      : 175,
            labelWidth : 40,
            layout     : 'form'
        },
        items    : [
            {
                items : {
                    xtype      : 'textfield',
                    fieldLabel : 'Office',
                    anchor     : '-10',
                    name       : 'officePhone'
                }
            },
            {
                items : {
                    xtype      : 'textfield',
                    fieldLabel : 'Home',
                    anchor     : '-10',
                    name       : 'homePhone'
                }
            },
            {
                items : {
                    xtype      : 'textfield',
                    fieldLabel : 'Mobile',
                    anchor     : '-10',
                    name       : 'mobilePhone'
                }
            }
        ]
    };
},
```

We've finished the factory methods. Next, we'll finish this class with the four on methods and the single utility method.

Listing 16.32 The final five methods for the EmployeeForm class

```
onNew : function() {
    this.clearForm();
    this.fireEvent('newemp', this, this.getValues());
},
onSave : function() {
```

```
        if (this.isValid()) {
            this.fireEvent('saveemp', this, this.getValues());
        }
    },
    onReset : function() {
        this.reset();
    },
    onDelete : function() {
        var vals = this.getValues();
        if (vals.id.length > 0) {
            this.fireEvent('delemp', this, vals);
        }
    },
    loadFormAfterRender : function() {
        this.load({
            url     : 'employees/getEmployee',
            params : {
                id  : this.record.get('id')
            }
        });
    }
```

In the final listing of this chapter, we construct the final five methods of the EmployeeForm class. Like the other classes we've constructed thus far, the on methods will be executed when the Buttons in the Toolbar are clicked. Also, as discussed, the loadFormAfterRender method will invoke an Ajax load of the form via its own load method. Recall that we configured the initComponent to register loadFormAfter-Render only if this.record is set.

This concludes the construction of the final and largest class in our reusability layer. Although it didn't contain a lot of class-specific logic or utility methods, it contained a whole lot of configuration for the form elements, which is expected for large forms such as this. Because this class has so much configuration, you can rest assured that it'll require less code to implement this class, allowing our application layer to be more focused on user interaction and workflow.

16.8 *Summary*

In this chapter, you learned a lot about what it takes to construct an application that's easily maintained and extensible.

We began by discussing namespaces in JavaScript and some patterns to use when developing different sized applications with Ext JS. We chose to use the segmented namespace pattern for the application that we began building, which allowed us to create a layer for the reusable widgets and a layer for the application logic. We did this because it gave us an area to place our reusable widgets, reducing the clutter of the application layer.

Before constructing the application code, we took an in-depth look at the application requirements and executed some decision branches to lay out the reusable layer namespace. While doing this exercise, you learned how to decide when to create abstract base classes, reducing code complexity and code duplication.

After reviewing the requirements, we constructed all of the classes in the reusable layer. You learned how to create classes that generate their own events and relay events from internal instances of widgets. We also gained experience in constructing base classes, and you learned two different patterns for creating classes that promote reusability within this layer.

In the next chapter, we'll pull everything together as we construct the application layer. This is where you'll see it all come together.

The application stack

In the last chapter, we discussed how to develop a scalable and maintainable application architecture with Ext JS by dividing the code into layers and segmenting by namespace. We examined mockups of the application, identified and created all of the reusable widgets, and placed them in the reusable layer of our application stack.

In this chapter, we'll implement those reusable components and see the benefits of segmenting reusable components from the workflow components that we'll soon create. We'll begin with a quick review of the application screens, designing and laying out the application layer namespace architecture as we determine what classes to create. This will give you a holistic view of how the application stack will be constructed and guide you through the development process.

After the application analysis, we'll develop the application in layers, screen by screen, starting each with an in-depth analysis of the desired interaction model that comes from the requirements. We'll use this knowledge to implement our reusable classes and "wire up" and construct the workflow logic.

426

In the end, we'll tie things together by developing our own custom navigation and authentication controller. This chapter will be the most challenging thus far. On the flipside, I think it'll also be the most rewarding because you'll get to experience first-hand how all of the work you did in the last chapter will allow you to focus on the setup of the application workflow, which is the majority of the application layer code.

If you want to take a break at any time along the way and see how all this is supposed to work, you can visit the application online at http://app.extjsinaction.com.

17.1 Developing the application namespace

To kick things off, we'll begin with a quick review of the application screen mockups. This exercise will give you a good understanding of how to lay out the application namespace and refresh your memory.

17.1.1 Reviewing the application screens

After the user is successfully logged in, they will be greeted with the company Dashboard screen shown in figure 17.1. This screen will implement the Company-Snapshot and DepartmentBreakdown custom ChartPanel implementation classes. We'll do a deep analysis of each screen before we begin construction. We'll call this class Dashboard.

Users will be able to navigate between screens by pressing the Buttons located in the top Toolbar. This Toolbar will also contain a Button to allow users to log out of the application. To visit the other two screens, they will have to press the associated Toolbar Button.

Figure 17.2 shows the Manage Departments screen.

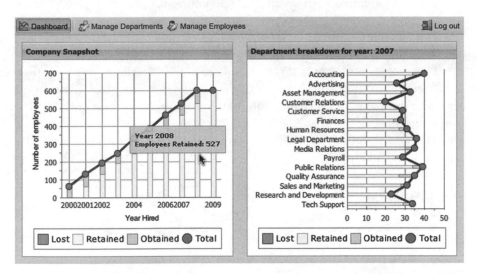

Figure 17.1   The Dashboard screen

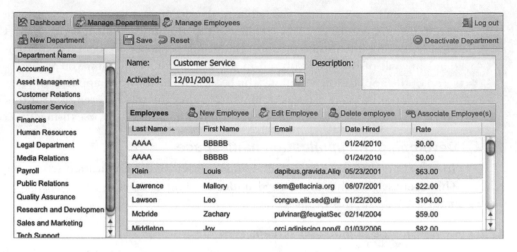

Figure 17.2   The Manage Departments screen

This screen will allow users to perform full CRUD operations for employees as well as move (associate) employees from other departments to the department selected on the left. This class will be named `DepartmentManager`.

When the user wishes to create or update employee records, the system will present a `Window` with an embedded `EmployeeForm`, as shown in figure 17.3.

When we discussed this widget in the last chapter, we decided that it would live in the application layer because of the necessary workflow logic, such as field checking. This widget will also have custom events to allow the `DepartmentManager` screen to know when an employee is created or updated so it can create or update `Records` in the `EmployeeGridPanel`. This class will be aptly named `EmployeeEditorWindow`.

The last screen, shown in figure 17.4, is designed to allow for quick CRUD operations of employees, and the class will be called `EmployeeManager`.

This screen implements three of our reusable widgets and has a context-sensitive left-to-right workflow, which means that we'll have to code quite a few event listeners to make this happen. Every function that this screen provides is contained within the screen itself.

This concludes the application UI refresher. We can now move on to lay out the application namespace.

Figure 17.3   The Edit employee `Window`

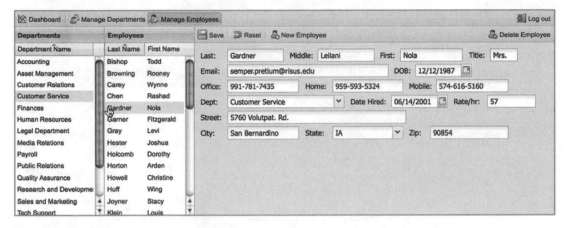

Figure 17.4   The Manage Employees screen

17.1.2 Designing the application namespace

The purpose of this application is to manage a company's department and employee association and is named Company Manager by the business. I generally like to name the application namespace in accordance with the application name, so we'll call our application namespace `CompanyManager`.

Using the information we gathered when reviewing the application, we can properly arrange the namespace layout, as shown in figure 17.5.

Each of the application screens is represented by a class; in addition, the `work-space` class manages the presentation of the three main screens, as well as navigation and authentication. Because this class is the glue that ties together the entire application, we'll work on it last.

You now have a good idea of how we'll organize our application namespace. We'll begin construction of this stack with the Dashboard screen.

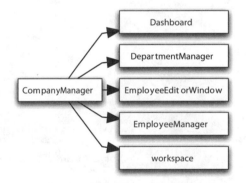

Figure 17.5   The application namespace layout

17.2 Building the Dashboard screen

Recall that the Dashboard screen will be presented to the user after a successful login. It'll implement the two `ChartPanel` extension classes, `CompanySnapshot` on the left and `DepartmentBreakdown` on the right. Because this screen doesn't contain anything other than these two widgets, we'll use a `Container` and implement the `HBoxLayout`.

Per the requirements, users can click a chart series node in the `CompanySnapshot` and view the department statistics for the selected year. This means that we'll have to configure an `itemclick` event listener to cause the `DepartmentBreakdown` store to load.

Now that you have an understanding of the UI and workflow requirements for the Dashboard screen, we can begin construction of the `Dashboard` class, shown in the following listing.

Listing 17.1   The `Dashboard` class

```
Ext.ns('CompanyManager');

CompanyManager.Dashboard = Ext.extend(Ext.Container, {
    border  : false,
    layout  : {
        type  : 'hbox',
        align : 'stretch'
    },
    defaults : {
        style : 'background-color: #DFE8F6; padding: 10px',
        flex  : 1
    },
    msgs : {
        deptBreakdown : 'Department breakdown for year: {0}'
    },
    initComponent : function() {
        this.items = [
            {
                xtype : 'companysnapshot',
                title     : 'Company Snapshot',
                listeners : {
                    scope     : this,
                    itemclick : this.
                        onCompanySnapshotItemClick
                }
            },
            {
                xtype  : 'departmentbreakdown',
                itemId : 'departmentbreakdown',
                title  : 'Department Breakdown'
            }
        ];

        CompanyManager.Dashboard.superclass.initComponent.call(this);
    },
    onCompanySnapshotItemClick : function(evtObj){
        var record = evtObj.component.store.getAt(evtObj.index);
        var dptBrkDwnChart = this.getComponent('departmentbreakdown');

        dptBrkDwnChart.loadStoreByParams({
            year : record.get('year')
        });

        var msg = String.format(
            this.msgs.deptBreakdown,
            record.get('year')
        );
        dptBrkDwnChart.setTitle(msg);
    }
});
Ext.reg('dashboard', CompanyManager.Dashboard);
```

① itemclick event handler

② Load the Chart Store

The entire `Dashboard` class fits inside listing 17.1. This is the first time that you can see and enjoy the benefits of a well-designed reusability layer. To create the `Dashboard` class, we only needed to implement the preconfigured `CompanySnapshot` and `DepartmentBreakdown` classes via XType configuration objects. In addition to the layout of these two classes, we set up the `itemclick` ❶ event handler, which will cause the instance of `DepartmentBreakdown` to send a request ❷ to the server based on the year that was clicked in the `CompanySnapshot` panel.

That's all there is to it. There are a few reasons why this code is so short. The first is that the `ChartPanelBaseCls` does most of the heavy lifting for the `Charts`. Another is that the `CompanySnapshot` and `DepartmentBreakdown` classes are preconfigured, so we needn't put any of that gunk in our application layer. Last, this screen, relative to its cousins, doesn't contain a lot of interactivity.

NOTE If you want to test this screen in a browser, you can place it in an `Ext.Viewport` with the `FitLayout`.

As you'll see with the next screen, writing the code for user interactivity can take a lot of effort, when there are a few workflows to enforce in the application. We'll continue our application construction with the Manage Employees screen because its workflow is much smaller than that of the Manage Departments screen.

17.3 The Manage Employees screen

The Manage Employees screen is designed for easy CRUD operations for employee records for the company. Before we can begin coding, you'll need to understand the UI workflow requirements for this screen. This will guide us in making the proper decisions for coding UI interactions, such as the context sensitivity of the different widgets.

17.3.1 Discussing the workflow

The Manage Employees screen implements a common left-to-right workflow, where the two rightmost widgets are context sensitive to the leftmost. Please look at figure 17.6, because it illustrates the selection workflow for the screen.

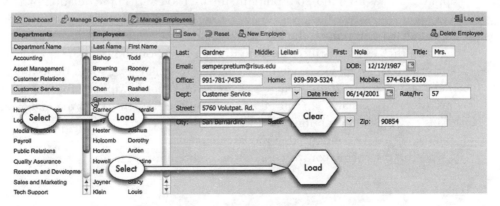

Figure 17.6 The Manage Employees screen context sensitivity

When this screen is shown, the DepartmentsListView (left) will load, gathering a list of the departments within the company, and the EmployeeList (middle) and EmployeeForm (right) are cleared of any loaded data. To load or create an employee Record, the user must first select a department. This sets the first context, where the selection of a department will trigger the EmployeeList class load, displaying all employees for the selected department on the left.

From here, the user can update or delete an employee by selecting an employee Record in the EmployeeList. Selecting an employee Record sets the second context, triggering the EmployeeForm to remotely fetch and load the data for the selected employee.

Along with the event model for the three widgets, we have to be concerned with capturing any successful CRUD operation made against an employee Record. For instance, when a new employee is added to a department, instead of reloading the EmployeeList, we'll use the createAndSelectRecord utility method (defined in the ListPanelBaseCls) to create a new data.Record and set its values accordingly. This will ensure that the traffic to the server is minimized and the UI is much snappier.

The same goes for editing or deleting an employee Record. To update a Record, the user must select an employee from the EmployeeList, make changes to the form, and then click Save. If the save is successful, we'll refresh the Record with the new data. When a user deletes an employee, the Record is removed from the data Store of the EmployeeList and the form is purged of its data.

Whenever the user makes a change that has been successfully committed by the server, we'll prompt them with a successful change alert. This will give them ample notification that their change was successful.

> **TIP** Some application developers are fine with just silently making changes to the UI whenever a CRUD operation occurs, but I like to give feedback to users in the form of an alert dialog box. This ensures that they're aware of the status of the requested change.

We'll post a confirmation dialog box when a user decides to delete an employee. This application has no undo, so prompting the user to confirm the deletion of a Record is a good idea, because this gives the user an opportunity to verify that they're performing a delete operation on the intended employee.

Last, the reset will cause the form to reset based on the last state the form was in. For instance, if data was loaded, pressing the reset Button should undo any changes that the user made. If the form was cleared, reset should wipe the form again, returning it to a virgin state. This all will come from the framework via the trackResetOnLoad configuration option that we set in the FormPanelBaseCls constructor extension that we configured in the last chapter.

We can now begin construction of this component.

17.3.2 Constructing EmployeeManager

This class will have quite a few methods and configurations. We'll begin by defining and examining the template. Afterward, we'll code clusters of methods until we've finished.

Listing 17.2 The `EmployeeManager` screen class

```
Ext.ns("CompanyManager");

CompanyManager.EmployeeManager = Ext.extend(Ext.Panel, {
    border : false,
    layout : {
      type  : 'hbox',
      align : 'stretch'
    },
    msgs            : {},                                        ❶ Object for
    initComponent : function() {},                                reusable messages

    buildDepartmentListView : function() {},                    ❷ Factory methods
    buildEmployeeListView   : function() {},
    buildEmployeeForm       : function() {},

    onDepartmentListClick     : function() {},
    onEmployeeListClick       : function() {},
    onEmployeeFormLoadFailure : function() {},                  ❸ Event handler
    onNewEmployee             : function() {},                     methods
    onDeleteEmployee          : function() {},
    onConfirmDeleteEmployee   : function() {},
    onAfterDeleteEmployee     : function() {},
    onSaveEmployee            : function() {},
    onEmpFormSaveSuccess      : function() {},
    onEmpFormSaveFailure      : function() {},

    setDeptIdOnForm : function() {},                            ❹ Utility methods
    clearMask       : function() {},
    cleanSlate      : function() {}
});

Ext.reg('employeemanager', CompanyManager.EmployeeManager);
```

If you examine listing 17.2, you'll see a `msgs` configuration object ❶, in addition to the typical factory ❷, event handler ❸, and utility methods ❹. The purpose of the `msgs` object is to place reusable strings, most of which contain placeholders that can be filled in with the little-known `String.format` utility method. As you'll see when implementing the CRUD operation workflows, having this type of centralized container for messages to the user will help rid us of the dependency of having to manually concatenate strings, cleaning up our code quite a bit.

Last, this class implements the `HboxLayout` with the `align:'stretch'` configuration. Looking forward, the following listing contains the `msgs` object and `init-Component` method.

Listing 17.3   The `msgs` object and `initComponent` method

```
msgs : {
    immediateChanges : 'Warning! Changes are'
        + '<span style="color: red;">immediate</span>.',
    errorsInForm     : 'There are errors in the form.'
        + 'Please correct and try again.',                    ❶ Message string
    empSavedSuccess : 'Saved {0}, {1} successfully.',              templates
    fetchingDataFor  : 'Fetching data for {0}, {1}',
    couldNotLoadData : 'Could not load data for {0}, {1}!',
    saving           : 'Saving {0}, {1}...',
    errorSavingData  : 'There was an error saving the form.',
    deletingEmployee : 'Deleting employee {0}, {1}...',
    deleteEmpConfirm : 'Are you sure you want to delete'
        + 'employee {0}, {1}?',
    deleteEmpSuccess : 'Employee {0}, {1} was deleted successfully.',
    deleteEmpFailure : 'Employee {0}, {1} was not deleted'
        + 'due to a failure.'
},
initComponent : function() {
    this.items = [
        this.buildDepartmentListView(),               ❷ Factory methods
        this.buildEmployeeListView(),
        this.buildEmployeeForm()
    ];

    CompanyManager.DepartmentManager.superclass.initComponent.call(this);
},
```

Listing 17.3 contains our `msgs` object along with the `initComponent` method. If you examine the contents of the `msgs` object ❶, you'll see that some of the strings have so-called tokens, which `String.format` will use to fill in portions of the string later on.

> **TIP**   Ext JS adds a few more utility methods to the `String` class that are useful for managing string format. To read about them, visit the API documentation at http://www.extjs.com/deploy/dev/docs/?class=String.

The `initComponent` method calls upon the three factory methods ❷ to construct the `EmployeeForm`, `DepartmentsListView`, and `EmployeeListView` configurations and sets them all as the local `this.items` array.

In the next listing, we'll construct the three factory methods described previously.

Listing 17.4   The three factory methods

```
buildDepartmentListView : function() {
    return {
        xtype    : 'departmentlist',            ❶ DepartmentList
        itemId   : 'departmentList',               View XType object
        width    : 190,
        border   : false,
        style    : 'border-right: 1px solid #99BBE8;',
        title    : 'Departments',
        listeners : {
```

```
                       scope : this,
                       click : this.onDepartmentListClick
                   }
               };
           },
           buildEmployeeListView : function() {
               return {
                   xtype      : 'employeelist',
                   itemId     : 'employeeList',
                   width      : 190,
                   border     : false,
                   style      : 'border-right: 1px solid #99BBE8;',
                   title      : 'Employees',
                   listeners : {
                       scope  : this,
                       click  : this.onEmployeeListClick
                   }
               };
           },
           buildEmployeeForm : function() {
               return {
                   xtype      : 'employeeform',
                   itemId     : 'employeeForm',
                   flex       : 1,
                   border     : false,
                   listeners : {
                       scope   : this,
                       newemp  : this.onNewEmployee,
                       delemp  : this.onDeleteEmployee,
                       saveemp : this.onSaveEmployee
                   }
               };
           },
```

2 Listener for relayed click event

3 EmployeeListView XType configuration

4 Listener for relayed click event

5 EmployeeForm XType object

6 Listeners for CRUD operations

Listing 17.4 contains the three factory methods used to configure the three custom widgets implemented by this screen. They all follow the same pattern, where the component is configured and event listeners are registered.

The buildDepartmentListView method will configure a DepartmentsListView XType **1**, which will have a static width and a listener for the relayed click event **2**. When fired, the onDepartmentListClick method will be responsible for loading the EmployeeListView and clearing the EmployeeForm.

Following the pattern above it, buildEmployeeListView will configure an Employee-ListView XType **3** and register the relayed click event **4** with the onEmployee-ListClick handler. This method will call upon the EmployeeForm to remotely load via Ajax.

Finally, the buildEmployeeForm method will configure the EmployeeForm **5** and register three event listeners for each of the CRUD operations **6**. onNewEmployee will clear the form of its values, whereas onSaveEmployee will submit the data contained in the form. onDeleteEmployee is somewhat of a special case, because it'll request confirmation from the user via Ext.MessageBox.confirm. As you'll see later, the callback method, `onConfirmDeleteEmployee`, will be used to perform the Ajax request if the user clicked Yes.

With our factory methods complete, we can move on to developing the 10 event handler methods. We'll first focus on the `ListView` click event handlers, starting with `onDepartmentListClick`, shown in the following listing.

Listing 17.5   `onDepartmentListClick`

```
onDepartmentListClick : function() {
    var selectedDepartment =
            this.getComponent('departmentList').getSelected();
    this.getComponent('employeeList').loadStoreByParams({
        id : selectedDepartment.get('id')
    });
    this.getComponent('employeeForm').clearForm();
    this.setDeptIdOnForm(selectedDepartment);
},
```

Load list
and
clear form

In listing 17.5, quite a bit of work is being done to perform the desired left-to-right workflow and handle any exceptions that may occur from the `EmployeeForm` load operation.

Recall that `onDepartmentListClick` will be called whenever the `Departments-ListView`'s click event is fired and a `Record` is selected. We leverage the selection model from the `ListView` via the `getSelected` utility method introduced by the `List-PanelBaseCls` we constructed in the last chapter to set a reference to the selected department.

Once the `Record` reference is created, we use it to load the `EmployeeListView` via another utility method found in the `ListPanelBaseClass` named `loadStoreBy-Params`, where we pass an object with a single property, the `id` of the selected department. This causes the data `Store` of the `EmployeeListView` instance to request the employees for the selected department and refresh its views.

Last, this method calls the `EmployeeForm`'s `clearForm` method, which ensures any loaded data is purged. It then calls `this.setDeptIdOnForm`, which is a convenience method that will fill in the selected department and the current date. This allows the user to create a new user as soon as they select a department, reducing their workflow by one click.

In the next listing, we'll focus on the `EmployeeListView` click workflow.

Listing 17.6   Handling the `EmployeeListView` click and `EmployeeForm` load failure

```
onEmployeeListClick : function() {
    var record = this.getComponent('employeeList').getSelected();
    var msg = String.format(
        this.msgs.fetchingDataFor,
        record.get('lastName'),
        record.get('firstName')
    );
```

Mask the page
and load the form ❶

```
        Ext.getBody().mask(msg, 'x-mask-loading');

        this.getComponent('employeeForm').load({
            url     : 'employees/getEmployee',
            scope   : this,
            success : this.clearMask,
            failure : this.onEmployeeFormLoadFailure,
            params  : {
                id : record.get('id')
            }
        });
    },
    onEmployeeFormLoadFailure : function() {
        var record = this.getComponent('employeeList').getSelected();
        var msg = String.format(
            this.msgs.couldNotLoadData,
            record.get('lastName'),
            record.get('firstName')
        );

        Ext.MessageBox.show({
            title   : 'Error',
            msg     : msg,
            buttons : Ext.MessageBox.OK,
            icon    : Ext.MessageBox.WARNING
        });

        this.clearMask();
    },
```

❷ Handle load exceptions

onEmployeeListClick ❶ is responsible for loading the EmployeeForm when an employee Record is clicked. It does this by obtaining a reference for the selected employee Record via the getSelected utility method. It uses this reference to dynamically format a string, which will be used to mask the entire document body, informing the user that the form is loading. By masking the entire body, we ensure that the users can't click anything else in the UI, which could cause another Ajax request and possibly an exception.

When the EmployeeForm load method is called, an object is passed, which contains the typical success and failure handler references. The success method is a reference to the local this.clearMask method, which we'll construct later. The failure method, onEmployeeLoadFailure ❷, is more involved, providing a friendly exception to the user if the load request were to fail.

We've finished the ListView event handler model. Still to be created are the CRUD operation handlers, which we'll start next. We'll begin with create and delete in the following listing.

Listing 17.7 onNewEmployee and onDeleteEmployee

```
onNewEmployee : function(selectedDepartment) {
    this.getComponent('employeeList').clearSelections();
    this.prepareFormForNew();
},
```

❶ Prepare for new employee

```
onDeleteEmployee : function(formPanel, vals) {
    var msg = String.format(
        this.msgs.deleteEmpConfirm,
        vals.lastName,
        vals.firstName
    );

    Ext.MessageBox.confirm(
        this.msgs.immediateChanges,
        msg,
        this.onConfirmDeleteEmployee,
        this
    );
},
```

❷ Display delete confirmation

To handle the creation of an employee, the onNewEmployee ❶ method accomplishes two tasks. First, it causes the EmployeeListView to purge its selected nodes. Purging the selection will allow us to determine what mode (create or update) the Employee-Form is in down the road, when we work on the code that's fired after a successful save request.

The second task is clearing the form of any value and setting the departmentId and dateHired fields accordingly, which is what the yet-to-be-developed prepareForm-ForNew method will do. By clearing the form, we erase the ID hidden field, which tells the server-side code that this is a new Record. Setting the departmentId allows new employee Records to be associated properly to the correct department, and setting the dateHired field is a convenience for the user. Effectively, the form sits dormant in create mode until the user saves the data via the Save Button.

Recall that the onDeleteEmployee is bound to the Delete Button of the top Toolbar. It then presents a customized confirmation dialog box to the user using MessageBox.confirm ❷. In order to capture and process the response from the user, we pass the yet-to-be-developed callback method, this.onConfirmDeleteEmployee, and the scope, this, as the second and third parameters to the MessageBox.confirm method.

Next, we'll code the onConfirmDelete callback method and onAfterDelete-Employee, which is the success callback for the delete employee Ajax operation request.

Listing 17.8 onConfirmDeleteEmployee and onAfterDeleteEmployee

```
onConfirmDeleteEmployee : function(btn) {
    if (btn === 'yes') {
        var vals = this.getComponent('employeeForm').getValues();

        var msg = String.format(
            this.msgs.deletingEmployee,
            vals.lastName,
            vals.firstName
        );

        Ext.getBody().mask(msg, 'x-mask-loading');
```

```
        Ext.Ajax.request({                              ◁─┐  Request to
            url           : 'employees/deleteEmployee',  ❶  delete user
            scope         : this,
            callback      : this.workspace.onAfterAjaxReq,
            succCallback  : this.onAfterDeleteEmployee,
            params        : {
                id : vals.id
            }
        });
    }
},
onAfterDeleteEmployee : function(jsonData) {
    var msg,
        selectedEmployee = this.getComponent('employeeList').getSelected();

    if (jsonData.success === true) {            ◁──❷ Post delete changes
        msg = String.format(
            this.msgs.deleteEmpSuccess,
            selectedEmployee.get('lastName'),
            selectedEmployee.get('firstName')
        );
      Ext.MessageBox.alert('Success', msg);

        selectedEmployee.store.remove(selectedEmployee);
        this.getComponent('employeeForm').clearForm();

    }
    else {
        msg = String.format(
            this.msgs.deleteEmpFailure,
            selectedEmployee.get('lastName'),
            selectedEmployee.get('firstName')
        );

        Ext.MessageBox.alert('Error', msg);
    }

    this.clearMask();
},
```

onConfirmDeleteEmployee checks to see if the passed button ID (btn) is equal to
'yes'. If so, it formats a friendly message and masks the entire page with it. It then
performs an Ajax request ❶ to the server to perform the delete operation, passing
the employee id as the only parameter.

Saving code when doing Ajax requests

The callback method reference passed to the Ajax.request method will perform a
custom two-phase check to verify that the web transaction was successful, where
only if the returning HTTP status code is favorable and the returning stream is valid
JSON will the custom succCallback method get called, executing any after-request
workflow logic. Performing this type of check can help prevent any duplicate code
from performing the aforementioned verification steps during each Ajax request.

onAfterDeleteEmployee will be called after the server returns a valid JSON stream. If it returns at least {success:true} ❷, a customized alert dialog box is displayed to inform the user that the delete operation was a success. Immediately afterward, the employee Record is removed from the Store and the form is purged of any values using the clearForm utility method. If for some reason the server returned valid JSON data but success was equal to false, then we'd alert the user that the delete operation failed, using a friendly formatted message.

> **TIP**   When developing the server-side code, there's no reason why you couldn't publish a failure code or a string explaining why it failed. For this, you can set something like a message string to the returning JSON stream and reference it via jsonData.message in the alert to the user located in the else block of onAfterDeleteEmployee.

This completes the create and delete portions of the workflow. In order to update or save a new Record, we need to develop the save portion of the workflow, which is what we'll do in the next listing.

Listing 17.9   Handling the save workflow

```
onSaveEmployee : function(employeeForm, vals) {
    if (employeeForm.getForm().isValid()) {
        var msg = String.format(
            this.msgs.saving,
            vals.lastName,
            vals.firstName
        );

        Ext.getBody().mask(msg, 'x-mask-loading');               ❶ Submit form
                                                                    if it validates
        employeeForm.getForm().submit({
            url     : 'employees/setEmployee',
            scope   : this,
            success : this.onEmpFormSaveSuccess,
            failure : this.onEmpFormSaveFailure
        });
    }
    else {
        Ext.MessageBox.alert('Error', this.msgs.errorsInForm);
    }
},
onEmpFormSaveSuccess : function(form, action) {
    var record = this.getComponent('employeeList').getSelected();
    var vals = form.getValues();

    var msg = String.format(
        this.msgs.empSavedSuccess,
        vals.lastName,
        vals.firstName
    );                                                           ❷ Update existing
                                                                    Record if present
    if (record) {
        record.set('lastName', vals.lastName);
```

```
            record.set('firstName', vals.firstName);
            record.commit();
        }
        else {
            var resultData = action.result.data;
            this.getComponent('employeeList').createAndSelectRecord(resultData);
            this.getComponent('employeeForm').setValues(resultData);
        }
        Ext.MessageBox.alert('Success', msg);

        this.clearMask();
    },
    onEmpFormSaveFailure : function() {
        this.clearMask();
        Ext.MessageBox.alert('Error', this.msgs.errorSavingData);
    },
```

**❸ Create new
employee Record**

Listing 17.9 has three methods that will handle the save operation of a new or existing employee Record. onSaveEmployee is called when the EmployeeForm's saveemp event is fired. If the EmployeeForm is valid, a submission ❶ of the data is attempted. If the form isn't valid, a friendly message is displayed to the user and no submission attempt is made. We set both the success and failure callback methods to manage the response from the server.

onEmpFormSaveSuccess is the submission success callback method. This method is responsible for figuring out whether the employee data was for a new Record or an existing one and has two branches of logic depending on each. Here's how it works.

> **Using the workflow to your advantage**
> This logic can determine whether the form is in edit mode or not by getting the selected Record from the EmployeeListView. Recall that to edit employees, a user must select a Record in the EmployeeListView widget, and when a new employee is created, any selections in the EmployeeListView are purged via the onNew-Employee method we created earlier.

For existing employees, all that needs to happen is an update of the Record data ❷ in the EmployeeListView to reflect any changes made for the last or first name. But for new employees, things get a little tricky and need to be handled accordingly to prevent duplicate Records from being created if any edits to a newly created employee needed to be made immediately after the Record was created.

For new employees, we need to get the data returned from the server, which contains the ID of the newly created employee row in the database. Instead of refreshing the EmployeeListView widget, use its createAndSelectRecord utility method, passing in the request result data. This will create the Record ❸ and select it in the view. Next, we set the values of the form using that same result data. This allows us to apply any changes to the data that may have been made by the server, such as inappropriate word filtering.

In case you're wondering

The reason we're rolling out our own CRUD code instead of using the framework-supplied `DataWriter` is that at the time of this writing, `DataWriter` has some undesirable behaviors such as creating a `Record` for a `Store` even if the create action failed in the backend.

The last method, `onEmpFormSaveFailure`, will handle any failure conditions returned by the server. This could mean anything from a bad HTTP status code for the request or a good HTTPD status code along with JSON containing {success:false}. Because our backend doesn't currently support intelligent error messages, we show a static error message to the user if this condition is met.

The code to manage saving data is complete. We can now move on to develop the three utility methods, which will complete this screen.

Listing 17.10   Handling the full save cycle

```
prepareFormForNew : function(selectedDept) {
    selectedDept = selectedDept ||
            this.getComponent('departmentList').getSelected();

    if (selectedDept) {                                        ◁──  Prepare form
        this.getComponent('employeeForm').setValues({       ❶  for new employee
            departmentId : selectedDept.get('id'),
            dateHired    : new Date()
        });
    }
},
clearMask : function() {
    Ext.getBody().unmask();
},
cleanSlate : function () {
    this.getComponent('departmentList').refreshView();
    this.getComponent('employeeList').clearView();
    this.getComponent('employeeForm').clearForm();
}
```

Listing 17.10 contains two methods that will be used by various portions of the code that we developed thus far and one that will be used by the master application controller, `workspace`, which we'll develop at the tail section of this chapter.

As discussed earlier, `prepareFormForNew` ❶ will be called by `onNewEmployee` and is responsible for setting the `departmentId` and `dateHired` values in preparation for a new employee. It will do this only if a selected department is detected in the `DepartmentsListView` widget.

The `clearMask` method is used to remove the mask from the `document.body` element and is called from various points in the workflow code above. Finally, the `cleanSlate` method will be called by the workspace every time this screen is displayed, because it's responsible for refreshing the `DepartmentsListView` widget and clearing the `EmployeeListView` and `EmployeeForm` widgets.

NOTE This behavior is put in place to fulfill requirements for the application globally, where the Manage Employees and Manage Departments screens are to be placed in a virgin state when chosen for display.

This concludes the development of the Manage Employees screen. You learned how to implement three of the classes from our reusable layer and apply asynchronous workflow bindings and constraints to them. You also saw how the use of utility methods like `String.format` can help keep our code clean, eliminating the need for messy string concatenation to create dynamic text strings to inform the user.

Next, we'll tackle the most complex screen of this application, Manage Departments, where you'll learn how to utilize the workflow bindings we implemented in the `EmployeeManager` class. We'll take things a step further and show how to bind to this screen two of our custom `Window` widgets, one of which we created in the last chapter and another that we'll work on after the `DepartmentManager` class.

17.4 The Manage Departments screen

Out of all of the screens in this application, Manage Departments contains the most workflow logic. This is because the user can perform CRUD operations for department and employee `Records` as well as move (associate) employees from one department to another.

With the development of Manage Employees, you became familiar with coding complex CRUD workflows. Because Manage Departments employs many of the exact same techniques, we won't be reviewing the code but rather discussing how the workflow logic works, aided by workflow diagrams.

We'll start by stepping through the department CRUD workflows.

17.4.1 The navigation and department CRUD workflows

To refresh your memory and as a point of reference, figure 17.7 shows the Manage Departments screen in action.

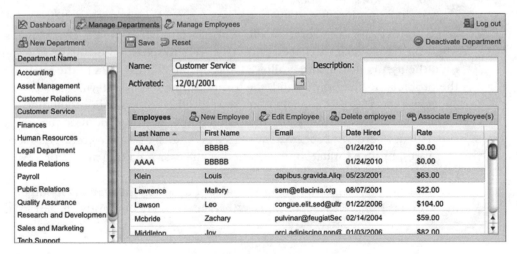

Figure 17.7 The Manage Departments screen

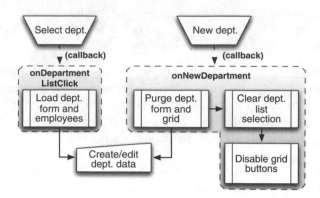

Figure 17.8   The Manage Departments navigation and new department workflows

The navigation and create department workflows both lead to the same point, where the screen is left in a state in which users can enter or edit data for a department. The new department workflow, however, is a lot more involved, including making some changes to the UI. To make discussion easier, I've included the flowchart in figure 17.8, which illustrates in a simple way how the navigation and new department workflows operate.

The navigation workflow is managed by onDepartmentListClick and is called whenever the user selects a department in the DepartmentsListView. This action causes the DepartmentForm to load, allowing the user to edit the data for the selected department.

onNewDepartment is invoked when the user clicks the New Department Button and purges the DepartmentForm of all of its data. Because the user is creating a department, the DepartmentsListView is cleared of any selections and the Employee-EditorGrid's Toolbar Buttons are disabled.

Both of these workflows place the screen in a state that allows users to create or edit information. From here, users can elect to save their changes. Figure 17.9 shows how the save workflows operate.

After the user modifies data in the DepartmentForm, they must click the Save Button to invoke the save workflow illustrated in figure 17.9. onDeptFormSave is called when the Save Button is clicked and first checks to see whether the form is valid. If it isn't, the user is alerted and is allowed to return to edit the data in the form to correct the problem. If the form is valid, the form is submitted, registering onDeptFormSave-Success and onDeptFormSaveFailure as respective success/failure handlers.

onDeptFormSaveFailure has the simple job of alerting the user that the submission failed, whereas onDeptFormSaveSuccess is much more involved. The success handler is responsible for determining whether the user is editing an existing Record and performs work accordingly.

If an existing Record is being modified, the selected Record is modified accordingly. Otherwise, a DepartmentsListView Record is created and selected in addition

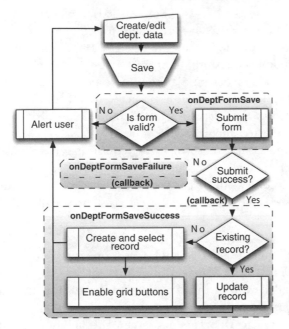

Figure 17.9 The department save workflows

to the `EmployeeGridPanel Toolbar Buttons` being enabled. Both result in the user being alerted to the successful `save` event.

The final workflow revolves around deleting a department and is illustrated in figure 17.10.

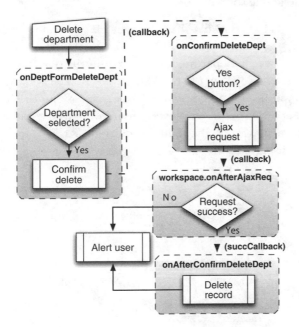

Figure 17.10 The delete department workflow

The delete department workflow for the `DepartmentManager` is identical to that of the delete employee workflow in the `EmployeeManager`, where only if a `Record` is selected will a confirmation dialog be presented when the Delete Department `Button` is clicked. To complete the deletion request, the user must click the Yes `Button` of the confirmation dialog box, which will invoke an Ajax request to perform the deletion of the department in the backend. If that request is successful, then the `Record` is deleted and the user is alerted of the successful transaction. Otherwise, the user is alerted of the failure and the selected `Record` is kept intact.

By now, you've started to see a pattern evolve, where confirmations in addition to status alerts coupled with UI changes make the UI interactive for the user. The employee CRUD workflows will follow similar patterns. But because creating and editing use an external editor, it's worth having a quick overview of how it all works.

17.4.2 *Employee CRUD workflows*

The Manage Departments screen is designed to allow CRUD operations for employees without requiring users to switch to the Manage Employees screen. To facilitate this requirement, three `Buttons` at the top of the `EmployeeGridPanel` are embedded in the `DepartmentForm`, one for each CRUD operation.

The class that gives the Manage Departments screen the ability to create and update employees is called `EmployeeEditorWindow`, and it has create and edit workflows that are similar to those of the Manage Employees screen, but greatly reduced.

> **NOTE**   In order to save you time, `EmployeeEditorWindow` is already developed and available in the downloadable source code.

As a visual reference, figure 17.11 shows what the `EmployeeEditorWindow` looks like when rendered onscreen.

For a user to create an employee, a department must exist in the database and be selected in the `DepartmentsListView`. When the New Employee `Button` is clicked, the `EmployeeEditorWindow` class will display an empty `EmployeeForm`, asking the user for data for the new employee `Record`. To edit employees, users will either double-click the `Record` or select a `Record` and click the Edit Employee `Button`, causing the `EmployeeEditorWindow` to be displayed with data.

Figure 17.11   The `EmployeeEditorWindow` widget in action

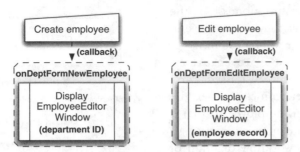

Figure 17.12 The create and edit employee workflows

Figure 17.12 shows the workflow diagram for this user interaction model.

As you can see in figure 17.12, both the create and edit employee user actions result in the display of the EmployeeEditorWindow, but each has a subtle difference.

The difference is in two configuration properties set when EmployeeEditorWindow is being instantiated. EmployeeEditorWindow requires either the ID of the selected department (create) or the Record of the selected employee (edit) to know how to display the embedded form.

Because this widget is responsible for saving new or existing employee data, you should take a quick look at its internal workflows, shown in figure 17.13.

If the form is valid when the user clicks the Save Button in the window, it will submit the data via the implemented

Event communication for loosely coupled components

When the EmployeeEditorWindow is instantiated, DepartmentManager doesn't keep a reference to it, which is what I like to call a loosely coupled component. This means that DepartmentManager relies on the EmployeeEditorWindow's custom employeesaved event to be published so it can create or update a Record in the EmployeeGridPanel accordingly.

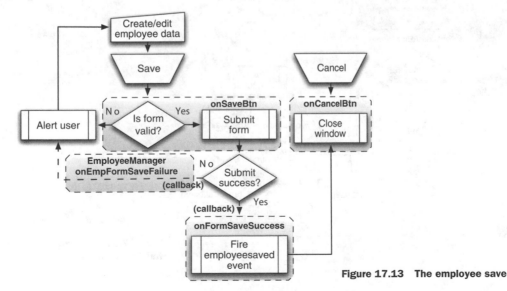

Figure 17.13 The employee save

EmployeeForm. Upon successful submission, the window will fire a custom employeesaved event, for which DepartmentManager will be listening.

When this event is fired, the EmployeeEditor-Window will automatically be dismissed, and DepartmentManager will determine whether the save operation was for a new employee so that it can create a Record or update an existing one.

Figure 17.14 is a quick workflow diagram of how this works. As illustrated in the figure, the onEmployeeWindowSaveSuccess method is a listener to the EmployeeEditorWindow employee-saved event, and when invoked, it will determine if action has been taken on an existing Record. If so, it's updated; otherwise, a new Record is created. Either way, the user is made aware of the successful change.

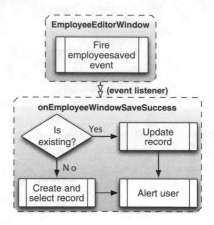

Figure 17.14
The DepartmentManager employee save workflow

To delete an employee, the user can select one or more Records in the Employee-GridPanel and click the Delete Employee Button, invoking the workflow shown in figure 17.15.

The act of clicking the Delete Employees Button while having one or more employees selected will result in a confirmation dialog box. If the person clicks the Yes Button, an Ajax request is invoked to delete the employee records from the database. If the server returns favorably, the selected Records are removed from the EmployeeGrid and the user is alerted to the success of the request. If the server

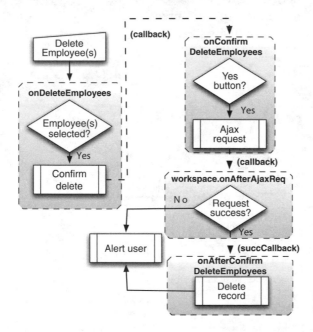

Figure 17.15   The delete employee workflow logic

returns unfavorably, the user is alerted of the failure. This workflow is nearly identical to the delete department workflow, except it deals with one or more selected `Records` in a grid.

We've completed the employee CRUD workflow. Next, we'll cover the final workflow for the Manage Departments screen, where users can associate one or more employees from one department to another.

17.4.3 *Employee association workflow*

The last bit of functionality that the Manage Departments screen will give to its users is the ability to associate employees from one department to another. To do this, users will have to select a department in the `DepartmentsListView` and click the Associate Employee(s) `Record` in the `EmployeeGridPanel`. This will display the `Associate-EmployeeWindow`, illustrated in figure 17.16.

When this window is rendered onscreen, it will display all of the departments via another instance of `DepartmentsListView`, except for the department selected in `DepartmentManager`. This will help prevent user requests from accidentally associating employees with a department to which they already belong.

The `Window` follows the same workflow as all others, where the context for the screen is set by the selection of a department. The department selection will trigger the loading of the `EmployeeGridPanel` in this window.

Figure 17.17 diagrams the workflow logic.

To associate employees, the user must select one or more `Records` and click the Add `Button`. This will cause the `EmployeeAssociationWindow` to fire its custom `assocemployees` event, for which `DepartmentManager` has a listener setup known as

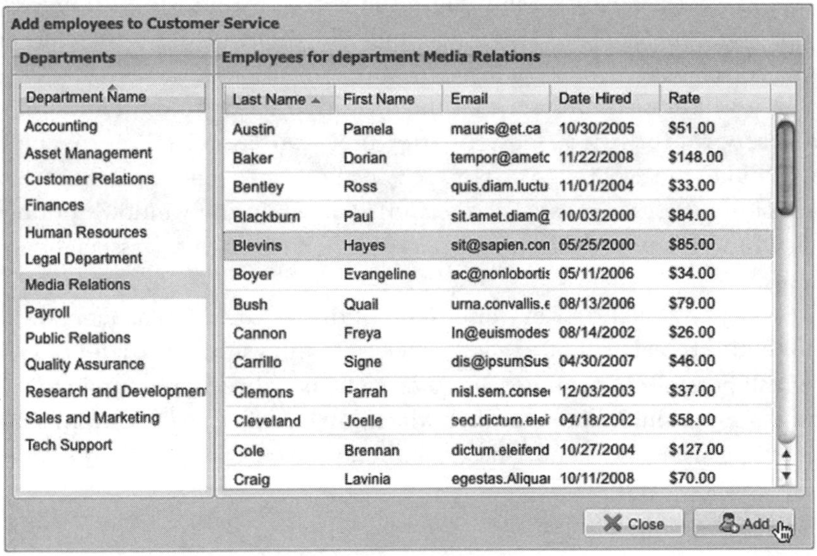

Figure 17.16 The `AssociateEmployeeWindow` in action

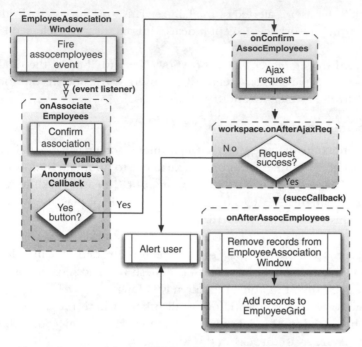

Figure 17.17
The employee association logic workflow

`onAssociateEmployees`. When this method is called, a confirmation dialog box will be displayed.

Only if the user presses the Yes `Button` will `DepartmentManager` invoke an Ajax request to the server to associate the employees with their new department. If the web server responds favorably, because the association operation is more of a move operation, the `DepartmentManager` will remove the `Records` from the `EmployeeGridPanel` inside the `EmployeeAssociationWindow` and add them to the `GridPanel` inside its own `DepartmentForm`.

Finally, it will inform the user that the operation was successful and will keep the `EmployeeAssociationWindow` alive so the user can associate more employees if desired. Unlike the `EmployeeEditorWindow`, the `EmployeeAssociationWindow` will never self-close; the user must click the Close `Button` in the window's bottom button bar to dismiss it. It's set up this way so users can loop through the association workflow more easily.

We've reached the end of our discussion of the `DepartmentManager` workflows. As you can see, this screen will offer a lot to the users and will require a lot of logic wiring to make it all possible. We can now move on to tie our three screens together by developing a workspace singleton controller, which will handle the global application workflow, including navigation and generic authentication. Hang in there. We're almost finished.

17.5 *Piecing it all together*

All of the work we've done thus far has led us up to this point, the grand finale, where we combine all the pieces of our application layer and see them come together as a single, unified application. To make this happen, we'll create a singleton that will be called upon to bootstrap the application, implement the screens we've created thus far, and control the navigation workflow.

> **Why use a singleton for the workspace class?**
> Recall that a singleton is a JavaScript design pattern where a class is constructed and can be instantiated only once, and it's referred to via a reference that can be accessed globally. Because that workspace needs to live only once per page load, this design pattern is perfect for placing all of the logic in one container, called a *closure*.

We'll begin by having a quick discussion of the various workflows and then move on to developing the singleton.

17.5.1 *The workspace workflows*

The workspace singleton, which will be referred to as workspace from now on, will be in charge of two rather simple but important areas of our application. The first is providing a lightweight authentication mechanism. This application will be used by a limited and static set of users in the company; their usernames and passwords have already been set up in the database, so we need not create a registration page.

To ensure users log in, workspace will check for the presence of a login cookie that will be created and provided by the server. Only if the login cookie is present will workspace display the application. Otherwise, a login window will be dynamically generated to request the user's credentials.

Once users are logged in, the login window will be destroyed and the viewport created, revealing the application dashboard as the first screen. From there, the user can refresh the page, and as long as the login cookie is still present in their browser, they'll be greeted with the application upon page load.

Users can then click the Log Out Button at any time after a successful login. The logout handler will first request confirmation from the user. If the user confirms, the Viewport and all of its contents will be destroyed along with the login cookie, and the login window will be instantiated and displayed.

> **Invoking a sense of familiarity for the login process**
> If the authentication workflow we've just discussed seems familiar, it's because we're mimicking the current authentication design pattern that's implemented in modern UI desktops.

The navigation workflow is the other main piece of functionality that `workspace` provides. Instead of using a `TabPanel` as the main view controller, we elected to use a generic `Panel` with a top `Toolbar` with `Buttons` that, when clicked, reveal the screen to which they're bound. To make this happen, we'll implement the `CardLayout`.

With the workflows now covered, we can move on to create `workspace`.

17.5.2 Constructing the workspace singleton

Because this is the first time we've covered such a class, we'll walk through the code. We'll begin the construction of the `workspace` singleton in the following listing by observing the class template, and then we'll move on to code the various factory, workflow, and utility methods.

Listing 17.11 The `workspace` class template

```
CompanyManager.workspace = function() {
    var viewport, cardPanel, loginWindow,          ⟵──❶ Reusable variables
        cookieUtil = Ext.util.Cookies;

    return {
        init : function() {},                ⟵── Application
                                                ❷ bootstrap method
        buildLoginWindow : function() {},
        buildViewport    : function() {},

        onLogin        : function() {},
        onLoginSuccess : function() {},
        onLoginFailure : function() {},

        onLogOut      : function() {},
        doLogOut      : function() {},
        onAfterLogout : function() {},

        onSwitchPanel : function() {},
        switchToCard  : function() {},

        onAfterAjaxReq : function() {},
        destroy        : function() {}
    };
}();

Ext.onReady(CompanyManager.workspace.init,          ❸ Bootstrap the
    CompanyManager.workspace);                   ⟵─  application
```

When reviewing the code in 17.11, you'll see four variables set at the top of the singleton ❶. These are considered private, lexically scoped variables and they'll be used by the methods returned in the object below them.

In that return object is the `init` ❷ method, which will be the bootstrap method for the entire application and is registered with `Ext.onReady` ❸. Along with the `init` method and factory methods are the login, logout, and navigation workflow controller methods. Additionally, there are two utility methods, one of which is `onAfterAjaxReq`, which is used extensively by the app tier.

We'll look at the shorter `init` and `buildLoginWindow` methods in the next listing, and then we'll move on, developing `buildViewport`, which is rather lengthy.

> **Listing 17.12   The workspace `init` method**

```
init : function() {
    if (! cookieUtil.get('loginCookie')) {
        if (! loginWindow) {
            loginWindow = this.buildLoginWindow();
        }
        loginWindow.show();
    }
    else {
        this.buildViewport();
    }
},
buildLoginWindow : function() {
    return new TKE.window.UserLoginWindow({
        title   : 'Login to Department Manager',
        scope   : this,
        handler : this.onLogin
    });
},
```

The `init` method is responsible for bootstrapping the application. It first checks to see if a valid `'loginCookie'` exists. If the cookie doesn't exist, then a `loginWindow` is created and displayed. Otherwise, the `buildViewport` method is called, which constructs and renders the main application body onscreen.

The `buildLoginWindow` factory method will instantiate and return an instance of `TKE.window.UserLoginWindow`. This preconstructed class does something special, where it binds the Enter key from the form input fields to the pass handler (`this.onLogin`) method.

This is more of a convenience for the users, allowing them to press the Enter key when focused on any of the input elements to submit the contents of the form. I like to do this for login forms, but it can be implemented on any form. `UserLoginWindow` also binds the `handler` to the Login `Button` in the footer bar of the window.

With the login window complete, we can construct the workspace viewport. This listing is lengthy but mainly consists of configuration, so it's an easy read.

> **Listing 17.13   The workspace `buildViewport` method**

```
buildViewport : function() {
    cardPanel = new Ext.Panel({           Create Panel
        layout     : 'card',           ❶ using CardLayout
        activeItem : 0,
        border     : false,
        defaults   : { workspace : this },
        items      : [
            { xtype : 'dashboard'         },     Initial child
            { xtype : 'departmentmanager' },  ❷ component
```

```
                { xtype   : 'employeemanager'    }
            ],
            tbar        : [
                {
                    text            : 'Dashboard',
                    iconCls         : 'icon-chart_curve',
                    toggleGroup     : 'navGrp',
                    itemType        : 'dashboard',
                    enableToggle    : true,
                    pressed         : true,
                    scope           : this,
                    handler         : this.onSwitchPanel
                },
                '-',
                {
                    text            : 'Manage Departments',
                    iconCls         : 'icon-group_edit',
                    itemType        : 'departmentmanager',
                    toggleGroup     : 'navGrp',
                    enableToggle    : true,
                    scope           : this,
                    handler         : this.onSwitchPanel
                },
                '-',
                {
                    text            : 'Manage Employees',
                    iconCls         : 'icon-user_edit',
                    itemType        : 'employeemanager',
                    toggleGroup     : 'navGrp',
                    enableToggle    : true,
                    scope           : this,
                    handler         : this.onSwitchPanel
                },
                '->',
                {
                    text    : 'Log out',
                    iconCls : 'icon-door_out',
                    scope   : this,
                    handler : this.onLogOut
                }
            ]
        });

    viewport = new Ext.Viewport({
        layout : 'fit',
        items  : cardPanel
    });
    Ext.getBody().unmask();
},
```

③ Bind Buttons to screens

④ Logout Button

⑤ Create Viewport

In listing 17.13, a lot of configuration is stuffed into the buildViewport factory method. It's this way because I was trying to reduce the overall complexity of the workspace singleton. Here's how it works.

This method first constructs the main application Panel, which is the application, cardPanel ❶, which implements the CardLayout. This Panel will also instantiate all of the screens as the child items ❷ as well as a top Toolbar with the three navigation Buttons and the logout Button ❹.

> **NOTE** Notice that we're setting all the workspace property child items as this, which is workspace. This is so all of the child items can use the workspace's onAfterAjaxReq utility method, reducing code duplication.

Because the Dashboard will be the first screen that users will see when the application renders, we need to ensure that the associated Button looks depressed (selected). To do this, we set the associated Button's pressed configuration option to true.

All of the screen-associated Buttons are bound to the onSwitchPanel method ❸, which will act as the main navigation logic controller. We needed a way to somehow to tell onSwitchPanel what type of class each of these Buttons should be associated with. Because xtype is a reserved option, I had to get a little creative, so I chose itemType.

This itemType property will be transposed into an xtype property in onSwitch-Panel. When these screen-associated Buttons are clicked, onSwitchPanel will use the itemType to search cardPanel's child items for an instance of the class named in the itemType property. If the class exists, the active card is switched accordingly. Otherwise, a new instance of the class described by itemType is instantiated and then set as the active card.

The final task that this factory method will complete is instantiating a Viewport ❺, whose only child item is cardPanel. In order to stretch cardPanel to the size of the browser's viewport, the Viewport will use the FitLayout.

That's it for the construction and configuration of the widgets and screens for this application. In the next listing, we'll work on the login workflow.

Listing 17.14 The workspace login workflow

```
onLogin :  function() {
    var form = loginWindow.get(0);
    if (form.getForm().isValid()) {
        loginWindow.el.mask('Please wait...', 'x-mask-loading');

        form.getForm().submit({                          ◁─┐  Submit
            success : this.onLoginSuccess,                  ❶  login form
            failure : this.onLoginFailure,
            scope   : this
        });
    }
},
onLoginSuccess : function() {
    loginWindow.el.unmask();

    if (cookieUtil.get('loginCookie')) {                 ◁─┐  Login is
        this.buildViewport();                              ❷  successful
        loginWindow.destroy();
```

```
        loginWindow = null;
    }
    else {
        this.onLoginFailure();
    }
},
onLoginFailure : function() {                    ❸ Handle
    loginWindow.el.unmask();                       failed login
    Ext.MessageBox.alert('Failure', "Login failed. Please try again");
},
```

The login workflow in listing 17.14 is logically segmented into three methods. First is onLogin, which is bound to both the login form fields and the containing window button. Its job is to mask the login window and submit the login form ❶ if it's valid. The other two methods are callback methods that will handle the response of the submission.

onLoginSuccess ❷ will unmask the window and check for the presence of the login cookie. If it's there, then this.buildViewport is called, the login window is destroyed, and its reference is set to null. Otherwise, the this.onLoginFailure ❸ method is called. I've configured this callback handler this way because even if the server returns the minimal response ({"success":true}), the response may not contain the loginCookie. This method is configured this way because the presence of the cookie is the only indication that the login was truly a success.

onLoginFailure, on the other hand, has a simple job: alert the user that the login attempt was a failure. Because the login window is already rendered, it only needs to be unmasked to allow the user to reattempt a login once the alert is dismissed.

The login workflow is now complete; we can move on to work through the logout workflow, shown in the following listing.

Listing 17.15   The workspace logout workflow

```
onLogOut : function() {
    Ext.MessageBox.confirm(
        'Please confirm',                           ┐ Request
        'Are you sure you want to log out?',        │ confirmation
        function(btn) {                             ❶ from user
            if (btn === 'yes') {
                this.doLogOut();
            }
        },
        this
    );
},
doLogOut : function() {
    Ext.getBody().mask('Logging out...', 'x-mask-loading');
                                                    ❷ Request to
    Ext.Ajax.request({                                log out user
        url          : 'userlogout.php',
        params       : { user : cookieUtil.get('loginCookie') },
        scope        : this,
        callback     : this.onAfterAjaxReq,
```

```
                succCallback : this.onAfterLogout
        });
    },
    onAfterLogout : function(jsonData) {
        this.destroy();
    },
```

③ Call destroy after logout

The logout workflow in listing 17.15 is relatively simple. onLogout is bound to the Logout Button and when called will request confirmation from the user **①**. If the user clicks the Yes Button, this.doLogout is called.

doLogout is charged with masking the document body and invoking an Ajax request **②** to the backend to clear the user's session. The backend will return an expired cookie as well as {"success": true}, ultimately causing onAfterLogout to be invoked **③**. afterLogout is simple; it will call this.destroy to destroy the Viewport and reinitialize the application workspace.

With the logout workflow finished, we can develop the navigation workflow methods in the following listing and then move on to code the utility methods, completing this class.

Listing 17.16 The workspace navigation workflow

```
onSwitchPanel : function(btn) {
    var xtype    = btn.itemType,
        panels   = cardPanel.findByType(xtype),
        newPanel = panels[0];

    var newCardIndex = cardPanel.items.indexOf(newPanel);
    this.switchToCard(newCardIndex, newPanel);
},
switchToCard : function(newCardIndex, newPanel) {
    var layout         = cardPanel.getLayout(),
        activePanel    = layout.activeItem,
        activePanelIdx = cardPanel.items.indexOf(activePanel);

    if (activePanelIdx !== newCardIndex) {
        layout.setActiveItem(newCardIndex);

        if (newPanel.cleanSlate) {
            newPanel.cleanSlate();
        }
    }
},
```

① Use button's itemType

② Search for matching child

③ Add new component

④ Set reference to panel

⑤ Switch to new index

⑥ Get index of active child

Listing 17.16 contains the logic to handle the switching from one card to another. Recall that onSwitchPanel is bound to the three navigation Buttons. Because the Buttons pass themselves as references (btn) to their click handlers, we can set a reference to the xtype of the screen that's to be displayed via the custom itemType property **①**.

Next, we use the Container findByType utility method to search the child items MixedCollection for anything that matches the xtype for the Button pressed **②**. If no matching child is found, then a new child is added to `cardPanel` using the `xtype` property **❸** and is set to the `newPanel` reference. If there is a matching child, then the `newPanel` reference is to it **❹**. Last, the `index` of the newly added or existing child item is fetched and passed on to `this.switchToCard` **❺** along with the reference for the child item to be displayed.

`switchToCard` is responsible for getting the `index` of the current active item **❻** and testing to see if the current active panel index (`activePanelIdx`) matches the desired `index` (`newCardIndex`). If this test is `true`, then a switch to the desired card `index` is made via a call to the `CardLayout`'s `setActiveItem` utility method. Last, if the screen contains a `cleanSlate` (method) reference, then it's called, placing that screen in a virgin state.

That's all there is to the navigation workflow. In the following listing, we'll work on the two utility methods for the `workspace`.

Listing 17.17   The workspace utility methods

```
onAfterAjaxReq : function(options, success, result) {
    Ext.getBody().unmask();                              ❶ Is transaction
    if (success === true) {                                  successful?
        var jsonData;
        try {
            jsonData = Ext.decode(result.responseText);  ❷ Try to convert
        }                                                    text to JSON
        catch (e) {
            Ext.MessageBox.alert(
                'Error!',
                'Data returned is not valid!'
            );
        }
        options.succCallback.call(options.scope,         ❸ Call custom
            jsonData, options);                             succCallback

    }
    else {
        Ext.MessageBox.alert('Error!', 'The web transaction failed!');
    }
},
destroy : function() {                                   ❹ Destroy viewport
    viewport.destroy();                                      and clean up
    viewport = null;
    cardPanel = null;
    this.init();           ◄──❺ Show login window
}
```

In listing 17.17, we wrap up `workspace` by developing the last two methods in the singleton, which are utility methods. `onAfterAjaxReq` is often used throughout the Manage Employees and Manage Departments screens as well as `workspace`'s logout workflow to perform a two-phase check on any Ajax request made within the application. Here's how it works.

After unmasking the document body, it tests to see if the `success` property is equal to `true` ❶. Sometimes servers will respond unfavorably, returning a non-200-ish HTTP status code. If this is the case, then no further processing is necessary. We know something went wrong, so we'll post an alert to the user stating that the "web transaction failed."

If the transaction is successful (`success === true`), an attempt to convert (decode) the inbound string data into a JSON object is wrapped in a `try/catch` block ❷. If there's no exception, the custom `options.succCallback` method is called, passing along the decoded `jsonData` and the options passed to the `Ajax.request` object. We use `succCallback` ❸ instead of `success`, because `success` is a reserved key for the Ajax requests.

The last method, `destroy`, is in charge of the cleanup of the application after the logout workflow has completed. To make this happen, it destroys the `Viewport` ❹ and sets the reference to the `Viewport` and `cardPanel` to `null`, because they're no longer needed. Finally, it calls the `workspace`'s `init` method, effectively bootstrapping the application again, causing the login window to display ❺.

This concludes the `workspace` class and the rest of the application. Congratulations! Because you have a pluggable architecture in place, making improvements or changes should be a breeze now. For instance, to add another screen to this application, you'd follow the same pattern where you'd create the reusable components, placing them in the reusability layer. Then, you'd implement them in the application layer and finally plug them into the workspace by adding a `Button` with an associated custom `itemType` property.

17.6 Summary

In this chapter you learned how to implement the reusability layer, allowing you to focus on coding workflow logic for the application layer. We developed and implemented three screens as well as a custom navigation and authentication `workspace` controller.

We started by developing the Dashboard screen, where we enjoyed the benefits of having most of the hard work done by the reusability layer. Next, we developed the Manage Employees screen. This is where, after a deep analysis of the workflows, you got to see what it takes to develop navigation along with CRUD workflows. When discussing the construction of the Manage Departments screen, you saw how you could employ reusable CRUD patterns from `EmployeeManager`.

We tied everything together with a `workspace` singleton that served as both navigation and authentication controllers. While developing this class, you learned how to set up basic authentication and application bootstrapping.

There you have it, an application using Ext JS!

index